Maike Oergel
Zeitgeist – How Ideas Travel

Culture & Conflict

Edited by
Isabel Capeloa Gil, Catherine Nesci and
Paulo de Medeiros

Editorial Board
Arjun Appadurai · Claudia Benthien · Elisabeth Bronfen · Joyce Goggin
Bishnupriya Ghosh · Lawrence Grossberg · Andreas Huyssen
Ansgar Nünning · Naomi Segal · Márcio Seligmann-Silva
António Sousa Ribeiro · Roberto Vecchi · Samuel Weber · Liliane Weissberg
Christoph Wulf · Longxi Zhang

Volume 13

Maike Oergel

Zeitgeist – How Ideas Travel

Politics, Culture, and the Public in the Age of Revolution

DE GRUYTER

I gratefully acknowledge that the research for this study was funded by a Leverhulme Research Fellowship 2015–2016.

ISBN 978-3-11-073673-1
e-ISBN (PDF) 978-3-11-063153-1
e-ISBN (EPUB) 978-3-11-063093-0
ISSN 2194-7104

Library of Congress Control Number: 2018967111

Bibliographic information published by the Deutsche Nationalbibliothek
The Deutsche Nationalbibliothek lists this publication in the Deutsche Nationalbibliografie; detailed bibliographic data are available on the Internet at http://dnb.dnb.de.

© 2020 Walter de Gruyter GmbH, Berlin/Boston
This volume is text- and page-identical with the hardback published in 2019.
Typesetting: Integra Software Services Pvt. Ltd.
Printing and binding: CPI books GmbH, Leck
Cover image: March to Hambach Castle on 27 May 1832 / AKG73492

www.degruyter.com

Contents

Introduction —— 1

1	Johann Gottfried Herder – the "Inventor of Zeitgeist"? —— 8	
1.1	Herder's work as a site of convergence —— 8	
1.2	The genealogy of zeitgeist – Barclay and Bacon —— 21	
1.3	Praising or critiquing the age – *Genius Saeculi* and the *Querelle* —— 25	
2	The Making of Zeitgeist – Culture and Public Spirit between Enfranchisement and Control —— 27	
2.1	*Geist, l'esprit,* spirit – public spirit and collective identity —— 27	
2.2	Montesquieu's *L'esprit des loix* – collective spirit against despotism —— 31	
2.3	Blackwell's *Enquiry* – communal spirit and cultural context —— 35	
2.4	*Culture* – conflating collective identity, the spirit of the times, and cultural history in Bodmer, Hurd, Mallet, and Percy —— 38	
3	The Public and Zeitgeist – Public Spirit and Public Opinion 1790–1800 —— 50	
3.1	Zeitgeist, public spirit, and public opinion —— 50	
3.2	The political role of public opinion in Britain and Germany – the guardian of lawful government and the risks of demagogy —— 56	
3.3	The uses of public opinion – Georg Forster and Christian Garve —— 64	
3.4	The battle over public opinion in 1790s Britain —— 73	
3.5	Zeitgeist, public opinion, and the masses – manipulation or the public will —— 81	
4	Zeitgeist in Germany – Public Opinion, History, and the People in Franz Josias von Hendrich, Ernst Brandes, and Ernst Moritz Arndt —— 85	
4.1	Restoring the public good – similarities between Thelwall and Arndt —— 85	
4.2	Hendrich and Brandes – zeitgeist and historical conditions —— 87	

4.3	Arndt – zeitgeist and the role of intellectual elites —— **105**	
4.4	Zeitgeist – public opinion and history —— **126**	

5   **Zeitgeist in Britain – The Spirit of the Age and Social Reform in Julius Hare, William Hazlitt, Thomas Carlyle, and J. S. Mill —— 129**

5.1	Arndt's *Geist der Zeit* in Britain —— **131**
5.2	Reform politics and zeitgeist in England – the rise of a new elite —— **141**
5.3	Julius Hare – public politics and Arndt's *Geist der Zeit* —— **144**
5.4	William Hazlitt – "paradoxical" German literature and the spirit of the age —— **166**
5.5	Thomas Carlyle – the "Age of Mechanism" and the French Revolution —— **190**
5.6	John Stuart Mill – the "Spirit of the Age" and the "Age of Transition" —— **219**
5.7	Zeitgeist in Britain – politics and public opinion —— **230**

6   **How Ideas Travel (in Theory): The Zeitgeist Dynamic —— 234**

7   **How an Idea Travels (in Practice) – A Case Study: The Germanic and the Gothic – The Life and Times of the "Northern" Identity of Liberty and Duty in Germany and Britain 1770–1870 —— 243**

7.1	The emergence of the terms Germanic and Gothic —— **246**
7.2	The "Germanic-Gothic" identity project 1770–1830 – a social and cultural challenge —— **251**
7.3	National self-determination and social emancipation – the Germanic Europe, chivalry, and constitutionalism —— **257**
7.4	Paths to institutionalisation in Britain and Germany – *Germanistik*, the Christian gentleman, and the Gothic Revival —— **271**
7.4.1	*Germanistik* – traditions of liberty in laws and poetry —— **271**
7.4.2	The Christian gentleman and English liberty – Kenelm Henry Digby's *Broad Stone of Honour*, J. M. Kemble's *Saxons in England* and the Germanist historians at Oxford and Cambridge —— **277**
7.4.3	The Gothic Revival – the Palace of Westminster and Cologne Cathedral —— **286**

7.5	The "Germanic-Gothic" identity project and its cultural patterns – summary —— **288**	
7.6	The propagators of the Germanic-Gothic identity – the profile of an "elite" —— **294**	
7.6.1	The British "elites" —— **296**	
7.6.2	The German "elites" —— **306**	
7.6.3	Elites, ideas, and getting established —— **322**	
7.7	How an idea travels (in practice) – conclusion —— **324**	

Works Cited —— 327

Index —— 338

Introduction

Most people have a sense of what the word zeitgeist means. It is used frequently in both contemporary German and English.[1] Basic definitions of the term, such as those on *Wikipedia*, focus on what zeitgeist *is* and what it *does*, "the dominant set of ideals that motivate the actions of the members of a society in a particular time".[2] Similarly, the German entry reads, "[d]er Zeitgeist ist die Denk- und Fühlweise (Mentalität) eines Zeitalters. Der Begriff bezeichnet die Eigenart einer bestimmten Epoche beziehungsweise den Versuch, diese zu vergegenwärtigen." [Zeitgeist is the way of thinking and feeling during a specific age (its mentality). This term describes the character of a specific epoch, or the attempt to present this character.][3] Neither definition addresses *how* zeitgeist works, both describe *what* it does: it produces a cultural coherence which does not last, it is epochal, dominant, and transient.

Despite the evident popularity of the term, there is no research in English into the concept of zeitgeist. Recent German research, which is not voluminous (but perhaps on an upward trajectory), has the tendency to dismiss zeitgeist as a manipulative concept whose chimeric qualities allow those who use it to pretend that things occur, or need to be done, due to some form of higher necessity or irresistible force, thus shifting responsibility and agency into a realm that is both unaccountable and beyond control.[4] Much of this dismissive and negative

---

[1] While frequency levels are higher in German, in English they are not very far behind. A basic search with Google NGram shows levels in German between 0.00028% and 0.00053% for the years 1960–2008 across German-language publications in the Google books corpus compared with around 0.0035% for the same period across the English-language publications, with both curves rising in the 1990s. (Search conducted 22 July 2018).

[2] Cf. <https://en.wikipedia.org/wiki/Zeitgeist> (accessed on 7 February 2018). The English-language definition focuses on Hegel's contribution to the idea of zeitgeist, mentioning Herder, Spencer, and Voltaire as contributors. It suggests a potential contrast – curious in the context of this study – between zeitgeist and Carlyle's ideas on "Great Men".

[3] Cf. <https://de.m.wikipedia.org/wiki/Zeitgeist> (accessed on 7 February 2018). Unless indicated otherwise, all translations are my own. The German page focuses on Herder's contributions as a starting point before moving on to describe zeitgeist's effects by giving examples of cultural changes. (The page has recently been updated; while two years ago it heavily relied on Hermann Hiery's introduction to his edited collection *Zeitgeist und die Historie* (Hiery 2001), it now prominently lists the volumes edited by Achim Landwehr (Landwehr 2012) and by Michael Gamper and Peter Schnyder (Gamper and Schnyder 2006) in its bibliography.

[4] Recent assessments frequently focus either on the pretended – invented or imagined – nature of any zeitgeist coherence or display a resigned acceptance of its "Unfassbarkeit" [the impossibility to grasp it] (Gamper and Schnyder 2006), or else warn of its dangerousness by insisting that the term serves to veil the manipulative interests of power. For Jost Hermand

assessment, often levelled at the term "Geist" too, is a reaction to the heyday of the notions of "Zeitgeist" and "Geist" in late nineteenth- and early twentieth-century historical studies, notably in the work of Wilhelm Dilthey. His *Einleitung in die Geisteswissenschaften*, published in 1883, set out to provide a theoretical foundation for the study of history and society. This tradition is based on the notion that "Geist" cannot be captured with the empirical methods of the natural sciences alone, because its metaphysical attributes are held to be characteristic of human existence in history. It is *this* notion that has been so heavily implicated in the German tradition of prioritising the state, the nation, and communal structures over the individual, leaving the term rather contaminated, at least from a German viewpoint. The legacy of the more positive nineteenth-century view of zeitgeist, however, lingers in the two mid-twentieth-century studies of zeitgeist by Hans-Joachim Schoeps and Eugen Böhler. Both, Schoeps' *Was ist und was will die Geistesgeschichte. Theorie und Praxis der Zeitgeistforschung* (1956) and Böhler's *Psychologie des Zeitgeistes* (1972) hold on to a neutral sense of the historical and social reality of zeitgeist. Schoeps calls for increased study of zeitgeist because he regards it as a tool for historical research; the aim of his book is to show how to identify the *content* of zeitgeist in history, arguably something Hegel, one of the founders of the tradition of prioritising the state, had already engaged in. Böhler deals with the impact of what he defines as a *mythic* (non-rational) concept of zeitgeist on individual (and collective) behaviour and understanding, drawing on the twentieth-century fields of psychology and sociology.

The research presented in this study seeks to qualify the idea that zeitgeist is a purely manipulative concept, or tool, used by self-interested agents to simplify complexity, disavow responsibility, and mislead. This book makes the case that the notion of zeitgeist has, to a large extent, a rational and empirically verifiable existence in modern societies in that it describes a dynamic by which ideas are successfully disseminated. This is less a reintroduction of Hegelian concepts through the backdoor than an acknowledgement that forms of social consensus, the basis of all forms of culture, tend to be powerful players in human societies. Such acknowledgement does not deny elements of manipulation. My proposal of an intellectually useful concept of zeitgeist derives from my discovery that in the minds of the early zeitgeist investigators around 1800 zeitgeist could not be

---

"Zeitgeist" is based on "eine betont verschleiernde und pseudo-demokratische Sehweise" [Zeitgeist is based on a decidedly obscuring and pseudo-democratic perspective] (2007: 72). However, the two recent essays by Theo Jung and Markus Meumann in Achim Landwehr's *Frühe Neue Zeiten* (Landwehr 2012: 283–317 and 319–355) take a more historically descriptive approach.

uncoupled from the functioning of social collectives and was approached from something of a sociological perspective.

The case for such a concept of zeitgeist is based on my investigation into the emergence of the modern idea of zeitgeist in the aftermath of the French Revolution. This emergence is intricately bound up with the reception of the Revolution in Germany and Britain. In both countries, the contemporaries of the period between the 1790s and the 1830s were developing a sense of a social dynamic in which new ideas succeeded if they addressed contemporary conditions in a way that made sense to a critical mass, often a majority, of people affected by them. The spread of revolutionary ideas, or of a (more moderate) desire for change, prompted intellectuals, whether they were conservatives, moderates or radicals, to investigate how this process worked. In Germany the majority of them considered this an investigation into forms of "Zeitgeist"; in 1790s Britain this investigation was conducted around the term "the public", perhaps a significant difference and a clearer "sociological" focus. However, in the 1820s and early 1830s the continuing British debate was conducted by addressing the "spirit of the age". This study shows that this change of terminology was due in large measure to a German influence on some of the key writers involved in the 1820s debate. In this regard the journey of post-Revolution zeitgeist, term and concept, from Germany to Britain is itself an example of how ideas travel.

The writers around 1800 did not pluck the zeitgeist concept out of thin air; they drew on the eighteenth-century debates about general and public spirit and the new concept of "culture". The word zeitgeist itself derives from the Latin *genius saeculi*, a common term throughout the seventeenth and eighteenth centuries, *genius saeculi* existed as calques in German (Geist der Zeit/Geist der Zeiten), English (spirit of the times), and French (l'esprit du siècle). As a social dynamic, zeitgeist was closely bound up with peoples and communities. This is the reason why around 1800 forms of zeitgeist were frequently linked to descriptions of human collectives and equated with *Volksgeist* or national spirit. This connection, no longer readily evident today, is fundamental for understanding the idea of zeitgeist as it developed at the end of the eighteenth century. To a greater or lesser degree (the) time was always conceived as embodied by people, and time was, through people, ascribed an identity.

During its gestational history in the seventeenth and eighteenth centuries, zeitgeist incubated a number of inherent tensions, all of which are linked to its connection with people. The first is the tension between an older diachronic aspect and its synchronic aspect. The diachronic aspect relates to longer temporal units, which may encompass a collective's entire history, the synchronic aspect relates to shorter, frequently generational timespans, which define a generation or the period in which a "generational" identity becomes visible. A group's identity was thought to imprint itself on time when their culture was firmly established internally, and possibly trendsetting externally. In the diachronic approach Hegelian thinking is clearly visible – Hegel's work developed out of this matrix -, but the notion that people as a collective shape time was well established 200 years before Hegel.

The tension between diachronic and synchronic focus is palpable in the different terms that at the end of the eighteenth century began to coalesce around the idea of zeitgeist in both German and English: on the one hand there is "Geist der Zeiten/Geist der Zeit" and "spirit of the times", all three tend towards the larger historical units, without excluding the possibility of a shorter period. On the other hand, we find "Geist des Zeitalters" and "spirit of the age", both of which are closer to today's meaning of zeitgeist and tend towards the short, possibly generational, timespan. While "Geist der Zeiten" and "spirit of the times" were common during the eighteenth century (one occasionally finds "Geist des Jahrhunderts"), "Geist des Zeitalters" and "Zeitgeist" only began to appear in larger numbers from the end of the eighteenth century, with "spirit of the age" only becoming frequent in English after 1820; both Zeitgeist and "spirit of the age" went on to predominate in the nineteenth century.

The second tension follows on from the first, it sits between the different functions that a collective spirit can fulfil: controlling the collective in order to maintain its identity on the one hand and changing its identity and culture in line with a new situation on the other. History and tradition, which develop over longer periods, exert control in order to maintain established notions, while new needs and coherent interpretations of these trigger and underpin change. Both functions aim at controlling the collective, but both functions can also lay claim to being an expression of the collective's identity, so that a tension arises between control and (self-)expression.

The third tension revolves around the use different agents – writers, intellectuals, political elites – make of zeitgeist definitions. These uses are invariably aimed at the "now", i.e. tend toward the short-term, and seek to influence their audience (or public) and, through them, the current conditions. These agents either seek to criticise their time or to promote positive changes, often the two aims go together. Here the link between zeitgeist and manipulation is most obvious, but it is important to note that these interventions are not *necessarily* selfish or self-serving, but frequently made, or believed to be made, in good faith.

In the discussions of the zeitgeist idea around 1800 (and in those of its eighteenth-century predecessors) there is considerable slippage between a focus on *the* zeitgeist, i.e. the features that characterise the current period, and the *principle* of zeitgeist, i.e. the dynamic, or process, of zeitgeist, that explains how it works. This slippage proved productive, however; the *principle* emerged in eighteenth- and early-nineteenth-century texts from investigations of the *concrete example* of the present. This study is concerned with both aspects of zeitgeist. As a comparative historical investigation it traces the origins of the modern idea of zeitgeist in the historical specifics of the aftermath of the French Revolution and necessarily identifies the key features of *that* zeitgeist, namely concern about the public sphere and the nature of public opinion, coupled with a fear of "despotism" and the erosion of social bonds. In this, it is a contribution to the intellectual history of Reinhart Koselleck's *Sattelzeit*, or transitional age. As an investigation into the socio-cultural dynamics of the circulation of ideas, this study is interested in establishing the ways in which such dissemination works. This was very much in the minds of the original zeitgeist investigators, too, because *they* wanted to understand what they saw as a dissemination of unprecedented intensity. In this respect, it is a contribution to cultural and social theory.

The idea of zeitgeist turned out to be an example of its own process. Everybody was interested in zeitgeist because it addressed a critical contemporary issue: understanding radical change. However, providing examples of the dynamics of zeitgeist is primarily the role of specific case studies, of which this study provides one in the final chapter.

The considerations about the process that drives zeitgeist, as a consolidating force *and* as an agent of change, among writers and thinkers around 1800 identify a pattern of this process: an idea, or a set of ideas, is promoted by an influential elite, for public-spirited or for partisan reasons; the idea contributes to an interpretation of contemporary "reality". The idea "succeeds", i.e. has or finds support within the collective or polity to which it is addressed, if it makes sense to enough individuals. If there is not enough support, the "idea" does not circulate readily and will have little impact. (If it is "made" to spread, there is the risk that the coercion needed to enforce it may eventually outstrip the enforcers' powers.) If it *does* make sense to enough people, it will disseminate well, within the collective or polity *and beyond* its immediate linguistic or national borders towards other collectives to whom it also makes sense. If an idea succeeds and becomes an established view, or "opinion", it will soon impact on people's thinking and their actions, which will in turn impact on collective practice, cultural, political or social. Zeitgeist was conceived not only as what people think but also as what they do. It is based on a certain level of uniformity between accepted or acceptable thinking and accepted or acceptable practice, which in turn produces a recognisable contemporary cultural coherence. Crucially for my enquiry, this impact on practice makes it possible to trace zeitgeist empirically, by looking at how an idea becomes institutionalised.

"Making sense" is my summary of the process of acceptance which is at the heart of this study. While the role of elites, be they influential reformers, capable and charismatic leaders or manipulators, is crucial, the role of the "audience", or the "public", is equally important in this process. The role of the "public audience" consists in their acceptance or rejection of "ideas". This process is highly interactive: anyone who accepts the idea as making sense may become its propagator or find ways of applying it practically, anyone successfully propagating an idea may accede to political or cultural power or, if the idea ceases to make sense, lose such power. The role, nature, and size of the "appropriate" public audience was a matter of much debate around 1800.

Measuring the public acceptance of ideas has its difficulties; in this study evidence of acceptance will be drawn from two empirically observable things: the spread of terms – who uses them, how, and why – and the cultural practices they help to change or create. For example (and these are *very* broad brush strokes), the discussions about the role and nature of the public turned on the tension between the Enlightened public, the arbiter of reason and the public tribunal which would guard against error and abuses, and the gullible mob, which was thought to be easily manipulated and which was newly prominent on the streets of European cities. The events at St. Peter's Field, Manchester, on 16 August 1819 caused a "public" outcry. A large, mainly lower-class audience demanding social reform and listening to a series of public speakers had been forcefully dispersed by mounted militia, resulting in casualties. The outcry indicates that the authoritarian practice of violently dispersing large crowds who (peacefully) demand social and political change as if they were an immediate threat to public order was no longer acceptable without incurring public opprobrium. This unacceptability was expressed in the name by which this event became known. "Peterloo Massacre" captured the public outrage as well as the desire to slay tyrants. The name, adopted by public consent, suggested that *some* of the sense of the enlightened public, guardian of the public good, now adhered to the public audience at St. Peter's Field and that this guardian had been silenced by a despotic force. The allusion to the historic victory over Napoleon at Waterloo four years earlier, which had been styled as a victory for liberty against a tyrant, effectively suggested that in 1819 this liberty had been massacred. The name Peterloo Massacre illustrates that in 1819 liberty, despotism, and who had the right to speak (and listen) publicly were contested entities. The name, which was in circulation immediately, *was* initially contested, libel for some, the truth for others. Its adoption indicates that the interpretation of these events as a massacre of liberty, registering public concern, commanded then, and in years to come, a large measure public approval.

"Making sense" does not prejudge whether the conclusion that something does make sense is "right" or "wrong", it does not prejudge whether it is based on fact or wishful thinking. It merely asserts that individuals, or groups of individuals, have concluded that they accept a given interpretation of a situation or event as sensible and appropriate. Making sense of a situation or event in specific historical conditions gives rise to all forms of zeitgeist.

The key evidence of public acceptance remains the *institutionalisation* of ideas, the link between ideas and cultural practice, which has been defined as *Kulturmuster*, or cultural patterns (Fulda 2010). Such a link may be an anthropological feature and perhaps happened anywhere and anytime in human history, but in the eighteenth century the link between culture, spirit, and collectives of people came into sharp focus. Social changes (questioning established social hierarchies), which eventually led to the Revolution in France, sparked discussions about how a well-run polity works; cultural practice, institutions, and community ought to be linked in harmony. The question whether this "social culture" needed to be adjusted, needed to be made "right" for the "times", was at the time closely bound up with the desire to define and enfranchise new forms of publicly run and publicly accountable polities. Such harmonisation would inevitably be the basis for new ideas about communal (and national) spirit and identity and its cultural institutions.

Equally important to this investigation are considerations about how ideas (and practices) cross linguistic and national borders. The notion of zeitgeist provides a conceptual model of how cultural transfer processes operate and of the role of networks within these processes. It offers the opportunity to read history not just comparatively, but horizontally by looking at how historically specific ideas travel from place to place rather than (just) how they develop over time. Zeitgeist is itself and quite literally a "travelling concept" in Mieke Bal's sense (Bal 2002). Bal's volume focuses on the usefulness of "concepts" *per se* for discussing interdisciplinary transfers within the humanities. "Travelling" in my investigation is more functional: it discusses where, why, and how concepts travel.

Finally, what is an "idea"? In this study, an idea is a concept expressed in a particular term. As both term and concept exist in the human mind and imagination, ideas are eminently portable, under the right conditions they travel easily. This study explores the complexities of these conditions and summarises the principles that this exploration has yielded.

A final note on capitalisation: in the following, zeitgeist is not capitalised if it refers to the general idea; however, when it refers to the German term in German it *will* be capitalised.

1 Johann Gottfried Herder – the "Inventor of Zeitgeist"?

The concept of zeitgeist describes an at once animating and permeating social force. It originates around the turn of the seventeenth century but was conceptually re-deployed in the late eighteenth century, so it can now appear as if the term we use today emerged in the ambit of the French Revolution. This is reinforced by the fact that in German the word *Zeitgeist* was at this time beginning to oust other forms denoting this concept, such as "Geist der Zeit(en)" [spirit of the time(s)] or "Genius des Zeitalters/der Zeit" [genius of the age/of time], and has remained current ever since. And to a large extent, this narrative of the emergence of the term (and concept) of zeitgeist at the *end* of the eighteenth century holds true. Yet three key aspects of the early seventeenth-century concept survived the terminological changes and established a continuity between the early seventeenth- and the late eighteenth-century understanding of zeitgeist: firstly, that the concept denotes social influences on human activity, secondly, that it is focused on culture, and thirdly that it is integral to constructing identities. The contextual background of zeitgeist was, and largely remained, the post-sixteenth-century secularisation process, the development of modern historical thinking, and the emergence of modern social collectives, such as the nation, the republic, and other constitutional entities.

1.1 Herder's work as a site of convergence

Much ink has recently been spilled as to whether the twenty-four-year-old Johann Gottfried Herder was the first to use the term "Zeitgeist" in 1769.[1] While Herder did clearly *not* "invent" either the term or the concept, despite the many

---

[1] The passage featuring the famous "Druck des Zeitgeistes" comes from Herder's lengthy review of Christian Adolph Klotz' study of taste based on numismatics, *Beitrag zur Geschichte des Geschmacks und der Kunst aus Münzen* (1767) in the third of Herder's *Kritische Wälder* (Herder 1878 [1769]: 424). Herder criticises the material Klotz uses to trace the history of taste, not the effort itself. His criticism is nevertheless irascible and severe – his implacability is linked to a feud between the only slightly older but far more established Halle professor and the young Herder, which had been sparked by Klotz' negative review of Herder's (anonymously published) *Fragmente* (Maurer 2014: 35). Markus Meumann (2012: 285–290) takes Hermann Hiery to task for claiming that Herder plagiarised the zeitgeist-concept from Klotz (Hiery 2001: 1–6), who had published a satire entitled *Genius Seculi* [sic] in which he censored contemporary vices.

claims to the contrary,² it is indisputable that his work is the site where different approaches to the concept, and a plethora of related terms, converge and develop. It will become clear in the following that when he uses the word "Zeitgeist" in 1769 he does so on the back of a host of contemporary and historical deployments of the concept and that he would not, in all probability, have considered himself particularly original.³

The recent discussions about Herder's status in the history of zeitgeist have highlighted the fact that the *concept* of a "genius" or "spirit of the age", which distinguishes periods from each other and which unifies one period and its contemporaries, the "Zeitgenossen", in perceptible ways, is much older. It emerged in the early modern period, when historical time was no longer exclusively conceived as a single providential development but was coming to be regarded as a chain of distinct and fundamentally different eras. This development began with the notion of the Renaissance as the rebirth of antiquity after the intervening and different "Middles Ages".⁴ A new term was coined in (neo-)Latin, the *lingua franca* of the educated early modern world, to name what makes a period distinctive: *genius saeculi*. This term was the linguistic and semantic basis from which a variety of vernacular terms were eventually derived. In German these were "Geist der Zeit(en)" [spirit of the time(s)], "Geist des Zeitalters" [spirit of the age], "Säkulargeist" [secular spirit/spirit of this world/age], "Genius der Zeit" and "Genius der Zeiten" [genius of the time and of the times] as well as "Zeitgeist", French translated it as "l'esprit du siècle" and "l'esprit du tem(p)s", Voltaire uses the latter frequently in his *Essai sur les moeurs et l'esprit des nations*, and in English there appeared "spirit of the times" (Hurd and Percy) and "genius of the age" (Hume).

Genius saeculi emerged at the beginning of the seventeenth century, most prominently in the works of John Barclay (1582–1621) and Francis Bacon (1561–1626). The variety of terms derived from it suggests a large and fairly open semantic field well into the eighteenth century – Herder's work features most of the German derivations (Kempter 1990–1991: 51–61). This semantic and linguistic breadth

---

2 For an overview cf. Meumann (2012: 285, note 13). Even the blurb on the back of the most recent Herder biography by Marie-Elisabeth Lüdde (2016) states that he "coined" the terms "Volkslied" and "Zeitgeist".
3 For the most recent, and excellently researched, overviews of the history of the term, see Jung (2012) and Meumann (2012).
4 The idea of a succession of ages was of course not new: Christian providence had also divided the narrative of salvation into different periods (Joachim of Fiore's ages of father, son, and holy spirit) and in Greek antiquity Hesiod had distinguished between different ages, from gold down to iron.

is due to two things: a wide-reaching, well established *"genius"*-discourse (in the sense of l'esprit/spirit/Geist) and the fact that the Latin word *saeculum* harbours a number of ambiguities, which it acquired during its long usage passing from Roman Latin into ecclesiastical Latin, before being recoded in Protestant Latin and secularised historiography. *Saeculum* can mean "century" or "age". "Age" is the older meaning, rooted in the Roman usage of *saeculum* for the idea of "a lifetime" or generational cycle and the theological understanding of "ages of the world". In Christian thinking and ecclesiastical Latin it assumed the meaning of "worldly", in the sense of "this (mortal) life", which is responsible for the modern meaning of "secular" and for the often pejorative deployment of "secular spirit". When Protestant chronology needed to replace the reigns of popes with a more opportune measure, numeric centuries were adopted, a practice that was soon transferred into secular historiography. This is the reason for the double meaning of *siècle* in French (as well as in the other Romance languages), while English and German created new functional terms, century and *Jahrhundert*, which are differentiated from "age" and "Zeitalter" (Meumann 2012: 299–305). In the Latin *saeculum*, however, all educated early modern readers had access to the overlapping meanings of age and worldliness, which combined to a sense of human history and people's places within it.

The *genius*-discourse, under which I subsume the various usages of *Geist*, *l'esprit*, or spirit from the seventeenth century onwards, when Barclay and Bacon used these terms, reached a peak in the first half of the eighteenth century. Deriving its sense as an animating and dominating force from Christian metaphysics (Jung 2012: 322–323), "genius" or spirit informed the wide-ranging discussions of "culture" in their various national, legal, and intellectual manifestations, discussions which produced the many publications on "manners". Helvetius' *De l'esprit* (1758) and Voltaire's *Essay sur les moeurs et l'esprit des nations* (1756) are prominent examples of this, as is of course Montesquieu's *L'esprit des loix* (1748). The idea that such culture, and its empirical manifestation in peoples' activities, was subject to historical change and could be empirically observed in the present, or by diligent and imaginative historians in past ages, was never far from the surface.[5] In fact a desire to improve the writing of

---

[5] I disagree with Theo Jung on the point that "Ausdrücke wie Zeitgeist, Geist des Zeitalters, esprit du temps, du siècle or spirit of the age vermittelten […] vor der zweiten Hälfte des 18. Jahrhunderts zumeist völlig andere Bedeutungsdimensionen, als der moderne Sprachgebrauch vermuten lässt." (2012: 323) He suggests that pre-mid-eighteenth-century usage tends to focus on pejorative worldliness or individual genius and lacks the distinctly historical dimension of later meanings of zeitgeist (Jung 2012: 323–326). While this observation is correct as to the *degree* to which *historical* considerations tended to predominate from the later

history around 1600 initiated the rise of the idea of intellectual and cultural history, which was in turn responsible for the emergence of the modern understanding of "culture". This understanding was based on the notion that culture, as a surrounding context, conditions human conceptions and behaviour, i.e. possesses the power to shape thinking and behaviour, as Erich Hassinger succinctly summarised in 1978.[6] The full title of Voltaire's *Essay* makes clear this link between history, (national) culture, and manners: *Essai sur les moeurs et l'esprit des nations et sur les principeaux faits de l'histoire depuis Charlemagne jusqu'á Louis XIII.*

The intertwining of spirit and history, via human cultural identities, is the basis for *genius saeculi's* capacity to denote *both* synchronic and diachronic time, the specific age and the history of a nation or culture as a whole, which could then be allotted a place in general history. This accounts for the occasionally very long duration of an age, such as the "age of chivalry", in which the spirit of chivalry ruled, or the "age of the Old Testament". In their diachronic aspect "Geist der Zeit(en)", "l'esprit du siècle" and "spirit of the times" resonate with the emerging grandeur of the historical process, which will eventually develop into the Hegelian *Weltgeist*, incidentally a term Herder used, with the same meaning, a decade before Hegel (Herder 1991 [1793]: 89).[7] A focus on synchronic spirit, visibly animating a specific period, began to predominate towards the end of the eighteenth century, galvanised by the momentous events unfolding in France, although the notion of longer "ages" of coherence did not disappear. Both "Geist der Zeit(en)" and "Zeitgeist" inherit this dual capacity. Both aspects, diachronic and synchronic, have their roots in identity construction. As I will argue, this is already the case in Barclay.

Both time (Zeit) and spirit (Geist) share the features of impermanence, instability, and intangibility; their effects seem tangible, but *they* are not. They are never fixed and always open to challenge and contestation. They share these features with two other entities that rose to prominence in the eighteenth century and that are of key concern for zeitgeist: culture and the public sphere.

---

eighteenth century, this investigation shows how these different manifestations of "culture" (national customs, cultural specificity or distinctive and representative individual genius) all contributed towards an emerging sense of historicity.

6 Hassinger speaks of the "Vorstellung einer Kraft, die bewirkt, daß die Träger einer bestimmten Kultur in einer bestimmten Zeit Ähnliches denken, schaffen, und überhaupt andere Ziele anstreben als die Menschen vor bzw. nach ihnen [= ähnliche Ziele anstreben wie ihre Zeitgenossen, MO]" (Hassinger 1978: 5).

7 The editor of *Humanitätsbriefe* points out that the first use of this term in German occurs in a letter by Herder to Johann Heinrich Merck nearly twenty-five years earlier, dated 12 September 1770 (Herder 1991: 874).

Both the diachronic and the synchronic dimensions of zeitgeist are essential for one of the key functions this concept fulfils: a diagnostics of the present, which is more often than not a critique. The practice of criticising one's own times, by means of satire, alongside a diachronic panorama of different cultures, was modelled by Barclay. But in the minds of the mid- and late eighteenth-century thinkers another debate about culture and history provided a very similar model: the *Querelle*. Critiquing the current state of culture, and by extension of humanity, is a key trait of this cultural contestation. The position of the *anciens* contrasts the natural purity and vigour of Homeric times, or the mature artistic and intellectual perfection of the classical times, with an overrefined, decadent, under-achieving present, while the modern position exalts self-confident enlightened thinking that critiques the superseded nature of the past. Critiquing the present age informs the work of both Rousseau and Voltaire, it reached a fevered peak in the 1790s. The course of the revolution in France produced the need to explain the causes and the prospects of the Revolution, at this time the term "Zeitgeist" as we use it today burst onto the German discursive scene.

The deployment of *genius saeculi* and zeitgeist in both their positive and negative connotations ranging from satirical or earnest critique of the times to immanent world spirit is made possible by the instability of both spirit and time, especially in their relation to each other within this compound noun: connotations of worldliness (as opposed to religious eternity) clash with the notion of the historical immanence of a world-spirit; the historical process allows for both rise and decline, the present may inaugurate a better future or precipitate deterioration, it can *result* from progress or decline. Individuals, nations, and cultures are exposed to historical conditions, they *may* successfully or unsuccessfully try to mitigate or foster them. This tension between diachronic and synchronic dimensions lies at the heart of the zeitgeist concept.[8] It has a corollary in a tension between cultural and political control and agency, as we shall see, which is less recognised, because much of the existing discussion has located zeitgeist in a historical discourse, without considering its place in identity discourses.[9]

---

8 See Meumann (2012) and Jung (2012).
9 Ralf Konersmann comes close to identifying the sense of identity contained in the zeitgeist-concept. "Er [Zeitgeist] ermöglicht tiefe Bindungen in der partikularen Lebensform eines rein zeitlich definierten Wir. Der Zeitgeist bedient das Bedürfnis nach Zugehörigkeit. Die funktionale Betrachung gestattet folgenden Vergleich: Was im geographischen Raum als Heimat erlebt und bejaht wird, das ist der Zeitgeist im Raum der geschichtlichen Zeit." (2006: 248). Konersmann, however, focuses on the psychological bonds of the individual, rather than the constructed cultural identities of (historical) collectives.

The constructed cultural identities of collectives are key to understanding not just zeitgeist discussions, historical or otherwise, but also to understanding the functioning of the zeitgeist dynamic. These identities are the link between zeitgeist discussed in ongoing political and social contexts and zeitgeist as epochal historical identity constructed by historians who look back on past periods. Both kinds of zeitgeist share the same purpose, differentiation: they are constructed to differentiate historical or geographical identities, to claim progress or decline, establish cultural superiority or room for improvement.

Herder's work illustrates these developments between the mid-eighteenth century and the 1790s. From the 1760s to the 1790s he uses the various linguistic and conceptual forms of *genius saeculi* (Kempter 1990–1991: 52–61), and in his writing both diachronic and synchronic strands converge: he discusses both historical and contemporary identities, always based on cultural identity. Beginning in 1767 in the second collection of *Fragments*, when speaking of translating oriental poetry into a contemporary context, he pairs up "Sekulargeist", perhaps the closest possible calque of *genius saeculi*, with "Nationalgeist", and uses "Genie unserer Zeit, Denkart und Sprache" [genius of our age, way of thinking and language] (Herder 1877: 274). A little further on one also finds "Geist eines Zeitalters" (discussing the pointlessness of imitating ancient Greek poetic forms) (1877: 314). Kempter also attests Herder's use of "Geist des Jahrhunderts" *as well as* "Geschichtsgeist", "Gott der Zeit", and "Zeitgott" (1990–1991: 54–55). The latter group connotes the (divine) majesty of time and history and suggests an immanent world spirit. In line with the earlier observations regarding the use of "Jahrhundert" in the sense of "age" (saeculum), Herder speaks, in 1773, of "Jahrhundert des schönsten griechischen Geschmacks" [age of the most beautiful Grecian taste] (1891 [1773]: 638). In Herder's thinking, especially in the 1760s and 1770s (and perhaps throughout his life), the synchronic focus on an age tended to illustrate diachronic progression; ages are *phases* in the course of history. Most of his texts that feature these terms are histories of aspects of human culture. These phases are often lengthy, frequently encompassing whole cultures. In 1774, for example, he calls chivalry (Rittersinn) the "Blüthe des Zeitgeistes" [the flower of the spirit of the age][10] and oriental philosophy (Morgenländerphilosophie) "Element des Zeitgeistes",[11] the first informing the Middle Ages, and the second the Hebrew world of the Old Testament. Similarly, the "bleierne Druck des Zeitgeistes" [the

---

10 In *Auch eine Philosophie zur Geschichte der Menschheit* (Herder 1891 [1774]: 527).
11 In *Älteste Urkunde des Menschengeschechts* (Herder 1883 [1774]: 478).

leaden pressure of zeitgeist] – the famous 1769 quote – is a lengthy "Joch des Jahrhunderts" [yoke of the age][12] based on the longevity of tradition in the practice of fashioning coins. In the early 1790s, when the Revolution was entering its most radical phase, Herder (eventually) produced a definition of zeitgeist. The first two collections of *Humanitätsbriefe*, written and published in 1792–1793 provide a comprehensive summary of what zeitgeist had come to mean, and how it would be understood from Hendrich to Mill.

Zeitgeist, for Herder, addresses not just the relation between the diachronic and synchronic dimensions of collective identities, but also the tension between cultural and political control and agency, which finds expression in the relationship between elites and their public(s) and will be investigated further in Chapter 3. In *Humanitätsbriefe* he moves from defining the features of *Zeit* and *Geist* on to public spirit, "Gemeingeist" [public spirit] (1991: 89). In his early work Herder frequently conceptualised the relationship between elites with their publics around the notion of predominant "taste" (Geschmack), in the sense that general taste is decreed by elites and accepted by the public. In Herder's early work, taste is closely linked to zeitgeist. In 1767 he speaks of "Geschmack der Zeiten" [the taste of the times] in *Fragmente* (1877: 265) and of "Geschmack des Zeitalters" [taste of the age] in 1773 in "Ursachen des gesunkenen Geschmacks", noting that "so verschieden also die Zeiten sind, so verschieden muss auch die Sphäre des Geschmacks seyn" [the sphere of taste must be as different as the different times] (1891: 645).[13] In 1773 zeitgeist was expressed through taste, by 1793 his focus had become more political.

With the aim of reaching greater clarity about the progress towards greater humanity against the background of the ongoing revolution, Herder ruminates, in *Humanitätsbriefe*, on the interdependence of culture, politics, and society. The text form, a collection of letters circulating among friends, mimics the dynamics of the public sphere, i.e. a space of free discussion among rational minds to achieve a reasoned understanding, as the originally unpublished preface to the first version of collection 1 and 2 makes clear:

> Diese Freunde sagen auch ihre Meinungen, deren keine der Herausgeber ihrer Briefe verbürget, [...]. Keine derselben nehme man also als Gesetz oder Evangelium an: denn auch die korrespondierende Gesellschaft widerspricht oder berichtigt einander; [...]. Auf diesen

---

12 It is – of course – debatable whether this phrase should be translated as "yoke of the century" or "of the age".
13 Kempter points out that, while Herder does use formulations related to zeitgeist in this essay, e.g. "Geist der Zeitbedürfnisse" [spirit of the needs of the time] (Herder, 1891: 638), he prefers the term "Geschmack" in the same contexts (1990–1991: 55).

Konflikt der Meinungen zu ihrer Prüfung und Ausbildung gehet der Zweck der Briefe. (Herder 1991: 763)[14]

[These friends express their opinions, none of which are underwritten by the Letters' editor, […]. One should not regard any of them as law or Gospel: for the members of a corresponding society too contradict and correct each other; […]. The purpose of these Letters lies in this conflict of opinions in order to examine and shape them.]

Herder still uses the key zeitgeist terms interchangeably. He begins his discussion with "Geist der Zeit": "Mehrmals finde ich in Ihren Briefen den Geist der Zeit genannt." [Several times I find the term Geist der Zeit in your letters.] (Herder 1991 [1793]: 85). The respondent then refers to the "Geist der Zeit*en*" (1991: 85), only to move on to speak of the "geläuterte Zeitgeist" [purified zeitgeist] before returning in the next sentence to "der geläuterte Geist der Zeiten" (1991: 86). While he has one eye on the present, the perspective is historical; Herder's interest in a diachronic view remains dominant. The "Geist der Zeiten" is a "mächtiger Genius" [mighty genius] (1991: 85) which proceeds from the "Schoß der Zeiten" [lap of time], a quick panorama running from pre-Christian Europe via the Catholic Middle Ages, the Renaissance, the Reformation and the scientific revolution to the eighteenth century follows (1991: 86). This spirit is largely benevolent. "Er hat aus den vorigen Zeiten gesammelt, sammelt aus der jetzigen, und dringt in die folgenden Zeiten." [It has collected [things] from past times, is collecting from the present, and rushes on to the future.] (1991: 86) This suggests the power and cumulative quality of the historical process, in which different specific cultural phases are viewed as "eine Kette im Fortgange der Zeiten" [a chain in the process of time] (1991: 89). His concern for the historical specificity of human culture – what he is most remembered for – is rooted in this very perspective of succession and multiplicity: "das Rad [of time/history MO] rollet fort, ist immer dasselbe, und zeigt immer eine andre Seite" [the wheel [of time/history] rolls on, it is always the same, and yet it is constantly showing a different side] (1991: 87). The wheel of history is a recurring metaphor in this text.

Herder's definition of zeitgeist is focused on the historical process and takes a diachronic perspective. "Geist der Zeiten hieße also die Summe der Gedanken,

---

14 The preface belongs with the suppressed materials for *Humanitätsbriefe*, which have in part survived in Herder's papers. Between January and the spring of 1793 Herder decided to withdraw (or rewrite) some of the first two collections he had completed by the end of December 1792. He was determined for his *Letters* to pass the censors and toned down his lingering support for aspects of the French Revolution, but his views were probably also affected by the continuing radicalisation in France: January 1793 saw the execution of Louis XVI. See Maurer (2014: 149–153) and Herder (1991: 809–812).

Gesinnungen, Anstrebungen, Triebe und lebendigen Kräfte, die in einem bestimmten Fortlauf der Dinge mit gegebenen Ursachen und Wirkungen sich äußern." [One could call the spirit of the times the sum of all thoughts, attitudes, endeavours, drives, and vital forces, which find expression as causes and effects in a specific course of things.] (1991: 88) The "spirit" emerges in the process of events, their causes and effects. This also applies to the present. The link between agency, effects, and circumstances is crucial: it is the expression of human thought, understanding, and active will in response to circumstances, but there is also a suggestion of force beyond direct agency in "effects" (Wirkungen). This dual identity is discussed near the beginning: Letter 14 asks "Muß er [der Zeitgeist] herrschen? muß er dienen? kann man ihn lenken?" [Must zeitgeist rule? Must it serve? Can it be directed?]. Letter 15 replies: "Wir stehen alle unter seinem Gebiet bald tätig, bald leidend." [We are all under its dominion, sometimes actively, sometimes passively.] (1991: 85) This expression of human designs and their implementation (on others) is the basis for zeitgeist's ability to create the synchronic coherence of an "age", or "unsere Zeit", to create the historical specificity of culture.

Herder's perspectivism sees the historical process as a succession of specific "presents". To define the "spirit" of "our time", the text points out that one has first to agree the boundaries of this age – which are moveable, again depending on perspective: "so müssen wir erst bestimmen, was unsere Zeit sei, welchen Umfang wir ihr geben können und mögen" [first we have to define what our time is, which extent we can, and may, give to it] (1991: 88). He settles on "das christliche Europa" (1991: 88), which has grown from the Great Migrations and the establishment of Christianity and produced a tradition of feudal monarchies and ecclesiastical control, a tradition that has come under fire, successively, through the Reformation, the scientific revolution, and now the social unrest of his own time. Herder leaves no doubt that the questing spirit of exploration and reform that drives this challenge is the *Geist der Zeit* (and linked to truth), and its connection with the revolution in France would have been evident to all but the most obtuse contemporary reader, even from the toned-down published version.[15] In the unpublished version he continues with a concise definition of zeitgeist that is more clearly focused on the present situation:

> Denn allenthalben ist er [der Geist der Zeit] eine Folge vorhergehender Zustände, nach Lage der Dinge zu einem flüchtigen Jetzt modifiziert. Dies flüchtige Jetzt kann allerdings geleitet und gelenkt werden, so wie es an seinem Teile auch leitet und lenkt. Es wird gebraucht and gemißbraucht; es herrschet und es dienet. (1991: 765)

---

15 For more details see the editor's commentary regarding the unpublished parts of the second collection (Herder 1991: 761–806).

[For it [zeitgeist] is clearly a consequence of preceding conditions, modified into a transitory Now by the situation. This transitory Now, however, may be led and directed, as it itself also leads and directs. It is used and abused; it rules and it serves.]

The conjunction of historically grown conditions [eine Folge vorhergehender Zustände] with contingent events [Lage der Dinge] produces a "transient Now" that affects contemporaries as it is directed by (some of) them. Herder begins to home in on a much shorter, fragile, and less "geläutert" [purified] period of coherence. The first two collections of Letters were published at Easter and in May 1793 respectively, but their drafts had been finalised in November and December 1792, i.e. weeks after the September massacre in Paris, the defeat of anti-revolution forces at Valmy, and the creation of the French republic (Herder 1991: 810–811), all of which Herder followed closely, and which made him want to speak out.[16] The focus on the present is not entirely lost in the published version. The vast compass of "das christliche Europa" is not just divided into different nations, in the same sentence the compass of the common spirit shrinks, historically, geographically, and socially. "Spirits" vary between regions and peoples, and even between different social classes of one nation "Denken wir uns [...] das christliche Europa: so ist auch in ihm nach Ländern und Situationen der Geist der Zeit sehr verschieden. Er ändert sich sogar mit Klassen der Einwohner, geschweige mit ihren Bedürfnissen, Neigungen und Einsichten." [Let us consider [...] Christian Europe: here, too, the spirit of the time differs according to countries and situations. It differs even between the classes of a population, not to mention in relation to their needs, inclinations, and insights.] (1991: 88). Herder is keen to stress that any suggested coherence is general at the best of times; it is in fact constructed:

> Die Elemente der Begebenheiten sehen wir nie; wir bemerken bloß ihre Erscheinungen, und ordnen uns ihre Gestalten in einer wahrgenommenen Verbindung. [...] So ist Europa auch nur ein Gedankenbild, das wir uns etwa nach der Lage seiner Länder, nach ihrer Ähnlichkeit, Gemeinschaft und Unterhandlung zusammenordnen. (1991: 88)

> [We never see the elements of the events; we only see their phenomena and order their appearances in a connection we perceive. [...] Thus Europe, too, is only a mental image, which we order for ourselves according to the position of its countries, their similarity, community, and negotiations.]

In any case people are easily influenced by events and fake news, "ein einziger Umstand, eine vielleicht falsche oder übertriebene Nachricht, kurz ein Wink und Wahn stimmt oft die Denkart und Meinung des ganzen Volkes" [a single

---

[16] "Die Zeiten verbieten das Schweigen; sie reißen den Mund auf." [The times forbid silence, they make us open our mouths.] Letter to J. W. L. Gleim, 12 November 1792 (Herder 1991: 810).

circumstance, perhaps a false or exaggerated message, in short, one hint or illusion frequently determines the whole peoples' thinking and opinion] (1991: 88–89).[17] Zeitgeist suddenly becomes hard to distinguish from a potentially fickle and short-lived public opinion. The execution of Louis XVI appears to have effected a change in the way the political developments in France were seen in the Herder household.[18] While the 1792 version contains harsh criticism of existing social hierarchies and of the aristocracy, which stand in the way of social progress,[19] the *Letters* published in May 1793 only very cautiously suggest that progress might still be part of the spirit of the current age. In the suppressed Letter 12, one friend is hopeful that the current zeitgeist, despite its demonic appearance, might be the harbinger of the true genius of humanity (albeit with still some way to go).[20] In the published version this passage was changed to: "ich glaube es [...] nicht" [I don't believe it is], although some hope remains that it might *become* the harbinger of the genius of humanity, if people worked on this (1991: 87).[21] By 1793 zeitgeist has potentially become a short-term mood that may be exploited for political purposes, and a synchronic perspective is preoccupying Herder. The divine-like majesty of the "Geist der Zeiten" now also comes to be questioned:

---

17 The ambiguity of the German term "Volk" – in the sense of the people as nation and in the sense of the (ordinary) people as the lower classes, or indeed as general (English) "folk" – leaves room for interpretation; the passage reiterates yet again the close link Herder saw between the spirit of (the) time and collective identity, such as "Volksgeist".
18 See Karoline Herder's letter to F. H. Jacobi of 5 April 1793 (Herder 1991: 812).
19 "Nur ein Stand exsistiert [sic] im Staate, Volk (nicht Pöbel); zu ihm gehört der König sowohl als der Bauer [...]. Die Natur schafft edle, große, weise Männer [...], diese sind [...] Vorsteher und Führer des Volkes (Aristodemokraten)." [There is only one estate in the state, the people (not the mob); the king as well as the peasant are part of it [...]. Nature produces noble, great and wise men [...], these are the principals and leaders of the people (Aristodemocrats).] (Herder 1991: 768) and "Zu unserer Zeit glaubt niemand mehr, daß die Geburt gelehrt, edel, geschickt oder verdient macht." [In our times no-one any longer believes that birth makes anyone educated, noble, skilled or bestows merit.] (Herder 1991: 777).
20 "Ich wollte, daß der Dämon unserer Zeiten der echte Genius einer reinen allverbreiteten Humanität wäre; das ist er aber bei weitem noch nicht; wir wünschen, daß er sein Freund, sein Vorbote, sein Diener sei, und wollen, daß er dies mehr und mehr werde." [I would the demon of our times were the true genius of a pure and ubiquitous humanity; this it is not yet by far; we wish it to be its friend, its harbinger, its servant, and we want it to increasingly become this.] (Herder 1991: 772).
21 "'Geist der Zeiten, ist er der Genius der Humanität selbst: oder dessen Freund, Vorbote, Diener?' Ich wollte, daß er das Erste wäre, glaube es aber nicht; das Letzte hoffe ich nicht nur, sondern bin dessen fast gewiß. Daß er sein Freund, ein Vorbote, ein Diener der Humanität werde, wollen wir an unserem unmerklichen Teile befördern." ['Spirit of the times, is it the genius of humanity: or its friend, harbinger, servant?' I would it were the first, but don't believe it is; the

Sobald man dem Wort seine magische Gestalt nimmt, was bedeutet es mehr, als die *herrschenden Meinungen, Sitten, und Gewohnheiten unseres Zeitalters*, und sollten diese eines so hohen Lobes wert sein? Sollten sie so hohe und große Hoffnungen für die Zukunft gewähren? (Herder 1991: 103, italics in original)

[As soon as one takes away the word's magical appearance, what more does it mean than the *dominant opinions, customs, and habits of our age*, and should these be worthy of such praise? Should they admit of such high and great hopes for the future?]

This sense of crisis is polemically intensified: "Wie ich fürchte, strebt der Geist unserer Zeiten vorzüglich zur Auflösung hin." [I fear the spirit of our age is preferably tending towards disintegration.] (1991: 105)

Despite these fears the notion of the benevolent zeitgeist is not abandoned: zeitgeist is, or can be, directed by the principles and opinions of the most clear-sighted and sensible men ("Grundsätze und Meinungen der scharfsichtigsten, verständigsten Männer"), who "machten sich vom Wahne des Pöbels los, und lassen sich nicht nach jedem Winke lenken" [who have detached themselves from the madness of the mob and do not follow constantly changing views] (1991: 89). They form an invisible church ("unsichtbare Kirche"), which produces and leads public spirit, "diesen Gemeingeist des aufgeklärten oder sich aufklärenden Europa" [this public spirit of enlightened Europe or of Europe enlightening itself] (1991: 89). An intellectual and moral elite, which may still be in need of continued education, research, and intellectual exchange but is already well versed in history and in debate ("Gespräche") and has a growing sense of how historical and social developments are affecting politics ("eine gemeinschaftliche Bemerkung dessen, was vorgegangen ist und täglich vorgeht", 1991: 89), is capable of leading the late eighteenth century into a brighter future.

By intersecting the diachronic and synchronic dimensions, spirit animates communities over time and in the present; different communal spirits express different phases of the historical process. Ultimately, human agency drives spirit. This agency may be reasonable, led by "sensible men", or it may serve ulterior motives. At the same time there is a sense that spirit exerts control and determines human activity. By the same token, zeitgeist is the expression of a communal identity, a nation or an age, which is permeated by a sense of its own purpose defined by their elites and accepted, ideally after purifying discussion, by their public.

---

last, however, I do not only hope, I am almost certain of. That it will become its friend, a harbinger, a servant of humanity, to this we want to contribute our own tiny share.] (Herder 1991: 87).

This discussion in the second collection may well have been prompted by the high frequency with which the term zeitgeist (or Geist der Zeit) was now appearing in public discourse. The opening line of the first letter alludes to this frequency: "Mehrmals finde ich in Ihren Briefen den *Geist der Zeit* genannt" (1991: 85, italics in original). Herder is likely to have felt some ownership of the term, he had been dealing with it since the 1760s, and he may at this point have felt he needed to set the record straight. The collection is written with an eye on the events in France and a growing sense of turmoil, and Herder wants to get across a distinction. He seeks to differentiate the "Geist der Zeit" (and "Geist des Zeitalters"), which are led by elites of those "scharfsichtigsten und verständlichsten Männern", from the madness of the mob, the "Wahne des Pöbels". The latter are easily whipped up and manipulated, while the former are not. Herder, it seems, wants to guard the terms that have informed his work and his thinking against contemporary appropriation, which is turning them into transient fashions ("Lufthauch der Mode", 1991: 85), or worse, into the "Geist des Aufruhrs, der Zwietracht, den unreinen, abgeschmackten Pöbelsinn und Wahnsinn" [the spirit of revolt, of discord, impure and tasteless madness, the mentality of the mob] (1991: 85–86). At the same time Herder takes on the discreditation of "spirit" as a ridiculous or dangerous "ghost", a well-established eighteenth-century stick to use against the genius-metaphor:[22] the interlocutor who supports the zeitgeist notion rejects the idea of spirit being a "Poltergeist" (1991: 85).

Debate is of course the point of the dialogic text form, and hope is allowed to prevail through recourse to the turning wheel of time[23] and the irrepressible force of moral regeneration, expressed in the metaphorical image of recovery from fever. The belief in the benevolent efficiency of the historical process is reiterated by suggesting "was Eine Zeit nicht tun konnte, kann eine andere" [what one age could not achieve another one will] (1991: 117), when governmental reform and education will be capable of repairing any damage created on the way. The ability of zeitgeist to contain a difficult present in the historical process, which rests on its combined synchronic and diachronic perspectives, will be integral to its success in the age of revolution and reform. It makes zeitgeist equally useful for both reforming moderates and radical revolutionaries.

---

22 See Meumann (2012: 309–310).
23 "Es ist Ein und dasselbe Gesetz der Natur, das diese Seite des Rades hinunter, jene emporkehrt." [It is one and the same law of Nature that moves this side of the wheel up and the other down.] (Herder 1991: 115).

1.2 The genealogy of zeitgeist – Barclay and Bacon

As *genius saeculi* a concept of zeitgeist is recognisable in John Barclay's *Icon Animorum* (likeness of the spirits),[24] which was published in 1614. Two years later it was appended to Barclay's immensely successful semi-autobiographical picaresque novel *Euphormio*, written in Humanist Neo-Latin, which had been appearing, initially anonymously, in instalments since 1603 (Becker 1904: 37 and 111). Herder was well versed in "genius"-literature and owned, by 1769, three copies of Barclay's *Icon* (Meumann 2012: 298). The outrageous satire of Barclay's *roman á clef* made the young author well known throughout Western and Central Europe. *Euphormio*'s biting portrayal of contemporary institutions, figures, and preoccupations presents in many respects a caricature of the "age". It may well have been an influence on Klotz's satirical *Genius Seculi* [sic], and in hindsight appears as an ancestor of Hazlitt's *Spirit of the Age*. *Euphormio*'s success helped to disseminate *Icon*, and with it the term and concept of *genius saeculi*, widely,[25] *Euphormio* went through at least fourteen editions between 1616 and 1664.[26] When it appeared in 1614, *Icon Amimorum* was published simultaneously in London and Paris, which illustrates the high expectations publishers had of this volume. In addition to the combined editions of *Icon* and *Euphormio*, *Icon* continued to be published independently; it appears to have been particularly popular in Germany, with six editions between 1625 and 1774 (Becker 1904: 112). That it was widely read and taken seriously is evidenced by its use in education: Becker refers to the 1733 edition published in Germany as a regular school book (1904: 112) and unearthed the (Latin) programme of an undated school performance in honour of a history teacher based on *Icon* in the Library of the National Museum in Budapest (1904: 113, note 4). While the translation into English in 1631 preceded the first German version, German is the language into which *Icon* was translated most frequently, four times between 1649 and 1821.[27] This wide dissemination in multiple editions may explain why Herder owned three different editions of the work.[28]

---

24 See Hassinger (1978), Kempter (1990–1991), Konersmann (2007), Meumann (2012), Jung (2012). Hassinger has identified Barclay's term as "Novum" as no earlier instances have so far been traced (1978: 145). The first French translations of *Icon Animorum* render the title as "Le tableau des esprits" and "Le portrait des esprits".
25 Meumann traces references to *genius saeculi* in connection with ages and peoples in German, English, and French (2012: 295–297).
26 For a summary see Becker (1904: 111–112).
27 See Becker (1904: 111–113) for details. The English translation is *Mirrour of Mindes* by Thomas May.
28 Kempter points out (1990–1991: 60) that Herder mentions "Euphormio" in 1769 in *Erstes Wäldchen* (Herder 1878: 73); but it is not entirely clear how this relates to Barclay's work.

Barclay (1582–1621) was of transnational descent and well-travelled; his father William was Scottish and taught law in France and England, his mother was from Alsace; John lived in France, England, and Italy during his (short) life. By all accounts, he was a witty, highly educated Renaissance man, with a penchant for scandal and a hunger for fame, who enjoyed the high life of a transnational jet-setting diplomat – James I may have sent him on missions from the age of twenty-one. He had excellent connections to the (Protestant) King of England and Scotland as well as to the Pope.[29] He formed his ideas based on his observations of the cultures and characters of different European peoples; *Icon* is an early contribution to the genius-discourse. The book's focus is, as the English translator points out, the different "humane dispositions".[30] Beginning with the "Four Ages of Man", Barclay goes on to discuss the spirits that affect human thinking and activity before presenting a panorama of different nations. Barclay also discusses what he terms *genius saeculi*, a word he had already employed in part 1 of *Euphormio* (Hassinger 1978: 143).[31] Chapter 2 is based on the premise "That every age almost hath a particular Genius different from the rest; that there is a proper Spirit to every Region, which doth in a manner shape the studies, and manners of the inhabitants, according to itselfe" (Barclay 1631: 36)[32] He asserts that "every age of the world has a certain Genius, which overruleth the mindes of men, and turneth them to some desires" (1631: 45).[33] He is particularly amazed ("there is no diversity which is more worthy of wonder, then [sic] this", 1631: 44) that "men born to liberty [...] should also serve; their own dispositions, the fate of the times, wherein they live, forcing them as it were into certaine affections and rules of living" (1631: 44–45). The permeating power of the *genius saeculi* is clear, and all change proceeds from it (1631: 53–54), but it is not the only force affecting human thinking and activity. "There is another force, that ravisheth the mindes of men, and maketh them addicted to certain affections. Namely, that spirit which being appropriate to every region infuseth into men [...] the habit, and affections of their owne country." (1631: 54) The striking aspect about Barclay's descriptions is the control, the power to mould, that is exerted on the individual by the two spirits, national

---

[29] See Hassinger (1978: 38–40 and 89) and Becker (1904).
[30] Barclay 1631: "Epistle Dedicatory", no pagination.
[31] Hassinger points out that Barclay uses "genius saeculi" and "genuis aetatis" (genius of the age) interchangeably (1978: 144).
[32] "Secula paene singular suum genium habere, diversumque a caeteris. Esse praeterea cuilibet regioni proprium spiritum [...]. Hos spiritus investigari operae precium esse." As quoted by Kempter (1990–1991: 60) from the 1637 Leiden edition.
[33] "Nam omnia saecula genium habent, qui mortalium animos in certa studia solet inflectere" (Hassinger 1978: 144). Hassinger quotes from the 1637 Leiden edition. Kempter (1990–1991: 59–60) refers to the same passage.

spirit and the spirit of the age, or *Volksgeist* and *Zeitgeist*. Barclay must hence be seen as an early propagator of the two terms which are so commonly associated with Herder and which retained an element of synonymity into the early nineteenth century. While to the late modern reader the link between specific collective spirits and zeitgeist may appear somewhat random, in Barclay's text this connection is close: the different collectives embody time, history becomes visible only through them. The second German translator (1660) reinforced this point by adding to chapter 2 the running head "Von dem Geist eines jeden Saeculi, so an den Menschen zu sehen" [Of the spirit of each age, as it can be discerned in men].[34] Barclay's *aetates* are large historio-cultural ages, such as the ancient Greeks, the Romans, the Middle Ages, which indicates that he regarded these periods as parts of universal history. Herder's close reading of Barclay is evident, not least in his equation of "National- oder Sekulargeist" in 1767.[35]

From the start, zeitgeist was linked to identity and to identity construction, both of peoples and of "ages". Both are collectives, their character is encapsulated in their genius, their spirit, which is intangible, yet perceived as real, even if it is constructed. As "time" was no longer primarily seen as a function of divine providence, it became conceived as embodied by people, human communities, their activities, producing predispositions and character(istic)s. Focusing, in this respect, on national characteristics, as Barclay does, appears as the most obvious way of embodying historical time. This reciprocal conditioning between age and the people continued to inform notions of zeitgeist from Herder to John Stuart Mill.

The fact that it was thought sensible to combine the satirical novel of contemporary (high) life with a panorama of national cultures as they shape individuals and are expressed by them suggests a sense that the contemporary moment was embedded in a historical process. Yet in Barclay's *genius saeculi* there is no very sharp sense of a short and changeable present, this notion would only gain prominence at the end of the eighteenth century. But Barclay too focused on national spirit in history with the aim to understand the workings of (contemporary) society.

Francis Bacon's contributions to the zeitgeist concept, his *Proficience and advancement of learning divine and human* (1605) and *De dignitate et augmentis scientiarium* (1623), appeared at roughly the same time as Barclay's *Euphormio* and *Icon*. They were written in the context of his efforts to reform historiography

---

34 Kempter quotes from Ioh. Barclai, *Spiegel Menschlicher GemüthsNeigungen*, published in Bremen in 1660 (1990–1991: 60).
35 In "Von den Deutsch-Orientalischen Dichtern" (Herder,1877: 262).

and the concept of history, which, in his view, needed to move beyond recounting only the "gesta" of the powerful. Historiography should include cultural history, the history of literature and the sciences, a "historia literarum et artium", if it was to be a source of education and knowledge and help "make men wise in the use and administration of learning". Because a conception of history that does not include these aspects "doth not show the life and spirit" of history and remains a lifeless collection of disparate facts (Hassinger 1978: 40, 119–120). In Bacon's programme, laid out in these two publications, a notion of intellectual and cultural history emerges, which lays the foundation for the modern understanding of culture as a context created by humans and informing their actions, both mental and physical.[36] Inherent in this approach to history is the belief that human history is about human collectives and how they work and that these collectives are animated by a spirit. Herder still subscribed to this approach towards the end of his life, in his introduction to Friedrich Majer's *Kulturgeschichte der Völker* in 1798:

> Nur durch den Geist, den wir in die Geschichte bringen, und aus ihr ziehen, wird uns Menschen- und Völkergeschichte nützlich. [...] Geistlos zusammengestellte Facta stehen unfruchtbar da. (Herder 1880 [1798]: 340)
>
> [Only through the spirit which we bring to history and draw out of it can human history and the history of nations be useful for us. [...] Facts that are assembled without spirit are fruitless.]

For Bacon the understanding of previous cultures of knowledge and cognition, and their relation to the present, was a key concern. In his *Proficience and advancement of learning divine and human* he focuses on intellectual progress (Hassinger 1978: 119) and calls for a history of the "state of learning", which would comprise

> ...the antiquities and originals of knowledges and their sects [sections/disciplines, MO], their inventions, their traditions, their diverse administrations and managings, their flourishing, their oppositions, decays, depressions, oblivions, removes, with the causes and occasions of them, and all other events of learning throughout the ages of the world.[37]

Through this exercise the "genius illius temporis literarius" (the literary genius of that time, i.e. spirit that is contained in all kinds of writing), Bacon asserts in 1623 in *De dignitate et augmentis scientiarum*, could be reconstructed

---

[36] Bacon was not without prompts on this point from (near) contemporary writers, especially Le Roy and La Popelinière in France and Reiner Reineccius in Germany, as Hassinger points out (1978: 40 and 119).

[37] Quoted in Hassinger (1978: 120).

(Hassinger 1978: 120). Cultural contextualisation necessarily led Bacon to formulate the notion of an "age" held to together by one or more unifying dominant themes. Bacon's focus was slightly different from Barclay's, Bacon was interested in understanding history (and the present within it), rather than contemporary society. But both suggest that this can best be done by studying the nature of different ages and the characteristics of the people that live them.

Zeitgeist as a concept that defines characteristics of collective cultural coherence, irrespective of whether this identity was criticised or praised, was in existence by the early seventeenth century. But at that time this concept did not make anything like the overt impact, intellectually or culturally, which it achieved at the end of the eighteenth century when it became a catchword that inspired fierce passions and much debate. Its impact at this stage was more covert; although it was widely known, it appears that it was uncontroversial, which does not preclude satirical attacks on its "ghostly-ness" (Jung 2012: 341–346). It was widely regarded as a historical tool without being investigated in its own right.

1.3 Praising or critiquing the age – *Genius Saeculi* and the *Querelle*

Notions of *genius saeculi* informed one of the key cultural debates of the later seventeenth century, which came to a head around 1700: the Quarrel of the Ancients and the Moderns (Meumann 2012: 297–301). The *Querelle* focused on cultural difference in history, it unites the two concerns which prompted the concept of *genius saeculi*: a fuller understanding of history and of the specific cultural identities of distinct historical periods, and their carriers, human communities. The *Querelle* was a key site for the creation of a new – modern – European identity. The aim of the moderns was to define and establish a distinctly modern culture, which was not just equal but superior to its ancient predecessor, which would allow them to emancipate themselves from the cultural hegemony of antiquity instituted by the Renaissance. The *genius* of (the age of) antiquity, evident in ancient art and thought, was pitted against the *genius* of (the age of) modernity, which claimed intellectual and moral superiority.

The *Querelle* was, on both sides, based on defining the character of an age in relation to other ages. This provided the opportunity to praise or critique the age in question and establish a historical development, which could be either progress or decline. Optimistic and self-confident Enlightenment thinking celebrated the (superior) character of its own time, the "siècle des lumières" which had been preceded by "le grand siècle". Charles Perrault's *Poème sur le siècle du Louis le grand*, presented at the Académie Française in 1687 and traditionally regarded as the opening shot of the *Querelle*, made the case for the moderns. Two generations later, Voltaire's *Siècle du Louis XIV* (1751) set this era into its historical context.[38]

Alternatively, from the beginning of the century, *critiques* of enlightened (over-)civilisation found fault with excessive refinement and the dominance of rationality and praised "natural" and simple conditions instead; the early eighteenth-century *Querelle d'Homére* is an example of this. Both celebration and critique were reciprocal features of the *Querelle*. Criticism of the present was inherent in the *anciens'* praise of the unsurpassable ideals of antiquity which in the present age could only be emulated. Despite the shared preoccupation with a superior age, which encouraged a synchronic perspective, the diachronic perspective was kept within sight by the focus on the historical development of progress or decline.

The early uses of *genius saeculi* by Barclay and Bacon linked this concept with the characters of different peoples in history who were affected by the spirit of their time and the spirit of their people. Both "spirits" interlinked in their effects on human manners and outlook. They also interlinked in the panorama of history, creating both an historical and a contextual perspective. The capacity of *genius saeculi* to evoke historical development while at the same time capturing the unifying characteristics of an age was unremarkable at this stage. This capability would prove important for zeitgeist in the later eighteenth century when, in German, *Zeitgeist* began to focus on the immediate present and assumed a more social and political meaning which nevertheless needed an anchor in history.

This is dual focus is evident in Herder's use of the (different) terms derived from *genius saeculi*. Zeitgeist's capability is rooted in the ambiguity of "Geist der Zeit", which conflates history and the current age by referring to *both* the specifics of the present *and* its place within the historical process. This ambiguity pinpoints the key tensions of this concept: between the diachronic and synchronic approach to culture, between tradition and epochal change, and between social coercion and dynamic disruption. Chapter 2 will look at the source of these tensions, which all focus on how social collectives function politically and culturally and what role collective identity plays in these processes.

---

38 The Voltaire-Foundation's new critical edition (2015) of Voltaire's *Siècle*, produced to mark the 300th anniversary of Louis' death, celebrates Voltaire's innovative "perspective of the age as a whole rather than a parade of facts" and "the central role of the *Siècle* in the emergence of modern historical thinking" (Pierre Force), both <voltaire.ox.ac.uk>, accessed 2 September 2016.

2 The Making of Zeitgeist – Culture and Public Spirit between Enfranchisement and Control

2.1 *Geist, l'esprit*, spirit – public spirit and collective identity

Geist is arguably the more important element in the term zeitgeist. Not only is it the semantic base for all terms deriving from *genius saeculi*, such as spirit of the times, *l'esprit du siècle*, or Zeitgeist, it is also the engine of the concept it describes: without the animating and permeating qualities of spirit the various collective identities would be without energy. The idea of spirit as a *social* dynamic gained currency during the eighteenth century.

Much of the scepticism and suspicion towards the term and concept of zeitgeist in German research over the last few decades is rooted in a mistrust of the term *Geist*. Notoriously associated with a German way of thinking, which was supposed (by Germans and non-Germans) to prioritise intangible speculation over empirical rationality, it is implicated in not just the German catastrophes of the first half of twentieth century, but equally in the dangers of zealous metaphysics wherever they may occur. Its association with German ways of conceptualising is so entrenched in Anglophone thinking that *Geist* is considered one of the key untranslatables into English; it has exercised the translators of Hegel – is it "spirit" or "mind" or neither of the two? – for many decades. It has, however, no individual entry in Barbara Cassin's (French) *Vocabulaire européen des philosophies: Dictionnaire des Intraduisibles* (2004). One wonders whether one reason for this might be the fact that the French *l'esprit* shares many of "Geist's" eighteenth-century features. This suggests that "Geist", rather like Zeitgeist, is not as quintessentially German as has often been assumed.

The previous chapter has shown how the spirit of the times was, by the middle of the eighteenth century, considered a social construction determined by historical and contemporary circumstances, which influenced human activity and was instrumental in building collective (and potentially individual) identity. Its diachronic and synchronic dimensions, i.e. perspectives on history or the age respectively, were interlinked in the image of succeeding ages. Collective identity was conceived at once diachronically, as the result of a community's development over time, and synchronically, as an identity maintained, even forged, in the present. At the same time, different identities were thought to succeed each other in history. Collective identities were seen to embody (historical) time, closely linking the spirit of (the) time(s) and the spirit of the people.

While the tension between the diachronic and synchronic aspects of zeitgeist created a capability rather than a difficulty, the (related) tension between control and agency inherent in this concept was in the first half of the eighteenth century only just emerging. It is evident in Herder's considerations of zeitgeist at the end of the century, expressed in his juxtaposition of "tätig" [active] and "leidend" [passive/suffering] as the two ways in which the individual experiences zeitgeist. This tension has two facets; on the one hand, zeitgeist was thought to exert control over human behaviour but it could also be shaped by human activity. On the other hand, zeitgeist was considered the free expression of an existing, evolved collective spirit, but at the same time it imposed limitations on human agency, which is not quite the same as the social control of the first facet. The first facet focuses on *social* mechanisms: social pressures make individuals or groups conform to social rules while individuals or groups decide to make and enforce changes to them. The second facet focuses on more *essentialist* qualities: social groups freely and irrepressibly *express* an (historically grown, but now) innate identity, while the characteristics of the age limit human conception and cognition in such a decisive way that genuine thinking outside the box is difficult and rare. Both facets of this tension hinge on the level to which zeitgeist is believed to be determinable and manageable by human intervention. If it is, the "course of history" can be (re-)directed and social identities are deliberate expressions. If it is not and no extent of human agency can manage the complexity of historical existence and contingency, the social pressures of zeitgeist have their own dynamic and human thought is largely locked into its age.

The newly defined role of culture in forming and maintaining human communities emerged as a flashpoint of these interlinking tensions. In the form of established cultural traditions, culture exerts diachronic control, while as public spirit – a much debated concept in the eighteenth century, as we shall see – it shapes a community synchronically. On the other hand, communal culture was considered as the free expression of a people's identity, which maintained their specificity and independence. By the same token, (voluntary) participation in collective culture and in the collective endeavour, i.e. by *showing* public spirit, demonstrated the individual's engagement in and membership of their community (which may or may not be egalitarian but provided a sense of belonging and purpose). The modern notions of social and political engagement, which all promise forms of enfranchisement, hinge on this individual participation. Various modern collectives are still making use of this notion in their terminology of inclusion.[1]

---

[1] For example, the German term "Kamerad", used in the German military since the late eighteenth century as well as in other public forces (police, fire brigade) and in school contexts (Schulkamerad, Spielkamerad) is derived from sharing a room (camera), suggesting community and equality. Its English cognate "comrade" fulfils the same function in the terminology

The tension between agency and control surfaces, largely unresolved, in Montesquieu's *Spirit of the Laws* (1748), a text that was crucial for establishing the notion of culture as the seat of collective spirit as well as its role in successfully maintaining political structures. Thomas Blackwell's *Enquiry into the Genius and Writings of Homer* (1735), which preceded Montesquieu's *Laws* by over a decade, proposes that culture influences the individual most decisively through language. Culture is shaped by geographical, social, and political conditions and stored in the language used by the members of the cultural community and in its texts.

These aspects of collective culture are the home of "spirit" as it was thought by eighteenth-century observers to manifest itself in history. The coherence of this culture applied to the collective and their age at the same time and was covered by the term *genius saeculi*. In the mid-eighteenth century, zeitgeist was predominantly worked out for "past presents", in history. Discussions tended to focused on those ages and collectives that writers considered significant and relevant for their own time or audience. In the second part of this chapter four mid-eighteenth-century texts, all of which are concerned with spirit, provide evidence of the complex level on which the zeitgeist of past presents was debated. These discussions provided the tools for the zeitgeist analyses around 1800 when the focus shifted to the analysis of the *actual* present, the "current age".

In his 1975 study of the role of the (German) Enlightenment in bringing about the historical perspective, Peter Reill identified "Geist der Zeit, [...] national character, and the active spirit [...] of the original [individual] genius", or like-minded groups of them, as the concepts the eighteenth-century German *Aufklärer* [enlighteners] considered to be the drivers of historical change (Reill 1975: 162).[2] In this context he pinpoints the tension between communal tradition, embodied in the collective spirit, and innovation, residing in the individual of genius, or the like-minded group (1975: 162). Reill concludes that the focus of the German Enlightenment thinkers was marked by an inherent contradiction between their awareness of historical specificity and their desire for immutable truth, for normative value. This contradiction was resolved by historical perspectivism, where the historically unique found its (proper) place in historical development (175: 190–192), in a similar way as the tension in zeitgeist between the spirit of

---

of socialism and communism, where German, the originating context of these social projects, uses "Genosse", a Germanic term derived from Middle High German, (also) indicating sharing and enjoying something together.

2 See Reill 1975: 161–189. His starting point in this context are social historians of religion, "thinkers concerned with religious and ecclesiastical history" (1975: 162). Reill's study precedes Erich Hassinger's *Empirisch-Rationaler Historismus* by three years; both argue to push back the origins of historicism.

history and the spirit of the era was being accommodated. "Spirit" has a central place in the make-up of the historicist outlook – and, one might add, in the establishment of the human sciences and the study of culture. Driven to "establish an independent hermeneutic region for the study of man in society" (different from that appropriate for the natural world), their "paradigm of historical explanation [is] characterized by two basic propositions: (1) man and the social world that man constructs are composed of material and spiritual natures; (2) the spiritual nature that fashions man's experience in the world cannot be totally explained by the material world in which it subsists" (1975: 217).[3] The extra-rational and non-material status of spirit led them to conclude that "spirit was free and original". Reill's focus on explaining the *Aufklärers'* notion of the ingenious (i.e. spirited) individual who is capable of initiating changes in social conditions and cultural traditions assigns spirit a key role in the "intuitive grasp", which was thought to distinguish moral from rational understanding. This intuitive grasp was summarised in the term "inspiration", which also acquired a secular meaning in the eighteenth century. Such spirit animated the inspired individual, a figure that was of course to have a long and influential history from the original genius of the "Genieperiode" of the 1770s to the Romantic poet.[4] As the carrier of spirit, such individuals have, as Reill points out, a particular role to play in epochal changes in society.

> The *Aufklärer* evolved an idea of history that envisioned historical change as the result of a continual interaction between transmitted social values and intellectual forces and a spiritual drive that sought to transform them. In so doing the *Aufklärer* borrowed the idea of original genius from contemporary aesthetics to account for the specific manner in which qualitative change occurs. The original genius becomes the central agent in effecting spiritual revolutions. (1975: 219)

The tension Reill pinpoints here is the same that arises in the discussion of spirit and culture in Montesquieu's *Laws* and that dominated the later discussions of how zeitgeist works: as a constant interaction between individuals being shaped by collective traditions as they are operative in their present, i.e. in their age, and the transformative forces unleashed by "inspired" or "ingenious" individuals, or small groups – elites – whose new ideas successfully obtain public acceptance. By the same token, this is the tension *within* the (inspired) individual between the forces of tradition and their (own) transformative vision, a tension

---

[3] Reill clearly deals with the eighteenth-century foundation of the "human sciences", or humanities, which in German have been named *Geisteswissenschaften*. Michael Carhart has recently investigated this foundation with a more sociologically oriented focus (Carhart 2007).
[4] "Genius" has over the succeeding 200 years lost much of its seventeenth-century meaning of "spirit" in favour of the narrower notion of the extra-ordinarily gifted person.

experienced, it was thought by 1800, by all independently thinking individuals. The struggle between "being shaped" by one's environment and (the will to) "shape" it became central in the zeitgeist discussions around 1800. As Herder remarked in 1793: "Wir stehen alle unter seinem [des Geistes der Zeit] Gebiet, bald tätig, bald leidend." [We are all under its [zeitgeist's] dominion, sometimes actively, sometimes passively] (1991: 85). The idea of communities being animated by a specific communal character was not new in the eighteenth century; linked to *genius saeculi*, it already existed at the beginning of the seventeenth century. What *was* new was that this notion of communal, or collective, spirit – what it consists of and how it arises and is maintained – was becoming a widely discussed and visible *issue*.

The mid-eighteenth-century German *Nationalgeist*-debate is a visible instance of this public discussion. In this debate the geographical and temporal configurations of the collective, *Volksgeist* and *Zeitgeist*, overlap. While analysing communal spirit from the national-geographical perspective, as animating a people or a nation, had a long critical history, analysing temporal collectives, those that define an "age", was less well established. The 1760s debate about the German national spirit, or more to the point, its absence, discussed the *contemporary* German "collective" as lacking an identity animated by a communal spirit, something other nations possessed at this time. This identity was not only, perhaps not even primarily, an historical identity, but a contemporary one that (should) animate the *contemporary* polity, in order to give it coherence and, most of all, give energy to all its members to live by its codes and laws. I shall return to this debate in the section on public spirit. This prominence of collective spirit in contemporary discussions suggests that it was acquiring a new urgency. One of the key texts that, by dint of its wide reception, propelled the political importance of collective spirit into the limelight was Montesquieu's *L'esprit des loix* (1748).

2.2 Montesquieu's *L'esprit des loix* – collective spirit against despotism

Montesquieu discusses different forms of government, republican, monarchical, and despotic – the latter being his *un*-form of government – and their agencies, the people, the aristocracy, the monarch, and the despot. Republics can be either democracies or aristocracies, monarchies are distinguished from despotism by the fact that the law and its institutions are above the monarch, while the despot rules unchecked. The guiding idea behind Montesquieu's taxonomy of governments is the need to guard against despotism by ensuring a division of political power, which will guarantee the secure enjoyment of different kinds of individual liberty. Alongside, he provides his arguments of how these forms have developed in practice: linked to geography and climate, which condition the forms of physical and economic existence, the most appropriate, or at least thoroughly causal, laws evolve, which then shape their communities by the force of their tradition. As he explains at the outset, for Montesquieu the term "spirit" of the laws denotes their inter-relatedness with cultural, social, and natural conditions. Their spirit is the sum of their reciprocal connections with their community and its conditions:

> These relations [rapports] [between laws and the principles of government, civil institutions, their legislators, the climate, economy, religion, values and social customs] I shall examine, since all of them together constitute what I call the Spirit of the Laws. [...] This spirit consists in the various relations which the laws might have to different objects. (Montesquieu 2011 [1748]: 3)

The laws *reflect*, in their spirit, the conditions of their evolution and then, by means of their spirit, *work on* their communities. This is the tension between the notion of spirit as the essence of communal identity, expressed by the community as a whole and through individual members, and the force of coercion created by communal tradition and applied to its members, which also featured in the zeitgeist discussions investigated in the previous chapter. The nature and dynamics of zeitgeist as Herder discussed it in 1793 also wavered between expressing a particular nature and coercing pliable materials (humans) into a pre-set shape to maintain an identity or situation. It was, however, a tension that was already visible in Barclay's thinking.

That communal spirit, in the shape of shared characteristics and customs and based on a consensus on values, animates a collective was not entirely new in the 1740s, neither was the idea that climate conditions peoples (Hassinger 1978: 101–147). Within these ongoing considerations, Montesquieu focused on *political* concepts: liberty vs despotism. One of the "relations" [rapports] he set out to investigate was the "degree of Liberty the constitution can bear" (2011: 4). Associating particular political values with particular peoples, who have developed them due to their conditions and internalised them over time to such an extent that they have become innate, Montesquieu ranks these values on a scale between liberty and despotism. In doing this Montesquieu takes national characteristics out of their historical context and judges them by contemporary standards, which are conceived as universal. This contradiction reflects the dilemma of needing to combine historicity with normativity, which Reill pinpointed for the German *Aufklärer* above and which neatly describes the hybrid nature of Enlightenment historicism. It has a bearing on the tendency of historicist thinking to end up with essentialist universals, of which the development of eventually innate national or communal characteristics is an example.

Inherent in this development towards innate characteristics is an absolutist tendency of the spirit: it has the potential to become determining in an almost omnipotent way. The reach of determinism is the issue in *The Laws*: are the laws the iron moulds that shape a people in their image or would the same people's laws change in different circumstances, or even by the free will of human consensus? Once created, does a people carry their laws like millstones round their necks as they cannot escape its self-perpetuating grip? Are laws enabling in any given situation, or are they a limiting prison? Montesquieu considers both options. In Book 19 he provides many examples of how the laws of a people are (brought) in line, at least at their formative stage, with their current situation: with their manners, customs, and prevailing ideas. He maintains that laws *ought to* have a relation to manners and customs. He approvingly points to Solon who had given the Athenians "the best [laws] they can bear" (2011: 117) and insists that (good, useful) laws reflect the *current* needs of the community they govern, i.e. they may change: "When the manners of the Romans were pure, they had no particular law against the embezzlement of public money." (2011: 117) In fact when "those who govern establish things that are shocking to the *present* ideas of a nation" this is one of two forms of "tyranny" (2011: 112; italics mine). Yet at the end of the book he suggests that "Laws contribute to *form* the Manners, Customs, and Character of a Nation" (2011: 118; italics mine), which suggests that over time long-lasting, unchallenged laws will mould a people. And this can be a problem. Whether laws are enabling or disabling depends on the way they are: while in the case of European law they appear to be enabling, Chinese laws are now limiting (2011: 116). Here a sense of European supremacy makes itself felt. Montesquieu's view of Chinese laws is linked to a belief in the debilitating effects of historical stasis, a bugbear for the Enlightenment project of progress. At the same time, this assessment indicates that there was a recognition that enabling tradition can turn debilitatingly despotic when public or general spirit becomes ossified.

The same tension regarding adaptive potential (which presupposes a degree of self-determination) and contextual coercion is discernible in the case of the individual: does education, which Montesquieu considers particularly important for republican social structures, shape the individual irreversibly or can they re-educate themselves? This is not discussed. The cultural identity Montesquieu discusses sways between essentialism and constructed-ness. Is it the result of independent rationality in humans, or has it become the innate response of instinctive nature? This was also the crux of the question whether zeitgeist was an all-powerful, an essentialist force or whether it could be guided and changed, i.e. purposefully constructed. Put another way, is the power of the spirit generated by coercion or engagement? This is a question that neither Barclay nor Bacon asked themselves, but which would become critical at the end of the eighteenth century, when not only the connection between temporal and "national" collective identity needed to be worked out more clearly, but also the conditions and benefits of membership in such collectives.

For Montesquieu the motivating power of a collective is its "general spirit" (l'esprit général), which is equated with national spirit. Unlike Barclay and Bacon, Montesquieu discusses in some detail how its power works. Human behaviour is shaped by their physical environment, which determines manners and the forms of social interaction, which crystallise into a "spirit". Book 19 is entitled "Of Laws, in Relation to the Principles which form the general spirit, the morals and customs, of a nation" (2011: 111). "Mankind are influenced by various causes; by the climate, by the religion, by the laws, by the maxims of government, by precedents, morals and customs; from whence is formed a general spirit of nations." (2011: 112) Appropriate laws are in line with this spirit, which is why their spirit is the sum of their relations with the community. Montesquieu distinguishes between "laws" on the one hand, and "manners" (moeurs) and "customs" (manières) on the other. While it is not always easy to tell which precedes the other, it is clear that laws are *established* by positive acts of legislators, whereas customs *evolve* out of given situations. "Laws are established, manners are inspired; these proceed from a general spirit, those from particular institutions", "the particular and precise institutions of a legislator". "Manners and customs", on the other hand, "are the institution of a nation in general" (2011: 114). They are the substrate of society, which can only change gradually, any forceful and sudden change amounts to tyranny, and can only be accomplished by oppression and punishment.

This begs the question who makes and changes the laws? Under what circumstances and conditions are changes to laws, or law-making in general, legitimate? This is a tension, to some extent, between laws and manners and within the laws: are they appropriate expressions of a preexisting collective spirit or coercive forces that perpetuate the status quo? It resurfaces at the end of the book: speaking of the British, whose constitution, i.e. laws, he had celebrated in book 11 as the realisation of the (presumably pre-existing) spirit of liberty and moderation, Montesquieu proceeds to present "the *effects* which follow from this liberty, the *character* it is capable of *forming*, and the customs which naturally result from it" (2011: 118, italics mine). Here the spirit appears to be the starting point rather than the result. It appears that this tension remains undecided, perhaps even unnoticed in his thinking.

2.3 Blackwell's *Enquiry* – communal spirit and cultural context

Montesquieu's use of the term "manners", which proliferates during the eighteenth century, pinpoints a conception of culture in the modern sense. *The Laws* was widely read in both Britain and Germany and its seminal effect on how the cultural conditioning of laws became viewed can hardly be overstated. But Montesquieu was not the first to point out that communal and cultural context regulates and inspires human activity through cultural traditions. The notion of the determining power of a specific culture on intellectual and artistic outlook, quality even, had been developed in the *Querelle* around 1700. Montesquieu would have been keenly aware of this. This idea found a particularly vivid and influential expression in the 1730s in Britain, in Thomas Blackwell's *Enquiry into the Life and Writings of Homer* (1735), which was a late contribution to the *Querelle d'Homère*. While Blackwell himself uses the term "culture" still exclusively in the sense of the agriculturally inspired "cultura", of growing or tending something (or indeed *someone*), and by implication improving them,[5] for Herder, some thirty years later, the word had acquired its modern meaning of the "culture of a people".[6]

Blackwell's aim was to show that Homer was a product of his environment, in which circumstance and human activity conditioned one another. And he maintains that this is always the case:

> Young minds are apt to receive such strong Impressions of the Circumstances of the Country they are born and bred, that they contract a mutual Likeness to those Circumstances and bear the Marks of the Course of Life thro' which they have passed. [...] the Circumstances that may be reasonably thought to have the greatest Effect upon us, may perhaps be reduced to the following: First, the State of the Country where a Person is born and bred; in which I include the common Manners of the Inhabitants, their Constitution civil and religious, with its Causes and Consequences: Their Manners are seen in the Ordinary way of living, as it happens to be barbarous, luxurious or simple. Next the Manners of the Times, or the prevalent Humours and Professions in vogue: Those are publick

---

5 "Culture" occurs a handful of times in *Enquiry*: twice directly in connection with "education" (Blackwell 1735: 4 and 10), the first a quotation from Horace, and once linked with "improvement" ("admits of culture and improvement" (162)). The other instances are: "might rise by constant culture" (119), "spring up without other culture" (124), "the fair Chance he had for [...] a proportioned culture" (162) and "arise from the culture and disposition of the ground" (283).
6 For example in *Drittes Wäldchen*, in the Klotz-review discussed earlier, Herder speaks of "Cultur des Volkes", "unser Publikum ist aus diesem Gleise der Cultur, aus diesem Vehikulum der Denkart hinaus" (1878: 412).

> and have a common effect on the whole Generation. [...] From these Accidents, [...] Men in every Country may be justly said to draw their Character and derive their Manners. They make us what we are. (Blackwell 1735: 11–12)

Based on the idea of finding out what makes Homer's work so excellent that it has stood the test of time, Blackwell's book is nevertheless an exercise in historical contextualisation, investigating the relations between political, social, intellectual, linguistic, and artistic conditions and developments. He engages in defining what will shortly be summarised as "culture" and what was already known as "spirit". "We find that the Fortunes, the Manners, and the Language of a People are all linked together and necessarily influence each other." (1735: 54) In Homer's "age", the restless insecurity of small, primitive communities vying for dominance necessarily produced warlike, straightforward manners, and simple laws. Blackwell does not only provide a description of how "manners" arise, but also how they are maintained – through conferring social status on those who exemplify them.

> Let us now consider the Manners of the Times; by which I mean the Professions and Studies that are en vogue, and that bring most Honour to those that possess them in an eminent degree. [...] Arms at that time was the honoured Profession, and a publick Spirit the courted character: [...] The Man who had bravely defended his City, enlarged its Dominion, or died in its Cause, was revered like a God: Love of Liberty, Contempt of Death, Honour, Probity and Temperance, were Realities. [...] No Safety to Life or Fortune without them; while every State, that is to say, almost every City was necessitated either to defend itself against its warlike Neighbour, or shamefully to submit to Oppression and Slavery. [...] In most of the Greek Cities, Policy and Laws were but just a forming, when Homer came into the world. The first sketches of them were extremely simple. [...] The great Law of Hospitality made the chief part of the Institution. (Blackwell 1735/1736: 52–54)[7]

This simplicity is the basis for a noble primitivity.

> The Tribes were but beginning to live secure within the Walls of their new-fenced Towns, and had as yet neither Time nor Skill to frame a Domestick Policy, or Municipal Laws; and far less to think of publick Methods of training up their Citizens: They lived naturally, and were governed by the natural Poise of the Passions, as it is settled in every human breast. This will make them speak and act, without other Restraint than their own native Apprehensions of Good and Evil, Just and Unjust, each as he was prompted from within. (Blackwell 1735: 54–55)

One senses the – soon to be common – criticism of the negative influence of luxury, indolence, and avarice on human manners. In fact, Blackwell quotes

---

[7] The last sentence was added in the second edition (Blackwell 1736).

Longinus to this effect (1735: 53), concluding "no wonder [...] that the Representations of such genuine Characters bear the Marks of Truth and far outshine those taken from counterfeit Worth, or fainter Patterns." (1735: 54). Although Blackwell uses the term "spirit" mainly in the sense of "spirited" individual, the above passage makes clear that he shares with Montesquieu a sense of a "general spirit" which informs and serves the community. What Blackwell calls "publick Spirit" is closely related to (but not identical with) Montesquieu's "general" or "national spirit". As "Manners of the Times", it is also closely related to the condition of the current age.

Blackwell is convinced that the spirit of peoples or communities animates their entire social being. Speaking of Britain, he enthuses, like Montesquieu a decade later, about English liberty:

> ... with Joy we may view our native Isle, the happy Instance of the Connexion between Learning and Liberty. [...] We see our Arts improving, our Sciences advancing, Life understood, and the whole animated with a Spirit so generous and free, as gives the truest Proof of the Happiness of our Constitution. (1735: 61)

Blackwell addresses the question of how manners change, the "Progression of Manners [...] depends for the most part on our Fortunes" (1735: 13). Change is achieved through the game-changers of war and economic boom or bust.

> The greatest Revolutions in them [manners] produce the most conspicuous Alternations [...]. When by an Invasion or Conquest the Face of things is wholly changed; or when the original Planters of a Country, from a State of Ignorance and Barbarity, advance by Policy and Order, to Wealth and Power, it is then, that the steps of Progression become observable [...] the very Soul and Genius of the People rising to higher attempts, and a more Liberal Manner." (1735: 14)

Certainly in peacetime, such changes are led by elites, those that guarantee "Order" and make and implement "Policy". While the pinnacle of political and social achievement is liberty, Blackwell's focus is more cultural than political: he sees communal identity, spirit, reflected and embodied most evidently in language. In Homer's case, it is the language of early cultural development.

> These Manners afford the most natural Pictures, and proper Words to express them. While a Nation continues simple and sincere, whatever they say has Weight and Truth. [...] Their Passions [...] break out in their own artless Phrase and unaffected Stile. [...] We feel the Force of their Words and the Truth of their Thoughts. (1735: 55–56)

While Montesquieu's approach was ultimately political, Blackwell is predominantly interested in the impact of social and political context on culture: language, poetry, and ideas. He is convinced of the pervasive power of surrounding conditions on social and individual activity, especially if they have coalesced into a coherent recognisable form, a "Doctrine":

> We have frequent examples how much the firm Belief of any Sect makes man speak and write in the approved Idiom: they introduce it into their Business, allude to it in their Pleasures, and abstain from it in no Part of their Life, especially while the Doctrine flourishes. (1735: 52)

Although applied here to a social sub-group (sect, in a non-religious sense), this description of the impact of a "doctrine" on language, discourse, and activity, comes close to later descriptions of the effect of zeitgeist, especially when Blackwell's description of the rise and spread of a "spirit" is taken into account: "The Times of such Struggles have a kind of Liberty peculiar to themselves: they raise a free and active Spirit which overspreads the country" and which affects "Every Man" (1735: 65). Blackwell does not analyse the dynamics of dissemination beyond the notion of necessity, and the incentive of gaining social rewards ("bring[ing] most Honour"). While he is quite aware of the coercive side of this spirit – it "makes" man do things, "affecting" everybody – he appears to have no interest in how or by whom the "Doctrine" is controlled.

2.4 *Culture* – conflating collective identity, the spirit of the times, and cultural history in Bodmer, Hurd, Mallet, and Percy

Both Montesquieu and Blackwell had extensive receptions. This section looks at four different authors, one Swiss-German, one Swiss-French and two English ones, who each developed the ideas discussed above by linking collective cultural identities with the "spirit of the times". Each author was seeking to define an "age" of significance that had a key bearing on the collective identity he is concerned with in order to establish a "good" tradition. In doing this each author describes a zeitgeist in action in a past present, implying all the while – like Blackwell – that the same dynamic, albeit driving different content, was also at work in *their* present. The spirit of the times was first established in history, operating in a past present.

Johann Jakob Bodmer's text, the earliest of the four, preceding Montesquieu's *Laws* by five years, is heavily reliant on Blackwell. The younger three wrote their texts after both *Laws* and *Enquiry* had appeared. In all cases their constructions of cultural identities were continuations of the *Querelle*: they are setting up postclassical modern identities that can compete with "classical antiquity".

Blackwell's book was widely read, in Britain and on the Continent. It went into a second edition within a year and was republished regularly during the rest of the century. Bodmer eagerly took up Blackwell's idea that political and social conditions determine the "manners" of a community, which in turn shape their language. Manners and language are captured in texts. By the same token, specific conditions produce specific cultural products. Bodmer deployed Blackwell's ideas to propose that a specific type of cultural product, heroic epics, must necessarily have been created in thirteenth-century German speaking regions, *because* political, social, and hence cultural conditions were very similar to Homer's Greece. His 1743 essay *Von den vortrefflichen Umständen für die Poesie unter den Kaisern aus dem schwäbischen Hause* [Of the excellent conditions for poetry under the Swabian Emperors] is entirely based on Blackwell's book, from which he paraphrases extensively.

Bodmer uses the descriptions Blackwell had applied to Homer's cultural context to describe the conditions in thirteenth-century Germany. He freely acknowledges his source as the "gelehrter Mann" [learned man] who wrote the *Enquiry* (Bodmer 1943 [1743]: 67), but does not name Blackwell, possibly because he does not know who the author is, the *Enquiry*'s first two editions were published anonymously. It is worth showing in detail how dependent Bodmer's text is on Blackwell's. In the lengthy passage below Bodmer's paraphrases – not to say translations – of Blackwell appear in italics, the relevant passages from Blackwell's text are given in the notes.

> ...*die Zeiten, da Freyheit und Sclaverey mit einander um die Oberhand gestritten,*[8] [haben] der Welt gemeiniglich etwas Vortreffliches von Werken des Geistes geliefert. [...] *Die Verwirrungen und Gefährlichkeiten, die in solchen Umständen häufig sind, setzen alle ihre Leidenschaften in Bewegung.* [...] *Diese Zeiten der Fehden* [...] *verursachen einen freyen und hurtigen Geist, der sich im ganzen Land ausbreitet. Jedermann sieht sich dann als seinen eigenen Herrn, und daß er aus sich selber machen darf, was er kann.*[9] Diese Betrachtungen [...] haben mich die beste Hoffnung von den Scibenten, welche unter den Kaisern aus dem schwäbischen Hause gelebet haben, fassen lassen. Damahls that die deutsche Freyheit ihr Äußerstes, sich des sclavischen Jochs zu entschütten, das ihr von Rom angedrohet war. Die Deutschen waren nicht mehr diese Rohen und Halbwilden, die aller Gemächlichkeit des Lebens und politischen Veranstaltungen beraubet waren. Sie hatten

---

8 "While every State, that is to say, almost every City, was necessitated either to defend itself against its warlike neighbour, or shamefully submit to Oppression and Slavery" (Blackwell 1735: 53).
9 "But the Disorder and Dangers frequent at such Junctures, set all their Passions going [...]. The Times of such Struggles have a kind of Liberty peculiar to themselves: They raise a free and active Spirit, which overspreads the Country: Every Man finds himself on such Occasions his own Master, and that he may be whatever he can make himself" (64).

friedliche Zeiten, zwischen langen und zweyträchtigen Versuchen, gehabt, wo sie es mit Künsten und Wissenschaften auf einen gewissen Grad gebracht hatten. Doch waren sie von Zucht, Höflichkeit und Cerimoniel nicht zu enge eingethan. *Sie hatten noch vieles von ihrem unbändigen und ungezähmten Geist behalten und die Schranken der Religion oder der Policey hatten die natürlichen und einfältigen Bewegungen ihres Herzen nicht eingezwängt.*[10] Sie ließen ihren angeborenen Neigungen insgemein vollen Zügel und verstellten sich nicht sonderlich. [...] *Die Waffen waren im Ansehen, und die Stärcke setzte einen in Besitz.*[11] *Ein jeder Staat eiferte auf den anderen, und versuchte, was sein Geist im Frieden, und noch lieber, was seine Stärcke im Kriege, vermochte.*[12] Die Zeiten gaben einem viel zu sehen und viel zu fühlen. [...] *Es kann nicht seyn, daß dieser Charakter, diese Empfindungen und Regungen nicht in ihre Sprache und Schriften eingeflossen seyn. Ihre Sprache muß von ihnen dahin gebracht worden seyn, daß sie diese starken und tapfermüthigen Fühlungen haben ausdrücken können.*[13] [...] *Indessen war diese Sprache noch nicht so sehr auspoliert, daß sie dadurch wäre abgeschliffen und abgeschwächt worden.*[14] [...] Die besten Poeten copieren die Natur, und liefern sie uns so, wie sie solche finden. Ein Scribent von Friedrichs des I. oder II. *Zeiten habe nur mit der damaligen Sprache getreulich geschildert, was er gesehen und empfunden, so muss sein Werk anmuthig und nachdrücklich seyn.*[15] *Seine Vorstellung einfältiger und natürlicher Sitten, wird uns einnehmen, [...] sie wird uns die Bewegungen eines unverstellten Gemüthes vorweisen.*[16] (Bodmer 1943: 67–70)[17]

---

10 "In most of the Greek Cities, Policy and Laws were but just a forming [...] the first Sketches of them were extremely simple [...] as we should think unnecessary and barbarous. [...] They lived naturally, and were governed by the natural Poise of the Passions, as it is settled in every human Breast" (54–55).
11 "Arms at the time were the honoured Profession [...]. The Man who bravely defended his City [...] was revered like a God" (53).
12 "While each City was independent, rivalling its Neighbour, and trying its Genius in Peace, and its Strength in War" (22).
13 "These Manners afford the most natural pictures, and proper Words to paint them" (55).
14 "Before they [ancient poets] are polished into Flattery and Falsehood, we feel the Force of their Words, and the Truth of their Thoughts" (55–56).
15 "These Manners afford the most natural pictures, and proper Words to paint them. [...] Their passions are sound and genuine, not adulterated and disguised, and break out in their own artless Phrase and unaffected Stile" (55).
16 "And *this* I take to be the Reason, 'Why most Nations are delighted with their ancient Poets" [Horace]: Before they are polished into Flattery and Falsehood, we feel the Force of their Words, and the Truth of their Thoughts" (55–56).
17 [The times when liberty and slavery fought each other for victory have usually produced excellent works of the mind. [...] The confusion and dangers which are common under such circumstances set all their passions in motion. [...] These times of feuds [...] produce a free and agile spirit that spreads throughout the whole country. Everybody considers himself his own master and that he may take his opportunities as best he can. These considerations have allowed me to form the highest hopes of the writers who lived under the rule of the Swabian Emperors. Then German liberty did its utmost to throw off the enslaving yoke with which Rome threatened her. The Germans were no longer uncouth and half-barbarous, without all regularity of life and political activities. They had enjoyed peaceful times, between lengthy

Using Blackwell, Bodmer proposes a supposedly inevitable link between political and social conditions and language, which determines discourse in general and conditions cultural identity and literary production.

Together with his friend and collaborator, fellow Zurich writer and academic Johann Jakob Breitinger, Bodmer was looking for inspiration to renew contemporary manners and culture on the basis of (Calvinist) virtue. Ancient sources of unsullied culture, such as heroic epics, he felt, could function as models for a new cultural and literary awakening. To this end he sifted medieval manuscripts in search of European equivalents to ancient epics, preferably with a Christian theme. Christianity as lead culture was important to him: he admired Milton's *Paradise Lost*, Klopstock's *Messias*, and tried his own hand at a "Noachide". But his most significant contribution to establishing a European Christian antiquity was his publication of the first modern edition of parts of the *Nibelungenlied* in 1757. A thirteenth-century manuscript of the epic (known as Handschrift C) had been unearthed, at his behest, by Jacob Hermann Obereit in the library of Hohenems in Western Austria in June 1755.[18]

The idea that there was a striking similarity between Homer's Greece and the European Middle Ages as far as socio-political conditions and their corresponding "culture" was concerned was also being developed in Britain. Nearly twenty years after Bodmer (and probably without any influence from him), Richard Hurd's *Letters on Chivalry and Romance* (1762) put forward exactly this idea. Hurd's analogy between different *early* cultures was part of the contemporary discussion about the course of (universal) history during which different ages defined by specific cultures succeeded each other, each running through

---

periods of discord, when they developed the arts and sciences to a certain degree. But they were not too tied down by rules, courtliness, and ceremony. They still retained much of their unbound and untamed spirit and the restrictions of religion and policy had not bound the natural and simple emotions of their hearts. They gave full rein to their innate inclinations and did not much dissemble. [...] Arms stood in high esteem and strength produced possessions. Every state competed with the next and tested what its spirit in peacetime and even better what its strength in war could accomplish. These times allowed [everybody] to see and feel many things. [...] It is impossible that this character, these sentiments and feelings have not influenced their language and their writing. They must have shaped their language in such a way that it was able to express these strong and brave feelings. [...] Meanwhile this language was not yet so polished that it would be weakened by this. [...] The best poets copy nature and give it to us as they find it. If a writer of the times of Frederic I or II wrote down faithfully what he saw and felt in the language of the day, his work must be appealing and emphatic. His presentation of simple and natural manners will appeal to us, [...] it will show us the feelings of an undissembling mind.]

18 See Rainer Schöffl (2018) regarding the details of the manuscript's discovery (Schöffl 2018).

their organic "lives": "'Tis certain that in the Infancy of States, the Men generally resemble the publick constitution." (Hurd 1911 [1762]: 42) Like Bodmer, Hurd was interested in identifying specific eras that were of national significance and had a bearing on the present. His *Letters* form a continuation of his *Moral and Political Dialogues* of 1759, which he identified in his preface as a contribution to the discussion of the uses of the ancients for the moderns.

The fourth *Dialogue* focuses "On the (Golden) Age of Queen Elizabeth". Here Hurd puts forward reasons why the Elizabethan "age" exhibits the happy characteristics of the period between primitive (medieval) originality and emerging civilised refinement, which Blackwell had also identified as so conducive to great poetry. These favourable conditions are (again) derived from Homer's age and strikingly similar to how Blackwell had described them and how Bodmer had characterised the thirteenth-century *Stauffen* period.

> Homer had the good Fortune to see and learn the Grecian Manners, at their true Pitch and happiest Temper for Verse: Had he been born much sooner, he would have seen nothing but Nakedness and Barbarity: Had he come much later, he had fallen in the Times either of wide Policy and Peace, or of General Wars, when private Passions are buried in the common Order, and established Discipline. (Hurd 1911: 35)

Like Bodmer, Hurd was keen to establish a tradition, in his case for the contemporary Anglo-British polity, which illustrates its collective identity. In his two dialogues "On the Constitution of the English Government", where Montesquieu's ideas echo clearly, Hurd proposes that a history of English Government ought to be drawn up from extant sources ("authentic papers and public monuments", Hurd 1788 [1759]: II, 89), because this would reveal English government as "at all times [...] free" (1788: 89) – a desirable condition. Such a history would provide incontrovertible evidence of the "genuin [sic] spirit and temper of the constitution" (1788: 89). This spirit appears to be the expression as well as the result of English identity, of English manners and circumstances. Following Blackwell, Hurd suggests that this spirit is encoded in the English language, or rather in its Anglo-Saxon ancestor, which faithfully reflects the conditions of early liberty.

> Our Saxon ancestors conceived so little of government, by the will of the magistrate, without fixed laws, that the LAGA or LEAGA, which in their language first and properly signified the same as Law with us, was transferred very naturally (for language always conforms itself to the genius, temper and manners of the nation) to signify a country, district, province; these good people having no notion of any inhabited country not governed by laws. Thus Dane-Laga, Mercena-Laga. (1788: 116–117)

The "spirit" of English liberty, the guiding light of Hurd's dialogues on the constitution, was also aligned with the "temper of the times" (Hurd 1788: 321). When

Charles I attempted to subvert this liberty, its suppression could not last, because it ran counter to the spirit of the constitution and it contravened the "spirit of the times". This latter spirit had, since the Reformation, been marked by a growing "spirit of enquiry" (1788: 321): "Inveterate errors were seen through, prejudices [...] fell off in proportion to the growth of letters and the progress of reason." (1788: 321) Combined with the increasing wealth of the period, the "ballance [sic] of power soon fell into the hands of the people". "Our kings were sensible to the alternation: but instead of prudently giving way to it, they flew into the opposite extreme, and provoked the spirit of the times by the very reluctance they shewed on every occasion to comply with it." (1788: 322) This royal reluctance to comply, not so much with their political opponents' wishes, but with the "times", led to the English Civil War. Hurd's use of "spirit of the times" occurs in the context of a historical survey, it is linked to the specifics of a *past* present and thus tends towards the historical, diachronic notion of zeitgeist. But Hurd expresses a clear sense of the regulating power of zeitgeist, which he sees manifest in public opinion, a conjunction that will be a focal point of zeitgeist discussions at the end of the century. The political imprudence of political rulers who do not to take account of the "spirit of the times" would become a common theme in the discussions about the French Revolution.

Another publication that takes its cue from Montesquieu, whose *Laws* are quoted repeatedly, and perhaps from Blackwell is Paul Henri Mallet's widely disseminated *L'introduction à l'histoire de Dannemarc oú l'on traite de religion, des loix, des moeurs et des usage des anciens Danois* [Introduction to the history of Denmark treating the religion, laws, manners, and customs of the ancient Danes], which was published in 1755. It was followed a year later by a second volume entitled *Monuments de la mythologie et poesie*, which illustrates its author's interest in the link between social and political culture, language, and poetry. The lengthy title of the first volume signals its intent as well as its intellectual descent: laws, manners, and customs are its key concerns.[19]

---

19 Religion was emerging as a cultural marker at this very time: Robert Lowth's *Praelectiones*, published in 1753 but given as lectures in the 1740s, investigates the poetic aspects of the Old Testament, while Johann David Michaelis conducted research into the cultural and social context of the world presented in the Old Testament. Michaelis provided the academic backup for Carsten Niebuhr's research expedition between 1761–1767, the "Arabian Journey", which had been in planning since 1753 and was expected to shed light on the cultural conditions of Biblical peoples by visiting their descendants. The "Arabische Reise" was financed by the Danish King Frederic V and his successor Christian VII. Frederic V was the individual to whom Mallet dedicated his history of the ancient Danes.

Mallet (1730–1807), like Bodmer, was Swiss, but born and educated in French-speaking Geneva. In 1752, aged twenty-two, he accepted the professorship of Belles Lettres at Copenhagen and proceeded to write a history of the cultural origins of his employers. For Mallet, too, the spirit of a people reflected and animated their particular culture, it is one of the guiding tenets of his work. He sets out to "sketch the manners and genius of the first inhabitants of Denmark" to trace "the spirit that animated them", because without such knowledge one merely has "the skeleton of history", i.e. a very incomplete understanding of it (Mallet 1770 [1755]: l). He may have gleaned this idea from Bacon, but would have found it elaborated and implemented in Montesquieu and Blackwell. Mallet's book proved seminal for identity constructions all over Northern and Western Europe in the later eighteenth and nineteenth century, indicating that these ideas constituted an emerging discourse, which will be examined more closely in the case study.

Mallet himself felt that a European reception of his book was appropriate, remarking in his introduction that during the Dark Age migrations "new societies were formed animated so entirely with a new spirit that the history of our manners and institutions ought necessarily to ascend back, and even dwell a considerable time upon a period, which discovers to us their chief origin and source" (1770: li). It was a "spirit" that originated in the "forests of Scythia" and "continued unaltered in the colder countries of Europe" for many centuries, until, after clashing with the fading culture of the Roman Empire – the Romans themselves are presented as very distant cousins – "coalesc[ed] together and from their coalition sprung those principles and that spirit which governed afterwards almost all the states of Europe [...]" (1770: lii-liii).[20] For Mallet this spirit is characterised by "independence and equality", hence the "most flourishing and celebrated states of Europe owe originally to the northern nations what liberty they now enjoy either in their constitution or in the spirit of their government" (1770: liii).

To illustrate this spirit's pervasiveness Mallet furnishes as part two of his history the extant materials of ancient northern mythology and poetry. The "old poems" are animated with "the peculiar genius" that presents the "genuine mode of thinking of those times", i.e. the "original manners and spirit of a people" (1770: 404–405). Mallet contends that (non-revealed) religion exhibits the spirit of their human makers, and "their government and laws are another faithful mirrour [sic] wherein that spirit may be seen" (1770: 156).

---

20 This sentence, written in the mid-1750s, sums up key elements of what was to become the nineteenth-century master-narrative of European culture.

The cultural identity that shapes these communities is reflected in their institutions – government, religion, poetry – and expresses their communal identity. It represents in turn the thinking of "those times". People and times are inseparable. As with Hurd, this spirit of the times was discovered in history, i.e. as the zeitgeist of a past era. And like Hurd, Mallet had a sense of how this spirit impacted on individuals and collectives. But Mallet had more to say than Hurd about the tension between agency and control: addressing the tension between coercive control and expression of identity, which marks the spirit, he resolves it. For Mallet a powerful coercion is immanent in a fully aligned "genius", when the social organisation (the laws) and the characteristics of a community converge:

> It is obvious that the laws cannot long be contrary to a nation's genius. Sooner or later they will be impressed with its character or they will give it theirs. These are two streams very different in their sources, but which as soon as they unite in one channel have but one force and direction. (1770: 156)

Mallet allows for the "genius of a people" to be changed if it meets with a legal spirit that is stronger than its own characteristics. He comes down on the side of spirit as a coercive, controlling force, even though it may originate in the free expression of collective identity. Its controlling force can only be controlled by (another) spirit. This is an idea that will remain current well beyond the French Revolution, when the agency of spirit greatly exercised the thinkers trying to work out how the "spirit of the revolution" arose and how, if at all, it could be controlled. Herder declared in 1793: "Geist allein kann mit Geist kämpfen." [Spirit alone can fight spirit.] (Herder 1991: 89)

Thomas Percy (1729–1811) published his English translation of Mallet's *L'introduction a l'histoire de Dannemarc* in 1770. *Northern Antiquities*, from which I have quoted above, went through several editions before the end of the century. Percy's translation was supplemented with para-textual material, a forty-eight-page "Translator's Preface" and a re-focused title, which makes no direct mention of specifically *Danish* history. Instead it presents the pan-European import of a generally "Northern" original culture, with a particular relevance to Britain: the book provides a "Description of the Manners, Customs, Religion and Laws of the Ancient Danes and other Northern Nations including those of our own Saxon Ancestors". Percy dedicated his translation to his long-time patron, the Duke of Northumberland. Mallet had dedicated the original to Frederic V of Denmark. Percy had been familiar with Mallet's work for some time, its content closely corresponded to his own interests. I will return to *Northern Antiquities* in the case study.

While some of Percy's enduring fame is based on his seminal translation of Mallet's work, he is best remembered for his *Reliques of Ancient English Poetry* (1765), published before *Northern Antiquities*, but after *L'histoire de Dannemarc*. Like Bodmer's and Hurd's work, the *Reliques* would exert a strong influence over European "Romanticism", not least because it contributed to the (re-)discovery of the "bard" as original poet who had the capacity to be a secular seer-prophet. As an edited collection of mainly early modern British ballads, with extensive explanatory notes, and bookended by contextualising essays, Percy's collection was a major contribution to the contemporary "ballad revival", and as such very much of its time. It helped identify medieval and early modern culture as the original culture of modern Europe which was informed by the "spirit of chivalry" (Percy 1794: I, xxi and liv). Like Bodmer and Hurd, Percy found medieval poetry and culture analogous to the works and times of Homer (Oergel 1999). In this respect, Percy contributed to the extended *Querelle*, which was becoming less a battle for supremacy and increasingly an anthropologically minded enquiry into cultural history.[21]

Like Hurd, Percy identifies a recognisable spirit of the times for the Elizabethan age; it can be distilled from cultural items, just as Bacon had suggested.[22] In his explanatory notes to "Phillida and Corydon" and "In the merrie month of Maye", Percy refers to extant diaries of Queen Elizabeth's visits to the palaces of her great nobles (Elvetham in Hampshire owned by the Earl of Hertford in 1591 in this case) and concludes: "The splendour and magnificence of Elizabeth's reign is nowhere to be more strongly painted than in these little diaries of some of her summer excursions [...] which so strongly mark the spirit of the times and present us with sources so very remote from modern manners." (Percy 1794: III, 62–64) Percy considered the "little diaries" as suitable for tracing this spirit as any activities of high politics, presumably because this spirit was all permeating and, most of all, cultural.[23]

This eighteenth-century conflation of a significant historical epoch with national culture and national history, which makes that particular age

---

21 The "spirit of chivalry" occurs in the introductory "Essay on the Ancient Minstrels in England" (Percy 1794: I, xxi-cvi); "chivalry" is a frequent term in "The Ancient Metrical Romances" (Percy 1794: III, x-xlv), where Percy also speaks of the "ideas of chivalry" (xii and xvi). Percy agreed with Mallet that in the large family of Northern tribes, which he calls the "Gothic nations" (Percy 1794: III, xxii, and xvi) or "Gothic tribes" (xix), similar "customs, manners, and opinions" prevailed in "every branch of that people" (xii).
22 See Chapter 1, pp. 23–25.
23 Percy gives careful bibliographical references for both poems. "Phillida and Corydon", variously referred to as song, sonnet, and pastoral, is recorded in 1600, and ascribed to Nicholas Breton.

foundational, has so far not been commented on by zeitgeist research. Defining a significant past age went hand in hand with defining national identity, because both rely on constructions of collective identities. The synchronic perspective focuses on defining the age, such as the Elizabethan Age (Hurd and Percy), Homer's times (Blackwell), or the reigns of the Staufen emperors (Bodmer), the diachronic perspective focuses on defining national characteristics, e.g. the key elements of Northern culture in European history (Mallet and Percy), which have shaped (or should be shaping) contemporary identity. Both synchronic and diachronic constructions seek to embody time. These constructions laid, on the one hand, the well-known foundations for cultural essentialism. On the other hand, they produced the basis from which the concept of zeitgeist emerged.

There is a clear sense in Hurd of the coercive nature of the "spirit of the times" and in Mallet of the coercive nature of the spirit of communal identity, and there was interest in investigating the dynamics of the rise and spread of such spirits, investigating what or who controls them. The focus was on the historical conditions of geography, society, and politics. Zeitgeist was first "located" in history, it was discovered at work in past presents as a "spirit of the times", embodied in collective identities, but there was no reason to assume that similar dynamics were not operating in historically less distant periods.

In the eighteenth century these spirits of collective identity were in the main conceived as positive forces, especially where they were identified as foundational (for a desirable) contemporary culture. One suspects that in the mid-eighteenth century there still lingered some of the benevolence of Providence, which made agency and evolution purposeful, not least because revealed religion was not questioned or discarded by those thinkers discussed here. Notwithstanding, the "spirit of the times" had from the start, i.e. from the seventeenth and earlier eighteenth century, been ridiculed and used to satirise the present. Whether evidence of benevolence or folly, these historical considerations about how collective identities animate communities had the potential to be applied to analyse contemporary culture and politics. They provided the tools with which to interpret current affairs when the Revolution in France called upon intellectuals to explain this event.

When notions of zeitgeist became the toolkit for analysing the present, the spirit became considerably more ambiguous. The tradition of satirising the present, which often focused on individual failings and folly (albeit supported by a conducive spirit), shifted towards locating the "problem" in the collective identity that informed the times. The concept of the spirit of the current age became infused with the notion of a dominating dangerous spirit and was, to some extent, separated from the more diachronic spirit of time. In the 1790s zeitgeist became associated with forceful social coercion and control that was imbued with notions of (sinister) human agency. It became possible to regard zeitgeist as serving the ulterior motives of political power, while the spirit of the people(s) and the genius of history were relocated into the philosophy of history. The "spiritual" nature of these "esprits", the seemingly immaterial basis of their energy and power, made them suspect, while their perceived strength made them efficient. Around 1800 the uncertainty regarding the genuine immanence of spirit, which might be a fabricated construction, came starkly to the fore.

Again, Herder's discussion of zeitgeist in *Humanitätsbriefe* provides a summary of the situation, presenting the range of the different connotations and their implications. Zeitgeist emerges as a great power, "ein mächtiger Genius, ein gewaltiger Dämon" (Herder 1991: 84), it sways between being an historical spirit ("Geist der Zeiten", 1991: 84) and the spirit of an era ("Geist unserer Zeiten", 105), it exerts its power as external coercion and through individual or collective agency ("Wir stehen alle unter seinem Gebiet, bald tätig, bald leidend.", 1991: 85). Herder opts for human agency: "Indessen wird er offenbar gelenkt, nicht von der Menge, sondern von wenigen, tiefer als andere blickenden, standhaften, glücklichen Geistern." [It is being directed, not by the masses, but by a few steadfast and happy spirits who can see further than others.] (Herder 1991: 86–87). But doubt remains whether this human agency really *is* benevolent or destructive in a seditious and mob-like way: is it the "Genius der Humanität" or the "Geist des Aufruhrs, [...], des unreinen und abgeschmackten Pöbelsinn und Wahnsinn" [the spirit of revolt, [...] of the impure and crude rage of the mob] (1991: 85–86).

Herder's growing pessimism is evident in his increasing scepticism as to whether wise elites ("wenige, tiefer als andere blickende, standhafte, glückliche Geister") *will* be able to control historical developments for the common good. "Lassen Sie sich auch die Stimmen unserer Philosophen nicht bis zur Täuschung bezaubern; [...] Roußeau, hat er mit seinen stark-ausgedrückten, regegefühlten Visionen mehr Nutzen oder mehr Schaden gebracht? Ich wage es nicht zu entscheiden." [Do not allow yourself to be charmed by the voices of our philosophers; [...] Rousseau, have his strongly worded and deeply felt visions done more good or harm? I dare not decide this.] (1991: 105) One of Herder's voices proceeds to divest the "Geist unserer Zeiten" of all historical or benevolent grandeur, bringing it down to the level of common opinion, which is frequently guided by private or party interest.

> Sobald man dem Wort [Geist der Zeiten] seine magische Gestalt nimmt, was bedeutet es mehr als die herrschenden Meinungen, Sitten und Gewohnheiten unseres Zeitalters; [...]. Versuchen Sie's einmal und bringen die kleinste Sache, die [...] Entsagung von Privatvorteilen fordert, zu Stande. [...] Jede Zunft hat ihren Zunftgeist, der fesselt. [As soon as you

take away the word's magical appearance, it does not mean any more than prevalent opinion, customs and manners of our times; [...] Try to make the smallest undertaking happen that requires renouncing private advantage. [...] Every guild has its guild spirit to which it is chained.] (1991: 103)

Herder's assessment pinpoints the two social and political spectres that haunt the turn of the century: political radicalism that harbours anarchy and materialistic selfishness that undermines spiritual values, such as the public good. While critiquing the present by constructing superior and inferior conditions of culture and society or by satirising common individual behaviours had been common for nearly two centuries, those earlier critiques lacked the fear of a politicised and mobilised populace intent on revolution. In this context the concept of public opinion, which was as closely linked to the later eighteenth-century understanding of zeitgeist, underwent a critical shift. After being regarded as a constructive and incorruptible corrective to individual and collective error it now acquired the potential to become a manipulative instrument of demagogy. This change, which is the subject of the next chapter, affected the understanding of zeitgeist significantly.

3 The Public and Zeitgeist – Public Spirit and Public Opinion 1790–1800

3.1 Zeitgeist, public spirit, and public opinion

The preceding sections have shown how in the mid-eighteenth-century zeitgeist was closely linked to collective identity and collective purpose, or public spirit. Both collective identity and public spirit codified collective identity and collective purpose in different historical perspectives, collective identity emerged from a diachronic perspective over time, public spirit defined a synchronic collective purpose, often linked to the "manners of the times" in history. This section takes a closer look at the "public" aspect of public spirit and explores the shift of zeitgeist away from a spirit of history towards a more prominent association with public opinion by the end of the century. The association of zeitgeist with public spirit and history was not eliminated, and neither had the aspect of public opinion been absent from mid-century conceptions of zeitgeist. This shift reflects a changed emphasis; once the Revolution was underway, zeitgeist's centre of gravity moved towards a focus on the *present* age and *current* public opinion.

This shift did not affect the structural tension between coercive control and free expression, the enforcement or the voluntary enactment of a general consensus or identity, within the zeitgeist concept. It did, however, affect the relative benevolence which adhered to the eighteenth-century spirit of the times and which was rooted in its connection with (providential) historical progression and positive identity. This was not exclusively due to the Revolution alone. The aspect of benevolence became questioned because it was challenged by what was perceived as an increasingly dominant "spirit" of self-serving and manipulative self-interest (again, this was not *wholly* absent in the earlier considerations). This partisan spirit was considered to work as effectively as community-building public spirit but served its opposite: the benefit *not* of the whole, but of interested parties. The perceived possibility of a "bad" public and a "bad" public opinion put these entities up for discussion, making them debatable, problematic, and open to interpretation. The following shows that these debates, focused on public spirit and public virtue, were conducted transnationally. Tracing them illustrates not so much the differences between national and linguistic contexts, but the similarities in the ways contemporaries experienced their situation and engaged with its issues.

Around the 1790s, "public opinion" and zeitgeist were defined afresh as they emerged from the discussions about the nature and construction of social and political collectives. Ruth Flad noted some time ago, and with some surprise, the variety of terms available in the early 1800s to denote the spirit of a public collective. Discussing Freiherr vom Stein's phrase "aller Einsichten und Willen" of November 1808, which, as "the insights and will of all", describes the collective of the consensual reasoned general will, she pointed out that this entity could be named variously:

> The period offered Stein a number of words to describe the spiritual and intellectual force of the collective [geistige Kollektivkräfte]. Opinion Publique, l'Esprit Publique [...] also Zeitgeist; latterly also the word Volksgeist. [...] Stein uses "public spirit" [öffentlicher Geist] and "public opinion" most frequently. (Flad 1921: 8)[1]

This suggests Stein favoured the (slightly less) "historical" terms, which he evidently considered closely related. However, in this context Stein also investigates the "Geist der Bevölkerung" [spirit of the population] (Flad 1921: 9), so the link between "Zeitgeist" und "Volksgeist" was still understood in 1808. In the context of this investigation it is not surprising that contemporaries were readily making connections between all the terms Ruth Flad mentions. It is telling that she, from a twentieth-century perspective, seemed particularly surprised at the inclusion of *Volksgeist* in this group of near-synonyms. That the seventeenth-century connection between zeitgeist and *Volksgeist* was lost on her is evident from her assumption that the association between the two is recent, when in this investigation *Volksgeist* has emerged as the oldest, closest, and most original relative of zeitgeist.

One of the conceptual connections between public opinion, the public, collective identity, and zeitgeist is the eighteenth-century idea of "public spirit", a close relative of Montesquieu's more neutral "l'esprit général". It expresses the sense of a community's historically grown identity and purpose and informs the present. This concept of a historically formed identity that animates a collective in the present also featured prominently in Blackwell's *Enquiry*. For him "Publick Spirit" denotes serving the needs and purposes of one's community. This support is necessary for the polity to flourish. To remind ourselves of the relevant sentences:

> Arms at that time was the honoured Profession, and a publick Spirit the courted character: There was a Necessity for them both. The Man who had bravely defended his City, enlarged its Dominion, or died in its Cause, was revered like a God: Love of Liberty, Contempt of Death, Honour, Probity and Temperance, were Realities. There was, as I said, a Necessity for those Virtues: No Safety to Life or Fortune without them. (Blackwell 1735: 53)

---

[1] "Die Zeit bot ihm [Stein] manches Wort für die Bezeichnung geistiger Kollektivkräfte. Die Opinion Publique, der Esprit Publique [...], dazu der Zeitgeist; neuerdings auch das Wort 'Volksgeist'. [...] Bei Stein erscheint am häufigsten die Bezeichnung 'öffentlicher Geist' und 'öffentliche Meinung'."

This kind of "good" public spirit, or "public virtue", which relates to a community's needs, reappears further on in the book as a deeply engrained collective (national) characteristic. In the case of the Romans, Blackwell declares:

> Here the Force of the *Model* appears, and the Power of *Public Manners*. Virgil's Poem was to be read by a People deeply disciplin'd; whose early Necessities had taught them *political Forms*, and from being a Company of *Banditti*, had forced them into Publick Virtue. These forms had Time to take root in the Minds and Manners of the Nation; and *Constancy, Severity*, and *Truth*, was become a *Roman* Character. Even when the Substance was gone, when Luxury and high Ambition had stript them of their original Integrity, they were still forced to feign and dissemble. (Blackwell 1735: 327–328)

Similarly, for Montesquieu the "general spirit of nations", "formed by the climate, by the religion, by the laws, by the maxims of government, by precedent, morals and customs" (Montesquieu 2011 [1748]: 112), is in the types of polity he condones linked (or ought to be linked) to "virtue".[2] And virtue consists of loving and living the (positive) principles of one's polity, because this lived embodiment guarantees the polity's continued existence: "The love of our country is conducive to a purity of morals, and the latter is again conducive to the former." (Montesquieu 2011: 16)[3]

In the first half of the eighteenth century, public spirit was conceived as a real and influential dynamic operating for the overall benefit of a community, i.e. it is evident in specific acts which effect or combine to real and concrete outcomes, but which in total may amount to an abstract level of social success, such as prosperity, justice, safety, victory, or freedom. As such, public spirit was linked in theory and practice to a collective and integral to producing and maintaining a sense of a community's common good. By virtue of promoting the active pursuit of the latter, public spirit was understood to check excessive individual self-interest, or selfishness, which was increasingly seen as a key contemporary vice.

Public spirit was closely bound up with the concept of eighteenth-century patriotism. Its origin in British discourse – Blackwell's book precedes Montesquieu's – was well known in later eighteenth-century German circles. In the sixth collection of his *Humanitätsbriefe* Herder points out that "Gemeingeist (public spirit),[4] diese Benennung stammt von den Britischen Inseln" [General

---

2 One key point of his book was to show that the spirit of any laws must be in harmony with this general spirit of the community.

3 In a democratic republic this love focused on democratic equality, in an aristocratic republic on moderation, in monarchies on honour. Despotisms, however, are based on fear.

4 These are Herder's brackets. Sometimes the term occurs as "Allgemeingeist".

spirit (public spirit), this name originates in the British Isles] (Herder 1991 [1795]: 419).[5] Georg Forster, writing at the same time,[6] also drew attention to the British home of this term in *Parisische Umrisse* (s.b.). This is also the time and context (1792–1794), in which both Herder and Forster explicitly deal with the concept of zeitgeist. Forster's *Parisische Umrisse* discusses the French Revolution as marked by zeitgeist and Herder's remark comes from his dialogic discussion of zeitgeist discussed above. Forster and Herder, however, disagree as to whether public spirit exists in Germany. In 1793 Forster, linking public spirit with public opinion, thinks not:

> Wie es keinen deutschen Gemeingeist gibt, so gibt es auch keine öffentliche Meinung. [...] Diese Worte sind uns so neu [...], dass jedermann [...] Definitionen fordert, indes kein Engländer den andern mißversteht, wenn vom *public spirit* [...] die Rede ist.
>
> [As there is no public spirit in Germany, there cannot be any public opinion. [...] These words are so new to us that everybody is demanding definitions of them, while Englishmen don't misunderstand each other when they speak of public spirit.][7]

In contrast to Forster, Herder was keen to point out that the concept of public spirit had a long tradition in Germany, at least in German cities. In the same "Humanitätsbrief" he writes: "wir verehrten ihn [den Gemeingeist] aber lange vorher unter dem ehrbaren Namen, *der Stadt Bestes*" [we have honoured it [public spirit] for a long time under the honourable name of *the Good of the City*, literally: the City's best] (Herder 1991: 419, italics in original).

While Forster's view results from his belief that progressive social and political forces were absent in Germany, Herder's view reflects his historicist and comparative approach. He was fully aware of the constitutional and institutional differences between Britain and the German Empire, but he decides to look at a similarity of dynamics at different levels of public administration. Herder locates this spirit at local level, harking back to the German *Nationalgeist*-debate of the mid-1760s, which he had followed avidly from Riga. This debate focused on a related question: whether there existed a *national* spirit in Germany. The answer was overwhelmingly that it did not,

---

[5] Strictly speaking, Herder quotes from Johan Christoph Berens' *Bonhomien. Geschrieben bei Eröffnung der neuerbauten Rigischen Stadtbibliothek* (1792), a text that according to Irmscher is not extant (Herder 1991: 1011). Berens was a longstanding friend of Herder's from his days in Riga in the 1760s.
[6] As part of the "Sixth Collection", Letter 78 was published in spring 1795 but written in autumn 1794 (Herder 1991: 811).
[7] Forster was writing to a friend; this letter fragment is published as "Über die öffentliche Meinung (Fragment eines Briefes)" (Forster 1991: 365).

but there was equally no doubt that *public* spirit (in the form of local patriotic spirit) *did* exist. This reiterates the link between national spirit and general (public) spirit, which did not just exist in Herder's mind. In fact, the main disagreement in the 1760s debate was the territorial level at which national spirit currently existed, or should exist. This is, as Nicholas Vazsonyi (1999) has pointed out, a debate set in the aftermath of the Seven Years War (1756–1763) about whether something could be gained from *not* having territorial division in Germany, whether enabling, anti-despotic public spirit did, or should, exist at *Reichs*-level. That it existed at the local level, as e.g. Hessian, Saxon, Prussian public spirit, was not in doubt. The question whether *Reichspatriotismus* is conservative, the common view (Vazsonyi 1999: 234), or a harbinger of modern nationalism will not be discussed here. The interesting question in this context is in what respect this discussion was political or, put differently, to what extent it was focused not on "national" unity versus federal plurality, but on the best way to check a political executive from becoming despotic, self-serving or un-public spirited. It is this political aspect of national and public spirit that zeitgeist brought with it, when it assumed its modern, more short-term(ist) meaning during the late eighteenth-century political debate.

The "national spirit"- debate was part of the initial reception of Montesquieu's *Laws* in Germany. Most of the participants were jurists (Johann von Justi, Johann Heumann, Friedrich Karl von Moser, Johann Heinrich Eberhard), the other two key ones, Casimir Karl von Creutz and Johann Jacob Bülau, were public administrators,[8] which means all had a keen interest in the running of a polity, so a key aspect of their discussions focused on the relationship between polity and patriotism. Eberhard identified the whole matter as belonging to the realm of "Staatsrecht" [laws of the state] (Vazsonyi 1999: 236). Friedrich Carl von Moser called one of his interventions "Patriotic Letters" (1767). His interest was clearly political, in *Patriotische Briefe* he defines "Nationalgeist" as

> [D]ie Gesinnungen, welche den Häuptern und Vätern unseres Vaterlandes, allen ihren Gehülfen, Rathgebern und Dienern, allen Patrioten und ächten Söhnen Germaniens eigen sein sollten, *in Absicht auf unsere allgemeine Staats-Verfassung*, den deutschen National-Geist genannt. (Vazsonyi 1999: 238, italics mine)

> [the attitudes, which ought to be held by the leaders and elders of our fatherland, by all their assistants, counsellors and servants, by all patriots and true sons of Germania, regarding the general constitution of our state, this is called German national spirit.]

---

[8] Creutz was "Staatsrat" (state councillor) in Hesse-Homburg, Bülau "Stadtschreiber" (town clerk) in Zerbst.

The polity is held together and kept mutually beneficial, i.e. public, through its defining spirit, which all subscribe to.[9] The bone of contention is how the rule of law can be guaranteed. For Moser it is through an extra-dynastic German national spirit. He picks up on Montesquieu's idea that *political* communities, polities, are virtuously maintained by public political identities. All three of Montesquieu's favourable types of polity (monarchy and the two kinds of republic) are based on the rule of law, which is controlled by a "virtuous" public (national) spirit. Virtue, however, can become corrupted by the ambition or avarice of individuals or groups, who by example pass on their corruption to the rest of the polity's members (Montesquieu 2011: 42–51). The result is invariably despotism, i.e. the absence of such a spirit jeopardises the rule of law.

That public spirit is the guardian of legitimate government remained a key feature of political thought well into the nineteenth century (and beyond, of course). Two generations later, the Norwegian-born academic Henrik Steffens (1773–1845), whose career took him to civil service posts in Denmark and Germany, maintains exactly this point, when he writes, in 1817, that any form of "might is right"-politics amounts to lawlessness (Montesquieu's point about despotic governments). A state needs to protect the interest of *all* its citizens and this is best achieved through a "truly loving attitude of all parts". "The healthier a state built on its own foundations [is], the firmer is its national attitude." (Steffens 1817: 4–5)[10] Such a public-spirited state is also unlikely to wish to expand and attack weaker neighbours, for "patriotic love does not replace the general love of humanity" (Steffens 1817: 3).[11]

This link between virtuous public spirit and the rule of law, whereby the former guarantees the latter, i.e. whereby political power is checked by the consensus of the governed public, was the basis from which public opinion inherited its political function. For Montesquieu and Moser public spirit was positive, moderating, and stabilising. The shift towards a negative view of public opinion (and zeitgeist), which I explore below, was based on the fear that their power can also be used to destabilise and overthrow a political set-up or *maintain* despotism. The presence of political virtue, and the absence of individual or party

---

9 Vazsonyi (1999: 238) identifies the tension between collective control and free expression of collective identity in this discussion. There are "two competing narratives of national development. One suggests that national identity is constructed by an elite (academics, political leaders), then fed [...] to the people. The other insists that a national spirit exists *ab ovo* and arises organically from the people."
10 "wirkliche liebevolle Gesinnung alle[r] Glieder"; "je gesunder [sic] ein in sich gegründeter Staat, je fester seine nationale Gesinnung".
11 "Vaterlandsliebe die allgemeine Menschenliebe keineswegs aufhebt".

self-interest, on which public-spirited polities were thought to depend, lies at the heart of the emerging discussion about a "good" and "bad" public opinion. Bad public opinion, which no longer serves the public but individual or party interests instead, produces a corrupted public spirit. The ambivalence lies in the "spirit's" controlling tendency which harbours the possibility of "undue" influence resulting from the managed manipulation by a self-interested party. Even in Moser's statement above, there is a hint of coercion in his definition of national spirit, if one considers the hierarchical set-up of the collective he describes and the moral obligation inherent in his use of "sollten".

3.2 The political role of public opinion in Britain and Germany – the guardian of lawful government and the risks of demagogy

During the last third of the eighteenth century public opinion rose to prominence in political discourse. On the one hand, it inherited the balancing function of public spirit, on the other, it became feared as an instrument of manipulation. It was the guardian of liberty as well as the means of subjugation and oppression. In both instances it was recognised as a form of control.

Like the concept of spirit, the notions of the public, publicity, *Öffentlichkeit* and *Publicität* dominated eighteenth-century thinking and predated the preoccupation with zeitgeist. And like zeitgeist, they experienced a dip in esteem in the decade following the Revolution. As the Revolution played out, bringing not only a raft of controversial new political ideas but also a wave of wars, which for many German territories resulted in political dependence on France and for Britain in a serious threat to national security, these conceptual entities came to be regarded as the root of the many ills of the present. Mobilising large sections of the population for (revolutionary) political ends by controlling, or at least influencing, the "public sphere" by means of publications and discussions was seen as a key driver of contemporary political developments. There was a steep learning curve: it was quickly understood that *any* mass political mobilisation could be achieved through decisively influencing "public opinion". This understanding was put into practice in Britain in the pro- and anti-revolutionary propaganda in the 1790s and early 1800s and in the agitation leading up to the Wars of Liberation against Napoleon in Germany. Around 1800 it was clearly understood that zeitgeist expressed itself in public opinion, which reduced *some* of the "ghostly" nature of its force.

Jürgen Habermas has famously traced the genesis and formation of the term *opinion publique*/public opinion in Britain and France as part of the emerging public sphere, the place of public business (Habermas 1990 [1962]: 161–178). It is clear how its rise in importance was intricately connected to bourgeois self-consciousness and self-confidence, even if post-Habermas research has equally clearly shown that there were other, not primarily bourgeois, public spheres and opinions developing during the later eighteenth century. What they all share, and this supports Habermas' original argument to some extent, is their constituents' desire to be enfranchised, to participate in political and public decision-making. In this, all public spheres endorsed the view that the public, in its various collective incarnations, did represent a mechanism to control political power and mitigate despotic tendencies, on which the link between liberty and publicity was based.

Habermas also deals with the "dialectic" of the public, which sets its liberating tendencies against its controlling ones. He points to the inherent contradiction (Widerspruch) in the bourgeois concept: on the one hand it is based on the belief that markets were self-regulatory without force (Gewalt) and that hence executive rule (Herrschaft) would become obsolete, as self-interest was subsumed under general rationality. On the other hand, threats to bourgeois dominance made "rule", or the defence of this dominance, necessary.[12] In my context this dialectic is a version of the mid-eighteenth-century tension between public spirit and public control, and the desire to protect the public interest from partisan interest without being too sure how to make certain the guardians of impartiality really are impartial.

It has been frequently pointed out that a concept of "öffentliche Meinung" was formed later in Germany than its equivalents in France and Britain (Liesegang 2004: 16). Indeed, the term *opinion publique* appeared in French in the mid-eighteenth century, while "public opinion" is recorded in the *OED* already in the seventeenth and early eighteenth centuries (significantly in Thomas May's translation of Barclay's *Icon Animorum* and in the work of Shaftesbury, a political thinker concerned with "manners" and general spirit). Its modern meaning, however, emerged only when the term became established and frequent towards the end of the eighteenth century (Hölscher 1978: 449–450). At this point it also appeared in German as "öffentliche Meinung", namely in Christoph Martin Wieland's *Teutscher Merkur*, where it featured in 1790 as a translation from the French in a short anonymous piece by Gerhard von Halem (Halem 1790: 383).[13] By the end of the decade "öffentliche Meinung" was certainly no longer a "new"

---

12 Habermas 1990: 148–178. § 11 "Die widerspruchsvolle Institutionisierung der Öffentlichkeit im bürgerlichen Rechtsstaat".
13 "Die öffentliche Meinung (opinion publique) giebt der National-Versammlung beym Volke eine Festigkeit und Autorität, von der ich bisher nur einen schwachen Begriff hatte." (Halem 1790: 383).

and "foreign" term in German (as Forster had suggested it in 1793), instead it was on everyone's lips. Christian Garve, writing before 1798, noted that it had "become significant through its [frequent] use" (Garve 1974: 1268/296).[14] But it lacked clear definition, leading Wieland to observe in 1799 that it was a "term with many meanings that one hears so frequently these days".[15]

Von Halem in 1790, Forster in 1793, and Christian Garve before 1798 all indicate that the German "öffentliche Meinung" was a calque of the French term.[16] However, what this term, calque or original, eventually named had a longer (eighteenth-century) history. In all three languages the term's decisive *and* novel aspect was the link between "opinion" and the concept of "public-ness", as Garve points out in his essay "Über die öffentliche Meinung" (Garve 1974: II, 1265). The two terms "public" and "opinion" had longer histories, but the collocation was a new development.

Public-ness was linked to the early modern idea of the legitimacy of the power of the state. In the eighteenth century it became associated with the space in which mutual enlightenment took place through critical exchanges and discussion (Hölscher 1978: 413–445). The interest in such exchanges, and the will to organise and maintain them, is evident in the well-documented spread of periodical culture, which implied an appetite for information and discussion. Periodical, journal and newspaper culture developed in Britain, France, and Germany at different paces; in Britain the *Spectator* and the *Gentleman's Magazine* appeared at the beginning of the century and review organs, such as the *Monthly Review*, operated from mid-century onwards, while in Germany journals of similar stature and intention did not emerge until the last third of the century, e.g the *Teutscher Merkur* in 1773 and the review publication *Allgemeine Literatur-Zeitung* in 1785. These were, however, preceded by the early eighteenth-century German moral periodicals ("moralische Monatsschriften"), such as *Der Patriot* (1724–1726) or Bodmer and Breitinger's *Discourse der Mahlern* (1721–1723), which were only a few years behind the British *Tatler* and *Spectator*. Periodicals crossed national borders: Bodmer, for example, was a keen reader of the *Spectator*, which served as "model for his *Discourse*" (Wehrli 1943: 18).

In Britain, the political aspect of public-ness, with its legitimising powers, runs through British political philosophy from the seventeenth century, from William Temple, via Locke, to Hume. All three assumed that government had to be

---

14 "[ist] durch seine Anwendung so bedeutend geworden".
15 "vieldeutige Benennung, die man unserer Tage so oft zu hören bekommt" (Wieland 1799: 309).
16 For von Halem, see note 13 above, Garve 1974: II, 1265, Forster, *Parisische Umrisse*, see below.

legitimised by the assent of (at least part of) the governed (Hölscher 1978: 448–449). The particular British fear of political and ecclesiastical despotism, a result of the specific nature of the English Reformation which paved the way for the English Civil War, is largely responsible for this preoccupation. Hume had, after 1740, a sense that rulers were subject to the "general will" and that they could only defy it – unwisely – through violent civil conflict. "As force is always on the side of the governed, the governors have nothing to support themselves but opinion."[17] Still without the adjective "public" in Hume, which at this time was closely linked to "spirit" (as in Blackwell), opinion still lacked a clear political functionality. Hume would later liken this opinion to "the spirit of the times". Similarly Montesquieu had only a few years earlier defined as a tyrannical act the instance of a ruler ignoring the views generally held by the governed, which were "seated in opinion". This is the case "when those who govern establish things shocking to the present ideas of a nation" (Montesquieu 2011: 112).

On the road of conceptual travel from public spirit towards public opinion, the potential political clout of this evolving concept became manifest in revolutionary France, as Gerhart von Halem pointed out in relation to the French national assembly of 1790, which he had observed in action: "Public opinion (opinion publique) gives the [French] National Assembly a firmness and authority among the people, of which I previously had only a faint understanding." (Halem 1790: 383, see note 13)

In pre-revolution France there was an inkling of the political nature and force of *l'opinion publique* in the 1770s and 1780s. Hölscher quotes Du Marsais (1770), Diderot (1775), and Necker (1784), all of whom attest, with some concern, the political power of public opinion (1978: 450). This power increased significantly when it was no longer (just) a check on despotic tendencies, but became conflated with the general will, which was increasingly the case in the 1790s, as we shall see.

As the case of public spirit discussed above showed, in a conceptual (rather than a terminological) sense the political power of the public was not limited to French or British thinking: the debate about national spirit made clear that the idea of a publicly based control mechanism existed in mid-eighteenth-century German thinking too. Moral and intellectual enlightenment became political in

---

17 Hölscher quotes Hume's "Fourth Essay Of the First Principles of Government" (1978: 449). The roots of this realisation lie in the constitutional crisis of the 1680s. William Temple had reached a similar conclusion in 1680 in his "Essay upon the Original and Nature of Government": "Power arising from Strength, is always in those that are governed, who are many: But Authority arising from Opinion, is in those that Govern, who are few." (Hölscher 1978: 449). In 1680 Temple was reflecting on the political settlements of the English Restoration, he thoroughly approved of the Glorious Revolution when it occurred in 1688.

pre-Revolution German lands when the sum of reasoned (public) judgements, or opinions, became considered as the control instance of the political executive. This was not just evident in the *Nationalgeist*-debate but was also put forward – somewhat obliquely for today's reader – by the young Herder, who was clearly aware of the debate. In one of his earliest publications, "Haben wir jetzt noch ein Publikum und Vaterland der Alten" [Do we today still have a public and a fatherland like the Ancients],[18] an occasional piece written on the opening of the new courthouse in Riga in 1765 when the twenty-one-year-old Herder was teaching at the cathedral school, he compares the role of the public in the running of the polity (Vaterland) between ancient and modern (or rather the present) times, "unsere Zeiten". He concludes that real democracy does no longer exist and that the insolent ancient notions of freedom ("ungezähmte Frechheit"), which was "a boldness to want to take on the steering of the state, a stubbornness [Eigensinn] not to tolerate anyone above themselves " (Herder 1877 [1765]: 23),[19] has been replaced by moderate freedom ("gemäßigte Freiheit"), which is private, a "freedom of conscience" ("Freiheit des Gewissens") (1877: 24). Herder comes across as conservative, advocating paternalistic absolutism, perhaps mindful of the rights of his Russian Zarina, "die Monarchin", as the Hanseatic city of Riga belonged to Russia. (He may also have felt that it behoved a young Protestant cleric to foreground the spiritual freedom of conscience inaugurated by Luther's Reformation.) Herder's essay is predominantly a discussion of public spirit: everybody is called upon to help maintain and safeguard the polity for everybody's benefit, (not least against the demagogic "Zauberkünste eines Rednerischen Charletans", the magic arts of an oratorical charlatan (1877: 19). So, while patriotism still exists, a political public does not. In contrast to those paternalistic notions, however, there is also a note of regret, an underlying irony, in his description of the disappearance of this "immoderate" and "insolent" ancient public, which participated in politics ("de[m] Staat"), in public discourse, and in poetry, and which can no longer be found, or has fallen silent, and whose absence or silence makes the efforts of writers (like him) pointless: Herder speaks of a melancholy sight, a "wehmüthige[r] Anblick" (Herder 1877: 20–21).

---

[18] It needs further investigation to what extent this essay is a direct contribution to the national spirit debate, which does, however, seem likely for three reasons: Herder refers to Abbt's "kleines Buch; vom Tode fürs Vaterland" (Herder 1877 [1765]: 23), a key text in this debate, and to the "jüngere Herr von Moser" [Friedrich Karl von Moser], a chief participant (1877: 22), and his essay touches on the debate's crux of patriotism, public spirit, and the political organisation of a polity.

[19] "Erkühnen, selbst das Rad des Staates lenken zu wollen, ein Eigensinn, nur keine Namen über sich zu leiden".

Significantly for our context, Herder returned to this piece in the mid-1790s, thirty years later, when he includes a version of this essay in the sixth collection of *Humanitätsbriefe* (1795) as Letter 57, "Haben wir noch das Vaterland der Alten?". Again, he eulogises public spirit and, returning to the "silent member(s) of the public", part of his cause for sadness in 1765, he now demands that the "voice of the citizen" ["Stimme des Bürgers"] be heard, and published – this is part of patriotic freedom, "Vaterlandsfreiheit" (Herder 1991: 335). "Die Winke und Blicke Derer [Bürger], die weiter sehen" [the hints and views of those citizens who [can] see further], of the intellectual elite, are important for the polity. They are silent ("schweigen weiter") at the peril of the patriotic polity ("Vaterland"), because the latter needs this "accounting" ("Rechenschaft"), this public reckoning, for the polity to remain publicly beneficial. Otherwise there will be self-interested wars, bloodshed, and the "Vaterland" will be shattered and orphaned, "zerrüttet" and "verwaiset" (Herder 1877: 335).

> Sollte unser Vaterland dieser Rechenschaft nicht bedürfen? [...] Licht, Aufklärung, Gemeinsinn; edler Stolz, sich nicht von anderen einrichten zu lassen, sondern sich selbst einzurichten, wie andere Nationen es von jeher taten; Deutsche zu sein auf eigenem wohlbeschützten Grund und Boden. (Herder 1877: 335)

> [Should our patriotic polity not have need of such giving account? [...] Light, enlightenment, public spirit; noble pride not to let others arrange our affairs, but to arrange them ourselves, as other nations have always done; to be Germans on our own secure soil.]

Although aware already in 1765 of the potential of demagogy (those "oratorical charlatans"), Herder, in 1795, promotes a political public that has a role in safeguarding the liberty, independence, and security of individuals and their polity.

The interpretation of German public opinion has traditionally focused on its belated development, in line with the interpretation of the belated move towards a centralised nation state. And in line with the similarly traditional interpretation of the "unpolitical" nature of German "cultural" nationalism, it is tempting to assume that the investment of the public and public opinion with political power took different forms in British and German contexts.[20] While in British thinking this investment coalesced around "liberty", which was achieved in terms of political practice through parliament and a free press, in Germany it coalesced around "Vernunft" and moral education, which would bring about reasonable political rules and public states organised to serve the common good. But looking at the

---

20 See Ruth Flad for a summary of the assumed differences between German and West-European approaches to public opinion, based on the German writers Ferdinant Tönnies and Ernst Troeltsch in the 1920s (1921: 1–6).

eighteenth-century evidence presented here it is no longer clear to what extent such a neat division in approach and outlook existed. British considerations were equally concerned with reason and moral development, and German thinking was concerned about (political) liberty, as Herder's demands above make plain. In both settings there was a keen interest in establishing relations between liberty, reason, moral judgement, and polity. There are considerable similarities in the appreciation of public spirit, public opinion, and their political roles. In both contexts an incorruptible quality of this social force was being postulated, which would flourish under the right conditions. This common approach to polity and publicness changed once the "national" was no longer closely linked to public spirit, patriotism, and a homeland (as it had been in the *Nationalgeist*-debate), but instead became attached to a *national* collective based on a shared language and the culture that flows from this. While in Britain and France this change of focus could be easily performed by moving from eighteenth-century patriotism to nineteenth-century nationalism, as both could attach to their centralised states, in Germany, which lacked such a centralised state, this was a more difficult shift to accommodate. In this regard, the idea of patriotism had been easier to handle in Germany, because it could attach, and was attached, to any territorial unit.

By the early 1790s most political observers and actors had realised the immense power of public opinion when it came to influencing political and public activity. But there was considerably less agreement on how it should be treated, whether it should be obeyed and if and how it could it be guided, as Herder wondered in 1793 in *Humanitätsbriefe*. Of even greater concern was perhaps another issue: whose opinion and whose voice was it? The enlightened public's, the indoctrinated mob's, the majority's, or was it the voice of those who control a great enough share of publicly available information? An understanding was emerging that public opinion sat at the intersection between "elites" and the "public", where it played a key role in influencing the spirit of the age by – eventually – arriving at a generally accepted version of what had happened, was happening, and should be happening.

From the 1790s, the discussion focused on differentiating good from bad public opinion. While concern regarding its dangerous potential came to dominate, this never fully displaced its older positive attributes, not least because they were useful. Once the power of public opinion had been demonstrated by the Revolution, its new influence was eagerly utilised. "Good" public opinion, which supported the propagator's political aims, was always presented as the true expression of the public view and will, while disagreement with it represented its corrupted manipulation by interested parties who did not have the communal good at heart. This (somewhat cynical) description is not to suggest that individual actors within the public arena did not genuinely believe that their ideas represented the true, good, and beneficial voice of the public, which would best serve the aims of public enlightenment and social self-determination, while its improper counterpart would produce the opposite, namely a public duped by a small group of conspiratorial self-seeking or self-interested usurpers supported by two larger groups: unthinking individuals who echoed what they were told and selfishly immoral individuals who stood to profit from the rule of the manipulative elite. The idea of a constructive and trustworthy public opinion did survive the awareness of its potential appropriation.

The 1790s debate about dangerous public opinion was in both countries situated within the larger, politically highly charged debate about revolutionary sedition and political reform. For the British context, the developments that led up to the Treason Trials of 1794 are well researched and need not be reiterated here. The aspect of these developments most relevant to this enquiry is that of the different definitions of "the public" and the validity of "its" opinion. A marker in this debate was Edmund Burke's *Reflections on the Revolution in France* (1790), which sparked vigorous reactions. The debate focused on the ways and methods of achieving social change, and their desired or undesirable outcomes and triggered the formation of a number of "societies", among them the *London Corresponding Society* and the *Society of the Friends of the People*, both founded in 1792. This debate was in many respects really a battle over the definition of public opinion, and the mutual public denunciations of Edmund Burke and John Thelwall, which will be discussed below, are an illustrative example of this.

In Germany, this debate surfaced in the essays and articles that discussed the question whether *Aufklärung*, i.e. reading, discussing, being invited to think and form judgements, contributed to social unrest and could even cause revolutions. Johann Adam Bergk's article "Bewirkt Aufklärung Revolutionen?", which appeared in *Deutsche Monatsschrift* in 1795, is an example. Bergk, rather like Schiller in his contemporaneous *Aesthetic Education*, considers moral enlightenment – public virtue – the necessary preparation for political reform and progress, which it would be an injustice to suppress, because the objective of an enlightened society is enfranchisement of all enlightened minds. In the same volume Christian Gottlob Heyne considered the question "Sind die Wissenschaften den Regierungen gefährlich?" [Are the sciences a danger to governments?], evidently responding to suggestions that they cause seditious unrest. Heyne decides they definitely are not, provided they are handled sensibly. Similarly, Franz Josias von Hendrich, before he moves on to discussing zeitgeist and public opinion in 1797, argues in his *Freymütige Gedanken* [Free Thoughts] of 1794 that "a free, decent and public examination of the abuses and failings of the state administration [is] the only way to reduce the latter" (Hendrich

1794: 171).²¹ And if rulers do not submit to this, they lose the trust of their subjects, which is a dangerous thing in the present climate. *Freymütige Gedanken* achieved a high circulation, it is extant in numerous libraries in Germany, Britain, and the United States and went into a second edition within a few months. In the preface to the third edition, which appeared in 1795, Hendrich reiterates the above idea (1795: 3) and defends himself against accusations of being a Jacobin (1795: 7–8). For all their caution, these German writers all insisted that a morally advanced people required enlightened government, and that rulers needed to respect this, in fact that they needed to go with the times.

3.3 The uses of public opinion – Georg Forster and Christian Garve

Garve's "Über die öffentliche Meinung" (1802, written between 1794–1798)²² and Georg Forster's *Parisische Umrisse* (1793/1794) make an illuminating comparison in this context; both authors saw the dangers of a manipulated public opinion, but neither wanted to give up its energising and politically purifying power to the instigators of (misleading) partisan public opinion. They approach this common ground from very different political view-points and with different political visions: Forster as an (at least publicly) committed Jacobin, Garve as a moderate middle-class intellectual. Both saw public opinion as a function of zeitgeist.

For Forster, public opinion was a social good underpinned by public spirit, but the uses of public opinion of which he explicitly approved are not conducive to *balancing* power. Forster (1785–1794), whose life fell halfway between the 1760s national spirit debate and the conservative clampdown of 1819, thought that such political virtue did not exist in Germany. His concept of public opinion was based on the political and cultural difference between France and Germany, but he too was convinced that a polity had to be morally and politically ready for revolution if the latter was to succeed. For him the marker of such readiness was a functioning public opinion that served the public good, something that in his view revolutionary France possessed. And even in late 1793 Forster was, at least publicly, optimistic on this front.²³ Germany on the

---

21 "eine freye anständige öffentliche Prüfung der Mißbräuche und Gebrechen der Staatsverwaltung [ist] der einzige Weg zu deren Besserung".
22 The exact date of writing uncertain: Garve knew *Parisische Umrisse*, which appeared in sections in 1794, and died in 1798 (Liesegang 2004: 141). The essay was published posthumously.
23 Researchers have suggested that there are two motivations for Forster's apologia of the Revolution in late 1793: Forster's pro-Revolution stance made it necessary to explain the need

other hand had, in his view, no such uncorrupted public opinion, and was hence not ready for revolution. The view of public opinion Forster puts forward in *Parisische Umrisse*, written in 1793 and published (posthumously) in 1794, is a eulogy to its transformative power, notwithstanding the fact that he is very aware of its negative potential in the hands of people with selfish motives. Forster was imbued with the positive potential of the public. However, in his insistence on an all-encompassing collective he produces a description of totalitarian structures that represent the dark underside of the normative tendencies of enlightenment rationalism. The tension between free expression and coercive control emerges starkly in this text, it is responsible for its conceptual slippage on this point.

In its current incarnation in revolutionary France, public opinion is presented as an instructive example of its political importance; von Halem had already introduced the notion of its *political* nature to German readers. Forster eulogises its majestic power and moral incorruptibility, which gives – text-immanently at least – unequivocal testimony of his belief in its function as a collective conscience. The text is conceived as providing information and education about the meaning of the Revolution, and the role of public opinion within it, to still uncomprehending, and possibly misinformed German readers. Its hybrid textual nature has been pointed out,[24] as have its semantic slippages (Liesegang 2004: 136–137). Its conceptual unevenness resides in its use of metaphysical teleology, its insistence on defining the revolution as an event initiated and sanctioned by Providence, "Vorsehung", while at the same time claiming that France's political transformation was the result of the united, self-determined, and free agency of the French people. This unevenness reflects not just the tension between the expressive and coercive aspects of zeitgeist, but also the tension between its diachronic and synchronic aspects, i.e. the link between the monumental spirit of history and the spirit of the age. It is of course possible to consider human decision-making and activity as free, i.e. not primarily the result of human interference, interest or pressure, and still set this freedom of self-determination within the ultimate necessity of a providential plan. Self-determination is then conceived

---

for revolutionary violence, making clear all the while that such a practice would be highly unsuitable for German politics. This is on the one hand intended to calm a fearful public opinion in Germany and thus reduce the pressure on the young republic. On the other hand, this apologia has been seen as the result of Forster's own uncertainty in the face of the ongoing revolutionary radicalisation and as his effort to reassure himself that these processes were beneficial (Liesegang 2004: 126).

24 Gamper and Schnyder describe it as "swaying between report and statement of opinion, between essay and manifesto" (Gamper and Schnyder 2006: 12).

within a human context only, it is *perceived* as real, while outside of this context it may be subject to, and sanctioned by, other forms of (pre)determination.

In Forster's text, Providence is used to bolster the legitimacy and the grandeur of the revolution, even if it takes away from the self-determining agency of the people. Historical providence is presented as supporting the "Geist der Gegenwart" [spirit of the present time] (Forster 1967–1971: III, 729), which is for Forster the "Geist der Revolution" (III, 766), but also the "sign of the future" ["Zeichen der Zukunft"] (III, 729). The latter appears to need some support: to the question as to why the revolution occurred at this precise point in time, which was perhaps not the most promising, as a discrepancy ("Mißverhältnis") existed "between the untenability of the government [of the ancien régime] and the inability of the people to create a new one" (III, 737),[25] Forster replies:

> Wer anders kann Ihnen antworten als die unbegreifliche und unergründliche Weisheit der Vorsehung! […] unsere Revolution, als Werk der Vorsehung, [steht] in dem erhabenen Plan ihrer Erziehung des Menschengeschlechts gerade am rechten Orte, […] denn sie ist die größte, die wichtigste, die erstaunenswürdigste Revolution der sittlichen Bildung und Entwicklung des ganzen Menschengeschlechts. (III, 737)
>
> [Who else can answer you than the incomprehensible and unfathomable wisdom of Providence! […] our revolution, as the work of Providence, occupies just the right position in its august plan for the education of the human race, […] because it is the greatest, most important, most astonishing revolution of the moral culture and development of the entire human race.]

Humans are engaged in the self-empowering process of educating themselves out of all kinds of dependencies – the Enlightenment goal of history –, which is also the inscrutable aim of Providence. In Forster's account the self-determined reasonable individual's purpose is not just to be part of the plan of unfathomable Providence but also to align their individuality with the unconditional demands of the (reasonable) human-led collective. This collective appears in abstract singulars in this text: the revolution, public opinion, the people. The high frequency of the term "Geist" situates Forster's thinking within exactly the context of abstracting and collectivising human activity in history and the present, which had powered the spirit-discourse throughout the eighteenth century and was producing the contemporaneous notion of zeitgeist. Forster presents the power and legitimacy of his collective entities as arising from their united-ness: free individuals have combined to a collective in which individuals no

---

[25] "zwischen der Unhaltbarkeit der Regierung [des Anicen Régime] und der Unfähigkeit des Volkes sich eine neue zu schaffen".

longer matter. "Denn was ihre [der Regierung] Dauer und Stärke verspricht, ist ja gerade diese durch das Ganze jetzt unwiderstehlich herrschende Einheit des Volkswillens, verbunden mit der Repräsentantenvernunft." [It is exactly the unity of the people's will, now ruling irresistibly throughout the whole [state], combined with the reason of the [people's] representatives, which promises the strength and [long] duration of the government.] (III, 734) In his view the revolution was not carried by important individuals, but the collective. "Wie unabhängig bei uns das Ganze vom Einzelnen ist! [...] Wenn dort die Vernunft hier den Arm in Bewegung setzt, ist der Endzweck des Staates erreicht." [How independent the whole is of the individual here! [...] If reason over there sets the arm in motion over here, the final purpose of the state has been achieved.] (III, 755) This neatly does away with factions, interests, envy, and corruption, everything that has so far poisoned political systems. It also does away with opposition and discussion: all are of one mind. "Der Wille des Volkes hat seine höchste Beweglichkeit erreicht, und die große Lichtmasse der Vernunft wirft ihre Strahlen in der von ihm verstatteten Richtung." [The will of the people has reached its highest agility, the great light of reason throws its beams in the direction this will determines.] (III, 733) And further on:

> Allein jene Arbeitsamkeit, jene Luftmasse von Vernunft, jene sich nie verläugnende Energie im Augenblick der Gefahr, jenes vor Aller Augen aufgesteckte Beispiel der Selbstverläugnung – erhoben sie nicht auch den National-Convent auf eine Höhe der Unumschränktheit, wo sie nur die öffentliche Meinung erhalten kann? Ohne Auszeichnung, [...] ohne Vorzug, und selbst ohne Autorität außer ihrem Versammlungssaale, ohne prätorianische Wache, endlich noch des Vorrechts der Unverletzbarkeit beraubt, herrschen die Repräsentanten des Volkes durch die öffentliche Meinung ohne Widerrede über vier und zwanzig Millionen Menschen. Nie befolgte man ihre Dekrete mit unbedingterem Gehorsam, nie war der Nahme des National-Convents so die allgemeine Losung des Beifalls, das Zutrauen des republikanischen Stolzes. (III, 748)

> [Alone that industriousness, that air mass of reason, that energy which never absconds in the moment of danger, that example of self-denial set up before all eyes – have they not raised the National Convention to a height of absolute rule where only public opinion can keep it? Without distinctions, [...] without preferment, and even without authority outside their assembly room, without Pretorian Guard, and lastly deprived of the prerogative of immunity, the representatives of the people rule through public opinion, without opposition, over a population of twenty-four million. Never have their decrees been followed with more unconditional obedience, never has the name of the National Convention been the general cause of so much applause or enjoyed so much the trust of republican pride.]

Although Forster uses the vocabulary of Enlightened self-determination throughout, e.g. the revolution is based on the "Geist der bürgerlichen Gesellschaft" [spirit of civic society] and represents the "Vereinigungspunkt aller Intelligenzen" [point of union of all intelligent minds] (III, 750), all enlightened reasoning must lead to selfless submergence in the collective of the age and the general will.

> Aus dieser Anregung der Verstandeskräfte, die wir der republikanischen Regierungsform verdanken, und aus der [...] Gleichartigkeit der jetzigen Generation folgt [...] die Sicherheit und Dauer der Republik. Die Grundsätze der republikanischen Freiheit haben bei uns überall desto tiefere Wurzeln geschlagen, je mehr sie simplificiert worden sind, und sich daher von jeder Fassungskraft aneignen lassen. In Frankreich wachen wenigstens fünfmal hunderttausend Menschen über die Gesinnungen eines jeden Bürgers und die Anmaßungen eines jeden öffentlichen Beamten. Wer wäre jetzt so kühn, sein Haupt über die Menge zu heben? Wer wagte es, auch nur Demuth zu heucheln? (III, 753)

> [The security and duration of the Republic is based on this stimulation of the powers of understanding, which we owe to the republican form of government, and on the homogeneity of the current generation. Here the principles of republican liberty have grown roots the deeper the more they have been simplified and can be understood by any intellect. In France at least 500.000 people keep watch over the views of each citizen and the presumptions of each public official. Who would now dare to lift their head over the masses? Who would dare only to simulate humility?]

Clearly there is coercive control: stepping outside the collective will trigger immediate collective judgement and condemnation. This becomes explicit when Forster suggests that where public opinion cannot persuade or control, the revolutionary army will: "Was die öffentliche Meinung noch nicht erzwingen konnte, das ergänzt überall, wo es noch nötig ist, die Revolutionsarmee." [The forces of public opinion are complemented by the revolutionary army, wherever this is still necessary.] (III, 746) And yet the basis of this popular rule is free self-determination. "Die Äußerungen des freien Willens (öffentliche Meinung) [können nicht] erscheinen, ehe der Wille frei ist." [The expression of free will (public opinion) cannot come forward until the will is free.] (III, 738) Even under those conditions, Forster still equates public opinion with the expression of free (collective) will.

The role of public opinion as the guardian of the public good is clear from the above. Its functioning seems to depend on freedom, at least before the point of revolution, "dies alles bahnte der Denkfreiheit und der Willensfreiheit den Weg, daß schon eine geraume Zeit *vor* der Revolution eine entschiedene öffentliche Meinung über das ganze Frankreich, benahe unumschränkt regierte". [All this paved the way for free thinking and free will, so that already some time *before* the revolution a decided public opinion ruled, almost sovereign, over all of France.] (III, 739–740, italics in original) Fulfilling its public function of checking the abuses of government, French public opinion contributed to the outbreak of the revolution. Forster's answer to whether enlightenment, in terms of autonomous judgement and action, causes revolutions is the opposite to Bergk's, it is an emphatic and approving affirmative.

Public opinion continues its control function regarding the government during the revolution. The victorious Montagnards rule as "servants of the state, not as overlords" (III, 756).[26]

> Sie regieren; aber sie stehen under der wachsamsten Aufsicht, und die heiligste Verwaltung des Volksinteresses ganz allein kann ihnen die Stütze der öffentlichen Meinung sichern. [...] So müssen sie jetzt inne werden, daß die kleinste Anmaßung den Strom der öffentlichen Meinung gegen sie richtet und ihnen selbst das Schicksal ihrer Gegner bereitet. (III, 756)

> [They rule; but they are under the most watchful supervision, and only the most sacred administration of the people's interest can secure for them the support of public opinion. [...] They must now understand that the most minor presumption will turn public opinion against them and produce for them the fate of their enemies.]

For: "Die öffentliche Meinung verurtheilt, noch schneller als das Revolutionstribunal, jeden Volksverräther." [Public opinion condemns every traitor to the people even faster than the revolutionary tribunal.] (III, 753) It is more effective, and more virtuous, than any secret police. Forster's all-encompassing collective public opinion is the tool ("Werkzeug") as well as the "soul" of the revolution. The people, the National Convention, and public opinion are one. Forster's concept of a vigilant public opinion in a new revolutionary collective is an extreme and radicalised version of the moderate Enlightened public of the mid-eighteenth century, maximising the controlling grasp of the collective on its members.

Conversely, where the people are not free, as is currently the case in Germany, there can be no "proper" public opinion: "Bei Ihnen [in Deutschland] gibt es noch keine öffentliche Meinung, und es kann keine geben, wenn das Volk nicht zugleich losgelassen wird." [In Germany there is no public opinion yet, and there cannot be one until the people are set free.] (III, 736) Instead German "public opinion" is fabricated to serve the interests of those (unrightfully) in power. For Forster, it seems, the tricky question of how the general will is established, had been solved, in France at least: it is reflected in public opinion. In Germany, however, public opinion was still controlled by interest and not yet capable of fulfilling its function as collective conscience. This could be one reason why in *Umrisse* the spirit of the revolution appears to the uncomprehending German friend as a "ghost", its ghostliness merely the result of successful manipulation at home. One may conjecture that, given his interest in zeitgeist matters, Forster had read

---

[26] "Diener, nicht als Gebieter des Staates".

Herder's recent ruminations on zeitgeist before he wrote *Umrisse*; the first collection of *Humanitätsbriefe* appeared at Easter, the second in May 1793 (Herder 1991: 811). Forster seems to allude to Herder at the end of part 4:

> 'Wer ist nun aber dieser Geist des stürmenden Frankreichs? Ists am Ende ein guter Geist oder rein feindseliger Dämon? Ein Meteor, das blendend durch die Lüfte fährt, zerplatzt und keine Spur seines Daseins hinterläßt, oder ein kräftiger Hauch des Lebens, der in den Abgrund der Zeiten hinabsteigt und die kommenden Generationen zu einer noch nie gekannten Entwicklung vorbereitet?' [...] Ein helles Licht spielt um seine Locken [...] ich vernehme deutlich die Donnerworte: discite justitiam moniti! [learn justice, you who have been warned]. (III, 757)[27]

> ['But who is this spirit of raging France? Is it in the end a good spirit or a hostile demon? A meteor, which, dazzling, shoots through the air, bursts, and leaves no trace of its existence, or a strong breath of life, which descends into the depths of time and prepares future generations for a development that has never been known before?' [...] A bright light is playing around its locks [...] I can clearly hear the thundering words: discite justitiam moniti! [learn justice, you who have been warned].

This further illustrates the associative link between public option and zeitgeist in the minds of contemporaries. Forster seems convinced that on this occasion history will bring a development for the better.

Christian Garve's approach is more one of damage limitation in a political world where politically charged public opinion is rampant. His essay pinpoints the change in the political importance of public opinion, which emanates from France: public opinion is the measure of all political, legislative, and jurisdictive action. It has acquired an unprecedented power to rule, which he identifies as unstoppable and unchallengeable, subject to no control, "unaufhaltsam und unwiderstehlich" (Garve 1974: 295). Public opinion is now seen as "ein unsichtbares Wesen von großer Wirksamkeit" [invisible entity of great effectiveness] counted among the "verborgenen Mächte, die die Welt regieren" [the hidden powers that rule the world] (1974: 294). Garve considers such unaccountable omnipotence the dubious refuge of the revolutionary, who appeals to a "Qualitas obscura, die alles erklären, – und einer höheren Macht, die alles entschuldigen kann" [obscure quality that can explain everything and a higher power that can excuse everything] (1974: 295), pointing out the manipulative and obfuscating quality of such an entity. He is, however, prepared to allow its

---

[27] For comparison: "Ist er [der Geist der Zeit/Zeiten] ein Genius, ein Dämon? [...] ein Lufthauch der Mode, ein Schall der Aeolsharfe? [...] Ist er der Genius der Humanität selbst? Oder dessen Freund, Vorbote, Diener? [...] Woher kommt er? [...] aus dem Schoß der Zeiten. [...] Seine Macht ist groß, aber unsichtbar." (Herder 1991: 85–86).

legitimacy. To defuse its revolutionary (but not its social) clout, he historicises it: it has always existed, quite recently as "gemeine oder herrschende Meinung" [common or dominant opinion]. "Meinung" is here, however, deprived of the politically legitimating attribute "public". Instead, he situates it within the context of engrained manners and even public spirit, close to Montesquieu's and Blackwell's "manners" and shared consensus:

> Die Meinung, worin viele Menschen übereinstimmen, noch mehr die, welche dem größten Theile der Bürger eines Staates gemeinschaftlich ist, hat von je her eine gewisse Gewalt geäußert, die Denkungsart der übrigen zu leiten. (1974: 293)
>
> [The opinion, with which many people agree, even more one which is shared by the majority of a state's citizens, has always had considerable power to direct the views of the rest.]

Then he defines what he considers as properly politically active public opinion, which relies on the notion of the individual's critical judgement, which is different from the common opinion of "je her" (the past) he described above. Garve proposes that public consensus is based on the reasoned judgement of rational individuals. But in difference to Forster, for Garve the individual's reasoning and conclusions, if they are to be valid, must not be influenced by any form of coercion, neither from interested parties or party interest, nor by tradition. If individual opinions, reached in such a detached manner, converged in large numbers on one particular view, this would for him indeed constitute a powerful and legitimate mandate (1974: 324). The Protestant Reformation serves him as precedent. Luther was not the author of the Reformation (not its "Urheber", 1974: 300), instead "er wurde der Vereinigungspunkt" [became its point of convergence] (1974: 301). However, even such a critical mass of considered views that freely associate into consensus – Garve marks the closeness between public opinion and general will (1974: 302) – represents not necessarily *true* opinions, as all are subject to their historical conditions and limitations. Garve was keenly aware of the difficulty of finding reliable ways of establishing such a consensus, he wonders "durch welches Organ sich dieser allgemeine Wille hören läßt, und wie man, bey Erforschung desselben durch irgendeine Art von Stimmensammlung, vor Täuschungen, ja vor muthwilligem Betruge sicher ist" [through which organ the general will can be heard, and how one can be safe from errors, wilful deceit even, when determining it through some kind of collection of votes] (1974: 319). Although public approval (or disapproval) gives an indication of the "general" view (1974: 320), Garve is certain that this will probably be just the voice of those who can or choose to speak. In this context Garve uses "Geist der Zeit" as a synonym of public opinion: it represents the "hidden attitudes of the greater part of the population" (1974: 320).[28] Decisive, however, is in Garve's view the direction given by those in power. He points to the frequent changes of religion in England between the Act of Supremacy and the accession of Elizabeth I (1974: 321), which was not evidence of the spiritual fickleness of the English people, nor of their struggle to find their true faith, but the result of shifts in political power. By focusing on the influence of the ruling elites in determining prevalent attitudes, Garve takes a different view than Hume or Hurd, who had stressed the dependence of rulers on the consent of the governed: for views to be prevalent they need some backing from some form of political power.

Despite Garve's pessimism regarding the genuine and representative nature of public opinion, he retains his faith in Enlightenment thinking: the tribunal of the public ("Richterstuhl des Publikums", 1974: 331) is, if it is an enlightened public, a legitimate court, and disinterested enlightened publicists and writers have an important and responsible role in this judicial process. They help their readers reach reasonable judgements and themselves voice such judgements, which amounts to a public opinion that commands respect.

> Ohne Zweifel haben auch auf diese [...] achtungswürdige öffentliche Meinung [...] besonders die Weisern, die Gelehrtern, und die Beredtern der Nation viel Einfluß. Und hier ist insonderheit der Einfluß der Schriftsteller bey einer lesenden Nation unverkennbar. (1974: 328)
>
> [Especially a nation's wiser people, the more educated, and the more eloquent, have great influence on this respectable public opinion. Here the influence of writers on a reading nation is easy to see.]

Like all moderates, he favours evolutionary change: the change of law must be prepared by a gradual change of opinion (1974: 324).

Although public acceptance is key, ultimately, for Garve, elites make public opinion, and those parts of the elite that have political power make the final decision on what it is. Indebted to Enlightenment ideals, Garve hopes that rulers and elites will make morally enlightened decisions and that if they don't, an enlightened public will correct them. For Garve, enlightened, individually critical public opinion remained the guardian of political and moral reason.

---

28 "die verborgenen Gesinnungen des größtern Theils der Menschen".

3.4 The battle over public opinion in 1790s Britain

In Britain, the debate about public opinion and public spirit followed a similar trajectory. British views drew on the legitimising qualities bestowed on public spirit and (public) opinion by eighteenth-century British political philosophy, which had invested an incorruptible collective power in them. Post-1789, however, a rancorous debate unfolded about the dangers of "the public", both as people and as an institution: the public was easily misled and corrupted by self-interested party-politics. Such corrupting of the common good was suspected across the political spectrum, by radicals, moderates, and conservatives, each accusing the others of pernicious opinion-mongering, or political propaganda. John Thelwall's engagement with Edmund Burke's running commentary on the developments in France and on home-grown Jacobinism provides a snapshot of this debate.

Thelwall, political radical and prominent member of the *London Corresponding Society*, disagreed vociferously with Burke's conservative views. Although the issues associated with public opinion and its impact on political activity are the same as those discussed by Forster and Garve, neither Thelwall nor Burke explicitly or consistently used a zeitgeist-term in this context. Thelwall's "spirit of the people", however, comes close to the concept of *Volksgeist*, which has been identified as synonymous with not just public opinion, but also zeitgeist. The mid-eighteenth-century usage of "spirit of the times" did not go through the same politicisation process as *Geist der Zeit* in German until "spirit of the age" became a catchword in the 1820s. The reasons for this will be explored in Chapter 5, but in a nutshell they are the following: a political term that links collective identity, historical process, and social change did not appear to be needed in Britain at this time and German "imports" were politically suspect as Britain shut down in its "defence of the realm" against Jacobinism, atheism, and Napoleon.

In this section I will focus on two texts by Thelwall, his mid-decade public lectures, which were swiftly published in his programmatically named *Tribune* (1795), and his contemporaneous *Rights of Nature against the Usurpations of Establishments* (1796). Both publications were part of Thelwall's response to Burke's views on the Revolution, the French Republic, and what Thelwall considered representative government. *Rights of Nature* in particular responded to Burke's first two *Letters on a Regicide Peace* (1796–1797). Both Burke and Thelwall are particularly interesting cases in the context of this investigation: while Thelwall, the radical English Jacobin, displays some interesting similarities to both Georg Forster and Ernst Moritz Arndt, whose *Geist der Zeit I* will discuss in the next chapter, Burke, who by 1790 was an anti-revolution "conservative", had highly liberal political origins. In the 1770s he had supported the grievances of the American colonists and was opposed to the use of force to discipline "American Liberty" because it was an off-shoot of English liberty. All of this went some considerable way towards making him support the *American Revolution*. His credentials of opposing despotism went further than this: he was a key figure in the impeachment of Warren Hastings, the first Governor-General of India and operative of the British East India Company who, according to Burke and other Whigs, had tarnished, not to say betrayed, British principles of good government by setting up an unaccountable, despotic rule in India. *Both* Burke and Thelwall were imbued with a sense of public spirit.

Thelwall frequently invoked the innate "rightness" of public opinion, very similar to Forster above, which made it the most, perhaps the only, legitimate political voice. His speeches share key political and conceptual features with Forster's text. Both are in favour of the Revolution and see it as a conflict of world-historical import between the people and their "establishment" oppressors. They differ on a linguistic feature, however. For Thelwall the seat of "rightness" and power is not called "the public", but "the people", and although he *does* use the term "public", he speaks of "popular opinion". On the one hand, this difference suggests that he supported the radical enfranchisement of all classes, rather than just the bourgeois middle classes, on whose self-definition the idea of the eighteenth-century public relied. On the other hand, focusing on the "people", the "spirit of the people", and "popular opinion" shifts Thelwall's perspective towards the communal collective, as expressed in "Volksgeist", which in the German context would be a perfectly possible conceptual configuration, and lexical choice.[29]

Conceptually Thelwall's "people" share the characteristics of the enlightened public, in them resides the frequently invoked "enlightened spirit of the people". This "spirit" clearly refers to the eighteenth-century spirit discourse: "popular opinion", guided by the "enlightened spirit of the people", is the disinterested guardian of the common good, and the conscience of legitimate political public action. In his 1796 *Rights of Nature*, which directly responds to Burke, especially to the first letters on a "Regicide Peace",[30] Thelwall extolls the incorruptible corrective of popular opinion as the only defence against tyranny and despotism.

---

[29] In German the cognate terms *Volksgeist* and *Volksmeinung* thrived in the heated atmosphere of insurrection and political struggle that developed after 1806. To what extent this similarity is owed to the similarly heated political contest between subversive radicalisation and establishment control requires more research.

[30] Thelwall refers to the first two *Letters* published by Rivington in 1796 (Thelwall 1796: 1).

> I do wish to uphold the salutary awe of popular opinion; [...] in whatever country this salutary awe does not operate, not only upon the tools and dependants of government, but upon the government itself, *even to its highest head*, there tyranny, in its essence, is already established, and liberty is but a name. (Thelwall 1796: 5, italics in original)

Thelwall believes that the people are the seat of reason. This "salutary awe" is to be "enforced"

> [b]y the manly energies of the people – by their active vigilance in watching the conduct of their governors, [...] by that intellectual courage, [...] that exertion of the inalienable prerogative of reason [...]. These are the means by which a brave and enlightened people overawe their governors [...]. These are the true and genuine checks of a free government. (Thelwall 1796: 5–6)

He uses the term "awe" with deliberate political intent – it puns on the phrasing of the 1795 amendment to the *Treasonable Practices* legislation, which now, in 1796, prohibited any activity that "over-awes" either House of Parliament, an amendment which Thelwall considered self-serving and servile, i.e. corrupted (Green 2014: 41). In fact, the "tribunal of popular opinion" is a court which the "hireling Burke" needs to "learn to respect" and to "bow" to (Thelwall 1796: 10). For Thelwall, patriotism in its proper sense is an attachment to the "spirit and virtue of the people, not the letter of the law" (Thelwall 1795: II, 96).[31] His idea of the "people" is saturated with the notions of public spirit and public virtue. Like Forster, Thelwall believed that individuals could ultimately not control public opinion: "opinion", he says, "burst its chains in France" (1796: 74), and "no Robespierre [...] [who by the time of Thelwall's speaking had been guillotined] could subdue the enlightened and philosophic spirit of a nation panting for freedom" (1795: I, 114). Individuals, especially those in power, are too affected by self-interest to make sound decisions, only *public* entities can be trusted to see clearly and work disinterestedly (1795: 69–70). Speaking of the wars which are currently taking place in the service of vested political interests, he concludes: "It is, therefore, from the virtuous energies of the public mind, from the bold and manly spirit of the general investigation, from the spirit and good sense of the people that we are to expect a thorough exposition of the horrors of war." (1795: 70) Like Hendrich (who was no Jacobin) the year before, Thelwall proposes that the people should be called upon to judge the abuses and failings of the state and that they are capable of doing so. In his reliance on abstract forms of general

---

[31] This passage comes from his *Tribune* lecture on "Barracks and Fortifications, with sketches of the character and treatment of the British Soldiery" given 10 June 1795 (Thelwall 1795: II, 84–108).

unity (the energies of the public mind, the philosophic spirit of the nation) Thelwall invokes, like Forster, the rule (and vigilance) of a unified collective.

Although he criticised Burke for using history and national tradition to bolster his claims, Thelwall himself did not pass up on the persuasive power of an ancient precedent. Their deployment of history, setting the present (age) in relation to "past presents", connects their argument to the diachronic aspect of zeitgeist, which also featured in the German discussions.

For Thelwall (English) history amounts to the constant struggle to safeguard the rights of the people, which were frequently threatened by despotic rulers, temporal and spiritual.[32] In much of this he follows Hurd and Hume. First the (Catholic) Church and then absolutist-minded seventeenth-century kings repeatedly dismantled the people's rights, often for long periods of time, but never indefinitely. The Reformation saw off the Catholic Church, and it is Thelwall's hope that the Enlightenment will do the same for those lingering notions of "divine right", which have been passed down from Stuart kings to create the "infallibility of ministers" and are asserted as "the divine right of 162 oligarchic proprietors of the rights and suffrage of the nation" (1795: I, 267). Crucially, the people's victories are conceived as restorations. Thelwall – in fine Enlightenment fashion – was convinced that the "tendency of the human mind is [...] to perpetual improvement", but "public good can become subverted to personal interest" (1795: I, 261), and history also "presents us with retrograde motions in the political and intellectual revolutions of nations" (1795: I, 262), which need to be reversed. He links the "present exertions of the advocates of the principles of liberty and the freedom of the human intellect" to the "virtuous spirit" of the "martyrs" of the Reformation (1795: I, 265). Here the contemporary political struggle – the activity *of the age* – and a historical panorama are intersected to form a historical trajectory for a national master narrative. Although Thelwall avoids the word "spirit" in connection with political terminology, preferring "principles", he conflates collective (national) history and identity with specific political struggles in the same way as Blackwell and Hurd had done. But while *they* had established the spirit of past presents, Thelwall used this technique to justify activities in the present.

To make his point of the need for, and entitlement of, a political and constitutional "restoration", Thelwall published the *Natural and Constitutional Rights of Britons to Annual Parliaments, Universal Suffrage, and Freedom of Popular*

---

[32] See "Lecture on the System of Terror and Persecution adopted by the present Ministry" given 30 May 1795 (Thelwall 1795: I, 261–278, 264).

Association in 1795, which he composed as his "vindication" speech at his trial in 1794.[33] The title suggests a political continuity not dissimilar to the eighteenth-century historians of liberty nor to the Victorian historians Stubbs and Freeman. Thelwall represents the gist of this in his lecture on "The System of Terror and Persecution": the "absurd doctrines of divine right of Kings, passive obedience and non-resistance" (1795: I, 265) were introduced, when "till this time the usual language with philosophers, lawyers and historians wont to be [sic] the Commonwealth of England. It was the constant language of our old constitutional writers, who considered the king as no other than a president with regal powers; the first magistrate of the republic of England." (1795: I, 266)

This master narrative was less indebted to Providence than to the manifest destiny of (English) history. Both approaches, however, intertwine the "rightful" path of history with the political struggle of the day. Thelwall also intertwined the historical identity of the collective with their purpose in the contemporary struggles the collective was currently facing. This conflation of historical process, collective (national) identity, and contemporary political struggle was also employed by Ernst Moritz Arndt, who will be discussed in the next chapter. Thelwall's perspective was historical – and hence in this respect not so different from Burke's – considering the current struggle as a restoration of what had been corrupted. Forster, on the other hand, saw the revolution in France as a genuinely new development on a theoretically obvious road of human progress. Both take their justification from a historical narrative, Thelwall from historical precedent, Forster from a speculative political and cultural theory of history.

The reason for Thelwall's oratorical exhortations was his belief that in Britain this righteous public opinion was being silenced through the tyrannical legislation of William Pitt and William Grenville and duped by their "hireling" opinion makers (Thelwall 1796: 7), such as Burke. "In this [Burke's] excursive frenzy of composition there is much deep design and insidious policy. [...] His intention is at once to instruct and to confuse." (1796: 12). For Thelwall, Burke was a demagogue.

But the current situation in Britain was not only due to direct despotic state control. In Thelwall's view, the (theoretically) incorruptible voice of the people

---

33 Its full title reads "Natural and Constitutional Rights of Britons to Annual Parliaments, Universal Suffrage, and Freedom of Popular Association; being a Vindication of the motives and political conduct of John Thelwall, and of the London Corresponding Society, in general. Intended to have been delivered at the bar of the Old Bailey, in confutation of the late charges of High Treason", London, 1795. "Vindication" is of course a signal term used from Wollstonecraft to Hare to denote "liberal" or progressive revisions to conservative points.

was also being disabled by the condition of the current collective: unlike their valiant ancestors, the British people were reduced to "an abject and degraded progeny. The evil is here. A greedy and unsocial selfishness absorbs our faculties. As base timidity bows our soliciting necks to the yoke [...] palsies every effort of patriotism" (1796: 8). These were the consequences of an unfree, despotically run collective.

Burke was himself equally anxious about the wrong kind of public opinion, which would corrupt a good, wise, and legitimate public. His *Regicide Peace* letters (1796–1797)[34] evince an intense fear that Jacobin politics would win out on the Continent and eventually destroy British political traditions. Hence no peace must be made with "Republic of Regicide" (Burke 1892 [1796–1797]: 8). The situation was dangerous because "our constitution provides greatly for our happiness, [but] it furnishes few means for our defence" (1892: 340) and (revolutionary) France was intent on achieving international political dominance. Investigating the "genius and character of the French Revolution" and its "evil spirit", he concluded that the aim of its philosophers and politicians was "not to make France free, but dominant" (1892: 104ff). Like Thelwall, Burke equates liberty with British identity, both need to be defended with "fortitude and wisdom" (1892: 340–341). Like Thewall, Burke affirms the legitimate power of the people, which is enshrined in its ancient constitution. In contrast to France, which has no true "publick voice" (1892: 203), in Britain, "by the judicious form of our constitution", "publick contributions" are only raised by "publick will", "according to the will and wisdom of the whole popular mass" (1892: 214). Significantly, Burke focuses on taxes and, by implication, on a property-owning public. In France, the situation is entirely different: "the world knows that France has no publick", instead it is comprised of "audacious tyrants and trembling slaves" (1892: 203). In France political battles only occur between different tyrants. Burke nevertheless uses the term "public" in connection with France. Here, however, it denotes "bad" public opinion: it is linked to unwise, if not corrupt, influence, a state of affairs predating the Revolution. Louis XVI, Burke says, was not a bad or particularly stupid person, his failure was due to seeking "his ministers [...] upon publick testimony" (1892: 133). "He gave himself over to a succession of the statesmen of publick opinion" (1892: 134). The French public is no good because at its (absolutist) court, full of "caballers", "the publick is the theatre for mountebanks and impostors". (1892: 133) *Even*

---

34 The first two letters were published in 1796, the third letter followed in 1797; the fourth letter, which was only published in 1812, fifteen years after Burke's death, however, was written first, in late 1795. See Payne's extensive introduction regarding the dating (Burke 1892: XXV).

the propertied middle classes, whom Burke at home sees as a mainstay of the good public, were dangerous in France. Marked by a "more violent" "spirit of ambition" than anywhere else, they control the "mercantile world" as well as the "academies" and have split up the unity of "the great and the populace" by pushing between them. The power of the French press, with their "electrical communication", "has made the very government, in it's [sic] spirit almost democratick" (1892: 134).

So, while France had all the hallmarks of a modern polity – a strong middle class active in business and education, an active media-driven public sphere, an enfranchised people (democratick government), for Burke, in France these markers were the pernicious inversions of their true (British) likenesses. Political forces that in Britain worked for the public good had a perverted form in France already before the Revolution, a situation which Burke sees as largely responsible for the political turmoil that followed. In a twist of the contemporary (German) view, such as Schiller's in *Aesthetic Education*, that salutary moral changes had to precede political ones for the latter to be successful, Burke declares that in France "a silent revolution in the moral world [for the worse] preceded the political and prepared it." (1892: 134) For Burke, revolutionary France was now a pariah among the monarchic nations of Europe and must not be accepted as an equal.

Thelwall and Burke agreed on the basic structure of modern government: both affirm the need for an engaged public, for a space for this public to articulate itself, and its rightful function to check the executive. But they differ sharply over who – or rather how inclusive – this public, or the people – should be. Much of Thelwall's invective against Burke in *Rights* focuses on Burke's calculations (in *Regicide Peace*) of a British electorate of 400.000 as appropriate, excluding (as well as all women) all men without property (Burke 1892: 14–15). To Thelwall and Burke, and perhaps to every politically minded person at the time, this difference of scope was so fundamental that it positioned them at opposite ends of the political spectrum. In hindsight, however, the conceptual similarities are rather striking: both believe in the unconditional rightness of the people's disinterested judgement when this is not fettered or deliberately corrupted, both fear the perniciousness of corrupting propaganda by vested interests, and both share a firm belief in the public collective as the path to improve everybody's prosperity and safety. Conversely, both denounce egotism, party-politics, and a partisan interest that supports only one faction. (To what extent they practised what they preached is another matter.) Both shared a general belief in the power and reality of "spirit", and a fascination with the ghostly aspect of the collective which becomes apparent when the collective is not constituted or handled properly. Burke describes the French Republic as a "spectre":

> Out of the tomb of the murdered Monarchy in France, has arisen a vast, tremendous, unformed spectre, in a far more terrific guise than any which ever yet have overpowered the imagination and have subdued the fortitude of man. Going straight forward to its end, unappalled by peril, unchecked by remorse, despising all common maxims and all common means, that hideous phantom overpowered those who could not believe it was possible she could exist at all. (1892: 7–8)

Thelwall exhorts the discontented people, the true "pillars of the nation" to shake off their suppressed ghost-like discontent (which in its chimeric form worries the establishment enough to promise fake improvements) and make concrete public demands.

> ... to appease this opinion, this wandering ghost of popular discontent, the simulator, Pitt, has drawn once more around him this magic circle of delusion, with charms and spells of pretended negociation [sic]. [...] But lift up your voices, ye artificers, ye mechanics, ye manufacturers, ye genuine props and pillars of the nation! [...] Wear not your lungs with sighs and sullen murmurs – let not only the nocturnal phantom, but the living body of your complaints appear before your oppressors. (1796: 30–31)

Thelwall believed that the enfranchising structures of popular representation and popular opinion were being realised in revolutionary France; Burke saw the new French state as a perversion of the political structures which in a moderate form were working well in Britain and which needed protecting at all cost.

Despite the perceived risks of public opinion being high-jacked by (self-)interested parties, the notion of public opinion as the legitimate guardian of liberty and public morality survived the political (and military) rollercoaster of the Napoleonic Wars, albeit in its "enlightened", bourgeois guise. Francis Jeffrey, the editor of the liberal *Edinburgh Review* affirmed this "good" public opinion in his review of Mme de Staël's *De la litérature considerée dans ses rapports avec les institutions sociales*, which appeared in the *Review* in February 1813.

> It is quite true, as Mad. de Staël observes, that the power of public opinion, which is the only sure and ultimate guardian either of freedom or of virtue, is greater or less exactly as the public is more or less enlightened. [...] It is in the intelligence of the people themselves that the chief bulwark of their freedom will be found to exist. (Jeffrey 1813: 7)

Although Jeffrey remained rather sceptical as to what extent all, or even the majority, of a people could be raised to the level of "intelligence" required to produce such politically legitimate and beneficial public opinion, he continued to subscribe to this political concept in principle.

3.5 Zeitgeist, public opinion, and the masses – manipulation or the public will

The British discussion about public opinion appears more politically concrete than its German counterpart because it took place in a specific political context, the discussions of reforming Parliament, a political institution that was already in existence. In Germany, divided into many political entities with different representative institutions, the discussion focused on the (right) moral, cultural, and political conditions for political change in a context of varying political structures. However, this difference should not obscure the fact that in both contexts the discussion *was* about politics and about the question of how to create participatory government, useful public engagement, and appropriate enfranchisement.

Across the political spectrum and different national contexts, different types of public opinion were constructed, which however all shared the same tension: the belief that *in principle* public opinion was a political good because it protected liberty and the common good by preventing abuses of power was tempered by the acknowledgement that manipulation by self-interested parties was a decided risk. How best to avoid this risk turned out to be the sticking point that divided views. The disagreement hinged on *whose* opinion should be included or excluded. Whom to include depended on how confident the speaker was that all who were, or would be, enfranchised members of the public polity would make sound decisions. Who were the (right) public?

The answer to this question was always given in the context of what to do with the "masses", who had recently entered the public arena in a number of iconic incarnations, as the revolutionary Parisian "mob" or the Copenhagen House crowds who demanded parliamentary reform in 1795. Whether to enfranchise, contain, or fear these newly agitated and agitating social groups, who may be economically deprived or socially disenfranchised, or both, were key questions. The answer, again, tended to depend on the extent to which the speaker believed they were capable of partaking of enlightened reason and to what extent they would be susceptible to demagogic manipulation.

In German, the terms prominently used around 1800 to describe the masses were "der große Haufe(n)" and "die Menge".[35] In the second collection of *Humanitätsbriefe* Herder outlines to what extent he thinks they can, and should, be politically enfranchised. Both Schiller (1795) and Fichte (1808) develop their education programmes as direct responses to the political project in France which, in their view, failed due to lack of mature citizens. In this

---

[35] These terms gradually gave way to "die Masse(n)" in the course of the nineteenth century.

respect, the educational project of the bourgeois eighteenth-century public sphere continued, feeding into the programmes of mass education that developed first in Germany and then in Britain in the course of the nineteenth century.

In English, the idea of the "masses" as the "people" went back to the contrast between the "Few" and the "Many", a terminology dating back to late seventeenth-century English political thought. Enfranchising the many could also be achieved in more economically or socially focused ways. Adam Smith, albeit pre-revolution, proposed that moral action and individual freedom could combine in a free market to benefit the common good: increasing prosperity for all by free and unfettered (economic) participation. Jeremy Bentham proposed sweeping legal, social, and political reforms that would, through the liberalisation of social practices, produce the "greatest happiness for the greatest number of individuals" by focusing on the welfare of all citizens. What these German and British projects share is a focus on a common good that needs to benefit all members of the collective, who in turn need to have a stake in their collective in order both to contribute to it and benefit from it.

And yet the concern over the manipulation of the "people", and by extension of public opinion, by demagogy was shared on all sides of the political spectrum. Even *within* the "radical" camp there was no agreement on what counted as demagogy and what did not. The political philosopher William Godwin, erstwhile friend of Thelwall, disagreed with Thelwall about the practice of whipping up emotion at political assemblies. Not unlike Garve, and not unexpected in the context of Godwin's own thinking, he found the excitement and agitation produced in large crowds and fanned by impassioned orators detrimental to reasoned and rational inquiry, which should be the basis of enlightened political considerations and was best achieved by calm, and solitary, reflection. Thelwall, on the other hand, found exactly the commonality of aim and purpose between orator and audience an expression of realised collective identity. To Godwin, however, the enthused crowd was under a non-rational spell, and hence prone to manipulation, i.e. could be easily mobilised to attempt to assert their – manipulated, unreasoned – will.

Despite the firmly held convictions on display here – certainly Burke, Thelwall and Forster were very certain as to who constituted the right public and articulated the true public opinion that would ward off self-interest, corruption, and party-politics – the lingering uncertainty about the success of demagogues was damaging the esteem of public opinion: the greater the assumption that it was or could be manipulated, the lower the esteem. While public spirit retained its positive connotation in these debates, public opinion became ambivalent. Public opinion becomes the site of conflict between manipulative control and independent collective decision-making. This conflict is familiar from the older discussions of spirit and zeitgeist, it is reflected in the tension between social control and free expression.

Despite the absence of explicit references to a "spirit of the times", there is in both Thelwall's and Burke's discussions of the public and public opinion a palpable sense of the concepts that in the German discussions of public opinion emerged as "Zeitgeist" und "Volksgeist". Both employ the idea of native liberal traditions as the engine of good public opinion in their respective argument. Both describe a collective (national) identity whose entitlement is based on historic roots and which has the strength to assert itself in the face of distraction or oppression, such as the present struggles of the 1790s. For Thelwall the threat is internal, the "establishment", for Burke it is external, the ideas and military threat of the French Republic.

Burke also captures a sense of zeitgeist when he focuses on the political and cultural conditions in France, which have been created by the French intellectual and ruling elites and which have led to the revolution and unleashed the destructive powers which are now dominating French politics and threatening Britain's polity. In the opening paragraphs of the first *Regicide Peace*-letter he speaks of "unpleasant appearances [...] indicating the state of the [British] popular mind; and they are not at all what we should have expected from our old ideas even of the faults and vices of the English character" (1892: 3). The "public" – elites and their audiences – determines the direction of travel, even if, as was the case in pre- and post-revolution France, this is a "bad" public. "Commonwealths are not physical, but moral essences," Burke observes, "they are artificial combinations; and [...] the arbitrary productions of the human mind" (1892: 5), acknowledging the power of ideas.

Even when the spirit of the age is not specifically mentioned, the discussions about public opinion were interwoven with notions of zeitgeist. The link between these two concepts is based on three shared features: their invisible "spiritual" nature, their inherent ambivalence, and their social and political force. In the last decades of the eighteenth century both public opinion and zeitgeist emerged in the form we think of them today by partly detaching from the older entities from which they were derived: *genius saeculi* and public spirit. Their parent concepts retained for the period in question, and for much of the nineteenth century, their positive connotations, of which zeitgeist and public opinion still partook in the early nineteenth century, as Freiherr vom Stein's interchangeable use of "öffentliche Meinung" and "öffentlicher Geist" demonstrates and as the persistent awe aroused by the *Geist der Zeit*, and its Hegelian transformation into *Weltgeist*, suggests. At the same time zeitgeist and public opinion developed a detrimental and dangerous dimension, which consisted of manipulating views and decision-making for un-public ends. This focus on the contemporary social, political, and cultural context made zeitgeist and public opinion less venerable and more liable to being dissected as human-made constructs than their parent concepts. This, however, did not significantly reduce their power, or the fear they inspired. *Geschichtliche Grundbegriffe* puts forward a related aspect linking public opinion and zeitgeist (and the general will): all three were no longer considered unequivocal expressions of universal truth (Hölscher 1978: 452). Instead, truth might be found in the "good" incarnations of public opinion and in a secularised historical providence. (Forster's views are an example of this.) The contention in *Geschichtliche Grundbegriffe* that "Zeitgeist" *enters* (eintritt in) "political language" in the wake of the French Revolution is confirmed by this research in so far as at this time a complex pre-exiting concept was politicised. But it was not a new concept and it brought with it considerable conceptual baggage, of connoting an historically evolved communal collective and a public that was originally self-governing rather than manipulated. These connotations were not immediately lost. This is the context in which expressions such as "Richterstuhl der Publicität" (Fichte), "heiliges Feuer der Publicität" (Arndt) or Thelwall's "tribunal of public opinion" were ambiguous terms. And among the many new abstractions and singulars which the eighteenth century created, zeitgeist, public opinion, public spirit, and even *Volksgeist*, genuinely overlap: all of them describe a public collective.

The power of these concepts was believed to lie in their "spiritual" nature, a legacy of the eighteenth-century spirit-discourse. Spirit guaranteed their permeating quality, their impact and effect, which amounted to a real presence. This ephemeral nature, which they share with their fully political cousin, the "general will", makes them notoriously difficult to determine and makes their concrete political application difficult. The next chapter investigates the definitions and uses of the concept of zeitgeist in Germany, which are intricately connected to the political concepts of public opinion, the public, and (national) history.

4 Zeitgeist in Germany – Public Opinion, History, and the People in Franz Josias von Hendrich, Ernst Brandes, and Ernst Moritz Arndt

The previous chapter ended on a sceptical note: the ephemeral nature of "spirit" makes all concepts associated with it hard to pin down, and hence difficult to "prove". In the understanding of late eighteenth-century contemporaries, this appears to have been less of a problem. As the spirit-discourse makes plain, many felt that with spirit they were dealing with something that had concrete manifestations in history and in the present, rather like time. The more concrete entity that all eighteenth-century writers who investigated spirit discuss is the relatively new concept of "culture", which to them comprised laws, language, literature, and "manners", i.e. the elements that structure and define collectives. Culture itself is a vague concept, and as we saw, it emerged in its current meaning in the second half of the eighteenth century. While Blackwell still used it metaphorically in the sense of Latin *cultura*, by the end of the century histories of culture began to appear.[1] The idea of spirit being manifest in concrete collective culture formed the background of the zeitgeist discussions. In the foreground were the considerations about the social phenomena of public opinion and public spirit. While "spirit" and "culture" have historical depth, the latter are focused on contemporary society. Both the contemporary and the historical approach to zeitgeist were used to deal with the most significant event in late eighteenth-century Europe: the French Revolution. These approaches were used to work out what the Revolution "meant" for contemporary politics and for the longer-term political future. And this working out was to be achieved by looking at how the zeitgeist that produced the Revolution arose.

4.1 Restoring the public good – similarities between Thelwall and Arndt

I have already noted the relative absence of the terms "spirit of the times" and "spirit of the age" in British discussions of public opinion around 1800. There appears to be a hiatus of these terms between Hurd's use and Julius Hare's

---

[1] Such as Johann Christoph Adelung's *Versuch einer Geschichte der Cultur des menschlichen Geschlechts* (1782) or Johann Gottfried Eichhorn's *Allgemeine Geschichte der Cultur und Literatur des neueren Europas* (1796–1799).

interest in them, but this should not obscure the fact that very similar discussions about the "meaning" of the French Revolution took place in Britain. British discussions focused directly on the terms "public" and "public (or popular) opinion", and foregrounded public spirit, as Thelwall's engagement with Burke's "effusions" made clear (Thelwall 1796: subtitle). The fact that there are also considerable similarities between Thelwall's and Ernst Moritz Arndt's approach to the political situation further illustrates the point that there was substantial overlap between public opinion, public spirit, and zeitgeist in British and German discussion around 1800.

Both Thelwall and Arndt created highly operative texts, Arndt's *Geist der Zeit* and Thelwall's *Tribune*-lectures were the efforts of political activists to explain to their audiences the contemporary situation and to persuade them to take action. Both constantly address their readers and listeners directly: Arndt, suitably, as "Zeitgenossen", in line with his focus on the present age, Thelwall, similarly suitably, as "citizens", in line with his support for French political reforms. *Citoyen* and *citoyenne* briefly replaced *Monsieur* and *Madame* as forms of address in France. *The Tribune* and the four parts of *Geist der Zeit* are mixed-genre publications, changing between prose (essays and speeches) and political poetry or song. But perhaps most specifically both deploy the connection between the political "now" and collective (national) history to create their impact, as discussed for Thelwall in the previous chapter. (Forster used the same technique, but the on the grander scale of *human* history.) Both Thelwall and Arndt support their analysis of current political affairs with historical excursions to legitimise their calls to action by drawing on historical precedents and suggesting that their struggles are part of the history of their (pre-existing) legitimate collective identity. This is the hallmark of the zeitgeist approach in the later eighteenth century.

In terms of content both texts focus on the culture of selfishness enabled by arrogant and *un*-public-spirited rulers, which has produced oppression and inequality. Their cause is to bring about the liberation of their oppressed peoples; liberty and collective identity are key ideas. Most significantly, Thelwall and Arndt agree that a pernicious mechanism of exploitation, which is politically and physically enforced by despotic rulers and governments, is turning human beings into oppressed slaves and fostering a slave mentality. However, there are also differences between the two texts: although both deal with ideas *and* economic and political facts, Thelwall's argument in the *Tribune*-lectures is more focused on economics, whereas Arndt's in *Geist der Zeit I* prioritises ideas; Thelwall focuses on liberating the economically and politically oppressed British people, Arndt on liberating a German people that is oppressed politically, intellectually, and nationally.

The similarities between Thelwall and Arndt are not limited to their approach to the political situation but extend to their personal profiles. Both writers pursued their radical activities at considerable personal risk, and both were persecuted by the authorities. Thelwall was imprisoned and tried in the Treason Trials and, although acquitted, eventually hounded out of direct political activism. Arndt fled into exile to Sweden six months after *Geist der Zeit I* had been published to escape the grasp of Napoleon. In difference to Thelwall, though, the powers Arndt fled in 1806 were foreign. However, by the time Arndt clashed with the "establishment" again, after *Geist der Zeit Vierter Theil* had appeared in 1818, he was suspended from his university post and tried for demagogy by *German* authorities.

4.2 Hendrich and Brandes – zeitgeist and historical conditions

The three German sources discussed here are taken from a lively zeitgeist debate. Writing in 1808, Ernst Brandes points out in the opening paragraph of his own contribution to this debate that numerous publications on "Zeitgeist" have appeared recently (1808:1), albeit without actually naming any.[2] Franz Josias von Hendrich's *Über den Geist des Zeitalters und die Gewalt der öffentlichen Meinung* (1797), Brandes' *Betrachtungen über den Zeitgeist in Deutschland* (1808) and Arndt's *Geist der Zeit I-IV* (1806–1818) were key interventions in a discourse that tracked the progress of the Revolution, in intellectual, political, and military terms, up to the point of their appearance. The texts were written at different points during these political developments, i.e. post-revolution (1790s), during the Napoleonic hegemony (1806–1812), the Wars of Liberation (1813–1814), and from three different political perspectives: by an enlightened

---

2 In addition to the texts treated in this chapter and in Chapter 1, notable publications from the relevant time-frame are: Johann Wilhelm Ludwig Gleim, "Geist der Zeit" (1794); Johann Ludwig Ewald, *Wie nützt man am besten den Geist seines Zeitalters? Eine philosophisch-historische Abhandlung* (1799); Hölderlin, "Der Zeitgeist" (1799); [Ignatz Heinrich von Wessenberg], *Der Geist des Zeitalters. Ein Denkmal des achtzehnten Jahrhunderts, zum Besten des neunzehnten errichtet* (1801), Johann Gottlieb Fichte, *Grundzüge des gegenwärtigen Zeitalters* (1804–1805); Georg Ferdinand von Cölln, "Über den Zeitgeist" (1808); [H./anon.], "Einige Bemerkungen über den Geist des Zeitalters" (1812); Carl von Dahlberg, "Betrachtungen über den Zeitgeist" (1816).

moderate reformer (Hendrich), a political radical (Arndt) and a political conservative (Brandes). Hendrich's *Über den Geist des Zeitalters* and Brandes' *Betrachtungen*[3] represent views from different moments in the relationship between France and its non-revolutionised European neighbours. Ernst Moritz Arndt's *Geist der Zeit* covers a longer period, moving through the phases of Napoleonic dominance in Europe, the period of resistance to and the gradual defeat of Napoleon (with all the hopes this engendered), into the onset of the *Restauration* and the struggle of the national liberal counter-movement to restrain it. Arndt's contribution was the most influential, the most widely received – *Geist der Zeit I* even made it into Britain at a very early stage (1806–1808). And it is probably the only one that is still remembered today; the same goes for its author. But it is also the least systematic discussion, addressing contemporary issues in ad hoc fashion, and in this it is more akin to journalism than academic enquiry. Of the four volumes the first was the most influential and it is the most relevant here. All three authors analyse the causes and consequences of the French Revolution in relation to German political developments and the spirit of the age. All three examine the conditions for revolution, and the role of elites and the public in this process. Reading the texts, it becomes clear that contemporaries discussed zeitgeist as a *social* phenomenon rather than a *metaphysical* force and that considerable consensus existed regarding the dynamics of zeitgeist.

The above summary of the key content of Arndt's and Thelwall's texts also holds true for Franz Josias von Hendrich's *Über den Geist des Zeitalters* and Ernst Brandes' *Betrachtungen über den Zeitgeist*. Incompetent rulers did not see the revolution coming. They had allowed a culture of selfishness to develop, which had eroded the public spirit and collective bonds of their communities and in turn reinforced selfishness. These views were to some extent commonplaces, not just in Germany, but also in Britain. These conditions were seen by the German authors – transnationally – as the reason for the violent dissolution of political and social structures in France; and all three discuss whether something similar might happen in German lands and, equally important, what *should* happen next in Germany.

Although occupying different positions on the political and intellectual spectrum and a decade apart, both Hendrich and Brandes argue for a compromise: for reforms that make the current monarchical system more liberal but do not abolish it. Arndt, on the other hand, calls for a German revolution that will

---

3 And its sequel *Über den Einfluß und die Wirkungen des Zeitgeistes auf die höheren Stände Deutschlands* (1810).

reconstitute the German political structure (without necessarily resulting in a republic). All three claim that the "Zeitgeist" demands and supports the changes they are proposing. And all three are keen to explain why this is the case and *how* this support materialises, each of them grappling with the question of how zeitgeist works. All agree that it exists because it is empirically observable. They argue, historically (like Garve), that there has always been a "herrschende Denkart" [dominant way of thinking], which helped to normalise this phenomenon, but all are aware that they are dealing with a newly inscribed (and ubiquitous) term that describes something new and very current. Because it describes something current, they need to consider "public opinion". While all three want to explicate what the spirit of the current age consists of – describe its content – they share an urgent sense to explain how it works. A key question in the German discussions is who controls zeitgeist and how. To answer this question, the three investigations all focus on the involvement of elites and their ability to engage with their audiences and influence public opinion. It has been pointed out that the discussions of zeitgeist are themselves a sign of the times, and an indication of what the age was about (Kempter 1990–1991: 62). So, inevitably, these discussions were conducted by and among intellectual elites, i.e. by those in a position to survey and interpret cultural and political processes. For this reason, it is important to situate the writers in their social contexts when considering the contemporary meaning and reception of their texts.

Franz Josias von Hendrich (1752–1819) was a high-ranking civil servant in the Duchy of Saxe-Meiningen and a member of its government. Saxe-Meiningen was one of the small Saxon principalities in central Germany ruled by different branches of the House of Wettin. The Wettin princes were in the main liberal and enlightened absolutist rulers; Goethe was serving one of them. Hendrich was actually a native of the neighbouring Duchy of Saxe-Coburg-Saalfeld, but joined the administration of Saxe-Meiningen as "Mitglied des Geheimen Rates" (member of the privy council) in 1775 at the age of twenty-three and remained in its service until his death in 1819. He served in 1815 as representative (Bundestagsabgesandter) of the Saxon courts at the *Bundestag* in Frankfurt. Very little has been written about him,[4] yet the high circulation of his publications, evidenced by their ready availability on digital platforms, suggests he was a much-read political publicist at the time, Goethe was certainly aware of him (Stadler 2006: 217, note 14). The progress of the Revolution in France galvanized him into publishing his thoughts in 1793/1794. His *Freymüthige Gedanken über die allerwichtigste*

---

4 He is mentioned by Ulrich Stadler (2006) and in more detail by Theo Jung (2012).

Angelegenheit Deutschlands (1794), mentioned in the previous chapter, went into its second edition in under a year, with further editions in 1795, 1796, and 1806. *Freymüthige Gedanken* is present in considerable numbers in German, British, and US university libraries and on digitised platforms holding eighteenth- and nineteenth-century print works. Perhaps due to his position in government, he published this book, like his *Geist des Zeitalters*, anonymously and without a concrete place of publication, in "Germanien". The reformist gist of the book would in any case have demanded caution. Its reassuring (but equally programmatic) subtitle reads *Seinem und andern guten Fürsten desselben ehrerbietig zur Prüfung und Beherzigung vorgelegt von einem Freunde seines Vaterlandes* [presented humbly to his own and other good princes to be examined and heeded, by a friend of his fatherland]. As I have already noted, the author of *Freymüthige Gedanken* was attacked as a "Jacobin".

Ernst Brandes (1758–1810) is less obscure, although his *Betrachtungen über den Zeitgeist in Deutschland* and its sequel *Über den Einfluß und die Wirkungen des Zeitgeistes auf die höheren Stände Deutschlands* did not go into any further editions beyond their first.[5] Brandes' greater publicity is largely due to his personal and political association with Edmund Burke, which kept him on the radar of historical research. Brandes was a life-long (conservative) observer of the French Revolution who published his views *before* Burke as *Über einige bisherige Folgen der französischen Revolution, vorzüglich in Deutschland* in 1790, a second edition appeared in 1792. He had met Burke as a young man on a visit to Britain in the mid-1780s and remained in contact with him until Burke's death in 1797 (Skalweit 1956). Politically they largely agreed with each other.

Brandes descended from a well-established family of bourgeois Hanoverian administrators in the service of their Hanoverian-British rulers. Brandes and Hendrich were the same generation, both were born in the 1750s, they had the same upper middle-class background and occupied similar positions in the administrations of their respective German homelands. Their interest in politics was doubtlessly a corollary of their professional lives in government administration; both considered "Staatswissenschaft" as the key science of the day. Both grappled with the meaning of the French Revolution and its impact on social and political developments; for both it was the most important event of their times, and possibly of modern history, Hendrich refers to it as "große Weltbegebenheit" [great event in world history] (Hendrich 1797 [facsimile 1979]: 54),

---

[5] Although copies are quite numerous in German university libraries, there are only a handful in UK research libraries, and none on the major US platform archive.org. Both volumes were reprinted in 1977 in the Scriptor Reprints series.

Brandes as "größte Weltbegebenheit" [greatest event in world history] (Brandes 1808: 184, 190, 199). Both shared the basic Enlightenment views that forms of government needed to be appropriate for the polity they govern and needed to keep pace with change. Not surprisingly both were keen admirers of Montesquieu, Hendrich makes his veneration clear on the cover of *Freymüthige Gedanken* by signing as "un ami des loix" [a friend of the laws]. Both have a high regard for the "British constitution". But while Hendrich in the mid-1790s had difficulty concealing a general agreement with some of the aims of the Revolution, Brandes in 1808 had nothing but abhorrence for it. They diverge on the Enlightenment tenet of the progressive perfectibility of humanity through education and culture. Hendrich displays an unshakable belief in its achievability, not to say inevitability, and has outspoken praise for the achievements of the eighteenth century, while Brandes thinks such hopes are unrealistic and without foundation in empirical fact. In this regard, he thinks that Herder was a dreamer (1808: 201), although he credits him with being one of the "ersten Köpfe" [brightest minds] of a generation that rejuvenated German literature and thought between the 1760s and 1780s (1808: 34). Similarly, Brandes thought Kant was a great thinker, but spawned a dangerous school of speculative philosophy (1808: 104–107). Brandes appears well-versed in Herder's manifold oeuvre, so it is not surprising that he reponds to Herder's points on zeitgeist made in the second collection of *Humanitätsbriefe*, as does Hendrich. But while Hendrich subscribes to the idea of human progress in the name of Herderian "Humanität" and broadly agrees with many of the points in the second collection, Brandes fairly precisely disagrees with Herder's belief in the perfectibility of "Humanität". Herder's *Letters* were clearly a focal point of the zeitgeist discourse, not just bringing together the eighteenth-century discussions that preceded him, but inspiring responses for a decade to come.

Both Hendrich and Brandes use the terms "Zeitgeist" and "Geist der Zeit(en)" interchangeably. Hendrich also speaks of "Genius des Zeitalters" and "Genius der Zeit", betokening his closeness to the original term (genius saeculi) and his eighteenth-century roots. Brandes chose "Zeitgeist" for the title of his books, Hendrich "Geist des Zeitalters"; both make clear that they are talking not about a providential historical force, but current affairs. Stadler noted that Hendrich used "Geist der Zeit/der Zeiten", "Genius des Zeitalters", "Genius der Zeit/des Zeitalters", "öffentliche Meinung" and even "Geist der Nation" almost synonymously. This synonymous use illustrates that in the minds of contemporaries around 1800 zeitgeist remained linked to the more diachronic idea of national spirit as well as to the new and more synchronically potent notion of public opinion.

Hendrich was convinced that ideas ("Vorstellungen") rule the world (Hendrich 1797: 91–92) and that they cannot be crushed by violence *if* they have found sufficient levels of public acceptance. Under such conditions coercion and ideas are an unequal match; attempts at violent suppression will only make those convinced of the new ideas hold on to them more passionately. (1797: 128–129, 134) Once ideas have public acceptance, they represent "die Zeit" and determine historical processes.

> Die Grundsätze dieser beyden Explosionen des menschlichen Geistes [Reformation and Revolution] hätten vielleicht im Verborgenen noch lange geglimmt, wenn sie nicht durch gewaltsame Stürme zur lodernden Flamme befördert worden wären. Dies war die Folge des immer steigenden Drucks, welcher im sechzehnten Jahrhunderte und jetzt, den erweckten Geist empörte [...]. Man sah anfänglich die ersten Äusserungen der Reformatoren in Deutschland als unbedeutend an: denn man kannte weder die Natur noch die Kraft des menschlichen Geistes, noch weniger die Stimmung des Zeitalters. Man hielt es daher nicht für die Sache der Menschheit, sondern nur einiger Schreyer, oder allenfalls einer kleinen [...] unmächtigen Faktion. (1797: 127–128)

> [The principles of the two explosions on the human spirit [Reformation and French Revolution] may have simmered for some time longer if they had not been fanned into a blaze by violent storms. This resulted from the rising pressure which outraged the awakened [human] mind in the sixteenth century and now [...]. Initially the first stirrings of the Reformation were considered insignificant: because neither the nature nor the power of the human spirit was understood [by those in authority] and the mood of the age even less. It was not regarded as a matter of the human race but that of a few shrill voices, or at most that of a small [...] powerless faction.]

Hendrich pinpoints the moment when new elites, still mistaken for "Schreyer" or powerless factions by established but complacent elites, make an impact and gain public acceptance. The established elite's failure to understand the roles and motivation of new elites and their public is a key cause of the violent "storms", or revolutionary upheaval.

> Die Grundsätze der Reformation waren nun einmal vorhanden, sie konnten nicht wieder vertilgt werden, und wurden vielmehr von den besten Köpfen aufgefaßt und weiter ausgebildet. Wenn diese gleichsam eine unsichtbare Kirche ausmachten, so war dies die Ursach, daß die neuen Meynungen nicht nur unbemerkt sich unter dem großen Haufen einschlichen, sondern auch nachher, als sie gewaltsam ausbrachen, bis in die entferntesten Gegenden wiedertönten. [...] Ebenso ging es mit der Französischen Revolution! (1797: 125–126)

> [The principles of the Reformation did now exist, they could not be eliminated, on the contrary, they were picked up by the brightest minds and developed further. As these constituted something of an invisible church, this was the reason why these new opinions did not only spread unnoticed among the masses, but also why they later, after they had broken out violently, resounded in the most distant regions. [...] It was exactly the same with the French Revolution!]

4.2 Hendrich and Brandes – zeitgeist and historical conditions

For Hendrich it is of paramount importance to investigate how this process – of how ideas rise and spread – works because he is convinced that

> Revolutionen in den Ideen und Begriffen der Menschen äußern auf das Schicksal der Staaten öfters einen Einfluß, der weit stärker, ausgebreiteter und in der That furchtbarer ist als jener, den große Kriege und Eroberungen in dem wechselseitigen Verhältnisse der Nationen hervorbringen. (1797: Vorbericht, no pagination)
>
> [Revolutions concerning peoples' ideas and concepts often affect the fate of states in the changeable relations between nations more powerfully, widely, and indeed more fearsomely than great wars and conquests.]

This sentence opens the "Preliminary Note" (Vorbericht) of his 264-page long study dated "March 1797". Hendrich has concluded that a new zeitgeist arises "through a visible change in people's concepts and ideas" (Vorbericht),[6] and that such "changes" occur when established principles ("Grundsätze") are replaced by new ones, normally because the old ones have lost their hold, their power to convince, i.e. their legitimacy. John Stuart Mill will echo this idea thirty-three years later. Only when such a constellation occurs do new ideas have a chance of replacing the established ones. So while it is impossible to stop the spread of new ideas once a certain point has been passed, very specific conditions need to be in place first: the established and common ideas have to have suffered considerable damage, the "Zerstörung alter Gewohnheitsbegriffe" must be "vorausgegangen und beträchtlich" (1797: 83).

> Sobald also die Gewohnheits-Begriffe vernichtet sind, springt der große Haufe blindlings von einer Meynung zur anderen über, und giebt oft leichtsinnig das Wahre gegen das Falsche, und dieses wieder ohne Verdienst für das Wahre hin. Das dauert so fort, bis überwiegende Umstände ihn bewegen, bey irgend einem Gedanken-Systeme zu bleiben, und es in Gewohnheit zu verwandeln. [...] so erzeugte sich die Reformation und die französische Revolution. (1797: 82)
>
> [As soon as the commonly established ideas have been destroyed, the masses leap blindly from one opinion to another and often exchange the true for the false and back again without merit. This continues until prevailing conditions induce them to stick with one system of thought and turn it into common ideas. [...] in this way the Reformation and the French Revolution came about.]

These "Meynungen" [opinions] have to be presented to the "many" and they need to convince; if they do, only a little push is needed to set the mechanism

---

6 "durch die sichtbare Veränderung der Menschen in ihren Begriffen und Ideen".
7 "es bedarf nur einer kleinen Kraft, die Maschine nach Willkür in Bewegung zu setzen".

["Maschine"] in motion, at will (1797: 83).[7] This is done by the new elite. Revolutions are "das Werk der Minorität oder der kühnen Anführer, welche Zeit, Umstände und Volkscharakter zu berechnen wissen. Die Majorität ist immer das Werkzeug dieser Anführer." [Revolutions are the work of a minority or bold leaders who know how to calculate the time/age, the conditions, and the national character.] (1797: 82). There is more than a hint of calculation on the part of the new elites, but to a large extent they simply galvanize and then represent new notions in public opinion, whose "commonality [Allgemeinheit] would not have come into existence without sufficient cause" (1797: 77).[8]

For Hendrich, social, cultural, and political conditions play as decisive a part as effective leaders and elites who propagate the new ideas. These conditions are the basis for the acceptability of their ideas among their audiences. The leaders' effectiveness is due to the acceptability of their ideas as much as to their individual gifts (although these are vital). "Jene kühnen, ausserordentlichen Menschen, die Triebfedern großer Revolutionen, welche bloß die Wirkung ihres Genies zu seyn scheinen, mußten daher immer durch den Geist ihres Zeitalters und durch günstige Umstände unterstützt werden." [Those bold, extraordinary individuals, the drivers of great revolutions which only seem to be the emanation of their genius always had to be supported by the spirit of their age and favourable conditions.] (1797: 84) This is very close to Garve's (as yet unpublished) views on revolutionary leaders and their success with public opinion, which he formulated at the very same time: Garve thought that rather than its "author" Luther was the "point of convergence" of the Reformation. For Hendrich, as for Garve, there is one more aspect that needs to join the charismatic individual and the new progressive idea: *some* support from within the establishment, from within the ruling elite and established institutions. Speaking of the Reformation in Germany, Hendrich says:

> Die Sache erforderte also gerade diesen Mann [Luther], der sich an die Spitze einer Partey stellte, hinter der sich die hellen Köpfe der damaligen Zeit steckten, der von einem mächtigen Fürsten unterstützt ward, und an einem so ansehnlichen und öffentlichen Ort stand, als die Universität Wittenberg damals war. (1797: 87)

> [So this matter needed exactly this man [Luther], who was supported by a powerful prince and came from a respectable and public place such as the University of Wittenberg was in those days, to take up position at the head of a new party, behind which the bright minds of that age gathered.]

---

7 "es bedarf nur einer kleinen Kraft, die Maschine nach Willkür in Bewegung zu setzen".
8 "Allgemeinheit ohne zureichenden Grund nicht entstanden seyn würde".

This combination generates the public acceptance needed to sway public opinion and produce the enthusiasm that carries large "majorities". This, in Hendrich's view, is why ideas rule the world.

> Man kann wirklich sagen, dass den Vorstellungen allein die Herrschaft der Welt verliehen sey. Sie schaffen die Gewalt [ambiguous in German in this context, meaning force, not necessarily violence, MO] dadurch, dass sie zu Gefühlen, Leidenschaften oder zum Enthusiasmus werden. Sie bilden und verarbeiten sich in der Stille; durch den Umgang zwischen Individuen begegnen sie und entflammen sich einander. Sobald sie aber durch dieses Zusammentreffen Haltung und Vollständigkeit erhalten haben, stürzen sie mit einem unwiderstehlichen Ungestüme unter die Menge. (1797: 91–92)

> [One can truly say that ideas alone rule the world. They have such power because they become emotions, passions, enthusiasm. They form and develop quietly; through communication and intercourse between individuals they meet and catch fire from each other. As soon as these encounters have made them complete and given them structure [Haltung], they rush forth among the masses with irresistible force.]

While the power of public opinion must, and in Hendrich's view *can*, be guided by reason and moderation – this is the task of wise governments (1797: 188) –, Hendrich adheres to the idea that ideally public opinion and publicity are the best control mechanisms of power (1797: 170). In a free society public opinion tends to be right (1797: 64). And even an absolutist regime can – and should – be controlled by its public. In this respect he argues for a free press, from which good rulers have nothing to fear and everything to gain. This recalls Hume's notion that "governors have nothing to support themselves but opinion" and Temple's idea that "in those that govern" "authority aris[es] from opinion."[9]

With this comes the familiar concern for public spirit: states must engage their people, personal interest and public interest must be seen to be linked in the understanding of the governed, better even, they should be aligned. Party-spirit and corruption are the enemies of the public good and fair enfranchised government (1797: 74 and 146); selfishness, a corollary of party-spirit, is encouraged by inequality. In line with the engagement of the people, Hendrich supports a gradual rolling out of political enfranchisement. Even the masses need to be enfranchised, although their capacities are limited (1797: 60–65). This is his advice for enlightened governments. In principle Burke would have agreed that the public need to be enfranchised and that its judgement is a necessary check on the executive. But the question remains: who are the people to be engaged, and who is to be enfranchised? In light of the revolution in France, or

---

[9] See Chapter 2, p. 59.

rather in light of the changed ideas which caused that revolution, engagement and enfranchisement are imperative if more revolutions are to be avoided. But these changes should happen gradually and must be managed by the established, and no longer complacent, elites. While Hendrich does not call for universal suffrage, he *does* use the terms "großer Haufen" (1797: 64), "Menge" (62) and "Volksmassen" (60) in this context, which suggests he believes the "masses" should and can be involved in some form of political participation.

In his view, *both* intractable princes *and* radical revolutionaries were detracting from the public good, so, as he had already made clear in *Freymüthige Gedanken* (1794: 141, 147, 176), a compromise is called for. Public opinion engaged by new ideas will, especially in times of crisis such as now, become a torrent and need directing (Vorbericht).[10] Conversely, governments must not neglect public opinion, as no policy can be successful if it cannot secure public acceptance (1797: 76–77). For Hendrich the link between public spirit and public opinion remains close, not unexpectedly so, as he upholds the idea of the potentially incorruptible public. Public opinion must be taken into account by governments because it is based on publicly established and accepted notions of the common interest. A people is for him a public collective: "Ein Volk [ist] eine Versammlung von Individuen zu einem gemeinschaftlichen Zwecke" [a people [is] an assembly of individuals for a common purpose] (1797: 75). For Hendrich the link between public opinion and national character is similarly close, both are based on a shared historical experience (1797: 76–77). Public opinion thus supports and stabilises the public good, and public order. Upsetting this link and its balance causes public discussion of these engrained ideas, of current affairs and government actions (1797: 75–78).[11] This can be productive, Hendrich is convinced that an enlightened and engaged public is the appropriate control mechanism of the political executive, but too many abuses of power risk upsetting the governmental system altogether. In such anarchic conditions public opinion is liable to lose its reliability because it easily falls prey to the imbalanced influence of party-political opinion – he castigates "party spirit" and "political intolerance" (1797: 55) – and becomes capable of producing social upsets and revolutions. But even these can be necessary, and productive, like the Reformation, and Hendrich seems unsure how to frame the current situation: in these days of increased enlightenment more people notice

---

10 "Es ist jetzt wirklich Pflicht auf den einbrechenden Strom der neuen Meynungen aufmerksam zu machen, und auch von seiner Seite beizutragen, seinem Laufe Grenzen zu setzen."
11 For example, Hendrich argues that if inequality and unfairness are perceived, egoism increases and selfishness comes to dominate behaviour, so governments have an duty to reduce inequality, possibly by changing laws.

unjustified inequality, so rulers are more accountable and need to be careful. "Die Begriffe von Recht und Unrecht werden bei diesem Zustande deutlicher." [The understanding of justice and injustice becomes clearer in this [enlightened] condition.] (1797: 64) In 1797 Hendrich is concerned, perhaps more than in 1794, that his ideal case scenario of a balanced and beneficial interaction between public spirit, national character, and public opinion is fragile, questionable even, in the current context of selfishness, corruption, changing ideas, and a powerful public opinion. So he too engages with the common question whether (the) Enlightenment has caused revolutions, which he of course denies (1797: 151–174, 175).

Perhaps mindful of the accusations that had been levelled at him, Hendrich expresses abhorrence at the excesses of the French revolution, which to him are represented by the Convention, the Montagnards, and Robespierre, who violently succeeded the National Assembly: the "Jacobin republic" is the "most detestable of all governments" (1797: 107).[12] Yet his view of the revolution as a whole appears deeply ambivalent. Hendrich sways between historicising the revolution (it's like the Reformation) and making it an unparalleled event ("never has there been a crisis so dreadful before" (1797: 103–104)),[13] as well as between the rightness of public opinion and the dangers of one unchecked by "limits". The Revolution's "spring" (Quelle) was "die aus der Aufklärung entspringenden Ahndung eines wahren oder eingebildeten Bessern" [the idea of a true or imagined better [state of things] which had sprung from the Enlightenment] (1797: 92). The analogy between the revolution and the Reformation, which is a guiding principle of his enquiry, also has ambivalent aspects. Hendrich was most likely a Protestant. While the fact that in terms of "zeitgeist dynamics" the revolution and the Reformation arose in the same way passes some of the Reformation's "rightness" onto the revolution, the Reformation too had its undesirable excesses, due to the fundamental upheaval of principles (Grundsätze), which created an entirely new "mood of the age" (Stimmung des Zeitalters). This ambivalence also finds expression in Hendrich's presentation of Luther: he was a hero, "Luther's success does indeed [deserve] our admiration" (1797: 88),[14] but at the same time Hendrich links Luther to partisan activity.

> Er [Luther] mußte eine gewisse Kühnheit und einen gewissen Starrsinn verbinden [...]. Er mußte zugleich ein Mann für das Volk, kurz er mußte Luther seyn, der durch die

---

12 "abscheulichste aller Regierungen".
13 "noch nie war die Crise so schrecklich".
14 "Luthers Erfolg [verdient] allerdings unsere Bewunderung."

> Popularität seines Witzes und seine Gelehrsamkeit unmittelbar auf den großen Haufen wirkte. Die Sache erforderte also gerade diesen Mann, der sich an die Spitze einer Partey stellte. (1797: 86–87)
>
> [Luther had to combine boldness with stubbornness [...]. At the same time he had to be a man of the people, in short he had to be Luther, who could through the popularity of his wit and his erudition influence the masses. The matter needed exactly this man to lead a party.]

This suggestion of a partisan spirit in the Reformation, and in Luther, is intensified by a close link between the Reformation and the revolution, and an equation between Mirabeau and Luther as the chief and demagogical mouthpieces of each:

> Mirabeau brauchte alles verzehrende Hitze und hinreißende Beredsamkeit, sein unerschütterlicher Muth, seine Kühnheit, machten ihn zum gefährlichen Demagogen, kurz er war der Luther der französischen politischen Reformation. (1797: 131)
>
> [Mirabeau needed all the consuming heat and the enrapturing rhetoric [available to him], his unshakable courage, his boldness made him a dangerous demagogue, in short he was the Luther of the French political Reformation.]

While there is of course a clear distinction between the political aims of the National Assembly where Mirabeau worked his oratorical magic, the Assembly wanted a constitutional monarchy, and those of the Jacobin Republic, which Hendrich denounces, it does appear as if he cannot quite decide where he stands on the biggest political issue of the day, nor whether the current situation has historical precedents or whether it is uncharted territory, whether it is manageable or out of control. Hendrich aims at neutral analysis and argues for compromises to be thrashed out in the mêlé of the public sphere. He describes the advent of modern public politics: public debate is now a battlefield of "principles and opinions",[15] it is the "battle between two systems in which either one has to vanquish the other, or both sides have to modify their views down to a compromise" (1797: 104).[16]

Hendrich may have retained *some* goodwill for *some* aspects of the revolution because he was well disposed toward French thought. He has great praise not just for Montesquieu, but also for Voltaire, Rousseau, D'Alembert, and Diderot. He also admired the English constitution (1797: 205) and acknowledges

---

15 "Grundsätzen und Meynungen".
16 "Kampf zwischen zwei Systemen, die entweder eines das andere überwältigen, oder sich auf beyden Seiten zur Modifizierung herabstimmen müssen".

the ground-breaking British insights of Hobbes (1797: 11) and Hume (1797: 63). This does not stop him from using Britain as an example of how liberty can be corrupted by self-interest (1797: 206–210). His assessment on this point is strikingly similar to Thelwall's: the constitution is being eroded by the despotic actions of the current government, who have removed personal liberty (presumably a reference to the suspension of Habeas Corpus in 1794) and curtailed the freedom of the press (1797: 176). The labouring masses in Britain are exploited by a government intent on restoring and increasing "crown privileges".

In his survey of the power relations – both political and economic – within Europe, with which he concludes his book, he paints a grim picture of British economic greed and colonial exploitation. These activities have made Britain the biggest economic power in Europe, which is upsetting the European balance by potentially making all European nations dependent on Britain (1797: 211).[17] Hendrich clearly read English fluently, he quotes in English from English texts,[18] and he is well versed in British sources, so it is not impossible that he had read Thelwall. He was aware of the *London Corresponding Society* (1797: 176), cautiously describing its activities as marked by the restless spirit of the age, which however will prove to be irrepressible (1797: 176–177).

Brandes, who refers to Hendrich in his *Betrachtungen* as well-meaning but misguided (1808: 18), nevertheless shares key insights with Hendrich regarding how zeitgeist works. His *Considerations* are presented in 288 numbered paragraphs of varying length reminiscent of maxims. Brandes, too, approaches zeitgeist from the basis of historical specifics, but his analysis concentrates almost exclusively on the concrete political, intellectual, social, and economic conditions and developments of the past few decades rather than on a comparison between the Reformation and the revolution. These conditions, in his view, produced the political revolution in France, the intellectual revolution in Germany (Kant and post-Kantian Idealism), and the (bad) political and military situation in Germany.

In 1808 Brandes did not, like Hendrich, write under the immediate impression of the revolution, but faced the situation created by Napoleon's victories over Prussia and Austria in 1806. Although he does not suggest that a popular insurrection against the new ruler of Europe is required, as Fichte does at the same time in Berlin, his dissatisfaction with the situation is made clear at the outset. "Deutschland existiert nicht mehr, doch das Volk der Deutschen ist noch

---

[17] Hendrich discussed this in greater detail in *Historischer Versuch über das Gleichgewicht der Macht bey den alten und neuern Staaten*, which appeared in 1796 after *Freymüthige Gedanken*, and to which *Geist des Zeitalters* was conceived as a sequel.
[18] For example when quoting David Hume (Hendrich 1797: 63).

vorhanden." [Germany does not exist anymore, but the German people still do.] (1808: 1) This people is now only connected through their language. More explicitly than Hendrich, Brandes blames the spread of revolution and the current situation on the failure of the ruling elites to show political sense. "Eine tiefe, die Zeichen der Zeit recht würdigende Ansicht fehlte fast allenthalben, sowohl in Beziehung auf das [sic] Reichsverband, als in Rücksicht der inneren Staatsverhältnisse." [A profound view which correctly recognised the signs of the time was almost completely missing, with regard to the Imperial confederation and the internal conditions of the states.] (1808: 6) This is his key thesis, which runs through the entire book.[19] Rulers and their governments did not understand what was happening, what was at stake, and what needed to be done. They laboured under the illusion that they were sufficiently in control to weather these storms. Brandes, too, advocates a reasoned compromise based on an assessment of the facts. He shares Hendrich's view of the power and force of public opinion, which in itself is not surprising, because it had become a commonplace. What is more interesting is the fact that he also takes a very similar view of how new – challenging – elites are able to gain control of public opinion under a set of specific circumstances and that, once established, these opinions invariably influence the "many". New (revolutionary) ideas, here he almost paraphrases Hendrich, "never originate among the masses, [but] very strongly impact upon them",[20] they condense to a "mood" (Stimmung) (1808: 194), a term Hendrich also used. Excessive – or oppressive – pressure on the people and the educated classes will only increase their readiness to entertain ideas of revolutionary liberation, and effect the opposite from restoring calm.

Echoing Herder and Hendrich, Brandes presents the new elite as a "young church". Dealing with historical specifics, he suggests one such youthful, somewhat militant opposition, a "jugendlich-*streitende* Kirche" (1808: 37), had been rising from the 1760s to the 1790s.[21] While gradually gaining ground, their good new ideas were diverted by specific political conditions, which allowed them to be high-jacked for the wrong political ends. The key element of these conditions was, according to Brandes, a despotically run "Staatsmaschine" [state

---

[19] This view is repeated throughout the text, next on p. 31.
[20] "[sind] nie von der Menge ausgehend, auf die Menge unheimlich stark wirkend".
[21] "Auffallend dürfte es stets bleiben, wie viele der bessern Köpfe sich gerade in dem ersten halben Menschenalter nach dem siebenjährigen Kriege zeigten, wie viele sich auf einem Standpunkte zusammen fanden. [...] die erweckten Kräfte schafften sich Raum. Sie glichen einer jugendlich-streitenden Kirche, [...] sie sahen, wie sie immer mehr Land gewannen. [...] Die Beharrlichkeit darin lohnte sich selbst. Was im Reiche der Ideen, des Handelns, des Empfindens, gewonnen wurde, war in der Regel nicht Flugland." (1808: 37)

4.2 Hendrich and Brandes – zeitgeist and historical conditions

machine, or mechanical state][22] and a selfish aristocracy that jealously guarded its privileges from the rising middle classes and was not opposed on this by weak Prussian and Austrian rulers, who were guilty of favouritism.

"Staatsmaschine" is a relatively new term, it begins to appear in the middle of the eighteenth century and is initially used neutrally to describe the workings of a state. Around the turn of the century it is increasingly picked up to denounce the workings of an inhuman social system, so for example by Novalis in 1800 (Oergel 2015); it plays a key role in Arndt, as we shall see. Brandes identifies a serious decline of public spirit as a result of these political and social conditions, which is responsible for the current depressing and dangerous political situation. Engagement in the common good has disappeared, consequently the collective bonds have weakened. Brandes believes in the power of "spirit": "Der Buchstabe töthet, der Geist macht lebendig." [The letter kills, spirit enlivens.] (1808: 63) The weakening of public spirit affects rulers as well as the ruled: social cohesion has been severely reduced by the eighteenth-century practice of regarding, and organising, the state as a "machine". From mid-century (1763–1780) a gradual decline of religion and a new wrong-headed kind of pedagogy allowed the detrimental approach to the state as a well-run machine to develop. This has led to a "mechanism" (passim) in political and state business, which is devoid of true allegiance, not least because it only looks at "skills" (Fertigkeit, 1808: 58, 118), rather than respecting the human being as a whole. In the same development patriotism, both at the imperial level and at the level of the local state, has been weakened. Brandes is most worried about the loss of social cohesion, "festen Bürgersinn" [firm civic sense] (1808: 92) and the dismantling of the independent workings of civic communities, both stifled by over-regulation and state control.

> Gegen das wahre Beste des Staates[23] hatte der alles maschinenmäßig regulirende, in Alles unmittelbar eingreifen wollende Staat der Gesammtheit Einzelner eine freye, nur unter einer sehr liberalen Oberaufsicht stehende Wirksamkeit in manchen Fällen entzogen, wo die Wirksamkeit an der rechten Stelle war und der Bürgerberuf dazu anwies. (1808: 169–170)

> [In contravention of the public good, the machine-like state, wanting to control everything directly, has in some cases withdrawn from the collective of individuals an independent [frey] power where this power was in its rightful place, being only under the state's rather liberal supervision, and where the citizen's role demanded it.]

---

22 The term occurs passim: e.g. pp. 38, 50, 59, 60.
23 Compare to Herder's "der Stadt Bestes", see Chapter 1, p. 53.

Brandes clearly promotes elements of liberalism here. This "Bürgersinn" used to be supported by (Protestant) religion, patriotism, and the old "Empire" before it was weakened by the growing strength of its dominant principalities, which made its two central institutions, the Imperial Diet at Regenburg and the Imperial Law Court at Wetzlar, inoperable laughing stocks. The gist of the "Nationalgeist"-debate returns here, not surprising in this avowed admirer of Montesquieu (1808: 47). The corrosion of collective bonds by the mechanical machinery of the new state, combined with the decline of religion, has produced selfishness and materialistic sensuality.

> Der allgemeine deutsche Patriotismus war viel zu schwach [...]. Der Provinzial-Patriotismus [...] verlohr in den höheren Ständen bedeutend von seinem vorigen Gewichte. Merklich zeigten sich hier Ideen von Calcüls, aufkeimend aus den herrschenden sinnlichen Neigungen, unterstützt von Egoismus, unter der Maske des Cosmopolitensinnes. Das Vaterland war da, wo es gut war, das heißt, wo der Einzelne mehr Bezahlung, mehr Befriedigung seiner Eitelkeit oder Dominationslust, Aussichten zu einem schnelleren Advancement, erhielt. (1808: 166)

> [Common German patriotism was far too weak [...]. Provincial patriotism [...] lost much of its earlier strength among the higher classes. Among them calculating behaviour became noticeable, growing out of the dominance of sensuousness and fed by selfishness under the mask of cosmopolitanism. The fatherland was where it suited best, i.e. where individuals received more pay, could gratify their vanity or their lust for power, or saw better chances of advancement.]

So even provincial patriotism was anaesthetised by the "selfish speculations of vanity or mercenary considerations" (1808: 166).[24]

Another reason for this decline of social cohesion was the prevalence of metaphysical speculation, the "metaphyische Seuche" [metaphysical contagion] (1808: 236), which was contaminating all branches of the arts and sciences[25] and culminating in the rise of the new (Kantian) abstract philosophy that promoted speculation and unrealistic reliance on individual reason. While Brandes has great respect for Kant, he believes that speculative philosophy is of no use for the majority. Here Brandes diverges from Hendrich, he does not share the latter's belief in the perfectibility of human reason. Brandes also suspects metaphysical philosophy of neglecting the empirical facts of history, and most importantly, the role of historical contingency, the unpredictability of chance. Outcomes are often

---

[24] "Egoismus eitler oder merkantiler Spekulationen".
[25] "Sie hatte alle Wissenschaften ergriffen: Theologie, Naturrecht, positives Recht, theoretische und praktische Medicin, Physik, Geschichte, Politik, schöne Wissenschaften, schöne Künste" (Brandes 1808: 236).

the result of coincidences ("Zufällen", 1808: 176–177, 201). The general spirit of critical (and speculative) enquiry into nature, society, and religion, combined with the oppressive illiberality of the mechanistic state machine, have produced a "Geist der Unruhe" [spirit of restlessness] (1808: 85, 178 and passim) in the governed, which Brandes identifies as a key feature of the age and which has paved the way for the political and social convulsions of the day.

One of the key (collective) failings of late eighteenth-century German rulers has been their failure to check their aristocracies' selfish manoeuvring to protect their social position from infiltration by the rising middle classes. Himself a member of the ambitious and public-spirited upper middle classes Brandes regrets the "Mißverhältnisse" [wrong relations] between these classes, which had been on the way to being balanced in the middle third of the eighteenth century before this process was, according to Brandes, stalled, if not reversed, by a jealous aristocracy in the decade before the revolution.

In principle, Brandes agrees that public opinion, the "öffentliche Stimme", expressed by a free press and exercised by publicity, is a liberal good.

> Preßfreiheit und Publizität thaten in dieser Periode [1780–1790] große und zum Theil heilsame Schritte; nur das bleibt sehr bemerklich, daß in Geistesfreiheit wirkende Schriftsteller den diese tödtenden Mechanismus der Staatsverwaltung nicht zum Vorwurfe ihrer Untersuchung nahmen. (1808: 83)

> [Freedom of the press and publicity made great and partly very salutary advances in this period [1780–1790]; but it remains rather remarkable that those writers working in conditions of intellectual freedom did not make the deadly mechanism of the state, which was killing this freedom, the reproachful subject of their investigations.]

However, in the recent past public opinion has been the instrument of coercive demagogy:

> Wer den [wilden jakobinischen, 192] Grundsätzen, die zu dem Schreckenssysteme leiteten [der Terror, MO], öffentlich widersprach, ward mit dem ehrenvollen Namen eines Obscuranten belegt, und durch einen litterarischen Terrorismus wollten Schreiber des neuen Glaubens das Lautwerden der Gesetze der ewigen Wahrheit verhindern. (1808: 194)

> [Those who publicly opposed the [wild, Jacobin] principles, which led to the system of terror, were honourably called obscurantists. Through this literary terrorism the writers of the new faith wanted to suppress the laws of eternal truth.]

In this form, public opinion seems to rule in the totalitarian manner Forster described, albeit in Forster's description this was salutary because it propagated ideas he wished to see implemented.

While for Brandes the strong original "enthusiasm" of conviction cannot be artificially produced (here is the remnant of a true public who cannot be duped), once it has been kindled, it can be maintained and fanned by demagogues and selective information. To start with, the flame can be spread "through continued gross deceit" (1808: 200–201).[26] Once the passion is spent, efficient information management is capable of keeping the desired view dominant "by letting the masses only hear judgements that produce the desired effect and suppressing the opposing ones most strictly" (1808: 201).[27] Specific conditions may produce a tendency, a view, even a passionately held conviction in some, whether this becomes a dominant and system-changing force may depend on how it is handled.

Brandes is quite clear that intellectual elites – "writers" (Schriftsteller) – have a key influence on this handling of the public sphere (1808: 192–194), but he does not examine the role of intellectual elites in these dynamics in the same detail as Arndt did two years before him. Instead, Brandes prefers illness metaphors in this context: the "flame" of enthusiasm becomes a "fever" (1808: 200–201); Kantian philosophy, although fine when handled by exceptionally gifted thinkers, is a "metaphysische Seuche" when it spreads into general consumption. Brandes hovers between sociological analysis and metaphorical conceptions of intangibles spreading by contagion.

In his sequel to *Betrachtungen*, *Über den Einfluß und die Wirkungen des Zeitgeistes auf die höheren Stände Deutschlands*, which appeared in 1810, the year of his death, Brandes *does* investigate the effects of zeitgeist sociologically by tracing its (negative) impact on the higher classes, discussing different groups: princes, the aristocracy, state administrators, the clergy, writers, merchants, and higher-class women. While this approach clearly shares aspects with Arndt's, both investigate the role of an elite in the zeitgeist process, Brandes' analysis remains focused on the *effect* zeitgeist has on these elites and how they, as influential social groups, perpetuate it once it exists, without looking at their role in its rise, which is Arndt's focus.

The differences in opinion between Hendrich and Brandes hinge on their divergent views of the French Revolution. Brandes rejects the notion of the perfectibility of human reason, and considers democracy impossible, Hendrich doesn't. Independent of this political and philosophical difference, both arrive at similar conclusions of how the dynamics of zeitgeist works, even though Brandes cannot follow Hendrich in linking the Reformation and the French Revolution as

---

26 "durch die fortgesetzten gröbsten Täuschungen, Dauer und Ausbreitung verschaffen".
27 "daß man der Menge [sic] nur hierzu wirkende Urteile hören läßt, entgegengesetzte aber auf das strengste unterdrückt".

examples of similar social and political phenomena. For Brandes the Reformation, which as a Protestant he sees in a highly positive light, is essentially different from the revolution, because for him religious and political fanaticism are distinct (1808: 183, 201). The religious zeal of the Reformation concerned the inward being, individuals and their salvation, while the current political fanaticism is focused on material externality, and for him an expression of what is wrong with the current age.[28] For Brandes, German – middle-class intellectual[29] – enthusiasm for the principles of the Revolution, especially for republicanism, is based on fashionable lip-service, because in their current selfish and materialistic frame of mind these enthusiasts cannot be serious about the frugality of republicanism; in Brandes such enthusiasm comes across as a fore-runner of champagne socialism. He does allow, however, one solidly political motive for such enthusiasm: the middle classes supported the revolution because they were disgruntled by the aristocracies' tenaciousness at keeping them out (1808: 181–183).

4.3 Arndt – zeitgeist and the role of intellectual elites

Ernst Moritz Arndt (1769–1860), whose *Geist der Zeit* appeared in four volumes between 1806 and 1818, is the best-known of the three writers examined here. In the post-1945 Western context he became notorious for being a Teutomanic nationalist whose dangerous legacy had spawned ideas that paved the way for early twentieth-century German fascism. In the second half of the nineteenth century, on the other hand, he had been regarded as a respected commentator on cultural and political affairs both in Germany and in Britain,[30] while before

---

28 There are other noticeable agreements and divergences between Brandes and Hendrich. Brandes blames Prussia for instituting the socially and humanly corrosive "mechanism" of the *Staatsmaschine*; it was the work of Frederick William I and Frederick the Great. Brandes – in this context – considers Frederick a "despot" (although he also acknowledges him as an exceptional individual and ruler), while Hendrich praises Frederick as an enlightened monarch. Both rail against misunderstood equality and both clearly recognise the rise of modern public politics, where different systems of thought compete in an enlarged public sphere. Brandes fears that the vastly increased number of publications spread too many half-baked or dangerous ideas to too many readers who are not capable of processing so much information and consequently may be duped. The root of their divergent opinions, despite the common ground, remains in their different views of the perfectibility of humanity.
29 In "den sogenannten gebildeten, eigentlich verbildeten Ständen" (1808: 181).
30 For a summary of the Arndt reception in Germany and the United States cf. (Erhard and Koch 2007: 1–14). His extensive reception in late Georgian and Victorian Britain still awaits rediscovering.

1840 views of Arndt had been polarised: some saw him as a freedom fighter, others as a dangerous revolutionary. Arndt, the writer, academic, and political activist of the anti-Napoleonic German *Befreiungskriege* (Wars of Liberation), spent three and a half years in exile following the publication of *Geist der Zeit* I, four years in hiding and on the road (while writing and publishing *Geist der Zeit* II and III between 1809 and 1813), and twenty years in the professional wilderness of suspension from his academic post at the University of Bonn (1820–1840), before being reinstated and advancing to *Rektor* of the University within one year. In 1848 he received a mandate in the first all-German elections (which had a fairly inclusive male suffrage) to represent "the people" in the "Vorparlament" in St. Paul's Church in Frankfurt am Main, which was tasked with agreeing an all-German constitution. Arndt's biography is itself evidence of the changing currents of political and intellectual acceptability.

There is another key difference between Arndt on the one hand and Hendrich and Brandes on the other: as the son of a liberated serf on the Pomeranian island of Rügen, he originated from a considerably lower social class. Arndt's father prospered and by all accounts his parents were educated and his upbringing enlightened (Müsebeck 1914: 3–7). Tellingly, his first publication argues for the social need to abolish serfdom to create a more equal collective. He never fully disavowed his allegiance to the *original ideas* of the French Revolution, which did not stop him from becoming a famously outspoken Francophobe. His impressive upward social mobility, to university professorships and the highest level of European diplomacy, being a confidante of Freiherr vom Stein, is testimony to his talents, and the changing landscape of professional careers.

Geist der Zeit – especially volume 1 – is the publication on zeitgeist with the widest reception at the time, and it is still the one with which Zeitgeist around 1800 is most closely associated. If it is remembered today, it tends to be for its nationalist Francophobic stance, which was welcome in the nineteenth and early twentieth centuries, but which after 1945 in West Germany (and the West generally) became a byword for violent Teutomanic nationalism. In the GDR, however, Arndt remained identified with his liberal political ideas, especially his publication against serfdom and his aspiration to extend political enfranchisement down the social spectrum. Here he was seen as proto-communist.[31]

---

[31] His alma mater, the university at Greifswald, where Arndt was a student and a professor, continued under its name of Ernst Moritz Arndt Universität, which it had taken in 1933, throughout the GDR period, a continuity that would have been unlikely in West Germany.

Like the other two authors, Arndt was an admirer of Montesquieu, whom he repeatedly quotes to support his points.[32] While the other two publications discussed in this chapter are sober prose accounts aimed at an educated middle- and upper-class readership, Arndt's volumes are intended for a much more general audience. They contain highly operative texts, aimed at almost populist intervention, using general, frequently religiously tinged language and metaphors. The use of such religious language remained an effective method for political radicals to engage a broad readership including lower social classes. It is visible in the political agitation of the *Burschenschaft* movement 1815–1819 and was used to great effect in Georg Büchner's and Friedrich Ludwig Weidig's *Hessischer Landbote* in 1834.

Arndt's volumes are mixed-genre texts, including political and historical essays, speeches, and poetry. The texts are often preaching in tone, with fiery exhortations to civic, political, and eventually militant activism. In language, form, and intention, *Geist der Zeit* resembles, as I have already noted, Thelwall's *Tribune*. Both intend to stir up their audiences' emotions by engaging their sense of togetherness. Similarly appellative in intention and tone, Thelwall's ubiquitous address of his listener-readers as "citizens" is mirrored in Arndt's frequent use of "Zeitgenossen". At the same time, this pinpoints a difference. While Thelwall's approach is primarily and openly political, appealing to the values of the French Revolution, Arndt's term, although deeply political too (as we shall see), focuses on the sense of an historic moment. "Bürger" appears frequently in *Geist der Zeit* too, but rarely as a form of address.

Arndt's aim was to raise German opposition and eventually resistance to an oppressive feudal system[33] and an oppressive conqueror (Napoleon).[34] In 1805 Napoleon was gaining ground in central Europe, by 1809 he appeared unstoppable, but by the summer of 1813 he no longer seemed unassailable. Arndt sought to instil in his readers a conviction of their lawful right to a representative constitutional settlement in a politically independent polity. To illustrate this right Arndt turns, like Thelwall and Burke, to history, but not so much to historical precedent as to historical "preparedness": Germans bring excellent qualifications for a more liberal political set-up than they currently have. Arndt's radicalism is evident in his unequivocal advocacy of an armed struggle. The quatrain prefacing the first section of *Geist der Zeit II*, "Blick vor- und rückwärts", written in

---

[32] For example, "Ewig ist Montesquieus großes Wort: eine freie Nation kann einen Befreier haben, eine unterjochte bekommt nur einen anderen Unterdrücker." (Arndt 1806: 226). His definition of despotism is also entirely reliant on Montesquieu's, see p. 110 below.
[33] Feudalism is historically inappropriate and enslaving (Arndt 1806: 108).
[34] It is worth noting that in *Germanien und Europa* (1803), Arndt's view of "the French" was still rather ambivalent, they too were being duped and oppressed by Napoleon (Flad 1921: 60).

September 1806, reads: "Im Herzen Muth, Trotz unterm Huth, Am Schwerte Blut, Macht alles gut." [Courage in my/our heart(s), Defiance under my/our hat(s), Blood on my/our sword(s), Makes everything good.] (1813, no pagnation)[35]

Geist der Zeit follows, comments on, and interprets from the perspective of a German radical liberal the events surrounding Napoleon's progress and retreat across the continent, from his conquests in central Europe in the first decade of the new century through his disastrous Russian campaign and the successful German efforts to defeat him in 1813 at the three-day battle of Leipzig to the post-Congress of Vienna settlements, and the disappointment they sparked in liberal circles. "Dieses Buch ist ein wanderndes Bild der Zeit. [...] Geh nun hin, Buch, und thu deinen Dienst." [This book is a wandering image of the times. [...] Go, book, and do your duty.] (1813: iii-iv) These lines come from the preface to the second edition of volume 2 and indicate the running commentary and its activist purpose. The whole of *Geist der Zeit* is indeed a "wandering image", Arndt changes his tone and some of his views as events unfold over more than a decade.[36] The idea of duty, "Dienst" and "Pflicht" in German, with which he had programmatically ended volume 1, appealed to the "more noble and wise" contemporaries to "to their duty and show the despairing which way rescue lies" (1806: 461).[37] This signals his belief that the "Bürger-Zeitgenosse" has a moral obligation to serve the public good, the collective, rather than individual or partisan interests. It identifies his key theme: the struggle between enslaving self-interest and liberating service in an environment of spiritual scepticism and political despotism, where people are too clever to do good intuitively and where no common idea exists to inspire them to do this with deliberation. This is the familiar struggle between dominant selfishness, both individual and partisan, and the endangered forms of collective spirit, or, in short, the contemporary concern for spirit. In the following it will become evident that the shared concerns of the conservative Brandes and the radical Arndt extended beyond the widespread general notion of selfishness destroying public spirit. Both identified the mechanistic forms of state control and the destructive forms of disembodied intellectualism as the

---

[35] It will become the motto of the most radical branch of the newly constituted German *Burschenschaft* movement, the Gießen "Unbedingten", founded by the brothers Karl and August Follen in early 1815, from which the Kotzebue assassin Karl Sand emerged. MHBG, the acronym of the key words in these lines, was their emblem.

[36] For example, he changes his mind on Britain; being very critical of the British moral and political decline in volume 1, he speaks of "proud and free England" in volume 3.

[37] "Thut eure Pflicht und zeigt den Verweifelten die Rettung".

underlying causes of this development. And both believed that this situation had arisen due to the failures of the rulers, their governments, and the intellectual elites. It is more than likely that Brandes had read Arndt's *Geist der Zeit I* before he published his *Betrachtungen* (Stadler 2006: 281).[38]

Arndt has even harsher criticism for the German rulers than Brandes, they are cowardly self-serving "Franzosenknechte" (1806: 437–438). In 1806 he no doubt had the creation of the *Rheinbund*, a confederation of West-German principalities under the protection of Napoleonic France, in mind. According to Arndt, the unchecked selfishness of the rulers and ruling classes has weakened social cohesion not only by setting the people and rulers against each other, but equally pitting natural friends from similar social backgrounds, such as "Bürger" [citizens] and "Soldaten" [soldiers], against each other, who have become "enemies" (1806: 106). An un-public-spirited competition for advantage and advancement is facilitated by a mechanistic "Staatsmaschine", which is set up in the service of power. Those that operate within it become "Zurüster, Helfershelfer und Diener der Gewalt" [they prepare, aid, and serve state control] (1806: 99). "Gewalt" always hints at "violence", which is *one* of the meanings of the term. In its automated efficiency, this machine, however, threatens to over-power even its handlers, entangling the entire collective body in its net of strings. In dark Romantic irony, *Geist der Zeit I* is framed as an uncanny puppet show, part phantasmagoria, part shadow play, in which a concealed puppeteer (Arndt or Napoleon?) pulls the strings (1806: 14).[39]

---

38 Apart from their broad agreement on major issues, Arndt and Brandes also see eye to eye on a number of other things: Arndt shares with Brandes the regret over the ineffectiveness, *and* the dismantling of the Empire, which could have been a source of collective resistance to Napoleon. Arndt also points out that the "Zeitalter" judges by outcome, not by what is right (cf. Brandes 1808: 341), which was one of Brandes' distinctions between religious and political fanaticism.

39 "So kommt denn her und schauet! Ich stelle den Spiegel auf, und lasse in meinem Panorama einige bedeutende Bilder der Zeit als flüchtige Erscheinungen vorüberwallen. [...] es ist ein wahres Schattenspiel, nicht bloß eines zum Scherz, und nachdem ihr euch satt gesehen – satt lachen werdet ihr euch nicht – so weinet euch satt mit mir. Das Theatrum ist Deutschland, auch Germanien genannt; der Marionettenspieler steht hinter seinen Gardinen und zerrt ungesehen die Puppen hin und her. [...] Das Stück könnt ihr nennen wie ihr wollt, [...]. [es ist] die leibhafteste, doch bildliche Geschichte des jüngsten Tages." [So come and see! I put up a mirror for you and let some significant pictures of the age float past in my panorama of fleeting appearances. [...] it is a true shadow play, not just a joke, and once you have seen enough – you will not laugh much – come and weep with me. The scene is Germany, also called Germania; the puppeteer, unseen, is standing behind his curtain and is pulling the puppets this way and that. [...] You may call the play what you like [...] [it is] a metaphorical story of the last day, yet also real.] (1806: 14–15)

The "Staatsmaschine" disables liberty and independence, destroys public spirit and social cohesion, and makes any form of participatory government impossible by eradicating the mental conditions necessary for this: it produces "Sklavensinn" [a slave mentality] (1806: 111) with all its attributes of forced servility, venality, envy, and disregard for laws if they can be circumvented for one's own advantage.[40] The situation is degrading (1806: 111) and crippling (1806: 114), it morally corrupts. The "Staatsmaschine macht Menschen zu Mühlenpferden" [turns human beings into mill horses] (1806: 110). What is left is self-serving competitiveness for advancement – what Arndt calls "Aristokratismus" (1806: 113). It serves lazy rulers because, if supported by enough surveillance and military force, it creates "Stille im Staate", a quiet state. Such a state is without any true laws as rules are obeyed out of fear rather than respect for their rightfulness. These are the conditions of despotism as defined by Montesquieu. Political power is presented as a physical force which spreads unchecked if there is no resistance. Public spirit, which could achieve such restraint, is in short supply. Such a system is devoid of "Menschensinn und Bürgersinn" [human and civic sense/spirit] (1806: 111).[41] In his final chapter "Wahrheit und Versöhnung", Arndt outlines his vision of a good state, which is based on justice, virtue, humanity and a meaningful equality, supporting and protecting the individual.

> Damit durch Sicherheit und Gesetz würde, was der Einzelne nicht schaffen und erhalten konnte, damit das Edelste und Größte, was der Einzelne dachte und empfand, durch Begeisterung Vieler als That und Werk aufgehen könnte [...], damit das Gesetz des Allgemeinen, Schönheit und Gerechtigkeit, als die leuchtende Sonne der Menschheit aufginge, darum sind Staaten gestiftet. [...] Was ihn [den Menschen] erniedrigt, erniedrigt auch den Staat. (1806: 451–452)
>
> [States were created so safety and law would achieve what individuals could not achieve and maintain on their own, so the noblest and greatest which the individual thought and felt could flourish as deed and work through the enthusiasm of Many, [...] so the law of

---

40 "Dies Geschlecht gehorcht nicht aus Gehorsam gegen Gesetze, denn da muß man Gesetze *achten*, es gehorcht nur, so lange es muß. Feig und schelmisch aber umschleicht es sie, wo es kann und wohin die Strafe nicht reicht." [This race does not obey out of obedience for the laws, for that they would have to respect the laws, they obey only as long as they have to. Like cowards and rogues they evade them where they can and where punishment does not reach.] (1806: 115, italics mine).

41 The relationship between human community and national community is complex: the Bürger needs to be a Mensch ("ohne freien Bürger, kein freier Mensch" [without a free citizen, no free human being], 1806: 215, also 452), but the idea of universal humanity must not be used to create conformity which can be abused for despotic tyranny in a machine-like state (1806: 451–454); however, by the same token, "ohne Volk" "keine Menscheit" [without a people no humanity].

the common good, beauty and justice, would rise as the sunlight of humanity. [...] What degrades the individual, equally degrades the state.

In the first years of the new century, the idea that the modern state was a despotic machine that was gradually mechanising all aspects of human society was becoming established as a dystopian vision on different sides of the political spectrum. Both Arndt and Brandes vociferously complain about this, as had Novalis a few years before (1800),[42] and it will become a key argument in Carlyle's critique of the times in 1829.

For both Brandes and Arndt the other key reason for the erosion of public spirit is the thorough-going scepticism of eighteenth-century thought, which has produced this "geistige[s] Zeitalter" [intellectual age] (Arndt 1806: 11).[43] Brandes linked this intellectualism to the decline of religiosity, for Arndt the intellectual scepticism was in itself not necessarily a problem. He did not call for a return to earlier ages – his rejection of feudalism is evidence of this – and he did not suggest that human progress should be halted, although he does display a sentimental affection for earlier forms of culture, such as antiquity and aspects of the Middle Ages, but he is adamant that they are past. In order to fight the political and spiritual evils of the current age, one needs means that are appropriate to the age. "In dem geistigen Zeitalter [...] kann nur der Geist Schöpfer, Erhalter und Richter des Lebens sein." [In an intellectual age [...] only the intellect can be the creator, keeper and judge of human existence.] (1806: 11) Or a little later: "Ist das Zeitalter durch Geist verdorben, so werde ihm durch Geist geholfen." [If the age has been spoilt by the intellect/spirit, it can only be healed by the intellect/spirit.] (1806: 49). This recalls Herder's words in *Humanitätsbriefe*: "Geist allein kann mit Geist kämpfen." [Only spirit can battle with spirit.] (1991: 89)

However, excessive "Urteilen und Deuten" [judgement and interpretation] (Arndt 1806: 66) has produced "das hohle Nichts, woran sich alles blind und vertrauend lehnt" [the hollow nothing on which everybody is blindly and trustingly relying] (1806: 10). A focus on quantity rather quality has produced knowledge without beliefs: "Der Kopf ist voll, das Herz leer." [The head is full, the heart is empty.] (1806: 68) Like political despotism, this "desert of the heart" (Wüstenei des Herzens) (1806: 121) leads the individual, left on their own and without the ethics of communal bonds, towards selfishness and vanity. It is scepticism that has allowed the rulers to become despots, and the combination of scepticism and despotism has produced the currently prevalent selfishness and oppression.

---

[42] See "Political Aphorisms" (Novalis 1981).
[43] The German "geistig" can mean both "intellectual" and "spiritual"; in Arndt's context here, "intellectual" is the prominent meaning.

Although Arndt was suspicious of ungrounded intellectualism, he subscribes to the power of ideas, because they evoke a "spirit". To illustrate the power of ideas, or "spirit", Arndt reviews the activities, over the past centuries as well as the past decades, of those social groups who determine, propagate, and maintain the intellectual and spiritual super-structure of their times: the intellectual elites, the "writers" (Schreiber), whose "Hauptklassen" comprise philosophers, theologians, historians, journalists, and reviewers. Beginning with himself, he is "der Schreiber" who is breaking rank within his own professional "tribe" (Sippe) and the selfish materialistic consensus in general, "I am throwing down the gauntlet." (1806: 12).[44] These groups could have taken up "the high duty of being the watchman and timekeeper of the age" (1806: 10),[45] in fact Arndt had hoped that "the wisest and best" would have worked as "Richter der Bildung des Zeitalters" [judges of the culture of the age] (1806: 72–73), i.e. as an enlightened public, but they have not – hence the gauntlet. Arndt retains the ideal that a public-spirited elite should work towards the good of the community in the public sphere and that they should provide a check on all forms of despotic egotism. But currently, and especially in the "current war" (jetziger Krieg), "die deutsche Nation hat ihr letztes Gefühl von Gemeinschaft verloren" [the German nation has lost the last vestige of feeling like a community] (1806: 441).

Arndt is the only one to produce a detailed analysis of the elites who carry zeitgeist. Although the notion that the intellectual elites are crucial instruments in the dynamics of zeitgeist was well established – we have come across it in Herder, Hendrich, and Brandes –, none of them, at this stage, gave them and their activities the same detailed attention as Arndt. His review of the intellectual elites covers nearly eighty pages, but it appears to be the part of *Geist der Zeit I* least understood at the time. Contemporary reviews, even favourable ones, considered this section the least interesting, even the very positive review in the Jena *Allgemeine Literatur-Zeitung* is going to "skip" (übergehen) "what was being said about astronomy, theology, history, poetry, reviewers and journalists [...] to have more room for the more important matters" (*Jenaische Allgemeine Literatur-Zeitung* 1806: 186).[46] The reviewer in *Göttingische Gelehrte Anzeigen* feels "that the real subject of the book only appears in the second half" (*Göttingische Gelehrte Anzeigen*

---

44 "Ich werfe den Fehdehandschuh hin."
45 "die hohe Pflicht des Wächters und Stundenweisers der Zeit".
46 "Was von der Astronomie, Theologie, Historie, Poesie, was über Recensenten und Journalisten gesagt wird, so treffend und eindringlich es ist, [...] um mehr Raum für das Wichtigere zu haben".

1806: 1354).⁴⁷ Both the Jena reviewer and the reviewer of the Halle *Allgemeine Literatur-Zeitung* suggest that in this section Arndt is primarily reviewing *subject areas* rather than writers; "the author discusses areas of literature".⁴⁸ The 1808 English translation deliberately omits this part because the translator considers it irrelevant. (I will return to this in Chapter 5.) Instead, the reviews and the translation focus on the more familiar territory of surveys of nations, i.e. distilling zeitgeist from different national spirits, which had been common since Barclay. The Göttingen reviewer calls the section on the modern nations (neue Völker) the "Stärkste im Buche" [the strongest section of the book] (1806: 1354) and the Jena reviewer considers Arndt's discussion of the nations "the more important part" (das Wichtigere) (1806: 186). Less than two decades later, however, approaching the spirit of the age by looking at members of elites will become rather common in England, William Hazlitt's *Spirit of the Age* (1825) is the most famous example of this new approach. Despite the fact that Herder and Hendrich, and also Brandes, spoke of the workings of a "church" and despite the general agreement that "prevalent opinions" were crucial for understanding zeitgeist, their observations on this point remained general. The way in which elites are the key to understanding the shifts of these "herrschende Meinungen" did not appear to be fully realised in 1806.

Underneath Arndt's religious rhetoric of Providence ("Vorsehung") and apocalypse ("der Anfang des Fegefeuers der Welt") (1806: 90) and alongside his cultural criticism demanding a return to authenticity, truth, and genuine life, his text is deeply political. He sees himself as the defender of the true intentions of the revolution, which Napoleon has sacrificed to his own selfish aggrandisement, and whose positive potential still awaits realisation. Feudalism is inappropriate and exploitative (1806: 108), the *Fürsten* are selfish, cowardly despots who exploit their subjects and their lands, and both princes and intellectuals have failed in their duties to their people (and themselves). While the revolutionary ideas have not succeeded in France, they *have* led to a rethinking of public spirit and collective in Germany, which currently (1802–1805) is being crushed by Napoleon's military advance and the small-mindedness of the German rulers. The "Dienst" and "Pflicht" of his book is to encourage this realisation, and with it a sense of the need for public action, so that constitutional liberty and political participation can develop and (renewed) servitude can be avoided. Especially the princes, the self-serving, plundering "Franzosenknechte" (1806: 438) have failed

---

47 "der eigentliche Gegenstand der Schrift tritt erst in der zweyten Hälfte hervor." Müsebeck identified August von Rehberg as the Göttingen reviewer, who was a friend of Brandes (Müsebeck 1914: 201).
48 "der Vf. geht Theile der Literatur durch" (*Allgemeine Literatur-Zeitung* 245 (13 October 1806): 83.

their peoples: "Fürsten schieden aus dem Kampfe für das Allgemeine und Teutsche, feig und geizig gewinnend sahen sie nicht was sie verloren." [The princes left the field of the struggle for the common German good, cowardly and miserly, they did not see what they lost.] (1806: 437). But, Arndt suggests, despite their failures they would even now still find the volunteers they need to support their (tottering) thrones, if they would make them *constitutional* thrones. (1806: 453)

> Völker, glaubt für den Menschen und den Bürger Ein Gesetz und straft seine Uebertretung [sic] an euch und an anderen – Fürsten, lernt die erhabene Geduld der Wahrheit wieder und freie, gerechte Männer, fertig in Rath und That, mit dem Schwerdt und mit der Wage [sic] werden sich um eure wankenden Throne versammeln. (1806: 453)

> [Nations, believe in One law for human beings and citizens and punish its infringement in yourselves and in others – Princes, if you re-acquire the august patience of truth, free and just men, ready to counsel and support you, with the sword and the scales of justice, will gather around your tottering thrones.]

Although the reference to the French Declaration of human and civil rights ("Ein Gesetz für den Menschen und Bürger") is unmissable, Arndt's support for constitutional monarchy that stops short of republicanism keeps him, despite his harsh criticisms of the princes, from the total and lifelong exile of republican political radicals, such as Karl Follen.

While in 1813 the princes would indeed find their supporters, at least for a while, in 1806 they did *lose*. Arndt published the above in April 1806 (Müsebeck 1914: 171), before the Prussian defeat at Jena. Arndt claims he had written much of it by November 1805,[49] i.e. even before Austria's decisive defeat at Austerlitz, which opened the way for the creation of the Confederation of the Rhine and rendered the Holy Roman Empire de facto defunct. The book was certainly in circulation before Francis II abdicated as Holy Roman Emperor in August 1806, dissolving the Empire officially. To contemporary readers Arndt's words of loss (which had materialised in terms of losing battles and state structures) must have added considerable force to the prophetic tone of the book. Re-reading any of this in 1813, when the appearance of part 3 and the re-issue of part 2 gave part 1 renewed impetus, and when embattled monarchs *had* found

---

[49] "Dies Buch erscheint später, als es sollte. Seine Ideen sind die Geburt von Jahren und hängen nicht allein von der Entscheidung des Tages ab. Das Wenige, was die flüchtigeren Momente der Zeit berührt, ist im November 1805 geschrieben, und Ekel an der Gegenwart hat es nicht weiter führen mögen." [This book appears later than it should have. Its ideas are the product of years and do not depend on the decisions of the day. The small part that touches on the more fleeting moments of the age was written in November 1805, but the disgust I felt for the present stopped me from writing more.] (1806: Vorrede, no pagination).

popular support, would only reinforce this sense of the author's prophetic gift, or his close touch with the spirit of the age and the spirit of history.

According to Arndt, the only way to overcome the current misery was to foster public spirit, and mend the broken bonds between individual citizens, their elites, and rulers. In terms of zeitgeist, the dominant current was negative, marked by self-interest and materialism, devoid of spiritual content. Arndt interpreted the current situation as the result of an entirely consequential historical development, which was however contingent. This contingent nature meant that this course could be changed and that activism had a point.

But how would this work? Especially if one takes into account Arndt's insistence that the power of the age to affect contemporaries was enormous, and hard to resist. To illustrate this irresistibility Arndt employs metaphors of fast-moving waters: people are existing in a "wilde Zeitflut" [wild deluge of time] (1806: 80). "Die meisten Menschen, so auch die Schreiber, [lassen] sich ohne das Gefühl der Gegenwehr von dem äußeren Wogenschwall blind mit wegtreiben." [Most people, including the writers, are blindly and without defence caught in the drift of the swell of waves around them.] (1806: 19) Along with the writers, those failing guardians of the public weal, the princes are also subject to this zeitgeist drift. Indeed, Arndt suggests that even "the best float along on the deluge of time, believing that the age (or time) wants what is good and right" (1806: 75).[50] Arndt proposes that this "flood" is experienced as an external force, a necessity even, to which most submit. But at the same time most individuals experience an internal power of independent agency.

> [er] kömmt ganz natürlich auf die Bemerkung, daß er zugleich gemacht wird und sich macht, kurz, daß zwei Kräfte an ihm arbeiten, oft grade einander gegen minirend, von welchen er die eine als innigst in sich wohnend fühlt, die andere aber außer sich denken muß. [...] Hier wird der Mensch von einer mächtigen Nothwendigkeit geführt, welcher er blind folgt und wodurch er nur als ein Tröpfchen in dem unergründlichen Strome der Zeit mitschwimmt; [...]. Dort, meint und scheint er sich selbst zu führen, dort, wo er wohl am leichtesten finden könnte, daß eine weit höhere Nothwendigkeit [the divine, morality] ihn beherrscht als drüben. (1806: 18–19)

> [[he] quite naturally notices that he is being made and that at the same time he makes himself, in short, that two powers are working on him, frequently countermanding each other. One he experiences as residing deeply within himself, the other he has to think of as outside himself. [...] On the one hand the human being is led by a powerful necessity, which he follows blindly and through which he swims along as only a tiny drop in the unfathomable mighty river of time; [...] on the other hand he thinks, and seems, himself

---

50 "Die Bessten fließen mit der Zeitflut hin und in der Meinung, daß die Zeit das Rechte und Gute wolle".

to be leading, when here he could see most easily that a far higher necessity [the divine, morality] rules over him than in the former context.

The reference to a "far higher necessity", which is contrasted with the mundane pressures of life and society, illustrates Arndt's belief in the human moral compass, which all late Enlighteners (from Kant to Fichte) considered an innate human gift that needed to be fostered because it was liable to corruption. This moral capacity was vital for public spirit, and in it the difficulty of moral freedom converges: morally right action is a free human choice, but it ought to be an inner compulsion, the properly educated human being would unfailingly *choose* to do the right thing.

While it is hard enough to resist the "äußere Wogenschwall", even the inner moral agency has been corrupted by current external influences.

> [A]uch das Göttliche in ihnen [...] hat Klang und Weissagung verloren und feige Schlauheit scharmützelt, wo fromme Kraft kämpfte. Klug und knechtisch weiß man bestimmt, was man will; aber was kann man? (1806: 20)
>
> [Even the divine in them [...] has lost its sound and wisdom and cowardly slyness runs skirmishes, where once pious strength fought openly. Clever and slavish, one knows well what one wants, but what is one capable of?]

Here Arndt arrives at his key theme of the first half of the book, defining the experience of zeitgeist by the individual as friction between having (moral) agency and being coerced, which is familiar from the discussions of how "spirit" works, recalling Herder's "tätig und leidend". When Arndt discusses "Das Zeitalter und die Zeitgenossen" [the current age and its contemporaries], he returns to this issue. Although taking up the old notion of Barclay's that age and contemporaries are inseparable and identical,[51] that hence any suggestion of duality – considering the people and the spirit (or the age) as distinct entities – amounts to a deception ("Wahn" and "Täuschung", 1806: 82), he nevertheless proposes that the individual's divided experience of agency and coercive influence is genuine, because this is how it actually *appears* to individuals.

> Das aber, was sich in ihnen [den Menschen] und durch sie nur bewegt, was in ihnen mit ihnen nur Eins ist, den Geist und allgemeinen Schwung ihres Lebens stellt er [der Mensch] außer ihnen hin, gleichsam als eine Kraft, die sich um sie bewegt und wechselnd auf sie eindringt oder von ihnen abläßt, je nachdem sie dieselbe auf sich wirken lassen oder zurücktreiben. [...] Ich stelle mich mitten in diesen Schein und nehme das Zeitalter und die Zeitgenossen als zwei Dinge außer einander, die einander bearbeiten und auf

---

[51] "Zeitalter und Zeitgenossen in rechter Bedeutung sind eins. Durch die Menschen geht die Zeit." [Age and contemporaries are one. Time realises itself through people.] (1806: 80).

einander wirken, denn so erscheinen sie wirklich. Das Zeitalter wird in diesem Sinn bloß Erscheinung und kann nur so dargestellt werden. (1806: 81–82)[52]

[The spirit and the energy of their lives, which moves only in them [people] or through them and is one with them, they posit outside themselves, like a power that moves around them and changes between pressurising them and leaving them be, depending on how much they let it affect them or repulse it. [...] I embrace this semblance that takes the age and its contemporaries as two distinct things that work on each other and affect each other because this is how they actually appear. Only in this sense can the age actually appear and be presented.]

Arndt pinpoints the reciprocal dynamic of influence and agency as it appears in life and reflects on it as a "construction" of experience. The "spirit" appears to exist as an entity external to human beings, but it is also in them, so they can act on it as if it is their will, yet it also exists as an influence on them in the shape of other people's actions. It is this latter influence, which condenses to the "äußere Wogenschwall" and has the ability to drown out every other impetus, that interests Arndt. This is what draws him towards investigating intellectual elites, and this is why he believes the people – intellectuals and their audiences – are and make an age.

Arndt was convinced that intellectual elites, the "writers", were the key to prevalent opinions and practices, they were the producers of "culture", of laws, all forms of literature, public debate, and closely involved in the spirit of a period that was characterised by an expansion of the public sphere. They are subject to the same dual forces described above, but due to their position within society their experience is magnified by their impact. Arndt proceeds to describe the very effective mechanism by which "truth" and "sense" are arrived at and achieve the all permeating quality of zeitgeist.

Zuerst komme ich zu euch, ihr Viri illustrissimi, fulgentissimi und celeberrimi, Messieurs de l'Institut national, membres des Academies imperiales et royales, und zu euch, ihr Herren Professoren in Oxford, Upsala, Göttingen und Bologna. [...] Ohne Ziel und Maaß schwanktet ihr mit andern auf dem endlosen Wege hin und hörtet endlich thörigt damit auf, nicht das Beste, sondern das Meiste zu ergreifen. [...] Die Menge des Stoffes ist zu groß, sie erdrückt den Geist und das Urteil. [...] Alles hat sich in lieblose Form, in körperlosen Geist aufgelöst. Man ist mit hinein, ehe man es merkt, und treibt mit eben dem Eifer ein Ding [...]. Ich habe Leute gekannt, sonst ehrliche brave Leute, [...]. Diese hatten einen zur Lust erfundenen Schwank so oft und so lebendig erzählt, daß ihnen endlich eine wahre Geschichte daraus ward, [...]. Dies ist das eigenste Schicksal unserer Akademiker und Universitätsmänner. (1806: 39–42)

---

[52] In theory it is possible to consider these two entities as separate because "in der Idee ist der Mensch auch über und außer dem Leben." [in the idea man is also above and outside actual life] (Arndt 1806: 81–82).

> [First I come to you, Viri illustrissimi, fulgentissimi and celeberrimi, Messieurs de l'Institut national, membres des Academies imperiales et royales, and to you, professors at Oxford, Upsala, Göttingen and Bologna. [...] Without aim and measure you were swaying along with the others on the interminable path, and eventually, foolishly, began to focus on quantity rather than quality [das Beste]. [...]. The mass of data is too vast, it smothers judgement and spirit. [...] Everything has been dissolved into loveless form[ula] and disembodied spirit. One is drawn into it before one notices and joins in with the same gusto [...]. I have known people, otherwise honest and good, [...]. They had retold an amusing story made up for fun so many times so vividly that it became a true story to them [...]. This is the very fate of our university men.

Institutionalised intellectuals produce constructions that self-proliferate into assumed truth. It is a process that is like an irresistible current, reflecting the heterogeneity of agency and coercion, of "gemacht werden" and "sich machend" above. Arndt suggests that this duping is not (generally) done with malicious premeditation. If there is deception (Betrug), then the deceiver is also deceived, they are shaped by the "system" and then act to support it, by producing more of their own who will make sure the current beliefs are passed on to a wider public and perhaps the next generation. This does not just affect "university men", but all groups that make up the intellectual elites, as Arndt sets out to show in this survey of intellectuals: "aus allen sollt ihr dasselbe Echo vernehmen". [hear the same echo from all of them] (1806: 43–44). Elites are a vital support to any established system of ideas and practices.

Arndt rises above mere finger-pointing by including himself in their number – he too is a "Schreiber". But his "gauntlet" promises that from the old elite, who are cold and weak show-offs (1806: 44), a new one will emerge. They begin as a small dissenting group that recognises the failings of the current "Strom der Zeit". Initially they may only experience a paralysing sense of debility, which he is familiar with: "Daß man nichts geworden ist und nichts kann! [...] es ist das [Gefühl] der Besseren, die jetzt leben, es ist das meinige." [That one has become nothing and cannot do anything! [...] This is the [feeling] of the better ones now living, and it is mine.] (1806: 5) In moments when the established system runs into difficulty, these few tend to coalesce into a new elite who challenge the status quo. Initially they tend not to be understood (until more people come round to their view). Arndt describes these "few men" as "prophetic riddles" and as "unbekannte Gestalten, wie Bilder aus einer fremden Welt [...], die geblendeten Zeitgenossen gehen vorüber und begreifen euch nicht" [unknown figures like images from a strange world [...], your dazzled contemporaries walk by and do not understand you] (1806: 36). These figures are especially incomprehensible to those fully imbued with the current spirit. Arndt of course sees himself as part of such a vanguard elite. Overcoming the sense of paralysis he describes above, he also presents himself as an awakener in an age of rudderless "blindness" (1806: 13 and passim), taking up the traditional role of evangelising prophet. This is in line with his religious rhetoric, a choice of discourse that differentiates him from Hendrich and Brandes. His intention may quite genuinely be to (re-)establish truth and "life" in a world anaesthetized by sophistic hair-splitting, overwhelmed with empirical details, and rife with corruption. But one wonders to what extent Arndt uses the religious discourse to engage his audience. Notwithstanding the religious rhetoric, Arndt very effectively describes a *secular* mechanism of how truth, or at least "sense", is arrived at and circulated. In *this*, his analysis of the mechanics of zeitgeist is very similar to Hendrich's and Brandes'. In terms of dynamics, the mechanism Arndt describes applies to both the perpetuation of the "old" sense as well as his "new" truth, Arndt's business is equally to expose how errors and illusions are perpetuated and to spread his own, in his view truthful, ideas. His religious discourse and populist rhetoric have obscured his more complex sociological commentary to many later readers.

In parts 2 and 3, reflecting the gradually intensifying climate of German resistance to French occupation, the focus shifts towards identifying Napoleon as the (main) oppressor of German rights. Volume 4 appeared in 1818, after the longest gap between parts and almost as an afterthought. It comes five years after the Battle of Leipzig, the outcome of which Arndt would have seen as a fruit of his activism, and three years after the conclusion of the Congress of Vienna, which he would have considered as an undoing of some of these achievements. So not surprisingly in *Geist der Zeit IV*, the focus shifts back to the German princes who are failing their peoples *again*, this time in their obligation to provide the promised political enfranchisement. Predictably, this made Arndt, again, fall foul of the (reactionary) post-Vienna authorities. But he holds on to a belief that something has been achieved. While the essay "Verfassung und Preßfreyheit" is largely a biting satire on what he sees as quietism serving the princes' betrayal of their promises of political reform, he is confident that this will not last because public spirit (öffentlicher Sinn) has been restored.

Dahin ist es bei uns gottlob gekommen, so weit ist ein öffentlicher Sinn, ohne welchen ein Volk als Volk nichts ist, erwacht, daß der Bauer und Handwerksmann jetzt richtiger fühlt, worauf es in der Zeit ankommt und was das Vaterland und die Welt bedarf, als vor zwanzig oder dreißig Jahren der Gelehrte und Edelmann. Was so aus allen herausklingt, ohne daß es hineingebracht ist, [...] das liegt viel tiefer als Bücher und Polizeiminister tasten können. (1818: 89)

[Thank God that among us a public spirit has awoken, without which no people is a people. Peasants and artisans now feel more accurately what counts in this day and age, what the fatherland and the world needs, than the scholar or the nobleman did twenty or thirty years ago. What you can hear from everyone, without them having been told so, [...] comes from a much deeper place than books or ministers running the (secret) police can touch.]

Public elites have been enlarged, replaced even: the "people" (Bauern und Handwerker) now have a politicised public spirit with which they can rival the scholar and the nobleman of a generation ago. Because *they* fought for their convictions and aims ("Verfassung" [constitution], "Stände" [estates] und "öffentliche Verhandlung der Dinge" [public debate and negotiation], 89–90) during the *Befreiungskriege*.

> Er [der Teutsche] weiß jetzt, daß er [...] mit anderen für und um Recht und Ehre gekämpft und gestritten hat; er weiß, daß derjenige noch kein wilder und frecher Frevler [...] ist, welcher auf Vaterland und Freiheit und auf vaterländische Gesetze und Ordnungen stolz ist. (1818: 90)

> [The German now knows that he [...] has fought with his fellow countrymen for justice and honour; he knows that someone who is proud of his nation [Vaterland], liberty, and patriotic laws is no radical anarchist by a long stretch.]

In the new climate of conservatism Arndt feels compelled to make the point that liberal constitutionalism is not anarchic, nor Jacobin. He remains scathing of the forces of the restoration, "die Ankläger und Weissager deutscher Umwälzungen und Jakobinerklubs" [the accusers and prophets of German revolts and Jacobin clubs] (1818: 92), who, insulting and accusing the people, warn that any political adjustment would create revolution and bloodshed and that the people don't know what they want anyway, influencing the rulers and public opinion along those lines. Arndt is adamant that the people do know what they want – constitutional representation – but that the way of achieving this was undecided and that any proposals of utopian or unworkable solutions were due to the recent phase of (pre-Napoleonic and Napoleonic) despotism (1818: 91–92).

> Sie [das Volk] wollen eine gesetzliche Verfassung, sie wollen feste Landstände und geregelte Einrichtungen und Vertretung dieser Stände. Dies ist das Was, worüber vom Rhein bis zur Oder und Weichsel nur eine Stimme ist; aber über das Wie sind die Stimmen allerdings sehr verschieden. [...] Diese Verschiedenheit der Meinungen und diese Unkunde der politischen Dinge ist in Teutschland die allernatürlichste, wo alle sonst bestandene politische Ordnungen übereinander geworfen und zerrüttet sind und wo in vielen Landschaften seit lange [sic] keine ständischen Verfassungen mehr waren. (1818: 91–92)

> [The people want a legally binding constitution, they want guaranteed local diets and orderly institutions to represent the estates. This is the "what", about which there is only one voice from the Rhine to the Oder and Weichsel; but there are many different voices regarding the "how". [...] These differences in opinion and this lack of political understanding is only natural in Germany, where all earlier political order has been ripped up and broken, where in many lands there have for a long time been no estate-based constitutions.]

In this there is a Thelwall-like appeal to historic liberties. In keeping with his belief in public spirit, for Arndt this is not the partisan voice of the disenfranchised, who are trying to assert their rights against a ruling party, but a communal sense focused on a common polity, the *Vaterland*, which is, or ought to be, shared by all its members, rulers and the people, alike. This is the theoretical and idealistic basis for the feasibility of reform from above, in which Arndt, at the side of Freiherr vom Stein, had participated.

Arndt is convinced of the need for public debate and argument, even political agitation and discord are good, provided they are based on honest and public-spirited opinions, not self-serving propaganda to maintain a partisan status quo. For Arndt, promoting honest public debate and scrutiny is linked to his belief in the corrective nature of the public sphere. The "Turnwesen" (gymnastics movement), for example, is not pernicious or detrimental to the public good, because it is *public* and free.[53] The gymnastics movement also has the potential to inspire a potentially egalitarian national spirit. Arndt describes it as

> ... dieses freie öffentliche volkliche nicht in den Wänden eines Gymnasiums oder Reitstalles und Garten einer Erziehungsanstalt eingeschlossene [Turnwesen] [...], die große Idee der Oeffentlichkeit [sic] und Volksthümlichkeit und der Wiedererweckung und Belebung eines durch alle Klassen und Stände gehenden und durch diese Idee erfaßlichen Volksgeistes. (1818: 385)
>
> [this free, public and folkish gymnastics movement which is not enclosed by the walls of an educational institution's gymnasium, riding hall or garden [...], this great idea of being public, and national, of reawakening and enlivening a national spirit inspiring all social classes, which is grasped in this idea.]

Its publicness guarantees scrutiny and safety from (rulers') demagogues and disinformation. Everybody should make up their own mind about it, Arndt continues, somewhat rhetorically: "Ist das eine Tugend, so ehre man ihn [Jahn, den Stifter]; ist es ein Verbrechen, so strafe man ihn." [If this is a virtue, honour its founder; if it is a crime, punish him.] (1818: 385) This belief in the (in the end) incorruptible public Arndt shares with Brandes and Hendrich. Brandes, however, would have considered very different ideas and activities as expressions of a purified public spirit; *he* would not have agreed with Arndt in finding this awakened spirit in the student movement or the gymnastics movement, which Brandes would almost certainly have classed as the outcomes of radical demagogy.

---

53 For example, in reference to Friedrich Ludwig (Turnvater) Jahn and his gymnastics movement, in origin a radical paramilitary political organisation, Arndt is content for attacks to be made on founder and movement, provided they are based on open and honest dislike and disagreement and not serving covert ulterior political motives (Arndt 1818: 384–385).

The events of 1819, i.e. the assassination of August von Kotzebue and the Carlsbad Decrees, perhaps proved both of them right. The student movement *was* radicalised into violent, even criminal, activity, while reactionary forces (who had the upper hand since 1815) *did* respond by crushing any national movements, and Arndt himself was suspended from the post at Bonn University he had only just acquired.

In Arndt's text, "Geist", in the sense of an idea permeating society and producing a spirit, is ambivalent, it can be good or bad, but it is powerful.[54] His *Geist der Zeit* also exhibits the conflation of the diachronic and synchronic tendencies of zeitgeist. Arndt spends most of part 1 defining the "current age", what is wrong with it and how this human-made present has come about, yet his text oscillates between referring to a fast-moving spirit of the age arising from historical contingencies and the slower spirit of history, which appears ultimately guided, in resounding deployment of the religious discourse, by Providence and rooted in the "heilige Geist der Natur" [sacred spirit of nature]. Like the other zeitgeist enquirers, Arndt uses the ambivalence between the legitimising majesty of history (which can be an expression of revealed religion or of the growth of reason and morality) and wrong-headed current affairs and politics to *persuade*.

While the spirit of history must – not just in a Christian, but equally in an Idealist, or Rationalist-Enlightenment framework – be inalienable,[55] the spirit of the age, resulting from human activities and historical contingency, must be malleable, if there is sufficient communal will. If the spirit of the current age is selfishness and corruption, this cannot by ordained by Providence or Reason, but must be contingent. If the age is defined by its own potentially short-lived

---

54 In the case of the idea of *Humanität*, Arndt argues (1806: 453–459) that it is used seductively, as a catchword, in the service of French propaganda advancing with the *grande armée*, but that it has nothing to do with any "real" humanity, they say they bring humanity, but instead they are incompetent and arrogant constitution makers and tyrants whose rule and wars kill thousands (1806: 458). This was a common complaint after the turn of the century, when Herder's and Hendrich's positive views of this term were dissipating. Brandes complains in general that "man dunkle Phrasen und Wörter [...] dem Haufen der Sektierer für neue Begriffe gab" [opaque phrases and word were given to the dissectors of new terms] and that their twisting was endemic while new words were used without definite meaning (Brandes 1808: 241). He deals with the term *Humanität* in the context of the (in his view ill-founded) idea of human progress and perfectibility which underlies especially Herder's "Humanität" more generally (1808: 206–252). Almost exactly contemporaneous with Arndt's part 1 are Fichte's discussions of the ill-understood meaning of this word in his *Reden an die deutsche Nation* (Fichte 1846 [1808]: 322–327).
55 The dilemma of free agency in a (pre-ordained) world of necessities is here reflected in political thinking.

characteristics – the "signs of the times" which arise through human agency, not Providence, to dominate human collectives – it must be susceptible to opposition. In that case there is not only a point in acting, but a moral duty to do so. Arndt concludes in *Geist der Zeit I* that corruption, disenfranchisement and poverty will be overcome eventually by history in a distant future, but it could be overcome much sooner if a public-spirited intellectual elite raised its voice (for the right reasons and the right ideas) and inspired "Geist": "Laßt uns in unserem Himmel nicht faul seyn, wissend, was wir thun sollen [...]. Ihr Edlern und Weiseren, auf! [...] thut eure Pflicht und zeigt den Verzweifelten die Rettung und Erlösung." [Let us not be idle in our [spiritual-intellectual] heaven because we know what we have to do. [...] Up, you more noble and wiser people! [...] Do your duty and show the despairing the path to rescue and salvation.] (1806: 460–461)

This is clearly one of the reasons why for Arndt it had become so important to characterise not just human collectives, such as nations, but politically active groups, such as politicians and intellectuals, or gymnasts. In this view of history and the age *their* actions are key causes of historical development, influencing the ruin of virtue or the chances of deliverance, as religiously tinged language might put it. Barclay's *genius saeculi*, the original conflation of a "spirit of the age" and a spirit of historically generated national identity, lingers.[56] This ambivalence allows projecting a better future, possibly on the basis of a better past, on precedents of ancient liberties or ancient prerequisites. This ambivalence is the reason why the European peoples, or nations, feature in all discussions of zeitgeist discussed here. Arndt illustrates, like Hendrich had done (or indeed Barclay), and as Steffens would do in 1817, the workings of the present age through the characters, the current activities, and the resulting outcomes of the major European nations. He describes the French attempt at revolution as a glorious dream that was bound to fail because the French were not ready, or perhaps capable, to be free. This was a familiar theme, from Herder to Schiller and Novalis, which was rapidly becoming a commonplace. In *Reden an die deutsche Nation*, Fichte elaborated on this in 1807–1808, and Hegel would incorporate it into his *Philosophy of History* in the 1820s. *Because* the French were unsuited to moral and political liberty they allowed a despot – Bonaparte – to rise to the unchecked power with which he was currently (1805–1806) enslaving all of Europe.

There is little that is original in Arndt's description of the British. They are presented in Burkean fashion as the great nation of liberty and public spirit who

---

[56] In 1806, this conflation was about to become the Hegelian "world spirit", the new theodicy manifest in (the) peoples. Inalienable principle and human construction remained conflated. In 1818 Arndt pronounced "Geschichte ist eine Offenbarung Gottes und der Völker." [History is a revelation of God and the peoples.] (1818: 94–95).

had the finest constitution in the world (1806: 332),[57] but who have over the past fifty years – here Arndt diverges from Burke and agrees with Thelwall, Hendrich, and Hazlitt – become corrupted through their own greed: their colonial empire has made them materialistic, selfish, and shallow and they have become slaves to their own exploitative machine. "Am Ganges, am Senegal und auf Jamaika gingen die Sitten und Tugenden und die brave Verfassung der Engländer unter; aus Unterdrückern wurden Unterdrückte, aus Despoten, Sklaven." [On the banks of the Ganges and the Senegal, and on Jamaica the customs and virtues and the brave constitution of the English perished; oppressors became oppressed, depots became slaves.] (1806: 333) They have been successful under the current spirit of materialistic corruption and now bear its marks, which makes them morally weak and vulnerable. "Ihr werdet untergehen, durch keinen als durch euch selbst, [...]; die Zeit eures Adels und eurer Bürgerkraft scheint für immer vergangen." [You will perish through no other than yourselves, [...] the times of your nobility and your civic strength seem gone forever.] (1806: 343) Arndt nevertheless hopes that they will be able to recover enough of their strength not to fall to Napoleon's rule. By the time a (Russian-)Prussian-British alliance promised a real hope of beating Napoleon, in *Geist der Zeit III* (1813), the British are again "stolzes und freies England" [proud and free England] (1813: passim). A similar reflection of the zeitgeist is Frederick II of Prussia; Arndt's assessment conflates Hendrich's generally positive view of him with Brandes' generally negative one. Frederick is imbued with the spirit of the eighteenth century, is indeed its emblematic representation. Embodying its values as virtues he is – hence – eminently successful, for Prussia. But in *German* terms, he is the great divider who, by creating a North German superpower that is vying with Austria for dominance in the old Empire, ultimately paves the way for its complete break-up.

Geist der Zeit I was a controversial book. As a precautionary measure it did not give a place of publication (neither does part 2), and some secrecy on this point proved to be well advised when one considers that the execution of the bookseller and publisher Johann Philipp Palm on 25 August 1806 for publishing, rather than writing, an outspokenly anti-Napoleonic pamphlet was only four months in the future. Palm was sentenced to death in French-controlled southern Germany for publishing *Deutschland in seiner tiefsten Erniedrigung* in lieu of the pamphlet's anonymous author who could not be traced by the authorities. Arndt had not published *Geist der Zeit* anonymously. So when Napoleon's army swept north into Swedish Pomerania, following their victory

---

[57] Arndt also echoes Burke's fear that France does not intend to liberate but dominate (1806: 326).

over Prussia in October, and approached the Pomeranian cities of Stettin and Greifswald where Arndt was newly holding a university chair, he fled to the Swedish mainland, no doubt mindful of Palm's fate. But even *without* Napoleon's troops advancing across central Europe, Arndt's views were controversial. Referring to Arndt's pronouncement on the useless princes as "erschütternde Worte" [shocking words], the Jena reviewer admits that "we can only report little here" (*Jenaische Allgemeine Literatur-Zeitung* 1806: 192).[58] Due to the secrecy about *Geist der Zeit's* places of publication and its publishers, the books' actual publication history is still not entirely clear.[59]

By all accounts, *Geist der Zeit I* was a bestseller, going into its second edition within a year. This would not have come as a surprise to the reviewer of the influential Halle *Allgemeine Literatur-Zeitung* who predicted that the book would be popular because it dealt with a topical subject matter (which the reviewer dislikes) – "das allgemeine Geschrey über die Erbärmlichkeit unserer Zeiten" [the general clamour about the miserable nature of our age] – in a fashionable way.[60] Arndt's book will succeed because it is of its time. For the reviewer this is the mark of mediocrity; he criticises Arndt for being populist, superficial, and obscure, too often indulging in bombastic and empty language.[61] Despite many excellent insights, Arndt cannot deliver because he is neither thorough nor specific, he lacks academic and intellectual rigour.

---

58 "wir können nur weniges hier mittheilen".
59 Arndt research is curiously silent on this. British and German research library catalogues list as places of publication Altona, Berlin or London. Hammerich in Altona, well known for its readiness to publish politically controversial material since the Revolution and protected by Altona's status as an independent city in Danish-administered Holstein, just outside the gates of Hamburg, may indeed be a likely candidate, although Reimer and the Realbuchhandlung in Berlin, purveyor of much *Befreiungskrieg* literature, seem to have been identified as the actual – not just stated – publishers of the later volumes. The initially outlandish claim of London as place of publication for part 3 and the reprint of part 2 in 1813, as stated in the books ("by Boosey" in "London") is not entirely improbable. More on this in Chapter 5. All this reflects the precarious and restless atmosphere of these years, when (anti-Napoleonic) agitation and (Napoleonic) domination vie for the power to promote the "proper" potential of the revolution in the public sphere.
60 "Wenn [Schriften über die Fehler des Zeitalters] auch in der modigen Sprache abgefasst, und mithin in aller Absicht von den Fehlern der Zeiten selbst recht angefüllt sind, [werden sie] Lieblingslectüre." [When [publications about the failings of the age] are also written in a fashionable manner and thus fairly saturated with failings of the times, [they become] favourite reading.] (*Allgemeine Literatur-Zeitung* (Halle) 1806: 81–82).
61 "Die meisten Perioden enthalten Räthsel, die Rec. nicht vermocht hat aufzulösen. [...] mystische Dunkelheiten, von grossentheils falschem Pathos" (*Allgemeine Literatur-Zeitung* (Halle) 1806: 89).

The reviewer of the Jena *Allgemeine Literatur-Zeitung* also identifies the topicality of the book, but takes a positive view of this: in Germany's hour of need – these are "verhängnisvolle Tage" [fateful days] following a "schmachvolle selbstverschuldete Erniedrigung" [a shameful, self-inflicted humiliation] – he asks rhetorically whether "an age did ever have more need of free, uncompromising speech".[62] Arndt, possessed of an "elevated attitude and spirit",[63] delivers just that, "his powerfully moving speech, which penetrates into the innermost, communicates bold enthusiasm for truth and justice" (*Jenaische Allgemeine Literatur-Zeitung* 1806: 185).[64] In all probability, what the Jena reviewer praises – discussing a general talking point in exalted and excited language – is what the Halle reviewer criticises, i.e. the Halle reviewer's populism appears as the Jena critic's vademecum. While more recent critics have tended to agree with the Halle reviewer regarding Arndt's vague big words,[65] the Jena reviewer found Arndt's text "zugleich tief andeutend und klar" [clear and deeply suggestive at the same time], "mit wenigen sichern Zügen [springt] das Bild hervor" [from only a few lines the picture quickly emerges] (*Jenaische Allgemeine Literatur-Zeitung* 1806: 185). One wonders to what extent the reviewers' differing assessments of Arndt's style and historical importance are functions of their differing political views. The Jena reviewer was clearly sympathetic to the national-liberal cause, while the Halle reviewer puts forward the views of a cultural and political conservative.

4.4 Zeitgeist – public opinion and history

The key German analyses of zeitgeist discussed here were conceived as political interventions. They focus on the political and social dangers that were threatening German society, on how this situation had arisen and what the possible ways forward might be. The texts combine an analysis of the current – in all cases post-revolution – situation with a call for political and social change. While all three agreed that public spirit needed to be restored and "selfishness"

---

62 "bedurfte jemals eine Zeit mehr freyer, rücksichtsloser Rede".
63 "Hoheit der Gesinnung und des Geistes".
64 "kühne Begeisterung für Wahrheit und Recht spricht aus seiner mächtig ergreifenden bis ins Innerste dringenden Rede".
65 Stadler remarks that "sein durchschlagender Erfolg wird nur noch übertroffen von seiner begrifflichen Unschärfe, die zugleich wohl einer der Gründe ist für die enthusiastische Aufnahme der Schrift. Auch sucht man vergeblich nach einer terminologischen Klärung dessen, was Geist der Zeit eigentlich bedeuten soll." (Stadler 2006: 279).

needed to be reduced in all quarters of society, their visions of what a better Germany would look like were different.

All three address the question of how a spirit of the age arises and is maintained and all three discuss the notion of zeitgeist and public opinion in close conjunction: elites respond to social, political or cultural questions and challenges and if their ideas meet with sufficient public approval or acceptance, if their ideas or proposals appear right and appropriate to enough members of their public audiences, these ideas will become established because they are deemed to make sense. All three relate their analyses to historical developments, scrutinising recent *and* long-term social, political, and cultural changes for reasons that drive the processes of forming and accepting (new) ideas. This connection between historical development and the present maintains the link between the diachronic and synchronic aspects of zeitgeist and allows zeitgeist to be explained "historically" on two levels. On a more immediate level, it explains how a particular situation – e.g. the current one – has arisen from historical circumstances. Arndt and Brandes very explicitly focus on the immediate prehistory of the French Revolution in relation to their time of writing, analysing the cultural and political developments of the eighteenth century as the basis for the current situation. On a more conceptual level, focusing on longer, diachronic developments and pointing out that similar revolutions have taken place before allows the writer to suggest that the current age follows a discernible historical pattern. By utilising the link between the diachronic and synchronic aspects of zeitgeist in this way zeitgeist is itself effectively historicised: the notion of a "herrschende Denkart" becomes an historical, even anthropological, form of public opinion, making zeitgeist a common social phenomenon in history. Herder suggests this approach as a possibility, Garve and Hendrich embrace it.

This take on zeitgeist as a historical pattern de-escalates the emerging panic about a new and possibly unmanageable situation, engendered by the post-revolution context. Hendrich's sustained comparison between the Reformation and the French Revolution is a sophisticated example of this deployment of zeitgeist, designed to shed light on why the revolution occurred and how it may proceed, while at the same time reducing its unnerving singularity. Arndt's suggestion that traditional German liberties and public spirit, dismantled by recent despotisms, are prerequisite, and a justification, for a German constitutional shake-up – or German political and social renewal – operates along the same lines: history is used to reassure, give answers, and legitimise. In Arndt's view, history can explain why the revolution led to bloodshed and renewed despotism in France and what prerequisites would avoid such a course. Hendrich's and Arndt's surveys of peoples add to this approach, using the diachronic aspect to explain current conditions or justify actions required in the present. Hendrich and Brandes write as political pragmatists, Arndt as a politically committed intellectual activist. All three acknowledge the power of ideas *both* in the hands (and minds) of elites or opinion-makers *and* in the minds of these opinion-makers' audiences, as their proposals consolidate into public opinion, or "herrschende Denkarten", and begin to influence social, political, and intellectual activity.

Hendrich, writing a decade before the other two, makes the most explicit case for why and how ideas "rule" societies, explicitly analysing the dynamics of the zeitgeist process from the rise of a new idea to its consolidation in public opinion and practice. He is less vehement about the problem of selfishness and the lack of public spirit, although he is by no means silent on this. His criticism of the German princes, which he had carefully but clearly put forward in *Freymüthige Gedanken* is toned down in *Über den Geist des gegenwärtigen Zeitalters*, perhaps due to the negative reception of the earlier book in conservative quarters. Brandes had read him and it is very likely that Arndt had too. Arndt and Brandes elaborate on this dynamic with further historical, sociological, and political detail. Arndt's contribution to discovering the zeitgeist process is his detailed analysis of the role of intellectual elites, of their power and its instrumentalization. Their power derives from the general power of ideas that Hendrich analysed in *Über den Geist*. They can use their power to guard or restore the public good or they can, blindly or corruptly, support and sustain un-public conditions. Without the activities of such elites, Arndt realised, the zeitgeist process cannot be explained empirically.

Discussing zeitgeist as a form of contemporary coherence reveals how much overlap exists between the views of the conservative Hanoverian civil servant Brandes, who abhorred the Revolution, and the radical agitator Arndt, who, despite coming to hate everything French, wanted to disempower despotic (and even absolutist) rulers and their courts. Both inveighed passionately against princely incompetence and dereliction of duty, and against a general culture of selfishness and materialism that was destroying communities.

5 Zeitgeist in Britain – The Spirit of the Age and Social Reform in Julius Hare, William Hazlitt, Thomas Carlyle, and J. S. Mill

The term zeitgeist, which is so prominent in the discussions between 1790 and 1810 on the German side, lacks the same prominence in Britain over these two decades, although British discourse has the same eighteenth-century legacies regarding spirit and "of the times" as its German neighbour. This chapter charts the trajectory of the term "spirit of the age" from (relative) absence around 1800 to the saturating prominence it had achieved by the early 1830s. The chapter has three aims: firstly, to identify the paths on which the German term travels into British use; secondly, to show how the concept of zeitgeist maps onto existing British concepts; and thirdly, to explore the reasons for the increasing acceptability of term and concept. Identifying the paths of transfer, the landscape zeitgeist maps onto, and the conditions under which it does so will give an indication of what impedes and what accelerates the transfer and circulation of ideas. Or, put another way, it will give an indication of which conditions facilitate public acceptance.

In doing so this chapter investigates and describes the activities and motivations (as far as this is possible) of a disparate, yet recognisable elite who, despite disagreeing on politics and intellectual priorities, share familiar social concerns (the dominance of "selfishness" which destroys public spirit) and a clear understanding of the dynamics of the public sphere. The idea of zeitgeist, under which they subsume the established (British) notions of public opinion and public spirit, allows them to engage in a critique of the ills of the age while at the same time projecting a different future by utilising the diachronic aspect of zeitgeist focused on historical processes. This association of zeitgeist with historical process provides an extra layer of interpretation and public engagement, which the notions of the public, public opinion, or public spirit on their own do not have. This forward thrust is energised by the idea of *spirit*, which connotes dynamics.

At the same time the activities and intentions of this disparate elite show the zeitgeist principle in action: they promote a roughly defined "idea" (social renewal) in the contested space of the public sphere to their disparate audience(s) with a view to social implementation. They all want reform, which for Hazlitt, Mill, and Bulwer-Lytton is political, while for Hare and Carlyle it is largely, though not entirely, spiritual. Forming an understanding of zeitgeist and trying to influence it (always) go hand in hand, or put differently, those interested in zeitgeist "dynamics" are also interested in zeitgeist "content". The manipulative potential inherent in this link is for the zeitgeist researchers always mitigated by their awareness of the complexity and contingency of the myriad of interlinking factors, which cannot really be controlled by individuals or groups for very long periods.

Before embarking on the story of the reception of Arndt's *Geist der Zeit* in Britain, which is the early route along which the German concept of zeitgeist travels into Britain, it is worth reminding ourselves of the British context in which the debates about the ills and the currents of the present age were discussed. In general outline this context was the same as in Germany: the revolution in France and its evolving outcomes; this much is obvious from the section on Burke and Thelwall. As members of an "un-revolutionised" polity, the British ruling elite, and many conservative and moderate Britons, saw the war against the French Republic, and then against Napoleonic France, as a fight for their political and social way of life. Again, this these views are similar to the concerns about revolutionary tendencies voiced by the politically conservative Brandes and the moderate reformer Hendrich who rejected not just the violent, but also the politically disruptive aspects of the revolution. On the other hand, and also evident in the debate between Burke and Thelwall, there was initial approval of the aims of the revolution in Britain among not just radicals but also moderates. This approval had sparked more debate about the need for political and social reforms. The trajectory from enchantment with the revolution among intellectuals to disillusionment, or at least great caution, in both Britain and Germany is too well known to need-rehearsing.[1] As the war intensified, especially with Napoleon's successes, paranoia and xenophobia spread and the violent excesses of the revolution became conflated with military aggression, conquest, and the violent implementation of a radical political re-ordering. In this process, "Liberty", in the shape of political (national) self-determination and legitimate government, became the contested entity in different visions of political and social progress as well as in different visions of collective traditions. The spirit of the age was, everybody agreed, convulsed; or the zeitgeist was convulsion. What would animate the future? These convulsions and contestations were, of course, very evident in Arndt's *Geist der Zeit*.

---

[1] The attitudes of Coleridge, Wordsworth, and Southey or of Schiller, Fichte, and Hegel are well documented. Herder's changing attitude has been discussed above.

5.1 Arndt's *Geist der Zeit* in Britain

The introduction (for want of a better word) of part 1 of Arndt's work into Britain was thoroughly political. It illustrates two things: author and text were presented in line with British readers' expectations of contemporary German texts and with British perceptions of current affairs, and at the same time the text was used to attempt to influence British public opinion. Adapting the text's presentation to the British context was to render the latter aim more hopeful.

Geist der Zeit I was quickly brought to the attention of the British reading public: it was reviewed in the "Foreign Appendix" of the *Monthly Review* in December 1806. Its readers had little reason to assume that the reviewer was not British, although his identity remained unspecified, as all reviews in the *Monthly* were strictly anonymous. He has since been identified as Dr Christian Anton Schwabe (Nangle 1955: 51), who had since 1799 been pastor at the German Lutheran Church St. George's in Aldgate, the spiritual centre of the German colony of *Zuckerbäcker* in London's East End. Schwabe had begun reviewing for the *Monthly* only that summer and would be a regular contributor to the "Foreign Appendix" until 1813. Schwabe reviewed Arndt's book in conjunction with Fichte's *Grundzüge des gegenwärtigen Zeitalters*, no doubt due to the shared theme of assessing the "present age", whose failings were of course much debated in Britain too.[2] The Georgenkirche had connections with the Franckische Stiftungen and the University in Halle, so it is possible that Schwabe took his cue from the Halle *Allgemeine Literatur Zeitung*, which he may have been reading, and which, as discussed in Chapter 4, had reviewed Arndt's book two months earlier. The Halle *ALZ* had also reviewed *Geist der Zeit I* in conjunction with Fichte's *Grundzüge*.

Schwabe generally approves of Arndt's "frank confessions of his sentiments" and commends his fearlessness to speak his mind, and the truth, on political matters in a context of political persecution, "he by no means avoids the subjects on which it is now scarcely safe in Germany to speak or write the truth" (Schwabe 1806: 525). The fact that Schwabe fairly faithfully echoes the Halle *ALZ*'s views on Arndt's inappropriate and needless exaggerations as well as on his dispersiveness and obscurities in argument and language may be another indication that Schwabe was influenced by the Halle review.[3] Schwabe

---

[2] Schwabe discusses the two publications in relation to a third book, also concerned with how the present has arisen: Johann Gottfried Eichhorn's *Geschichte der drei letzten Jahrhunderte*, which is a history of the *Neuzeit*.

[3] "We do not, however, find M. Arndt's sentiments, and his way of stating them, so praiseworthy as we believe his intentions to be. [...] By the former [his lively imagination and ardent feelings] he has been led in the work before us to many exaggerations and gloomy views of

also agrees with the Halle reviewer that the best part of Arndt's book is his panorama of peoples, but he may of course have gleaned this from other reviews too, as we saw above. Schwabe does not mention Arndt's observations on how zeitgeist works and he quickly skirts over Arndt's discussion of the failures of the political and intellectual elites, merely reporting that Arndt "objects to the literary, political and moral qualities of his contemporaries" (1806: 525). Instead, Schwabe focuses on an issue familiar to his British audience: the alleged German predilection for overdone metaphysics. In an effort to make Arndt appear unaffected by this German foible, Arndt's *criticism* of the negative effect of too much speculative metaphysics is foregrounded, "he censures with great propriety the rage for proposing new systems, the separation of literary men from active life, their desire to know everything" (1806: 525). This would chime with his audience, and it serves to pre-empt their preconceptions about German thinking in relation to this writer.

Notwithstanding the above criticisms, Schwabe's aim is to promote the book, or rather its political implications: having established Arndt as honest and trustworthy, "the voice of truth" even (1806: 527), he presents Arndt as the courageous representative of those among the German public who share key views regarding the political landscape and especially Napoleon with Schwabe's British audience. In December 1806, the British public was digesting, with considerable alarm, the collapse of Prussia (October), which followed on the heels of the dissolution of the *Reich* (August), which had been preceded

---

things, and sometimes to great aberrations from his main subject; while the latter [affectation of strength and originality] seduces him into much less plain and dignified language, than he who assumes the office of the monitor of the age, and addresses in particular the enlightened part of the community, ought to adopt. [...] thus by blaming everything, he renders his correction unimpressive; and by laying the dark colours too strongly on his picture, he makes the features indistinct." (Schwabe 1806: 525) Compare this with: "aber diese [Stärke des Charakters] zu erwecken, ist ein solcher Vortrag, wie des des Hn. A. nicht geschickt. [...] Hr. A. Vortrag [sic] ist nicht ein politisches Räsonnement [...], der heftige Unmut über die Lage der öffentlichen Angelegenheiten macht sich Luft, und ergießt sich in einem wilden Strome höchst unreiner Beredsamkeit. [...] mit zu vielen unverständlichen Bildern, übertriebenen Wendungen, ungestümen Ausbrüchen der Empfindungen in über zusammengesetzten Phrasen vermischt, als daß sie bleibende Wirkung thun könnten." [But such speech as put forward by Mr A. is not suited to awake such [strength of character]. [...] Mr A.'s speech has not the features of political reasoning [...], intense anger about the conditions of public affairs vents itself and pours forth in a wild torrent of the most impure rhetoric. [...] [it has] too many hard to understand images and exaggerated expressions, mixed with unbridled effusions of emotions in over-complicated phrases, to have a lasting effect.] (Halle *Allgemeine Literatur-Zeitung* 1806: 92) Schwabe also reproduces the Halle reviewer's criticism of Arndt ignoring recent progress in the arts and sciences.

by the comprehensive defeat of Austria and Russia and the creation of the Confederation of the Rhine (December 1805), which was "protected", i.e. controlled, by Napoleonic France.

A commonality of views with Germans may not be obvious to his British audience, Schwabe feels, because the British have been told differently and because most Germans dare not speak out. "We have often been told that opinions abroad respecting the ruler of France differed widely from those which are prevalent among us; but we may conclude, from the pages of this writer, that many think, but few dare to speak or write, as we do." (1806: 527) Protected by the *Monthly*'s policy of anonymity, Schwabe could pose as a Briton, which significantly increased his trustworthiness as public-spirited insider.

Schwabe includes two long quotes, both from the section on Britain, to make his points. The quotations show Arndt, firstly, as adamant that it is in Germany's interest to support Britain, because Britain falling to France would produce an (even more) intolerable level of French dominance and, secondly, as an admirer of English liberty and nationhood. Schwabe does, however, not shrink from quoting Arndt's assessment of the recent British political and social decline, not least because these views were also current in Britain, and as a supposed Briton he might as well be honest.

In line with the other German reviewers, Schwabe focuses on Arndt's engagement with contemporary politics through the lens of national histories, i.e. the second part of the book, it is the "most interesting" section (1806: 526). He introduces Arndt's importance as a commentator on the present age and how it might develop by focusing on areas of British interest: Napoleon, the British, and the Spanish. The latter were of interest due to their geographical proximity to Britain's ally Portugal, which was crucial for British naval operations against the French and important as a transatlantic trading partner through their colonial possessions in Brazil. For these reasons the relatively recent alliance between Spain and the much more powerful France was highly alarming, it ended Spanish neutrality and threatened Portugal. (In fact, the Franco-Spanish occupation of Portugal, which was to precipitate the Peninsular War, took place in early May 1807). Schwabe devotes his third quotation from the book to Arndt's assessment of the Spanish. Arndt suggests that Spain has the motive and the fibre to throw off French domination, which would be a very palatable prospect to British ears. As a prediction of the Spanish uprising in May 1808, still seventeen months away at the time of Schwabe's writing, this would in hindsight appear as impressive political prescience on Arndt's part.

This prescience is used to promote an English translation of (part of) *Geist der Zeit I*, which appeared in London in 1808. Entitled *Arndt's Spirit of the Times*, it only renders less than half the source text. It does contain, however, most of the sections that reviewers valued so highly: the review of nations and the situation of contemporary politics, leaving out the review of elites and the observations on zeitgeist. The review of nations, however, is not complete either. It only includes Spain/Portugal, Sweden, the Germans, the Russians, the Turks, the French, and The Upstart, Arndt's chapter on Napoleon. The translation leaves out the ancient nations, the Italians, the Prussians, and the Hungarians, as well as the chapters on "Republics", "Edelleute und Fürsten" [nobility and princes], and the final chapter "Wahrheit und Versöhnung" [truth and reconciliation]. The deselections are as telling as the inclusions: the content is carefully chosen to engage, and not to scare, the target audience; it practises what modern translation studies calls domestication. Maximising the audience's engagement and understanding are features of an operative text, i.e. a text that aims to produce a speedy and uniform response that is readily translated into some form of action. In fact, the whole publication is a carefully managed introduction of Arndt's book into Britain. It is not just an exercise in domestication, but also in promotional spin. The carefully crafted preface and the title page are both telling illustrations of this approach.

It may have been published in haste, the somewhat dyslexic misspelling of Arndt's name on the cover as "Ardnt" was not picked up. Evidently, the translator wanted to create a stir around his translation by tapping into current anti-Napoleonic feeling. He refers to the execution of the bookseller Johann Philipp Palm in August 1806[4] not just to vilify Napoleon, who is given the epithet "Destoyer",[5] but also to suggest – wrongly – that Arndt's book was the very publication that led to Palm's death, which gives the book a sensationalist gloss. He could rely on Palm's fate being known in Britain. As he mentions in his "Preface", the execution generated a public outcry in Britain, which led to a collection for Palm's widow.[6] It was also the butt of Napoleon-jokes, such as Thomas Campbell's much rehearsed quote, "But Gentlemen – we must be just to our great enemy. We must not forget that he once shot a bookseller!" (Brendon 1975: 181).

Linking *Geist der Zeit* with Palm's execution is of course incorrect, it was the anonymous pamphlet *Deutschland in seiner tiefsten Erniedrigung* of similar

---

4 See chapter 4, pp. 124–125.

5 A strategy repeated in his introduction, where Napoleon is referred to as the "French Attila" and "modern Attila" (Arndt 1808: iv, vi).

6 "[...] the heroic Palm, the unfortunate bookseller of Erlangen, (whose fate, to the eternal honour of the British character, made so deep an impression on the minds of Englishmen, that a very considerable sum was generously collected here by subscription for his disconsolate widow and fatherless children)." (Arndt 1808: iii).

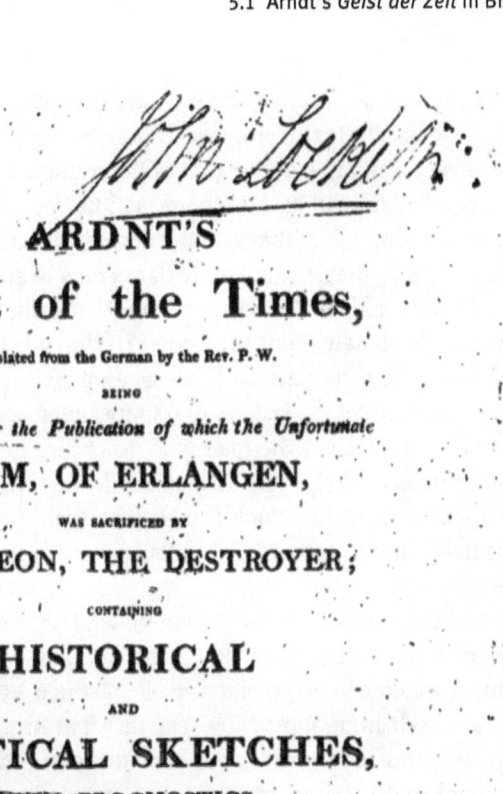

Fig.5.1: Front cover of the 1808 English translation of Arndt's *Geist der Zeit I*.

anti-Napoleonic content that led to Palm's death. This was no innocent mistake; the translator corrects his misrepresentation in the preface, but insists that Arndt's text is representative of the kind of literature that "had chiefly kindled the tyrant's rage" (Arndt 1808: iv). The reason he cannot present the British public with a translation of the actual "Corpus Delicti" is that it "had suddenly disappeared and that it was highly dangerous to speak of [it]" (1808: iii-iv). Even Arndt's book had to be procured from Denmark, and Arndt is only still alive because of his "timely flight to Sweden" (1808: iv). The translator was clearly keen to present the recent drama of persecution and repression to maximum effect, always mindful of the spectre of (Montesquieu-esque) despotism in his readers' minds – Napoleon is the man who "tramples under foot all laws, both human and divine" (1808: iii). To spark further interest, the cover describes Arndt's text as providing "political sketches with prognostics relative to Spain and Portugal", among others. This should draw in the politically interested reader because the situation in Spain had recently made headlines; the translator refers to the Spanish uprising (1808: iv), which means the translation must have been published after May 1808. The uprising was generally welcomed in Britain, it weakened Napoleon and, for liberals, represented a people's will to liberate itself from oppression. The fact that Arndt's "prognostics" were accurate gave author and text further kudos. Current affairs and Arndt's prescience were deployed to promote an English translation of (part of) *Geist der Zeit* in London in 1808. But deployed by whom, and with what aim?

On the cover the translator is given as "Rev. P. W.", in library catalogues these initials are identified as Peter Will (1764–1839), about whom little is known. He was a Protestant German clergyman, who according to his own words in the preface was in political exile in London.[7] Records show, however, that he had been in London for a while, he certainly arrived before Napoleon began to conquer continental Europe: he was minister at the German Reformed Church (St. Paul's) in the Savoy before 1798, and possibly as early as the early 1790s.[8] During the 1790s and early 1800s he translated numerous German novels into English as well as texts by Johann Kaspar Lavater and

---

[7] He explains that he does not give his name because his parents still live in Germany and he fears reprisals against them. He is, however, is happy to give his London address (8 Howland Street, Fitzroy Square), in case anyone wants to come and peruse the whole book in the original.

[8] A contemporary history of German churches in London, published in 1798, reports that Will succeeded Carl G. Woide in this post, who died in 1790 (Burkhardt 1798: 10–11). See Oergel 2018b: 43–44.

Adolph Knigge,[9] and he co-edited the *German Museum* (1800), a short-lived periodical to promote German literature in Britain, i.e. he very much lived off his Germanness. The German churches in London maintained links with each other, so it is beyond doubt that Will and Schwabe knew each other.

Will's intention was similar to Schwabe's: to point out commonalities between British and German views and interests, albeit in an (even) more determined fashion. What he starts on the title page he continues in his "Preface", which is an exemplary para-text: he very deliberately sets out the way in which Arndt's text is to be read. To an even greater degree than Schwabe, but in the same vein, he manages his target audience's preconceptions and expectations to give his aim the best chance of success.

In the preface Will turns directly to the anti-French uprising in Spain. Arndt is an important commentator, he says, because he is clear-sighted about politics: "his remarks on the Belligerent Powers [...] bespeak him a man of considerable knowledge of the world and the human heart, and of profound political penetration and judgement" (Arndt 1808: v), so much so that "other predictions of the author, that of the late glorious revolution in Spain, written in November 1805, was literally fulfilling" (1808: iv). To underline his point he quotes, in the prominent position between his preface and his translation, Schwabe's summary of Arndt's assessment of the current situation of the Germans, the Italians, and the Spanish. In Schwabe's words, Arndt "entertains great hopes" and "anticipates", through them, "the approach of better times" (Arndt 1808: verso page, no pagination). In the contemporary political context this must be read as an endorsement of national liberation from the control of Napoleonic France, which should, Will seems to suggest, perhaps be taken as

---

9 He translated Lavater's *Geheimes Tagebuch eines Beobachters seiner selbst* as *Secret Journal of a Self-Observer* (1795) and what appears to be a collection of Lavater's shorter pieces as *On the Nature, Excellency and Necessity of Faith* (1805), as well as Karl Grosse's *Der Genius* as *Horrid Mysteries: A Story* (1795), Cajetan Tschink's *Geschichte eines Geistersehers* as *The Victim of Magical Delusion; or, The Mystery of the Revolution of P-L* (1795). He published *Practical Philosophy of Social Life: or The Art of Conversing with Men*, after the German of Baron Knigge (1799), *Romulus: a Tale of Ancient Times translated from the German of Augustus Lafontaine*, (1800?) and *The Sufferings of the Family of Ortenberg: A Novel. Translated from the German of Augustus von Kotzebue* (1799), which went into several editions within a year, in London, Dublin, and New York. In the 1830s he turned to translating travel guides to German regions: *A New Guide through Baden and it's [sic] Environs for Travellers and Visitors by A[lois] W[ilhelm] Schreiber together with a history of the town by H. A. Schreiber*, translated by P. Will (1831), *A Complete Guide on a Voyage on the Rhine etc. New moulded for the use of English Travellers.* Translated by P. Will (1835?) and *Traditions of the Rhine etc.* Translated from the German by C. Incledon and P. Will (1836).

an inspiration. In any case, given his ability to anticipate such developments, Arndt's views must "be highly interesting to every loyal Briton at the present crisis" and "to the public in general" (1808: v).

Given the prominence of the Spanish uprising in the preface, in the motto-like quotation on the verso page and, by implication, on the title page, it is evident that Will was publishing his translation with a political agenda at a specific moment in political and military developments, which he judged favourable for his purpose of seeking to influence public opinion. The decision to leave out the chapter on Britain – with its condemnation alongside its praise – was no doubt intended to maximise the reader's empathy with the text. Will did not want to risk offending his "public", a risk Schwabe seemed happy to run.

Will frames the text's potential reception as a replication of what he describes as his own: after initial "aversion" to the "metaphysical criticism of [...] the present state of philosophy, history and divinity &c. couched in the unintelligible jargon of the critical philosophy" (1808: v), i.e. Arndt's discussion of the zeitgeist process, Will was engaged (unsurprisingly) by Arndt's comments on Spain, "which have amply repaid me for the difficulty I had wading through the mud of his sybillic [sic] style." (1808: vi). Regarding the difficult language he picks up on the reviewers' criticisms, including Schwabe's which some politically interested readers may have read. Diverging from Schwabe's view of Arndt as someone who is averse to too much metaphysics, and in line with British expectations of a German thinker, Will censors Arndt for engaging in "metaphysical criticism" in the first half of the book, which he has therefore not translated. This is probably intended to first engage and then neutralise the British reader's prejudices of German writing. Will opines that much of this part is written in the off-putting "unintelligible jargon of the critical philosophy" (1808: v). He seems to relay, almost to the point of caricature, the conservative British views of German thought, which were holding sway over much "sober" British thinking from the later 1790s to the time of Will's writing, despite the unabating popularity of German Gothic tales (which contributed to Will's income) as well as German plays on the London stage. In this context it is immaterial whether Will faithfully reports his own views or not because the outcome is the same: the British reader is led to the text through an approach tailored to their expectations and interests. Will claims he has omitted the metaphysics, because it was "not appearing to me to possess interest enough for an *English* reader" (1808: v, italics in the original), and it even "for a long while deterred [him]" as well as "several learned friends of [his]" (1808: v). Finally, Will presents himself as a grateful refugee from an intolerable regime, "I do not indeed desire ever to quit this hospitable country, where all the intended victims of the modern Attila are sure of meeting with a safe asylum."

(1808: vi) This panders to the British self-perception of providing a haven of "liberty" for those persecuted by tyrannical regimes. In summary, Will was deliberately and carefully trying to manage the reception of Arndt's text.

The translation was reviewed in the *Monthly Review* in 1809, again by Schwabe (Nangle 1955: 262). Schwabe censors Will for his sensationalist and extreme choice of epithets for Napoleon ("Destroyer" and "Attila"), ticks him off for using a cheap sensationalist trick (the Palm execution) to get the book noticed, and also points out that this is factually wrong. Schwabe agrees that Napoleon *must* be fought, but urges care regarding Arndt's incitement of violent struggle, and wants to retain the moral high ground, warning not to fight Napoleon with this own "weapons" of oppression and dictatorship as this will bring bloodshed, misery, and potentially recriminations (in case one does not vanquish the enemy), but most of all because it is a course based on injustice (Schwabe 1809). Although Schwabe considers Will's input too extreme and aspects of Arndt's thinking too radical, he reiterates the alignment of British and German interests. The review provided more publicity for Arndt's views, which, Schwabe notes (again), "seem to be not uncommon in this country" (1809: 109).

Arndt and his book, including its title, were presented to the British public in the context of anti-Napoleonic writing. Its dissemination was engineered by German nationals, with some help from within the London periodicals and publishing scene.[10] Irrespective of how much deliberate collaboration or planning there may have been between Schwabe and Will, the German term "Geist der Zeit" was presented to the British reading public in a new context, not as the "spirit of the times" that culturally summed up past presents, which they may be familiar with from their own mid-eighteenth-century writers, but under a *political* heading with direct application to current affairs, in the sense of "spirit of the current age". In the eighteenth century, "spirit of the times" had been used with less overt political charge, when it appeared in the context of the *Querelle*, making the case of the moderns and cultural progress.

The German-driven, anti-Napoleonic promotion of *Geist der Zeit* in London between 1806 and 1808 may also be a clue for the Boosey-imprint of volume 3 and the re-issue of volume 2 in 1813, which protected German publishers from

---

10 Ralph Griffith at the *Monthly Review* let Schwabe pose as British, the publishers Thiselton at Goodge Street co-published the translation with Will, and the bookseller-publisher Thomas Boosey allowed his business to be used to front the publications of *Geist der Zeit II* and *III*, see below.

persecution at a time when it may not have been fully clear just how disastrous Napoleon's Russian campaign in the winter of 1812–1813 had actually been. Thomas Boosey, a London bookseller and publisher involved in the foreign book trade, had a particular interest in French periodicals and émigré journals. Boosey's was a family business, its founder, John Boosey, Thomas' grandfather, was of Franco-Flemish origin and had settled in London in the 1760s as a bookseller. His son and grandson, both named Thomas, expanded the business, first to include a lending library (King Street No 39) and in the early 1800s branching into publishing (Burrows 2000: 67–68).[11] With their continental origins, and established business interests in foreign books, publishing foreign material would not be unusual for them. Politically one can perhaps assume that their initial interest in anti-revolution literature might have shifted to anti-Napoleonic literature, in which case they would be well-disposed towards Arndt's book. Boosey continued to have an interest in German topics: by 1816 Coleridge was in touch with them regarding his project of "fortnightly or monthly Letter[s] [...] concerning the real state and value of the German Literature from Gellert and Klopstock to the Present Year", a project incidentally not too different from Will's *German Museum* of 1800.[12]

One wonders to what extent Will's and Schwabe's interventions were the earliest harbingers of a change of mood, from entrenched ("*Anti-Jacobinical*") rejection of German thought and denigration of German literature to the Prussian-British collaboration at Waterloo and the growing interest in German ideas and literature from the late 1810s onwards. Without further research it is impossible to gauge whether Schwabe and Will helped prepare this change or whether their activities came too early, failing to convince a sceptical British public at this point. While I find it likely that Schwabe and Will were co-ordinating their interventions, it may be worthwhile to investigate whether their efforts were instigated by higher authorities with political motives. While there is no readily discernible increase in the use of the terms "spirit of the times" or "of the age" for over a decade after Schwabe's and Will's activities, by the 1810s Francis Jeffrey of the *Edinburgh Review* was relenting on his anti-German position. An established landmark of the beginning change of attitude towards things German was of course Mme de Staël's *De l'Allemagne*, which was published in London in 1813 (like, perhaps, Arndt's *Geist der Zeit* II and III).

---

[11] Boosey went on to become one of the most successful international music publishers of the nineteenth and early twentieth century.
[12] 31 August 1816, quoted in Ashton 1980: 27.

5.2 Reform politics and zeitgeist in England – the rise of a new elite

Despite Schwabe's and Will's activities, and the slow shift towards a more positive view of German thought and culture in the wake of military and political co-operation from the mid-1810s onward, the English phrase "spirit of the times" was no "Modewort" in Britain in the second decade of the nineteenth century. While critiquing the "age", which was such a key driver of "Zeitgeist's" rise in German at the end of the century, was just as widespread, as Burke's and Thelwall's texts show, terminologically their discussion focused on the words "public", rather than "time" or "age", and "opinion", with "opinion" semantically covering the aspect of energising force that in the German term was expressed by "Geist".[13] This approach of foregrounding public opinion and public interest is also visible in Schwabe's and Will's discussions.[14] By 1830, however, this had fundamentally changed, and the ubiquitous (over-)use of the term "spirit of the age" was the subject of a satirical essay in *Blackwood's Magazine* ("On the Spirit of the Age"). The following section traces this development, which was accompanied by the gradually growing acceptability of German ideas, as the latter began to lose their close association with Jacobinism, atheism, and useless metaphysical speculation.

In Germany, the discussion of zeitgeist between the 1790s and the 1810s critiqued the age from different political angles: from conservative quarters, such as Brandes', as well as reformist ones, such as Hendrich's, while Arndt's represents a radicalised version of aspects from both sides, i.e. an acceptance of the ideas of the French Revolution, especially in terms of rejecting what Arndt called "Aristokratismus" (a self-serving elite maintaining unfair privileges), combined with a thorough rejection of any form of co-operation with the French themselves. All three criticised those in power, either for incompetence

---

13 "Öffentliche Meinung" was in use too, of course, as we have seen, but it entered German as an import and was discussed in connection with Zeitgeist.
14 Schwabe summarises Arndt's objective as engaging "public opinion" and swaying it: "to lay before the public the fears and hopes of a heart warmly interested in the state of his own species, desirous of leading them to a consciousness of their real situation, and longing to kindle in others the flame that warms his own bosom" (1806: 524–525). Schwabe's summary of Arndt's book as "impressions which the times and men have left on his mind" (1806: 524–25), however, harks back to Barclay's concept of times and people and, like Thelwall's texts, produces a focus on *Volksgeist*. Will suggests that it is Arndt's "considerable knowledge of the world and the human heart" and his "profound political penetration and judgement" which is of interest to "every loyal Briton at the present crisis" (Arndt 1808: v), i.e. it is in the *public interest* to read this.

(Brandes), negligent disregard (Hendrich) or selfishness and oppression (Arndt). Such readiness from *all* sides to criticise the ruling elites indicated real potential for political change and, depending on how far demands were taken, a revolutionary situation.

Any such potential was kept under much tighter control in Britain around 1800, with conservative forces retaining the upper hand, not least due to the easy denunciation of any progressive change not just as Jacobin, but as High Treason against the "nation" in times of war. The centralised nature of the British state supported this control very effectively. Radicals such as Thelwall were driven out of politics, and out of the public sphere; early sympathisers of revolutionary ideas, such as Wordsworth, Southey, and Coleridge largely changed their minds. In Germany, radicals like Arndt did not suffer Thelwall's treatment from German authorities before the late 1810s (they did from Napoleonic ones), because they were willing to support German ruling elites in the fight against French occupation and control. In post-1806 Germany it was possible to combine political radicalism with anti-French propaganda, as both could be framed as anti-despotic and *for* the "nation". In Britain this circle was harder to square because it could be argued that the Glorious Revolution had already modernised and enfranchised the nation and, post-1815, that the political leadership *had* managed to protect the country from invasion and conquest. In the German context, enquiries into zeitgeist were associated, not just with conservative *Zeitkritik*, but equally with national-liberal tendencies. A similar revolutionary-reformist zeal would in Britain only be successfully combined with *some* form of established political power in the course of the 1820s, in the long run-up to the first Reform Bill.

In Britain, it is those in the next generation (born in the 1790s, rather than witnessing this decade's political events) that are interested in national-liberal reform: Shelley (born in 1792) on the radical end,[15] Hare and Carlyle (both born in 1795) on the moderate end. Hazlitt (born 1778) fell between these generations in terms of politics and spent his life suffering the complications stemming from this. These four were part of a larger group[16] of writer-journalists who

---

15 Shelley actually used the term "spirit of the times" in a political context in relation to the present age early on; he will, however, not be discussed in this study because his discussion of zeitgeist occurs in his *Defence of Poetry*, which, although written in 1815, was not published until 1840, i.e. too late to influence the discussions up to 1830. It is likely that, if Shelley had not died in 1822, he would have been active in or around the circle discussed here, which was emerging in the 1820s.

16 In this context, "group" is not to suggest that they were an organised body; they were disparate in terms of politics and specific aims.

coalesced in the early 1820s around John Taylor's *London Magazine*, Olliers' publishing house, and the short-lived ventures of the two *Quarterly Magazines*. Among those contributing to these magazines, Hare, Thirlwall, Carlyle, Shelley, de Quincey, and Sterling had – to varying degrees – been engaging with German thought and literature. Although far from being politically homogenous, they shared an aversion to individual or collective selfishness driven by materialism and the will to power, which on the individual level had its corollary in narcissistic, self-centred vanity. These negatives merged into the term "egotism" prevalent in their writing. The prevalence of this selfish attitude led, in their view, to social injustice, spiritual impoverishment, and a corrosion of communal bonds. As such it continued the debate about the decline of public spirit in Britain, which had been running for several decades. While their aversion to selfishness and self-centred vanity did not mean that they themselves were completely free from such tendencies, they were concerned that these attitudes did not just go uncensored, but were promoted priorities in public life, which made even those who are not naturally inclined that way behave in this manner, i.e. they traced the implementation of an idea into practical activity. This concern formed the backbone of their different social, cultural, and political critiques, which all viewed the British political leadership as wrong-headed, even dangerous, but with the power to influence, even control, public opinion. These critiques amounted, in effect, to an informal intellectual political opposition. Their interest in looking at similar tendencies across different fields – cultural, social, political – in conjunction led to their belief in something like a "spirit of the age": such a spirit informed those different fields of human activity and participation, the similar tendencies were evidence of this, and the fields mutually reinforced the shared spirit, or "culture". Their combination of social, cultural, and political criticism – again, in no way homogenous – was an approach they shared with German post-1790 zeitgeist investigators, who too were only united in their critical view of contemporary developments, but not in their political outlook. The one concrete concern they all share, in Germany and in Britain, was for the manifold failures of the ruling elite.

Against this background, these British writers became interested in understanding how the spirit of the age worked, because this would give them, in their view, the opportunity to have public influence. While this sounds very close to making zeitgeist a means of manipulation, I would argue that their interest was less cynical, because they all believed that such a spirit existed and that it was related to two potential positives: the spirit of history and the incorruptible essence of public opinion, both of them "authorities" that sanction and approve human actions and activities. For them, the spirit of the age partook of the grandeur of the spirit of history, from which it never fully detached in German thinking either, and which was even becoming imbued with aspects of revelation when it was interpreted as divine immanence in history, not just by Hegel, but equally by Carlyle.

Another aspect of this "grandeur" was the vastness and complexity of history, which served as a constant reminder that attempts to "influence" its course were in the long run beyond the capabilities of individuals or specific groups. However, they were all aware that the spirit of the age drew its operative power from public opinion, and for them this entity remained associated with incorruptibility. All of them shared a genuine desire to improve the age, and their contemporaries, so their interest in understanding zeitgeist was not driven by selfishly manipulative motives. At least that is how they would see it; anti-reform conservatives were much more ready to suspect manipulative conspiracies to influence opinion among them. All of them shared a mistrust of those in power, a mistrust of the established ruling elite which they blamed, variously, for incompetence, arrogance or despotic tendencies.

5.3 Julius Hare – public politics and Arndt's *Geist der Zeit*

Julius Charles Hare (1795–1855) is a particularly interesting case in point. Although he has not authored any texts that directly address the spirit of the age, nor is he particularly noted for using the term,[17] Hare must be regarded as one of the key conduits of German ideas on zeitgeist into Britain. This is not entirely surprising because he was a well-known Germanophile who is recognised as a key "Germaniser" of his generation. But his interest in the zeitgeist concept was quite specific: Hare was an admirer of Ernst Moritz Arndt, his aims, and much of what Arndt stood for. Hare's admiration for Arndt is virtually unknown. It has escaped notice because Hare kept it quiet. However, physical evidence of his interest can be found in his library; intellectual influence can be inferred from Hare's own preoccupations and his political development.

---

17 Although it is well known *that* Hare was an important mediator of German thought from the late 1810s, there is little research on Hare's mediating activities. Exceptions are Roger Paulin's and G.F. McFarland's essays (Paulin 1987 and McFarland 1964/1965). McFarland also traced Hare's early intellectual and literary development in the prequel to the above (McFarland 1963/1964). Research on Hare in general is sparse, too; it tends to focus on his involvement in the Broad Church Movement and his activities as a Victorian archdeacon concerned about the compatibility between knowledge and faith or, in a handful of articles, on his links with British writers and poets. An exception is N. Merrill Distad's biography of Hare (Distad 1979).

5.3 Julius Hare – public politics and Arndt's *Geist der Zeit*

Hare evolved from a youthful political radical towards a more conservative spiritual reformer, whose appreciation of German thought combined political focus with spiritual renewal, an approach that eventually fitted in well with the liberal part of the Victorian elite.

Hare's long silence on his engagement with Arndt illustrates the barriers to intellectual transfer and the reception of ideas, which Hare seems to have been particularly attuned to. While the extent to which he engaged with the political and cultural thinking of the German Wars of Liberation will become clear, what he presented publicly to his British readers was carefully calibrated. This calibration was to avoid coming across as revolutionary while preserving the impetus to initiate change. Hare showed tireless determination to safeguard the German ideas he valued (and their authors) from misrepresentation in the public arena. It is quite likely that some of his astuteness in dealing with publicity and public opinion was gained by reading closely what Arndt had to say not just on *the* zeitgeist, but on zeitgeist in general, i.e. on the social and intellectual processes by which new ideas emerge and establish themselves.

In Arndt (and in *Geist der Zeit*) Hare found ideas of progressive social restructuring and a firm belief in the inalienable nature of *Volksgeist*, both tempered with what appears as conservatism: adherence to constitutional monarchy and to religion. Arndt also appealed to Hare because he was a political activist who was fighting his battles in the public sphere and engaged in changing public opinion and the condition of his nation, a role Hare aspired to from 1820 onwards. Hare's reforming efforts – both politically and spiritually – focused on changing attitudes by engaging the (educated) public. To be effective in this he needed to understand how the public sphere, a key aspect of synchronic zeitgeist, worked and how historical progression, the diachronic aspect of zeitgeist, gave clues as to how the present fitted in between the past and the future. The German post-revolution zeitgeist concept, especially as Arndt summarised it, addressed all these issues. The following traces Hare's development in these respects as well as his activities that helped prepare the ground for the "spirit of the age" to become a catchword and a key concept.

Hare was not just part of an emerging new elite who would change and then dominate nineteenth-century British opinion, but also a key figure in helping this new elite to emerge. Although these days he tends to be known only to researchers of nineteenth-century Anglo-German literary relations or as a B-list Victorian, he was a well-connected and influential figure throughout his entire adult life, as a student and Fellow at Trinity College Cambridge, as a vociferous publicist, and eventually through his career in the Church of England.

Hare shared, with many of his contemporaries in Britain, and in Germany, a keen sense of the perilous state of "public spirit", of the prevalent pernicious dominance of "egotism", the corruption of the political class, and the social damage this was doing. Unlike many of his British contemporaries, though, Hare was already by the end of the 1810s convinced that German ideas could help mitigate this problem of the age, and he set about disseminating them. He was aware that there were considerable hurdles to overcome, and this made him interested in the mechanics of public influence, theoretically and practically. Hare knew that the right publicity was essential to win battles in the contested space of the public sphere. His exact contemporary Thomas Carlyle, born like Hare in 1795, was reaching very similar conclusions regarding things German at the same time and would become a key member of this new elite, but around 1820 Hare had two advantages over Carlyle: his excellent grasp of German acquired in childhood and his better connections.

Hare did not need Peter Will's translation to access Arndt's *Geist der Zeit* because he had learnt German during a stay in Weimar in the winter of 1804–1805 as a nine-year-old boy, which kindled an abiding interest in German literature. Even while a student at Cambridge the size of his German library was large, over his lifetime it grew to legendary proportions. Much of it survives at Trinity College Cambridge, following his widow's bequest of his library to his alma mater.

Hare grew up in an itinerant and impecunious upper middle-class family of intellectuals, who had close connections to people as diverse as the William Joneses – William's wife was Hare's aunt – the Wilberforces, Charles James Fox, and Georgiana Duchess of Devonshire. His parents were staunch republicans who welcomed the French Revolution, as so many liberals of their generation (born in the third quarter of the eighteenth century) did.[18] *Their* political radicalism, however, outlived the terror and transferred to Napoleon, at least in the late 1790s, much of which the family spent in Italy, observing the French advance with approval. They did not only approve of *contemporary* French republicanism, but equally idolised Switzerland as a model of a historical democracy and independent nationhood. And the Hares senior avidly politicised their children.[19]

---

[18] Schiller, Fichte, Coleridge, Southey, Wordsworth, Hegel, and Hölderlin were all between eighteen and thirty in 1789.

[19] According to Hare's biographer Distad, Francis jr.'s letters to his parents, when the latter made a trip back to England in 1797 while three of their children stayed behind in Italy, were regularly confiscated on their journey into Britain due to the republican slogans which adorned them. The child that accompanied them, the six-year-old Augustus, kissed the spot where Wilhelm Tell defended Swiss independence (Distad 1979: 11–12).

5.3 Julius Hare – public politics and Arndt's *Geist der Zeit* — 147

Hare was an undergraduate at Trinity College from 1812 to 1818. He became a member of a new, politically minded debating club, the Cambridge Union, which was founded in February 1815. The outline of a speech for a Union debate on "The Question of the Propriety of the War against France in the preceding year" from February 1816 is preserved in Hare's "Commonplace Book", a personal notebook he kept from 1816 to 1818.[20] The speech, written under the impression of the outcomes of the Congress of Vienna, castigates the current British policy of restoration, which had been set in stone at Vienna a few months earlier, as a repressive betrayal of liberal principles. It appears that apart from an openness to central European thought the young Julius had picked up *some* of his parents' political views.

> It may perhaps have been fortunate for the sovereigns of Europe that the attention of mankind was diverted from the iniquity of the Congress, by the re-establishment of Napoleon on the imperial throne; [...]. It may have been fortunate for them that Italy and Poland and Saxony were forgotten in the more imminent threat of France, and that the contempt, which their conduct may otherwise have excited, was swallowed up by the fear of Bonaparte. They might have been otherwise subjected to a scrutiny, which would have been neither easy nor pleasant to have undergone. It might have been asked, and fairly asked, [...] Why then is Saxony partitioned? Why is Genoa bartered? Why is not Poland set free? [...] It might have been urged [...], "We have overthrown oppression abroad, and we will not be oppressed at home. You have unfurled the bright banner of freedom. We hailed it, we followed it, we conquered under it [...]. If you attempt to re-erect the black flag of your despotism, we will tear it down and [...] dye it in blood." [...] In the days of moral deluge [...] England alone preserved his [sic] virtues, as in an ark. For during all this age of universal calamity England has always been free, and safe, and pious and happy. She has stood forth, amidst the perils of the world. [...] A magic circle has been drawn around her [...] by the genius of her Constitution. [...] Are we then, sir, to leap headlong from this sublime elevation [...]? Are we to degrade this Justice by injury, and to desecrate this High-mindedness in oppression? Are we to tyrannize, because France is weak? Are we to shed our own blood because she [France] desires to be free? [...] But then we hear of this tutelary genius of regenerated Europe, [...] this god Castlereagh. [...] I will let him quietly pursue his career of triumph amid the applauses of princes and contractors, while his chariot wheels trample over multitudes, and are dogged by the curses of Africa and of Ireland.[21]

Robert Steward, Lord Castlereagh, was regarded as one of the architects of the "restorative" outcomes of the Congress. Hare attacks the restoration as oppressive, despotic, and inhuman on several fronts. The Vienna settlement allows all

---

20 It remained in the possession of Hare's descendants, but Distad arranged for a photocopy of the notebook to be placed in the Wren Library in Trinity College Cambridge.
21 Hare, MS Commonplace Book: 22–25; also quoted by Distad.

European rulers to return to pre-Revolution politics, ignoring the rights of their peoples. It allows colonial exploitation in "Africa" and colonial oppression in "Ireland", and it allows the suppression of the British people at home ("trampling over multitudes"), which would happen quite literally three years later at Petersfield in Manchester. And the speech threatens revolution (tear down the black flag of your despotism and dye it in blood). Such sentiments were at home at the radical end of liberal reform. This decline of liberty and descent into oppression is presented as the result of the disabling of public "scrutiny". It is easy to see how close the ideas put forward here are to the liberal side of the German resistance before the *Befreiungskriege* and especially to the radical politics of the German student movement 1815–1819. One suspects that not just Arndt, but also Thelwall would have approved of such talk. (Hare was *debating*, of course, i.e. forcefully putting forward one side of the argument.) In this context, however, Hare's growing library of German books, which at Cambridge appears to have been a bit of a curiosity, takes on political connotations. Judging by what survived, most of them were recent publications. His conservative aunt Jones, imbued with the sense that German thought was atheist and Jacobin, was concerned that her nephew was being radicalised by what he was reading, as their quarrel about his books, discussed below (pp. 153–154), shows. As we shall see, her fears were perhaps not entirely unfounded.

The draft speech shares considerable ground with Arndt's view that the "princes" were failing to offer fair enfranchisement to their peoples and that those in power sought to retain their despotic and exploitative grip on the governed. Arndt made these points in the context of 1806–1809 and again in 1818. The draft also agrees with Arndt's (and Hendrich's) assessment of the decline of British liberty. It is not clear whether Hare gave the speech, which he describes in the notebook, rather cagily, as "fragments of a speech which might have been spoken in February 1816" (Commonplace Book: 19). A decade later Hare inserted the following note at the front of the book: "So far as I have examined it [the book] now (1826) it contains hardly anything of value: the greater part of it is vague, wordy and inaccurate, and much erroneous. I only preserve it as a memorial of former thoughts." (Commonplace Book: n. p.). This "examination" presumably took place for the preparation of *Guesses at Truth* (1827), a book Hare co-authored with his brother Augustus, where numerous passages from the erroneous, wordy and vague material in the Commonplace Book reappear (Distad 1979: 71).[22] His quasi-preface is an oddly self-conscious statement in a private notebook. It is unclear to

---

[22] The Commonplace Book itself has frequent (later?) annotations, referring to "Guesses" and giving volume and page references.

what extent Hare simply wanted to record a change of heart for himself or felt the need to distance himself from his statements to protect himself in case the book were to leave the privacy of his desk. He evidently kept the notebook until the end of his life, and it was considered important enough to be passed down several generations of descendants.[23] Hare would not make such strident attacks on British policies in print, but his continuing belief in the need for political and social change will emerge through a closer look at his publications and journalistic activities in the 1820s.

While Hare may have imbibed a mistrust of autocratic forms of government from his parents, to whose views the conservative influence of his maternal aunt Lady Jones and of his school, Charterhouse, would have been a counterweight,[24] he did not share his parents' initial admiration of Napoleon. The former French emperor is consistently reviled in the Commonplace Book, Hare describes Napoleon as an "inverted" blood-thirsty Aaron,[25] an image reminiscent of Peter Will's epithets and a view shared by Arndt (and of course by many others in Britain). This mixture of being anti-Napoleon without being against the principles of more democratic government, in which political power is balanced, checked, and rolled out, has the signature of the German liberation movement between 1806 and 1819, and it is what Arndt and Hare share. To be sure, Burke was anti-French (and would have been anti-Napoleon) and a great defender of the English liberty that Hare extols in his draft speech, but from Burke's clash with Thelwall discussed in Chapter 3 it is clear that his vision of liberty translated into a limited suffrage and tightly controlled franchise. However, Hare's "Burkean" reference to the "genius" of the English "Constitution" seems to suggest an anti-revolution, Whiggish approach to "old liberties", the traditional, historically grounded privileges that supported traditional estates. And to be sure (again), even at age twenty Hare can see nothing good in the French Revolution ("Everything was new, monstrous and unnatural."),[26] while Arndt, a generation older, who had been twenty at the outbreak of the Revolution, takes his time to relive the intoxicating enthusiasm of the early years of the Revolution and explain the innocence and naivety of the revolutionaries who emerged as a decadent and broken regime was collapsing (Arndt 1806: 339–340). In sharp contrast to Burke, both

---

[23] The last recorded owner was Robert Lane Bayne-Powell (1910–1994), whose great-grandmother was Hare's sister-in-law.
[24] Which he attended from 1806–1812 (Distad 1979: 29).
[25] MS Commonplace Book: 111.
[26] MS Commonplace Book: 10.

are united in their belief that *currently* oppressive despotism rules and needs to be fought.

Hare's library is testament to his intense interest in Ernst Moritz Arndt. Arndt tops the list of German authors in terms of numbers of individually published books in Hare's collection, there are thirty-three titles. No other author's oeuvre is assembled in individual publications in this manner. Most of Arndt's books are first editions, something that cannot be said for the editions of the works of Herder, Fichte, or Hegel Hare owned. He added to his Arndt stock over several decades. It seems, however, that Hare was particularly interested in the Arndt of the Wars of Liberation. The great majority of the titles – twenty-five of the thirty-three – were published between 1803 and 1818, the period when Arndt was particularly active and when he was at his most vociferous on political reform.

It is likely that Hare and Arndt met. In his "Memoir" prefixed to many of the posthumous editions of *Guesses at Truth*, one of Hare's most influential publications, Edward Plumptre reports that in the summer of 1828 Hare spent "some weeks" in Bonn, becoming "acquainted" with Niebuhr (whose *Römische Geschichte* he had just translated together with Connop Thirlwall) "and with others whose works either then or afterwards entered largely into his taste and judgment – with Welcker, and Arndt, and Schleiermacher, and A. W. Schlegel, and his old favourite Tieck" (Hare 1867: xxvii), which is in itself confirmation of Hare's engagement with Arndt, certainly in the 1820s. Plumptre's mention of Welcker, in first place, is also significant. It is not clear which of the two Welcker brothers Plumptre is referring to, Friedrich Gottlieb or Carl Theodor, both of whom were holding chairs at Bonn at the time. Friedrich was a classicist like Hare (and one of the first academically established archaeologists), his brother a professor of law.[27] But this makes little difference for my point: both Welckers had been closely involved in the ideological and military efforts of the Wars of Liberation and both suffered, like Arndt, consequences in 1819 during the conservative clampdown; both were arrested and had to defend themselves against charges of demagogy. Both were acquitted and, unlike Arndt, able to continue in their posts. Schleiermacher, whose sister became Arndt's second wife, had also been involved in the secret activities of building up the German resistance to Napoleon; like the others he was charged with demagogy after Napoleon's fall. This suggests quite a dedicated interest on Hare's part in the agitators of the *Befreiungskriege*.

---

[27] It was probably Friedrich Gottlieb: Arndt owned numerous works by him, whereas the Hare collection does not list any of Carl Theodor's.

5.3 Julius Hare – public politics and Arndt's *Geist der Zeit* — 151

Although Distad does not mention Arndt when dealing with the visit to Bonn (1979: 55–56), it is likely that Plumptre, who as a member of Hare's extended family knew Hare personally and was in all probability writing from personal memory, would not have reported these details if he did not believe them to be true. Both Friedrich Gottlieb Welcker and Schleiermacher are well represented in Hare's Library,[28] but not *quite* as voluminously as Arndt, it hence seems unlikely that Hare would pass up the opportunity of meeting the man whose books he so dedicatedly collected and read. Arndt was at that time not even halfway through his suspension from his professorial post at the University; although he had been acquitted before the Central Commission, the right to lecture had not been returned to him. He was, however, suspended on full pay.

Had Hare already read *Geist der Zeit I* when he drafted his Union speech in early 1816? The Trinity holdings have no records regarding when Hare acquired his individual copies, and possessing a first edition does not mean he bought or read it when it came out. The bindings, however, may provide some clues, bearing in mind that at the time books tended to be bought "flat-packed", i.e. consisted of just the pages, and the owner would instruct a bookbinder to bind them in the manner and order they wanted. Regarding the four volumes of *Geist der Zeit* the picture is as follows: part 1, in Hare's case the second edition of 1807, is bound together with the 1813 ("Boosey") edition of part 2 into a double volume, and parts 3 (1813) and 4 (1818) make up a second double volume. Both double volumes have the same binding (although the second volume's spine is darker), suggesting that Hare had both volumes bound at the same time to the same specifications, which in turn could suggest that he acquired all four parts together in or after 1818 (i.e. after part 4 had appeared). The appearance of the pages of parts 2, 3 and 4 from top, bottom, and side of the volumes have the same colouring (suggesting they are of similar provenance and age), but the appearance of the pages of part 1 is darker and, looking at Hare's first double volume from the side, one can clearly make out where part 1 ends and part 2 begins. While it was always unlikely that Arndt read part 1 at Charterhouse when he was in his early teens, the physical evidence *may* suggest that Hare's part 1 has a different history from the rest of his *Geist der Zeit*-volumes. This evidence is far from conclusive and Hare may indeed not have read part 1 by the time he composed his Union speech. It is entirely possible

---

28 The works by Schleiermacher and Friedrich Gottlieb Welcker in the Hare Collection include books published before Hare's visit in 1828. In Schleiermacher's case there is evidence that Hare diligently collected the volumes of his *Collected Works* as they appeared in the 1830s and 1840s, which suggests that Hare was as interested in him as in Arndt.

that Hare had gleaned the ideas put forward there from British sources. But we know that he read German ones, so even if he had formulated his ideas based on British texts, he would have found reinforcing confirmation in his German reading.

There are, however, good reasons why Hare might have been interested in Arndt already during his student days in Cambridge and in somewhat more radical politics than might be expected of a Victorian Archdeacon-to-be. After Napoleon had been defeated and sent into exile for a second time in 1815, student discussions of liberal politics were watched with great suspicion in conservative ruling quarters in Britain, as in Germany where a newly politicised student movement, the new *Burschenschaften*, was establishing itself. If Hare gave his speech in 1816, and if the views he puts forward were not uncommon among Cambridge students, it cannot come as a surprise that amid the general paranoia about sedition, which had led to the suspension of Habeas Corpus in February 1817 and the passing of the Seditious Meetings Act in March of that year, the Cambridge Union was closed down in a dramatic mid-meeting intervention by the University authorities on 24 March 1817. Hare's close friends William Whewell and Connop Thirlwall, who were president and secretary of the Union respectively at the time, even failed, despite spirited protests, to be allowed to conclude the ongoing debate (Distad 1979: 29–30).[29] It is not unlikely that Hare witnessed this measure at first-hand; if not, he would have had a detailed first-hand account of it from Whewell and Thirlwall. Such authoritarian acts would confirm any views Hare might have held about illiberal currents in England.

Against this background, Hare, as a keen observer of the German scene, might quite naturally have been interested in student activities in Germany. If so, it is unlikely that the *Wartburgfest*, which took place in October 1817 on the Wartenberg near Jena, only months after the closing of the Union Debating Society, would have escaped his notice. This student congress, put together by the new liberal and nationalist student organisations of the *Burschenschaften*, demanded the realisation of the constitutional promises the German rulers had made before 1813. To commit to liberal constitutional government is also a demand in Hare's Union speech, which so far was being disappointed, if not betrayed. The *Wartburgfest* ostensibly celebrated the 300th anniversary of the Reformation (the Wartburg is the fortress where Martin Luther had translated

---

[29] McFarland, however, reports that, based on Thirlwall's biography by John Connop Thirlwall, they *did* manage to persuade the VC to let them continue the debate of the day (1964/1965: 44). Distad is relying on a collection of other sources (1979: 29–30, note 17).

the Bible into German) and the 4th anniversary of the Battle of Leipzig (Napoleon's first defeat in central Europe). It served as a public platform for the (young) liberals to vent their anger and frustration about the illiberal, anti-constitutionalist turn in German politics, and culminated in the infamous book-burning. It signalled to the conservative authorities that the students, many of whom where veterans of the Wars of Liberation, saw themselves as a political force. Watched with alarm by the German authorities, this "seditious" student congress was attended or supported by a number of younger, liberal-minded Jena professors. Jakob Friedrich Fries attended and spoke, Lorenz Oken attended, and Heinrich Luden supported the event. All three were to experience some form of pressure from conservative authorities in the wake of their participation. All three are represented with several volumes in Hare's library.

Viewed against this background, there is a distinct possibility that the young Hare, and perhaps his friends, were politically more radical than has been assumed, and that they turned towards German sources for inspiration in the face of their thwarted political engagement after the Cambridge Union had been closed down. This would go some way towards explaining why they chose to read *German* texts while the Union was suspended, a choice that mystified Distad (1979: 30), but is less surprising considering the above. McFarland describes a scene of Hare teaching his friends Whewell, Thirlwall, and Hugh James Rose German before he left Cambridge for London in 1818 (1964/1965: 165).

The Union was turned into a "reading society" during its suspension between 1817 and 1821. It requires more research to establish whether this move was inspired by the "Teutsche Lesegesellschaft zur Erreichung vaterländischer Zwecke" [German Reading Society for Achieving Patriotic Ends], which was founded in Gießen in November 1814 by the leaders of the most radical branch of the *Burschenschaften*, Karl and August Follen, whose aim was to politicise their fellow students (Mehring 2004: 39). In any case, there can be no doubt that at this time German was becoming "fashionable" among a group of reform-minded young men at Cambridge, especially at Trinity, and that Hare was a prime mover in this development.

After leaving Cambridge, Hare continued to disseminate German thought, although for public propagation purposes he turned towards the politically slightly less sensitive area of literature. But even this continued to arouse suspicion, as his exchange of letters with his conservative aunt Lady Jones shows. In the winter of 1819–1820 Lady Jones was so appalled by her nephew's involvement with foreign sedition and blasphemy, for which German writing clearly stood in her mind, that she asked him to burn all his German books (McFarland 1963/1964: 48). In a letter of January 1820 Hare rebuts her in no uncertain terms, explaining that his German books were preserving his faith and moral virtue:

> As for my German books, I hope from my heart that the day will never arrive when I shall be induced to burn them, for I am convinced that I shall never do so, unless I have first become a base slave of Mammon, and a mere vile lump of selfishness. I shall never be able to repay a hundredth of the obligation I am under to them [...]. For to them I owe the best of all my knowledge, and if they have not purified my heart, the fault is my own. Above all, to them I owe my ability to believe in Christianity with a much more implicit and intelligent faith than I otherwise should have been able to have done; for without them I should have only saved myself from dreary suspicions, by a refusal to allow my heart to follow my head, and by a self-willed determination to believe whether my reason approved of my belief or not. (quoted in Augustus Hare 1872: I, 195)

Furthermore his "patriotism and his faith" were only endangered by British materialism.[30] If the ferocity of Lady Jones' outburst is a measure of her fear of sedition and revolution, this must, in the winter of 1819–1820, be seen in the context of at least two signal events: the widely reported assassination of the conservative German writer, civil servant, and diplomat August von Kotzebue, one of the best known German dramatists in Britain at the time, in Mannheim in March 1819 by Karl Sand, a politically radicalised student with a *Burschenschaft* background, and the Peterloo Massacre in August 1819.[31] Whether Hare's first publication, his translation of Friedrich de la Motte Fouqué's *Sintram* (1814), a "gothic" romance, which appeared in 1820, did anything to appease his aunt is doubtful; neither Augustus and Julius inherited any of her wealth at her death in 1829 (McFarland 1963/64: 49).

Hare claims that German thought helped him begin to solve the rupture between knowledge and faith, which was to become a central topic in Victorian thinking from Carlyle to Matthew Arnold, and to withstand the immoral onslaught of materialistic capitalism, which relies on, and produces, selfishness.[32] Thomas Carlyle evidently felt the same, and would publish his

---

[30] Quoted by Distad (1979: 17–18) from a source used by [F.D.] Maurice, which I cannot trace.

[31] Lady Jones would have been familiar with Kotzebue's name, possibly even his work. Whether she was aware that his assassin considered him a reactionary, i.e. politically conservative, is another matter. One might speculate whether her suggestion of burning those German books was a reverse reference to the book-burning at the Wartburg where a book of Kotzebue's had also been committed to the flames. She may have heard about the *Wartburgfest* through reporting in the press or from Hare himself.

[32] In the Commonplace Book Hare inveighed against selfish competitiveness, which he felt was encouraged by the socialisation of boys in British boarding schools. Such institutions, in

more famous ruminations on this topic ten years later. Hare's concerns about cynical and materialistic selfishness were of course nothing new, and almost identical to those expressed by Arndt, other zeitgeist-researchers from Hendrich via Brandes to Henrik Steffens,[33] or indeed Romantic writers such as Novalis, who was an important source for Carlyle. All of them boiled down their criticism to the dominance of the competitive selfishness that was destroying public spirit, which in their view was essential for a polity to function.

Against this background, it is not likely that Hare's interest in German texts was only literary, as which it might appear in hindsight when one focuses narrowly on the fact that he translated Fouqué and Tieck. His aunt, for one, was not taking his activity as anything other than political. That Hare was seeing his activities as embedded in a socio-political context is evident from his deliberate engagement with the public sphere, seeking out a broad audience with the intention to intervene and change public opinion. His early publishing activities in the 1820s, both as writer and editor, show him as closely involved with the creators of a new liberal public opinion.

Engagement with the educated general public occurred in the main in print. It was pursued by intellectuals for intellectual, moral, or political reasons and by publishers for commercial ones. Under the right circumstances this led to symbiotic relationships. Hare's Germanising activities are a case in point. The Ollier brothers, for example, were keen to publish Hare's *Sintram* in 1820 because the public taste for medieval "gothic" was still current.[34] Hare himself had a female audience in mind, who would not engage in further intellectual pursuits and, crucially, whose education would not (and should not, in his view!) include German, so they needed translations like his.[35] The medieval-gothic was at this point not yet identified with a consolidating conservatism, but still represented opposition to the political and cultural status quo (see Chapter 7). His intention in publishing translations of German Romances –

---

his view, bred "selfishness" as they instilled a "duty to surpass", regarding "merit not as a positive, but a comparative" and encouraged "a pernicious spirit of emulation, rivalry, and of contention." (MS Commonplace Book: 58–59).

33 Hare owned the first edition of Steffens' *Die gegenwärtige Zeit und wie sie geworden in besonderer Rücksicht auf Deutschland*, where Steffens makes this case (1817: 4–5).

34 More specifically, George Soane's translation of Fouqué's *Undine* (1818) had been very successful (Distad 1979: 37).

35 "Nor indeed is it greatly to be desired that language-learning should be greatly diffused among them. The spot wherein woman is most beautiful and most fulfils her duty is her home. And this is no less true of the mind than of the body." (Hare 1820: i-iii) Hare evinces a staunchly bourgeois sexism here.

Thirlwall and Carlyle would follow suit – was to influence his readers as a public morally, as his friend Whewell immediately recognised: it was "to diffuse valuable ideas and feelings".[36] The journal *Ollier's Literary Miscellany in Prose and Verse*, at Hare's instigation, joined these efforts (Distad 1979: 38). The *Miscellany* only managed one volume, which contained three contributions by Hare, including "August Wilhelm Schlegel on Romeo and Juliet".[37] German criticism on drama, and perhaps especially on Shakespeare, was well chosen to build on existing interest.[38] Hare's writing on German drama in this publication was picked up by Shelley, who had himself been busy reading and translating Goethe. Shelley was so impressed that he enquired with the publishers who the essay's author was (Distad 1979: 39 and McFarland 1963/1964: 53). Hare's publicity increased his connections: around this time he became personally acquainted with his (English) heroes, Coleridge and Wordsworth (Distad 1979: 39), on whose behalf he would ceaselessly campaign for approval and acceptance, although he was not uncritical of Coleridge's failure to fully realise his potential. Both Wordsworth and Coleridge represented ideas and values that Hare had found in his German reading; in his view their ideas were similar to those "German ideas" of anti-egotism, promoting a morality that was spiritually and socially conscious. It was an agenda that Thomas Carlyle would take up with vigour, and success, a few years later. In 1821 Hare began to contribute to John Taylor's (recently acquired) *London Magazine*, whose other regular contributors shared his social concerns, some even his interest in German literature: Thomas de Quincey, a keen reader of German literature, Carlyle, whose early essays on Schiller would appear here in 1823–1824, Charles Lamb, William Hazlitt, and John Keats. Getting the attention of a wider British public on these matters was clearly Hare's aim.

From the 1820s, Trinity College Cambridge became a hub not just for "Germanising", but also for the publicistic activities of a new "elite" who wanted to change culture and society. Following the discovery of an annotated copy of the short-lived *Metropolitan Quarterly Magazine* (1825–1826) in the early 1970s,

---

36 McFarland quotes from Isaac Todhunter's *William Whewell, An Account of his Writing* of 1876 (1963/1964: 55).

37 It also contained Hare's essay on Oehlenschläger ("German Drama No. 1: Oehlenschläger"), and another Fouqué translation by Hare, "The Siege of Ancona" (McFarland 1963/1964: 51–53).

38 The English translation of Schlegel's *Vorlesungen über dramatische Kunst und Literatur* (*Lectures on Drama*) had been widely noted when it appeared in 1815, with William Hazlitt writing an extensive review of it in the *Edinburgh Review* in 1816 (see below). Interest in Shakespeare was increasing, to which Coleridge's and Hazlitt's lectures on Shakespeare and the Elizabethan Age, in 1811/1812 and 1818/1819 respectively, testify.

attention has been drawn to the fact that this journal was entirely run by Cambridge students who belonged either to the Cambridge Conversazione Society or were associated with its members (Allen 1973: 26–27). The Conversazione Society was founded in 1820 as a private and entirely "free" debating club by Hare's students Frederick Denison Maurice (who would become his brother-in-law) and John Sterling, both from Trinity. It was influenced by both Hare and Thirlwall (Allen 1978: 10–11 and Lubenow 1998: 110–111). A club like the "Society" would no doubt have appealed to Hare and Thirlwall after their experiences with the Cambridge Union and the gagging of free debate. Both shared with the members of the new Society, who were soon nick-named "Apostles" on account of their "evangelising" tendencies, an abiding liberalism in social, political, and religious matters.

F. D. Maurice was the *Metropolitan Quarterly's* co-editor, among the magazine's frequent contributors were the keen Germanists Sterling (who was also a close friend of Carlyle's), and J. M. Kemble, "Apostle" and later professional Germanist (see below). Allen and Want note the determination across the magazine's content to "declare open warfare on the leading literary periodicals of the day", and point out a tendency, especially in Maurice's contributions, to make "egotism" "a prime target" (1973: 26). Here is palpable evidence of Hare's influence on the first generation of Cambridge Apostles. Activism for social change continued to be closely linked to the Apostles' endeavours: Maurice became closely involved with the emerging movement of Christian Socialism.

The *Metropolitan* was the successor of the even shorter-lived *Knight's Quarterly Magazine* (1823–1824), which had a similar "staff" (McFarland 1963/1964: 74–75) and which was itself succeeded by the long-lived Germanophile *Athenaeum* (1828–1921), whose first editors were, again, Maurice and Sterling (1828–1829). The short shelf-lives of *Knight's* and the *Metropolitan* reflect the fast-moving, commercially highly responsive periodicals market of early nineteenth-century Britain. Their commercial inviability also suggests that their "line" was at this time still without wide acceptance, as the journals were not able to establish themselves long-term. However, this group's tenacity in keeping up their publicising activities suggests that they were ready to contest public opinion. How *politically* charged cultural criticism was, is borne out by Henry Malden's comment on Hare's (unpublished?) essay-series on a "defence of Goethe".[39] Malden (1800–1876), another Trinity graduate, was in September

---

39 When Thomas de Quincey published a negative review of Carlyle's *Wilhelm Meister*-translation in the *Metropolitan* in 1824, which however did the translation little harm, Hare immediately resolved to publish a counter-account (Distad 1979: 83 note 10; McFarland 1964/1965: 168 and 1963/1964: 72).

1825 trying to persuade the publisher Charles Knight to resume publishing *Knight's Quarterly Magazine* (successfully, it re-emerged as the *Metropolitan*). To him Hare's essay was an example of critical work that showed that

> men may be good political economists, liberal thinkers in politics, without being raving democrats, without reviling *every*thing old, without renouncing the imagination and all its works, without being selfish and hard-hearted, and without being despisers of God and of all religion. (quoted by McFarland 1963/1964: 75)

Malden evidently tries to allay the publisher's concerns regarding political radicalism, atheism, and moral corruption that might be lurking in a defence of the German writer Goethe. He also advertises Hare's work as "a full and powerful assertion of *our* literary creed" (McFarland 1963/1964: 75, italics mine). The use of the word "creed", which is conceptually related to the metaphor of the "invisible church", suggests that here a group of like-minded individuals were working together to get their points across in order to influence public opinion and activity. In other words, *here* a new elite was consciously positioning itself to challenge established notions by trying to get public acceptance for their ideas, part of which was "normalising" German thought for the benefit of British public spirit. Their activities are interventions in the public debate, against established and powerful periodicals, which were supporting opinions they disagreed with. Such engagement with the educated public, as writers, teachers, and in public office, was a tradition carried on by generations of Victorian "Apostles" who had been members of the Cambridge Conversazione Society. Malden himself would join the staff of University College London in 1831 and be influential in establishing the University of London, which aligns him closely with reforming tendencies (see Chapter 7).

It is entirely possible that Hare gleaned some pointers as to how "opinion" is shaped in the public sphere from reading the section on intellectual elites in *Geist der Zeit I*. His copy bears the evidence of avid reading: it has an abundance of Hare's characteristic pencil markings in its margins. While there are no markings in parts 2–4, and Hare's double volume of parts 3 and 4 is so stiff as to suggest it was hardly ever opened, the binding of the first double volume containing *Geist der Zeit I* shows the effects of frequent use. It appears that Hare was particularly interested in the first two sections; in the first Arndt discusses the behaviour and public influence of writers and scholars, from philosophers to journalists, and in the second, "Das Zeitalter und die Zeitgenossen", he outlines his views on the dynamics of zeitgeist. These chapters have the most extensive markings, sometimes half pages or even whole ones. Tellingly, these were the sections that the German reviewers, including Schwabe and Will, considered the least interesting parts when the book was first published.

Hare, it seems, grasped the importance of these intellectual elites for generating impact and activity via the public sphere. In the context of his activities and intentions around 1820 this cannot be surprising.

In the review of nations, the sections on the English, the Germans, and the French have some markings, as does the final chapter "Wahrheit und Versöhnung".[40] On the whole, Hare was particularly interested in problems relating to religion, truth, and government, and how to express matters, i.e. speech and language. Within these topics he seems to investigate in particular the two interlinking aspects of political and spiritual reform. This tendency is also borne out in Hare's markings on Arndt's short-lived and little-known periodical *Der Wächter* (1815). Here Hare has marked numerous sections in the article "Die Aristokratie", which deals with different forms of government and is deeply influenced by Montesquieu's categories.[41] His particular attention is focused on Arndt's points on the pernicious aspects of the rule of hereditary aristocratic oligarchies, as well as his ruminations on Britain's uneven potential, on the one hand as the model of historical liberty, but on the other as currently morally corrupt, a view which also featured in *Geist der Zeit I*.

That Arndt's commanding presence in Hare's library has so far gone relatively unnoticed and that hence no influence by Arndt on Hare has been traced, in terms of zeitgeist, radical politics, or otherwise, is probably due to the fact that Hare avoided mentioning Arndt in his publications during the 1820s. There is, for example, no reference to Arndt in Hare's major publication of that decade, the first edition of *Guesses at Truth by two Brothers*, the collection of aphorisms and short essays he co-authored with this brother Augustus and published anonymously in 1827. *Guesses at Truth* reached a wide audience, it was a phenomenally successful publication, especially in the second half of the nineteenth century, twelve reprints appeared between 1851 and 1906.[42] In 1837 Julius reworked the book on his own (Augustus had died in 1834), resulting in the 1838 edition; he then enlarged and extensively revised the book for a third edition in 1847–1848.

While Arndt may not be mentioned in 1827, he may still have influenced Hare: in *Guesses* Hare describes the impact of the age on individuals and their actions in a way that is reminiscent of Arndt. "He [the historian] must also, since human actions are his chief theme, exhibit them at once as growing and

---

40 Pp. 332–35, 213–215, 354–355, and 448–449 respectively. Some sections, however, bear no markings.
41 "Die Aristokratie" appeared in issue 1 (Arndt 1815: 224–254).
42 Copac lists editions or reprints for the following years: 1851, 1855, 1859, 1866, 1871, 1873, 1876, 1878, 1882, 1884, 1897, and 1906.

as grown up, [...] so that human character as modifying and modified by circumstances, man controuling and controuled by events, will be the historian's ultimate subject" (1827: 228). Talking of human experience, Arndt pointed out in the first section of *Geist der Zeit I* that "[he] quite naturally notices that he is being made and that at the same time he makes himself, in short, that two powers are working on him, frequently countermanding each other" (1806: 18–19).[43] He returned to this in "Zeitgeist und Zeitgenossen", "like a power that moves around them and changes between pressurising them and leaving them be, depending on how much they let it affect them or repulse it. [...] I embrace this semblance that takes the age and its contemporaries as two distinct things that work on each other and affect each other because this is how they actually appear" (1806: 82).[44] Arndt describes how human beings experience zeitgeist and how this interaction manifests itself in history, Hare describes in very similar terms how this interaction is, or should be, recorded by the historian.

There are a two more general aspects in which Hare's *Guesses* is similar to Arndt's *Geist der Zeit*: it is an unstable text – Hare tended to change his mind, as we saw already regarding his Commonplace Book – and it has overt operative social and cultural intentions. *Guesses'* publication history is complex and the differences between the 1827 and the 1838 and 1848 editions are numerous and significant,[45] something Hare himself flags up in the different introductions, and which, as he freely admits, was due to the changes brought by social and political developments, and his reactions to them.

> On looking it [the work] over for the press [for the 1838 edition] I found much that was inaccurate and more that was unsatisfactory. [...] Ten years cannot pass over one's head, least of all in these eventful times, without modifying sundry opinions. A change of position too brings a new horizon and new points of view. (1838: xiii)

---

[43] "[er] kömmt ganz natürlich auf die Bemerkung, daß er zugleich gemacht wird und sich macht, kurz, daß zwei Kräfte an ihm arbeiten, oft grade einander gegen minirend".
[44] "[...] gleichsam als eine Kraft, die sich um sie bewegt und wechselnd auf sie eindringt oder von ihnen abläßt, je nachdem sie dieselbe auf sich wirken lassen oder zurücktreiben. Ich stelle mich mitten in diesen Schein und nehme das Zeitalter und die Zeitgenossen als zwei Dinge außer einander, die einander bearbeiten und auf einander wirken, denn so erscheinen sie wirklich."
[45] The differences between the 1827 and 1838 editions of volume 1 and the differences between volume 2 of 1827 and 1848 are especially significant, but they cannot concern us here.

For this reason, *Guesses* is a treacherous book from which to quote. Even a cursory look shows that the texts were adjusted in numerous ways, from changing individual words or phrases, to omitting sections, adding others and changing the positions or individual "guesses", sometimes drastically. A thorough study of all changes and their relations to Hare's views and the changing political and intellectual landscape is still outstanding.[46] So rather like Arndt's *Geist der Zeit*, *Guesses* is a "wandering image of the times".

Hare intended *Guesses* as a social and intellectual intervention; but in difference to his translation of *Sintram*, this was from the start conceived as a book for "young men", who needed guidance in "times" of "false philosophy" and "mechanical" intellectual pursuits.[47] In the introduction to the 1838 volume he reiterates that it "would be a delightful reward if they might help some of the young, in this age of the Confusion of Thoughts, to discern some of those principles which infuse strength and order into men's hearts and minds" (1838: xiii-xiv). Its operative function was to encourage its readers to think for themselves, hence the short sections only present ideas *in nuce*, providing a stimulus for further reflection. "If [you] read to be told what to think, let me advise you to meddle with the book no further. [...] But if you are building up opinions for yourself, and want only be provided with materials, you may in these pages meet with many things to suit you." (Hare 1827: I, v)

Hare's not mentioning Arndt in 1827, although Hazlitt's *Spirit of the Age* had just appeared and notions of zeitgeist were spreading in the intellectual and journalistic circles he frequented in early to mid-1820s London, *could* be taken as evidence that Hare was either indifferent to or even disapproved of what he read in Arndt (although clearly any such disapproval did not extend to Arndt's description of how zeitgeist affects human experience and actions). Neither would such an interpretation explain why Hare continued to buy books by Arndt. In the 1838 edition Arndt *does* get a mention, as that "honest and hearty German patriot, Arndt, which [sic] did such good service in kindling and feeding the enthusiasm during the war with France" (1838: I, 296). Hare compares Arndt to Cobbett, both are men of the people, not adulterated by too much

---

46 Another complicating factor is the dual authorship of Julius and Augustus, at least in the original edition. However, it is fair to say that overall Julius is the main author: all decisions on changes and additions were his, and judging by the signature "U" at the end of sections, which identifies Julius, it is clear that Augustus' share was small.

47 "The readers the book is chiefly designed for [...] are young men. [...] and they are the persons to whom I think I can afford the most help, and who want it the most. [...] young men are inundated with false philosophy, or else fall in a dreary habit of mere mechanical reading." Letter by Hare to Lucy Hare of uncertain date (Hare 1876: supplementary volume, 230).

schooling, which is certainly in Arndt's case not entirely true. This contributes to their ability to use straightforward language to effectively express truth, rather like, Hare suggests, Martin Luther, an association that conveys considerable merit on both Arndt and Cobbett.[48] The key aspect is to get at truth, which is also a principal theme in *Geist der Zeit I*, introduced in its first chapter about "Der Schreiber" and summed up in the final one "Wahrheit und Versöhnung", which is liberally pencil-marked. Irrespective of this specific topic, Hare introduces Arndt as the writer of German national and (inseparable from this) political agitation. It is not unlikely that Hare might have felt uneasy referring, in the 1820s, to a foreign political "radical" who had recently been removed from his university post and had faced trial for sedition in his homeland. By the late 1830s, on the other hand, Arndt was on the way to being exonerated and becoming a venerable "patriot" in Germany too: he was recalled to his professorial post in 1840 and advanced to *Rektor* (highest executive officer) of the University of Bonn in 1841.

In the 1820s, German thought was still suspect and Hare may have had good reason to be circumspect regarding whom he quoted and in what context. But his journalistic activities show that he did not shy away from direct intervention on behalf of German ideas, especially when there was a suggestion that these ideas were politically suspect. His (hard to trace) "defence of Goethe", mentioned above, may, based on Henry Malden's comments, be one example. A more prominent one is Hare's *Vindication of Niebuhr* (1829), whose programmatically liberal title recalls "revolutionary" texts such as James Mackintosh's anti-Burke *Vindiciae Gallicae* (1791), or Mary Wollstonecraft's radical (and equally anti-Burke) *Vindication of the Rights of Men* (1790), and *of Woman* (1792). Occasioned by a review of A. B. Granville's *Travels* in the conservative *Quarterly Review* in January 1829, in which Niebuhr was attacked as a blasphemer and a Jacobin and Hare as his translator ("St. Petersburg" 1829: 8–9), Hare's riposte resulted in the (so-called) Niebuhr-controversy. While the reviewer's comments on Niebuhr are more of an aside, they elicited from Hare a sixty-page defence of Niebuhr's character, persuasions, and *Römische*

---

[48] This comparison occurs in a new section on language use, appearing for the first time in the 1838 edition, which touches on the difficulties of translating, the pitfalls of over-complicating language, i.e. making it highly technical and specialised, or using foreign words. In 1838, the earlier discussions of "language", its uses, history, and uses in history were expanded, Hare's main concern is the immediacy of simple direct language which has not gone through numerous editing processes, of which he cites Cobbett and Arndt as good examples and which he recommends for intellectual discourse, because such language not only communicates effectively but also reveals the true nature of the writer. (Hare 1847: 289–298).

Geschichte, as well as a three-page postscript by Thirlwall (Hare 1829). Hare goes to great lengths to demonstrate that Niebuhr has "Burkean" views and that the reviewer is an unprincipled hack.[49] The allegations, however tenuous they may be, would not have been entirely unfeasible to British conservatives in the 1820s. Niebuhr's activities in the run-up to the Wars of Liberation at the new University of Berlin, although almost twenty years in the past, occurred very much in the context of politicising students to take up arms in the struggle for national liberation, which at the time was closely linked to constitutional reform. Significantly, and perhaps cunningly, the allegations against Niebuhr were linked to *recent* student unrest at the University of Heidelberg, and in Germany generally. This illustrates how vulnerable anyone who became associated with the wrong kind of revolutionary "patriotism" could be in 1820s Britain and how close the link between nationalism, constitutional change, and the French Revolution still was.

Obviously, Hare felt the need to rescue one of his heroes from such slander, whose *Römische Geschichte*, a work that dealt with the constitution of "culture", had been a revelation for him as a classicist and a cultural historian. But there was no doubt another motive: Thirlwall and Hare were just finishing their translation of volume 1 of *Römische Geschichte*, and any adverse press about its author might impact on the reception of their efforts. Continuing association with "Jacobinism" could potentially frustrate their efforts to bring German critical historical thought and method into Britain, which was one of the key motives for their translation. Niebuhr, who was following the translation process and the coverage of his activities in the British press, himself added another reason why Hare should act: Hare and Thirlwall needed to safeguard their chances of promotion in the Church, which could be at risk through allegations of radicalism.[50]

While the risks of the wrong public image are clear enough, the intensity of the contestation also emerges clearly: if association with Niebuhr, someone who (indeed) had never lost favour with his Prussian establishment employers, could be construed as "radical" in the British public sphere, how much more risky would it be to quote approvingly or to rely intellectually on a political

---

49 Niebuhr's political activities have always been patriotic, aimed at defending his native country against foreign domination, he is a respected civil servant of the Prussian government and the Prussian king (Hare 1829). Hare almost manages to make the *Preußische Correspondent*, of which Niebuhr was the first editor, sound like *The Anti-Jacobin*.
50 Letter to Mme Hensler, 14 June 1829 (Niebuhr 1854: 513).

activist from the same equivocal context of the German Wars of Liberation, such as Arndt, who had remained openly committed to the liberal aspirations of 1813 and to the student and gymnastics movement and who had lost his job as a consequence amid suspicion of demagogic activities? Such "evidence" of Jacobin radicalism might quite possibly sink any publication straight away. From this angle, not mentioning Arndt in the 1827 edition of *Guesses at Truth* makes sense. But it also begs the question of how committed to political reform Hare was in the later 1820s. A look at *Guesses* suggests a complex picture. Hare's (public) shift of focus from politics to spiritual renewal is emerging here, but it has become equally evident that much of this shift was necessary for (any) German ideas to be "allowed in" and taken seriously.

Hare was clearly aware of recent debates about public opinion, and this concept, in both its salutary and its pernicious aspects, is discussed in *Guesses at Truth*. The 1827 edition considers the "novelty of an opinion on any moral question a presumption against it" (1827: 143) because moral wisdom has the "deep and living roots of everything that is enduring" and is dismissed at the enquirer's peril. Burke is praised for being someone who did not dismiss such wisdom (1827: 144). Judging by the absence of the signature "U.", which identifies Julius' contributions, both of these points are made by Augustus, who may have held more conservative views. A few aphorisms later, the same writer likens the rapid spread of an "argument or opinion" to a contagious disease, in contrast to truth, or health, which cannot be caught, or "communicated easily", unlike errors or infections (1827: 157). Presumably truth and health need to develop within the individual, in their minds and their bodies. This consideration leads the writer to an unequivocal denunciation of popular rule:

> This being so, how much to be deplored are democratical elements in a constitution! Not unless the people are the head of state; and I have always fancied them the heart: a heart which at times may beat too fast, and perhaps feel too warmly, but still by its pulsations evinces and preserves the life and vigour of the social body. (1827: 157, *not* sighed off U.)

In the current political context these are a carefully crafted statements: careful not to attack British "liberty" which resides in the (non-populist) assembly of parliament, where representation is through the Few, who have influence or are supported by the powerful, i.e. who are not the "masses". "Democracy", one might infer, is not to be deplored if it does not involve the "people", but only if it means the people's rule, i.e. rule of the mob. Nevertheless, the people, including the lower orders, are a vital part of the social fabric, their lives, feelings, and emotions are the strength on which the Few rely to carry out their decisions. In the 1838 version these ideas are modified, this time U., i.e. Hare, reinstates the people into a more salutary function, which (re-)uses some of the vocabulary familiar from the radical discourse of the 1790s, such as Thelwall's. In the context of castigating the selfish and idolatrous narcissism of those in charge of the country or the press, he points to the incorruptible voice of the people:

> ... all who are heedless of that *vox populi*, which when it bursts from the heaving depths of a nation's heart, is in truth *vox Dei*, – all who take no account of the moral power, without which intellectual ability dwindles into petty cunning, and the mightiest armies, as history has often shewn, become like those armed figures in romance, which look formidable at a distance, but which fall into pieces at a blow, and display their hollowness. (1838: 213)

The incorruptibility, and the moral superiority of the *vox populi* is of course achieved by recourse to divine power, it is an affirmation of the power of God and religion, not an assertion of popular enfranchisement, or rule. Reading on, this is quite clear, the happiness of the people is not achieved by wealth, luxury, increasing production, nor learning, science, not even literacy, but in the recognition of God's omnipotence (1838: 213–214). *But* the statement acknowledges the power of the immaterial over the material and "mechanical", and the powerful *spirit* of the collective (the depths of a nation's heart) are clearly recognised and evoked in the argument's favour. This is close to Arndt's concept of the emotional bonds among the people who sustain the collective, but it does not share Arndt's political aim of constitutional enfranchisement.

The *vox populi* trope was key in the 1790s debates about sovereignty and political enfranchisement. From his Commonplace Book we know that around 1816 Hare appeared politically quite close to the concerns of the liberal radicals and the (German) student movement. Is this apparently conservative stance of the 1820s and 1830s a volte face, an apostasy or a mature "seeing sense"? Hare, it appears, employs a contested term to reclaim it. From his youthful radicalism he is well aware of the political fault-lines in public discussions and public opinion. His activity in the "Niebuhr controversy" of the late 1820s makes this plain. By "reclaiming" such terminology Hare attempts to defuse the earlier political radicalism into a new religious faith, which might heal not just the philosophical rupture between knowledge and faith, but also the political one between radical reform and conservative reaction. It allowed a way to suggest reform without being branded a revolutionary.

Hare has been, rightly, credited with promoting German thought; he also operated within a "bigger" social and intellectual context that encouraged this promotion. Imbued with a sense of the social and spiritual ills of the age, he found in the German thinking of the early 1800s confirmation, answers, and encouragement. The texts he read confirmed his diagnosis of what was wrong.

Their answers focused on social justice and spiritual renewal, ideas to believe in, which – often – could be drawn from (broadly) cultural history. Their encouragement consisted not least in attuning him to the role of intellectuals in the workings of the public sphere and how bringing about change without violent revolution needed like-minded people to work together and with their audience. In short, he gleaned much about zeitgeist.

The turn towards cultural history (such as Niebuhr's *Römische Geschichte*) aided a spiritual revival that did not want to ignore the progress in the sciences, which had led to increasing empiricism as well as to more knowledge. German historical criticism, of literature, antiquity, culture in general, offered a way of combining a scientific approach with a spiritual purpose (Forbes 1952: 1–11). Historical circumstances could be analysed as (historical) facts, not unlike natural ones, while the grandeur of history, not necessarily as Providence, nor as teleology, but bestowed by the sheer length of the human endeavour it chronicled, could provide a framework that went beyond the material. The historical aspects of German Romanticism also answered to this. Unsurprisingly in this context, the younger generation, born in the 1790s, would look to Coleridge, Wordsworth, and *German* thinkers for direction, as Hare, Thirlwall, Thomas Arnold, and Carlyle did. German thought was gradually being differentiated from "continental" radicalism and atheism of the "French" sort. This turning towards Germany continued in the first and second generations of the Cambridge Apostles, such as Frederick Denison Maurice, Arthur Penrhyn Stanley, or John Mitchell Kemble.

5.4 William Hazlitt – "paradoxical" German literature and the spirit of the age

William Hazlitt would give the English term "spirit of the age" public prominence when he made it the title of his collection of "contemporary portraits" published in January 1825. There is a critical consensus that this collection represents one of Hazlitt's "best" works.[51] It is certainly the one that endured

---

[51] A.C. Grayling calls it "one of [his] finest" (Grayling 2000: 312); similarly, Duncan Wu, the editor of the nine volumes of *The Selected Writings of William Hazlitt*, calls it "the most important of his works" (Wu 2008: VII, xxii). Early twentieth-century critics agreed: A.R. Waller, the co-editor of Hazlitt's works of 1902–1906, remarked that this text "contains some of the very best of Hazlitt's writing" (Hazlitt 1910: ix).

throughout the nineteenth century and which is still most readily associated with his name today.[52]

Unlike Hare, Hazlitt was a proudly pro-revolution political radical. Neither has he been particularly associated with Germanophilia. But he was moving in the same journalistic London circles, Hazlitt too contributed to Taylor's *London Magazine*, (although around 1820 he was of course an established writer for the *Edinburgh Review*). Hazlitt's choice of title for his most canonical publication is in all probability no coincidence. He shared with Hare, and with the German zeitgeist-enquirers, a keen sense of the decline of public spirit and a keen interest in the function and uses of public opinion and the public sphere. With the German writers Hazlitt shared an abiding interest in the historicity of culture and in the link between culture, general spirit, and collective identity. These interests and concerns made him highly susceptible to notions of a synchronic spirit of the age and a diachronic spirit of (cultural) history. Hazlitt, too, was interested in the dynamic between the "spirit", the people who make it, and the public who accepts it. The following section falls into two parts: in the first I will show that Hazlitt was aware of German ideas, in the second how *Spirit of the Age* is a sophisticated representation of zeitgeist in action.

Politically, Hazlitt appears the greatest outlier in the group of British writers discussed here. From a dissenting background, he did not only hold on to a belief in the ideals of the French Revolution – the same can be said for Shelley – he also transferred his faith from the revolution to Napoleon, not unlike Hare's parents had done in the 1790s, but Hazlitt persevered in this beyond 1815, mourning the defeat of his hero to the end of his life. His last, and longest, single work was a four-volume biography of Napoleon, which appeared between 1828 and 1830. Hazlitt's political views were considered extreme, not to say transgressive, and in the wake of the scandal surrounding the publication of his *Liber Amoris* in 1823 they were readily conflated in his public image with sexual transgression, or libertinism.

---

52 Hazlitt's son, William jr, brought out a third edition in 1858, and his grandson William Carew Hazlitt a fourth in 1886, with further editions in 1893, 1904, and 1910 clustering around the turn of the twentieth century. Before Wu's 1998 edition, two other scholarly ones had appeared: one as part of the 1930 "Centenary Edition" *(The Complete Works of William Hazlitt)* edited by P.P. Howe and a stand-alone one in 1969, edited by E.D. Mackerness. While the twentieth-century editions suggest academic interest in Hazlitt, i.e. a presence on university syllabi, the clustering of popular editions around 1900 indicate a more general interest in Hazlitt's portrait gallery. It seems that by then he had passed into some form of canonicity, which was no longer challenged by the political power-relations that had determined the reception of *Spirit of the Age* in his lifetime.

Hare could not have disagreed more with Hazlitt over Napoleon. The two also occupied very different positions in the social matrix. Hazlitt, eighteen years older than Hare, always remained critical, secular, and a political radical, who never acceded to any form of establishment, while Hare, from politically critical beginnings, opted to pursue a spiritual religiosity which he felt could help overcome the political and social ills he had identified, but which also allowed him to pursue a career in the Church of England. Despite these differences, both agreed that a prevalent culture of selfishness and widespread corruption of those in power exploited the people and the nation, politically, materially, and spiritually. In Hazlitt's early (and by all accounts largely unread) pamphlet *Free Thoughts on Public Affairs. Advice to a Patriot; in a Letter Addressed to a Member of the Old Opposition* of 1806, the author inveighs, anonymously and not unlike Hare in his Commonplace Book, against the new and continuing "war with France" as a betrayal of the nation by a power-hungry self-interested government, and elite, who are driven by "unbounded ambition" (Hazlitt 1930 [1806]: 99) and who dupe the people into a potentially disastrous war. Continuing the debate on public spirit, the content is similar to Thelwall's lectures in the *Tribune*.

> I will not pretend to censure the general practice of obtaining a war *under false pretences* [italics in the original]; [...] but I cannot help thinking that in a war which is to try the spirit of a people, they ought not to be tricked, or bullied, or unnecessarily forced into it. (Hazlitt 1930: 100)

Such leaders do not "feel", nor are they "capable of inspiring in others, either true patriotism" or "a sincere and manly spirit of independence" (1930: 99). Materialistic, self-serving elites "believe money to be the only substantial good, they are also persuaded that it is the only instrument of power" (1930: 117). "Ironically every thing in which they themselves are concerned [...] demands all our vigilance and attention, while every thing else dwindles into insignificance. I therefore think there ought to be as little connection as possible between the measures of government and the maxims of the Exchange" (1930: 118) because "a state cannot look to its commerce for its security [...]. The views of men altogether engrossed in such pursuits are low and mechanical" (1930: 117).

In its appeal to those with a share in power (politicians and rulers) and engaged members of the nation (patriots), Hazlitt's title is reminiscent of the political pamphleteering of the 1790s in both Britain and Germany, not least Hendrich's *Freymütige Gedanken* [Free Thoughts]. A key criticism coalesces around the term "mechanical", which summarises the detrimental nature of this machine-like approach to public spirit. Such rule contaminates the entire fabric of society, it breeds "servile dread which bows only to present power and upstart authority" (1930: 115), a slave mentality. This destroys the public spirit of the collective, which is its only true rock:

> A commercial spirit is a very weak as well as dangerous substitute for the spirit of freedom: a sense of self-interest, of mere mercenary advantage, can ill supply the place of principle. [...] Men who are actuated by this sole principle will [...] defend their wealth, [...] they will think nothing else worth retaining [...]. The common birthright which they receive from nature, in which every Englishman has an equal interest as such, appears of little value in their eyes. [...] They will defend England as connected with her colonies, [...] but will they defend her [...] as their country? [...] They would defend their country not as her children, but as her masters, as a property, not as a state. (1930: 114)

Identifying egotism in ruling elites and "mechanical" and "commercial" principles of government as destructive to community cohesion are of course stock "Romantic" criticisms, and one of the reasons why Hazlitt is considered imbued with concerns of the Romantic revolution (McFarland 1987: 3). These preoccupations are familiar not just from the young Hare and from Thelwall, but also from Arndt's *Geist der Zeit I*, which appeared at exactly the same time as Hazlitt's *Free Thoughts*, in the spring of 1806.[53]

Particularly striking are the similarities between Hazlitt's and Arndt's texts regarding the current defects of Britain and the importance of the national spirit to prevail in a war about survival. There can be no suggestion that Hazlitt might have read Arndt in 1806, Hazlitt had no German.[54] This congruence is more likely to be serendipitous. Such serendipity is significant, as it suggests a transnational context informed by what might be defined as zeitgeist. Although Hazlitt and Arndt have in part different motivations, bearing in mind their differing views of Napoleon and the French, and inhabit different national contexts, they *make sense* of the current *overall* situation in the same way. The correspondence in their assessment of the current state of Britain, or even the state of Britain and Germany generally, i.e. their assessment of the related plights of liberty, national representation, popular enfranchisement, and communal spirit, is based on their shared view that the *ideals* of the French Revolution have not been realised in their homelands, largely due to the

---
53 See Müsebeck (1914: 171) and Grayling (2000: 101).
54 He may have read Will's translation in 1808 or later, it is hard to gauge whether the disparaging of Napoleon on the title page would have repelled or intrigued him. But in any case, Will omitted the sections about Britain and the "Fürsten".

untrustworthiness of despotic ruling elites and the dehumanising effects of early capitalism.

Although Hazlitt had no German, it would be wrong to assume he was not affected by German thought, a circumstance that has received little attention in Hazlitt research, despite the fact that it is frequently pointed out that he wrote an extensive review of John Black's translation of August Wilhelm Schlegel's *Lectures on Dramatic Art and Literature* for the *Edinburgh Review* in 1816 and that he recycled what he had gleaned there in his own lectures on the dramatic literature of the Elizabethan age three years later. To what extent Hazlitt was directly influenced by German thought, or simply in tune with its preoccupations, which he could have also picked up from "Romantic" British sources, remains to be investigated. It is clear, however, that he did have a sense of what the new German ideas from the 1770s onwards were about, and that they were *German* ideas. Much of this is due to his emotional encounter with the two key literary texts of *Sturm und Drang*: Schiller's *Räuber* and Goethe's *Werther*. In this context I will focus on the overlap between the ideas Hazlitt put forward around 1820 and those put forward by Schlegel and, a generation earlier, Herder. This overlap will show that Hazlitt was more attuned to the German zeitgeist discourse as it arose in especially Herder's thinking than might have been expected.

The key ideas he shared with German writers concern the historicity of culture, especially the historical specificity of culture as a communal bond, which summarises and illustrates communal identity. As we have seen in Herder's work, this conflation of a historicist approach to culture and communal spirit, which Herder had gleaned from reading across Blackwell, Montesquieu, Mallet, and Percy, was the basis from which his diachronic approach to cultural history as well as his synchronic approach to the nature of an age had developed. Hazlitt's approach was similar, he too was keen to understand the historical trajectory of cultural identity and public spirit as well as the synchronic workings of culture. This predisposed him towards a diachronic spirit of the times and a synchronic spirit of the age, in both cases he was interested in how people responded to their times, and in responding shape them, be this galvanising, maintaining or challenging cultural, social or political conditions.

This conceptual overlap between Herder, A. W. Schlegel, and Hazlitt is particularly noticeable in his *Lectures on the Dramatic Literature of the Age of Elizabeth* (1819/1820). Their publication coincided with the emergence of the loose circle of writer-journalists around the publishers John Taylor and the Ollier brothers. In the last of his lectures in the above series, Hazlitt vividly commemorates his first experience of reading German literature, his reading of

Schiller's *Robbers*, as an excitable sixteen-year-old at the dissenting academy of New College in Hackney.

> The Robbers was the first play I ever read; and the effect it produced on me was the greatest. It stunned me like a blow, and I have not recovered enough from it to describe how it was. [...] Twenty-five years have elapsed since I first read the translation of the Robbers, but still they have not blotted the impression from my mind. (Hazlitt 1931 [1820]: 362)

The play's revolutionary content and powerful language, conveyed well in Alexander Fraser Tytler's translation of 1792, did not fail to make a deep impression on young Hazlitt.[55] As a drama critic in early nineteenth-century London Hazlitt had been experiencing the full brunt of the general obsession with German melodrama and gothic tragedy. But his detailed assessment of German literature in the last lecture on the *Age of Elizabeth*, entitled "On the Spirit of Ancient and Modern Literature – on the German Drama, contrasted with that of the Age of Elizabeth", makes plain his engagement with the historicist ideas of German literary criticism from Herder to August Wilhelm Schlegel. There are four kinds of tragedy, the ancient-classical, the gothic-romantic epitomised by Shakespeare, the French neo-classical, and the new German. His characterisation of the ancient as "natural" and unitary, the gothic-romantic as historical, epic and fanciful, the French as "declamatory" and "pompous" (1931: 347), and the difference between Shakespeare and ancient Greek tragedy as that between a "Doric portico" and "Westminster Abbey" owes as much to Herder, especially his essay on "Shakespear" in *Von deutscher Art und Kunst*, as to the Schlegels; he probably gleaned much of this from August Wilhelm Schlegel's *Vorlesungen über dramatische Kunst und Literatur*. However, his concluding description of German drama as "paradoxical" is all his own. German drama inverts all established notions.

> All qualities are reversed: virtue is always at odds with vice, [...] the internal character and external situation, the actions and the sentiments, are never in accord, you are to judge of everything by contraries, [...] opinions totter, feelings are brought into question, and the world is turned upside down, with all things in it! (1931: 361)

This reversal is based on a revolutionary liberation from all rules and maxims that have gone before.

---

55 Hazlitt was of course not alone in his response. At the same time, the young, still pro-revolution Coleridge wrote to his still similarly radical friend Southey, "who is this Schiller – this convulser of the heart?" after reading the play through in one session (Coleridge 1956–1971: I, 122).

> Is it wonderful that the poets and philosophers of Germany, the discontented men of talent, who thought and mourned for themselves and their fellows, the Goethes, the Lessings, the Schillers, and the Kotzebues, felt a sudden and irresistible impulse by a convulsive effort to tear aside this facticious drapery of society, and to throw off that load of bloated prejudice, of maddening pride and superannuated folly, that pressed down every energy of their nature and stifled the breath of liberty, of truth and genius in their bosoms? These Titans of our days tried to throw off the dead weight that encumbered them, and in so doing, warred not against heaven, but against earth. (1931: 362)

Notwithstanding the reference to Kotzebue, the nature of his engagement with German thinking becomes evident: he relates with great passion to *Sturm und Drang* ideas and what prepared them (Lessing),[56] to their iconoclastic irreverence for currently established wisdom. In 1819, this liberation ("throwing off", "breath of liberty") is for him intricately linked to the French Revolution. He continues: "The same [German] writers (as far as I have seen) have made the only incorrigible Jacobins, and their school of poetry is the only real school of Radical Reform." (1931: 362) He had already suggested earlier that

> Up to the present reign, and during the best part of it [...] tragedy wore the face of the Goddess of Dulness in the Dunciad, serene, sickly, lethargic, and affected, till it was roused from its trance by the French Revolution, und the loud trampling of the German Pegasus on the English stage, which now appeared as pawing to get free from its ancient trammels, and rampant shook off the incumbrance of all former examples, opinions, prejudices, and principles. (1931: 359–360)

While his words have more than a tinge of irony, he suggests, too, that German writing is at the forefront of the age. His engagement with *The Robbers* and his other favourite, *Werther*, was clearly heartfelt, if the lyrical intensity with which he recalls their effect on him is anything to go by. Although he is critical of Goethe, and even Schiller's later (classical) work does not measure up in dramatic terms – *Wallenstein* lacks enthusiasm and passion (1931: 363) – he would not "part with" *Werther* "at a venture" and proceeds to quote from it lovingly (1931: 363).

In terms of *Sturm und Drang* historicist preoccupations, this last lecture connects with the first on the Elizabethan age, where Hazlitt outlined the "General View of the Subject" (1931: 175): the point of these lectures is to reinstate

---

[56] Hazlitt's suggestion that those four writers belong "together" may in hindsight easily be taken to illustrate his limited understanding of later eighteenth-century German literature. But it equally illustrates how later criticism and canonisation erects barriers that did not yet exist in the minds of contemporaries and that may limit and skew the later observer's view.

an indigenous cultural origin, Elizabethan writing, into its rightful place in national memory, where the big names (Shakespeare, Bacon) already reside, but out of context and with little true appreciation: "it is the present fashion to speak with veneration of old English literature" (1931: 179). A better understanding of them, and their many brilliant contemporaries, is hampered by the ahistorical preoccupation with intellectual progress, which assumes contemporary rules and human nature to be universal and looks down on "Gothic darkness" and the "rudeness and barbarism" of the past. Their memory has been displaced by undue preoccupation with classical antiquity (1931: 177–180).

The qualities Hazlitt ascribes to this writing, and to the genius of their writers, chime with the notion of original, culturally specific genius put forward in *Von deutscher Art und Kunst*: "no tinsel and but little art; they were not the spoilt children of affectation and refinement, but a bold, vigorous, independent race of thinkers with prodigious strength and energy, with none but natural grace and heartfelt unobtrusive delicacy", they were original geniuses, who "did not lay aside the strong original bent and character of their minds" (1931: 175), which is important because "the first impulse of genius is to create what never existed before" (1931: 187). Not just current refinement, but also wrong-headed learning makes their appreciation difficult these days: "the very nature of our academic institutions, which unavoidably neutralizes a taste for the productions of native genius, estranges the mind from the history of our own literature" (1931: 179).

Hazlitt displays a historical sense that is close to Herder's and Blackwell's: the writer and their surrounding cultural and political context condition each other, brilliant poets are not exceptions that somehow measure up to the criteria of later – advanced – ages, but they are part and parcel of their time (1931: 179). Although Hazlitt's historicism was not quite as thorough-going as it sounds here, he was convinced that the Elizabethan context was favourable to strong, vigorous thought and highly expressive poetry. He may indeed have gleaned all this from Blackwell and Hurd, but what the latter two lacked, and what the *Stürmer* and *Dränger* had, and which clearly appealed to Hazlitt, was that urge for iconoclastic liberation from a "superannuated" restrictive authority, which Hazlitt, like them, conceived of as "foreign". Hazlitt speaks of "native genius" and "our own literature" in a similar way as Herder praises literature that is created "in accordance with its own history, its spirit of the age, according to manners, opinions, language, national prejudices, traditions" in his Shakespeare-Essay (Herder 1988: 75).[57]

---

[57] "nach seiner Geschichte, nach Zeitgeist, nach Sitten, Meinungen, Sprache, Nationalvorurtheilen, Traditionen". At the same time, Hazlitt is scathing in his assessment of the current

It is this historical approach that made Hazlitt receptive to the idea of a complex, dynamic spirit of the age, a longer-term diachronic spirit of national tradition, and a long-term diachronic spirit of history, all of which he presents in these lectures. The spirit of history appears in the last lecture as a compressed survey of the history of literary productions from the ancients, via medieval literature and neo-classicism to the "paradoxical" Germans, the other two emerge in the first and last lectures: in the Elizabethan Age and in German literature. The Elizabethan Age has its own spirit and is at the same time the foundational period of English literature. Its particular spirit animated and made possible the poetic, philosophical, and dramatic brilliance of the time of Shakespeare. (All) Elizabethan writers and their work "bore the same general stamp", it "had the mark of their age and country [...]. Perhaps the genius of Great Britain". He devotes several pages to analysing the historical "causes" of this particular context, and finds them, firstly, in the Reformation, which produced the first Enlightenment, by getting all Christians to think and instigating a mood of general enquiry and openness for even foreign ideas, secondly, in the discovery of the New World, whose exotic and novel geographies inspired the poetic mind, and thirdly, in the culture of chivalry, not yet extinct, which provided a "martial and heroic" storehouse for the poetic imagination (1931: 186–189). He could indeed have found much of these details in mid-eighteenth-century British writing, in Hume, Hurd, or Percy, but the clear sense of the historicity of culture he would have found succinctly presented in A. W. Schlegel's lectures. Lastly, he concludes that the "unity and common direction of all these causes was the natural genius of the country" (1931: 191). Hazlitt focuses quite explicitly on the connection between the "age" and the "people" ("mark of their age and country"), on the link between the spirit of the age and the spirit of the people, common from Barclay to Herder. While I have not found any reference to Hazlitt being aware of Barclay,[58] he would have found the same ideas in Bacon's *Advancement of Learning*, which he

---

German literary scene and the impact of its intellectual activities in Britain: German Goethe worship is "idolatry" (but this is the dull Goethe, whose plays "avoid all possible effect and interest") and he ridicules "those among ourselves who import heavy German criticism [...] in shallow flat-bottomed unwieldy intellects" (1931: 363).

58 It is, however, not implausible that he was, bearing in mind his interest in writers of Shakespeare's time and the fact that Thomas May's translation, *The Mirrour of Mindes*, although not reprinted since its second run in 1633 was, judging by the large numbers extant of both print runs, not rare.

discusses – "[it] is his greatest work" (1931: 328) – along with his reverence for Bacon in Lecture 7 (1931: 326–333).[59]

Hazlitt did not only define the spirit of the age historically, for a past present such as the Elizabethan period, he was also keenly interested in his own time. A permeating contemporary spirit, brought about by a combination of historical circumstances and the human reaction to them, was summarised in contemporary cultural products (drama) and intensified by their staging. The current spirit was summarised in German literature; the German plays spoke to their British audience because they embodied the spirit of the age, which was located in "floating opinions" that were held by a collective "public mind", i.e. that common understanding of the world, making sense of the contemporary conditions.

> There is something in the style [of these plays] that hits the temper of men's minds; that if it does not hold the mirrour up to nature, yet "shews the very age and body of the time its form and pressure". It embodies, it sets off and aggrandizes in all the pomp of action, in all the vehemence of hyperbolical declamation, in scenery, in dress, in music, in the glare of the senses, and the glow of sympathy, the extreme opinions which are floating in our time, and which have struck their roots deep and wide below the surface of the public mind. (1931: 360)

And Hazlitt tells his listeners what these opinions are: political and moral revolution and contestation.

> We are no longer as formerly heroes in warlike enterprise; martyrs to religious faith; but we are all partisans of a political system, and devotees to some theories of moral sentiments. The modern style of tragedy is not assuredly made up of pompous common-place, but it is a tissue of philosophical, political, and moral paradoxes. I am not saying whether these paradoxes are true or false: all that I mean to state is, that they are utterly at variance with old opinions, with established rules and existing institutions; that it is this tug of war between the inert prejudice and startling novelty which is to batter it down (first on the stage of the theatre, and afterwards on the stage of the world) that gives the excitement and the zest. We see the natural always pitted against the social man. (1931: 360)

He takes the proof for his assessment of the "times" as much from the popularity of these plays, from their public acceptance, as from their content: "such extravagant and prodigious paradoxes would be driven from the stage – would meet with sympathy in no human breast, high or low, young or old" (1931: 361) if they did

---

[59] Although he focuses here on Bacon's insights into the sweep and connectivity of historical development, in which "letters" "as ships, pass through the sea of time and make ages so distant to participate of the wisdom, illumination, and inventions the other of the one" (1931: 333).

not correspond to what was going on, "we feel this and we do justice to the romantic extravagance of the German Muse" (1931: 361–362). Hazlitt identifies the key tendency of the age as contestation, a "tug of war" between tradition and innovation. As we shall see in a closer reading of his *Spirit of the Age*, for Hazlitt this contestation was the mark of the contest of public opinion in the public sphere and in this respect "structurally" related to the emergence and maintenance of a spirit of the age.

While the term "paradoxical", a favourite of Hazlitt's, can – negatively – refer to an excess of abstraction and wilful contradictoriness,[60] in German drama this quality was not (entirely) toxic, although the key characteristics are the same: socially somewhat irresponsible flights of fancy and abstraction in thought and language, which are exciting because they are extraordinary and, more importantly, relatable because they represent a currently common state of mind.

> The German tragedy (and our own which is only a branch of it) aims at effect [...] and does this by going all the lengths not only of instinctive feeling but of speculative opinion, and startling the hearer by overturning all the established maxims of society. [...] It is the violation of decorum. [...] The action is [...] extravagant: the fable [...] improbable, [...] the language is a mixture of metaphysical jargon and flaring prose: the moral is immorality. In spite of all this: a German tragedy is a good thing. It is a fine hallucination: it is a noble madness. [...] they [the audience] have their eyes wide open all the time and almost cry them out before they come away, and therefore they go again. There is something in the style that hits the temper of men's minds. (1931: 360)

While there is a hefty layer of irony in Hazlitt's suggestion that German tragedy is good because, outrageous as it is, it sells ("they go again"), like a sensationalist tabloid headline, he quickly shifts into a more serious gear when he asserts that people are responding to something that they sense themselves, or that is preoccupying them: it "hits [their] temper".

Hazlitt had applied his historically contextual approach the year before to the contemporary literary scene. In his *Lectures on the English Poets* (held and

---

[60] In *Table Talk* (1821–1822) he devotes an essay to the difference between "Paradox and Common-Place", two terms he uses in the passages quoted above, which represent the two poles of the current public intellectual and political landscape. "Common-place" represents the conservative aversion to change and reform, holding on to received tradition for the sake of it or for preserving current power structures, while "paradox" represents the highly abstract and extravagant, and often irresponsible, schemes of theoretical reformers, frequently "poets". Paradox may also be the vanity-driven preoccupation of the narcissistic poser who seeks "singularity" for the sake of effect. The latter is represented, for Hazlitt, by P. B. Shelley, the former by George Canning. Both extremes poison the public sphere and public debate, thus hampering social progress and reform.

published in 1818) he identified the origins of Romantic literature in general, and English Romantic literature in particular, as the French Revolution and German literary influence. "This school of poetry [the Lake school of poetry] had its origin in the French revolution, or rather in those sentiments and opinions which produced that revolution; and which sentiments were indirectly imported into this country in translations from the German about that period." (Hazlitt 1910: 161) The nature and effect of this poetry was the same as those of the "German Muse" above. "From the impulse it thus received, it rose at once from the most servile and tamest common-place, to the utmost pitch of singularity and paradox." (1910: 161) If one adds the "speculative opinion" and "metaphysical jargon" from the above passage to the French Revolution and German literary influence, Hazlitt is not far off Friedrich Schlegel's 1798 pronouncement on the tendencies of the present age in *Athenaeum Fragment* 216, a more famous definition of the causes of Romanticism.[61] Ironically, this is also not far removed from the conservative assessment of what was wrong with the times: sedition and excesses of political and cultural extremism.

This is the background to the *Spirit of the Age or Contemporary Portraits*, the title Hazlitt gave to the collection of his pen-portraits of public figures, the first version of which was published in January 1825. Originally these essay portraits were not conceived to make a book, many of them had appeared individually in a variety of journals between 1821 and 1824.[62] A selection of them – Bentham, Irving, Horne Tooke, Scott, and Lord Eldon – had been part of a loose series of numbered "Spirits of the Age" published in the *New Monthly Magazine* between January and July 1824. These dates suggest that Hazlitt was thinking about characterising "spirits" or a resulting general "spirit of the age" at the time when he was closely involved with the *London Magazine*. In fact, the earliest portrait of the collection (Crabbe), appeared *in* the *London Magazine* in May 1821 – where the talk may well have been of zeitgeist. That the term was attention-grabbing is indicated by the fact that immediately following on from the last of Hazlitt's "Spirits of the Age", the newly founded *John Bull Magazine* launched a series entitled "Humbugs of the Age",

---

[61] "Die Französische Revolution, Fichtes *Wissenschaftslehre*, und Goethes *Meister* sind die größten Tendenzen des Zeitalters." [The French Revolution, Fichte's *Science of Knowledge* and Goethe's *Meister* are the greatest tendencies of the present age.] (Schlegel 1967: 198)

[62] *Crabbe* in May 1821 in the *London Magazine*; *Cobbett*, added in the May 1825 edition, had appeared in *Table Talk* in 1821, *Canning*, also added in the same edition, in *The Examiner* in July 1824. Those that had not appeared anywhere else before were written in the course of 1824, according to Herschel Baker, *William Hazlitt* (1962), quoted by Mackerness (Hazlitt 1969: 9).

lampooning public figures, starting with Thomas de Quincey. This series ran from July to October 1824.[63]

It is likely that there was a commercial motive for the *Spirit of the Age*, too, not just for Hazlitt but also for his publisher. The book-version was published by Henry Colburn, a highly successful publishing entrepreneur with an eye for developing trends, who was also the editor and proprietor of the *New Monthly Magazine*. The idea clearly had some currency, since John Taylor, editor of the *London Magazine*, had been hatching a similar idea for some time. Carlyle reported to his bride Jane in a letter dated 4 March 1823 that his portrait of Schiller was to be the first of "a kind of picture gallery of great literary men" which "Taylor of the London Magazine" was interested in publishing (Carlyle 1970: II, 300).

This interest in representative public figures suggests not just a focus on "great men", with which zeitgeist is sometimes associated as these individuals are styled to define a period, but equally a conscious or unconscious recognition of the powerful role public (intellectual) elites play in the creation of public opinion and the spirit of the age. While Herder and Hendrich had recognised their power, Arndt had attempted to present this power in greater detail. Although Arndt had characterised these elites conceptually as groups, and did not deal with individuals, his groups of "writing" intellectuals also come across as a "gallery". Hazlitt presents *only* such a gallery, in which both the nature of the age and the social dynamics that make it so unfold before the reader, without giving the reader much "guidance" on how to distil the spirit of the age.[64]

The line-up of individuals Hazlitt included in his gallery, and their order of appearance, were unstable. Of the three editions which appeared in 1825 – two in London in January and December and one in Paris in May – each was different.[65] It is difficult to reconstruct the *exact* reasons for the changes Hazlitt

---

[63] "The Humbugs of the Age No. 1 The Opium Eater", pp. 21–24; "No. 2 Dr Kitchener", pp. 52–55; "No. 3 Sir Humphrey Davy", pp. 89–92; "No. 4 Bishop the composer", pp. 140–143 (*John Bull Magazine* 1824).

[64] The portraits are presented without general introduction or para-textual material that might suggest how they relate to the title of the book, apart from a motto prominently displayed on the title page. "To know another well were to know one's self well" suggests there are indissoluble inter-relations between the identities of individuals, that self-knowledge can only be derived from knowing one's fellows. This in turn suggests that identity is not (fully) innate but constructed by context. The phrase plays on Hamlet's lines in act 5 (William Shakespeare, *Hamlet*, V, 2, ll. 139–140: "To know a man well were to know himself"). It alludes to the Socratian "Know thyself" and picks up from "No man is an island."

[65] *Cobbett* was added in the second British edition and the text of *Coleridge* was amended; *Canning* and the section on Sheridan Knowles only appeared in the Paris edition until the 1858

made, but it seems likely that they were a mixture of the topical and personal. Duncan Wu observed that "some of the alterations were made in response to criticisms of the first edition" and concluded that "the peculiar way in which this work evolved was determined at least in part by its hostile reception" (Hazlitt 1998: VII, xxii). It appears that the shifting nature of the collection is in itself an aspect of the ephemeral nature of the "spirit of the age". The portraits are expendable elements in evolving situations, rather like Arndt "wanderndes Bild der Zeit" and Hare's *Guesses*.

The list of individuals portrayed in his collection is disparate in every respect, in political orientation, individual motivation, and public aims. It includes poets (Wordsworth, Byron, Southey, Scott, Thomas Campbell, Thomas Moore), a poet-philosopher (Coleridge), philosophers (Jeremy Bentham, William Godwin), writer-journalists (Francis Jeffrey, John Gifford, William Cobbett, Leigh Hunt, Charles Lamb/Elia, Washington Irvine/Geoffrey Crayon), writer-politicians (Horne Tooke, Henry Brougham, William Wilberforce, Francis Burdett), politicians (Lord Eldon, George Canning), a writer-civil servant (James Mackintosh), a political economist (Thomas Malthus), and a popular Scottish Calvinist preacher (Edward Irving). Some of them, although they are no politicians, are committed political partisans (Gifford, Cobbett, Hunt, Burdett). What they all share, apart from being male, is that they have all "published", i.e. contributed directly to public debate. This is also true of Arndt's gallery of professional intellectuals, who, as groups, are equally male, "public" and "publishing".

Much in Hazlitt's characterisations pivots on the "public-ness" of his subjects, he devotes considerable attention to how they are perceived and regarded by others, i.e. by other public and/or powerful figures and by the public in general. This public standing directly affects their impact, and their chances of achieving any public or personal aim. Clearly, for him, a large part of their importance rests on this. His interest focuses as much on what they are *taken* to represent within the contemporary context of publicity as on what they themselves *intend* to represent, let alone on what they may really be like. This focus shifts the emphasis away from the individual, their (original) genius, or exceptionality, and makes them subject to collective public forces. It is this public aspect which most clearly relates to the "spirit of the age", pinpointing the inter-relation between a (public) individual's intentions and endeavour and

---

edition of the book (Hazlitt 1969: 11). The rather incendiary essay on Canning was frequently not included in later editions, for example not in the high-volume Everyman edition of 1910. For a full account of the textual history see Hazlitt 1998: VII, xx-xxiii.

their success, which in a reasonably free public sphere is determined by the public mood.

In many cases Hazlitt spells out that an individual's standing in public opinion is their key relation to the "spirit of the age". For example, Byron and Scott "are among the writers now living the two who would carry away *the majority of suffrages* as the greatest geniuses of the age" (Hazlitt 1910: 235, italics mine). In the case of Godwin, "the Spirit of the Age was never more fully shown than in its *treatment* of this writer – its love of paradox and change, its dastard submission to prejudice and to the fashion of the day" (1910: 182, italics mine). Hazlitt charts Godwin's changing fortunes from being the toast of the early 1790s liberal mood to becoming, by the end of the decade, a "Jacobin" under heavy surveillance, whose works are bywords for radicalism.

Malthus' "name undoubtedly stands very high in the present age" (1910: 269) because his work is useful (or reassuring) to those who wish to maintain the social and political status quo. Hazlitt's analysis of Malthus' famous *Essay on Population* focuses on the political exploitation of its key tenet – population growth is limited by the available resources of sustenance – which, according to Hazlitt, is not just a truism, but also plagiarised (1910: 273). This simple fact is useful for discrediting the project of human perfectibility and abrogating any social and moral responsibility, and with it any need for social and political reform. It supports the views of

> persons whose ignorance, whose fears, whose pride, whose prejudices contemplated such an alternative [a better and fairer world] with horror; and who would naturally feel no small obligation to the man who should relieve their apprehensions from the stunning roar of this mighty change of opinion that thundered at a distance, and should be able by some logical apparatus or unexpected turn of argument to prevent the vessel of state being [...] dashed to pieces down the tremendous precipice of human perfectibility. (1910: 272)

Hazlitt makes clear that in the public sphere publications relate to each other competitively, not just in a commercial but also in a power-political sense. Malthus' *Essay on Population*, and any public approbation of it, appears in relation to Godwin's *Political Justice* and its acclaim, "Mr. Malthus's first octavo volume (published in the year 1798) was intended as an answer to Mr. Godwin's *Enquiry concerning Political Justice*. [...] It was what in the language of the ring is called a *facer*." (1910: 271, italics in original) Godwin's book had "allured the gaze and tempt[ed] the aspiring thoughts of philanthropists and philosophers" and there was perceived a "danger that the proud monuments of time-hallowed institutions, that the strong-holds of power and corruption [...] might be overthrown and swept away" (1910: 271–272), which Malthus' *Essay* has prevented, "he

[Malthus] has not left opinion where he found it" (1910: 270). Likewise, the setting up of the conservative *Quarterly Review* occurred in response to the well-received liberal tendencies of *Edinburgh Review*. "The *Quarterly Review* arose out of the *Edinburgh*, not as a corollary, but in contradiction to it" because the *Edinburgh Review* "had stung the Tories to the quick [...] and something must be done to check these *escapades*" (1910: 292, italics in original).[66] Both publications are represented by their editors, Francis Jeffrey and John Gifford.

Similarly, *individuals* act competitively and contextually within the public sphere, adjusting their public actions to social power relations. Hazlitt reiterates the familiar diagnosis that servility to political power is particularly rife when there is no public spirit.

> The personal always prevails over the intellectual, where the latter is not backed by strong feeling and principle. [...] Where the public good or distant consequences excite no sympathy in the breast, [...] self-interest, indolence, the opinion of others, a desire to please, the sense of personal obligation, come in and fill the void of public spirit, patriotism, and humanity. (1910: 311)

This mitigates any chance of moral or political integrity. Servility becomes a (successful) career in its own right. Lord Eldon's

> only fault is that he cannot say Nay to power, or subject himself to an unkind word or look from a King or Minister. [...] His servility has assumed an air of the most determined independence, [...]. There has been no stretch of power attempted in his time that he has not seconded. (1910: 311)

Hazlitt presents those that adjust their decisions and public acts, including publications, to such power relations as the play-things of the powerful, "they claim the privileges of court favourites" (1910: 290). The *Quarterly Review* and its editor William Gifford are responsible for perpetuating "servility" in the public sphere, they "explode every principle of Liberty, laugh patriotism and public spirit to scorn [...] and strike at the root of all free enquiry and discussion by running down every writer as a vile scribbler and a bad member of society, who is not a hireling or a slave" (1910: 290).

Public standing, if it is not determined by constellations of political power, is conditioned by public acclaim, "popularity", which is the result of feeding a specific popular appetite, and not necessarily an indication of quality. Popularity is "almost unprecedented" in the case of the Reverend

---

[66] The *Edinburgh Review* was founded in 1802, the *Quarterly Review* in 1809.

Edward Irving, or of George Crabbe, who "is one of the most popular and admired of our living authors" (1910: 330), despite being "a repulsive writer", who "turns diseases into commodities" (1910: 331), while Thomas Moore satisfies "the craving of the public mind after novelty and effect" (1910: 336). Under this rule of naked power, censorship (self-imposed or otherwise), venal crowd-pleasing opportunists, and the selfish thrive, and those who do not pursue self-serving agendas, politically or commercially, remain in the minority (1910: 307).

Hazlitt's key concerns – paradox, extravagance, startling novelty – which he identified as characteristic of the current age in his *Lectures on the English Poets* and on the *Age of Elizabeth* reappear here. This take on public "success" links up with Hazlitt's concern for the unreliability of appearances, which he had identified as a key aspect of the age in the lecture on German drama.

> The world and every thing in it is not just what it ought to be, or what it pretends to be; or such extravagant and prodigious paradoxes would be driven from the stage [...] Opinion is not truth; appearance is not reality, power is not beneficence: rank is not wisdom: nobility is not the only virtue: riches are not happiness: desert and success are different things: actions do not always speak the character any more than words. (1931: 361–362)

As with the German zeitgeist researchers, his critique of the age and his investigation of the dynamics of its spirit overlap; Hazlitt weaves both into the crafting of his essays and his collection.

Hazlitt also discusses individuals' *actual* representativeness of the age – which is probably what most readers were expecting when looking for a definition or description of the spirit of the age. Only Wordsworth and the *Edinburgh Review* seem to encapsulate it with any claim to comprehensiveness: "Mr. Wordsworth's genius is a pure emanation of the spirit of the age" (1910: 252) and the *Edinburgh Review*'s criticism in political and cultural fields (in the shape of Francis Jeffrey) is "eminently characteristic of the Spirit of the Age" (1910: 293). With some of his subjects Hazlitt spells out that they embody defining excellence in specific aspects of contemporary activities. For example, Coleridge is, on the one hand, "the most impressive talker of his age" (1910: 196) in "the present [...] age of talkers" (1910: 194), which is on the other hand not affected by the fact that he has "a mind reflecting ages past" (1910: 195).[67]

---

[67] Walter Scott is "the most popular writer of the age" (1910: 223), and James Mackintosh "one of the ablest and most accomplished men of the age" (1910: 261), while Horne Tooke "links between a former period and the existing generation" (1910: 213) because he is "the finished gentleman of the last age" (1910: 214).

Indeed, the "paradoxical", Hazlitt's term for describing the key quality of the cultural and intellectual scene around him, is never far from the surface. The fact that people whose opinions and convictions are as far apart as Godwin's and Malthus' are both presented as part of the "spirit of the age" led contemporary reviewers, as well as later critics, to wonder whether Hazlitt actually managed, or intended, to describe something like a coherent general spirit. The reviewer of the *Monthly Critical Gazette* was looking for a clearer exposition of this "spirit", which he did not find, concluding, uncertainly, that "title and content are a variance – perhaps" (Hazlitt 1998: VII, xv). The reviewer of the *Monthly Review* came away bewildered: "Everything shines as through a prismatic medium. The result is, that we retain nothing distinctly of what he says. It is a sort of confused memory of sounds, like the clashing of musical instruments." (Chandler 1998: 184) A similar tension as between Godwin and Malthus exists between the two representatives of the spirit of the age, Wordsworth and Jeffrey. James Chandler pointed out that "Hazlitt's portrait of Jeffrey suggests, if one were to single out one antagonist more insistent in his opposition to Wordsworth than any other, it would surely be Jeffrey" (1998: 179). Hazlitt uses juxtaposition as a deliberate strategy, frequently pairing two individuals, always in some respect opposed to each other, either within one essay, by references between two essays, or through the essays' positioning. Again, the description of the characteristics of the age and the dynamics of its "spirit" overlap, both are defined by contestation, something Hazlitt had summed up in late 1823: the "spirit of the age (that is, the progress of intellectual refinement warring with our natural infirmities)".[68]

Many noticed the predictable bias Hazlitt brought to his characterisations, or character assassinations. The *Gentleman's Magazine* complained of Hazlitt's extreme political partisanship, the "mists of prejudice and passion" (Hazlitt 1998: VII, xxv-xxvi). And unsurprisingly, much of the contemporary critical reaction to *Spirit of the Age* divided along political lines, with all sides complaining about the unproductive party-spirit of the opposition. The greatest vituperation came, predictably, from the conservative *Blackwood's*.[69] The liberal publications were, again predictably, generally favourable (Grayling 2000: 313 and Hazlitt 1998: VII, xxv). The *Examiner*'s editor Albany Fonblanque did not miss the opportunity to denounce in the book's detractors as evincing "the

---

[68] "On the Pleasure of Hating" (Hazlitt 1931: XII, 127–136), published in the *Plain Speaker* collection in 1826, i.e. *after* the publication of *The Spirit of the Age*, but according to Howe written in November-December 1823 at Winterslow (Hazlitt 1931: XII, 400). See also Hazlitt 1998: VIII, 119.
[69] Focusing on Hazlitt's controversial attacks, John Lockhart's review implies that Hazlitt is an envious, "vulgar, low born hack" (Hazlitt 1998: VII, xxv-xxvi).

miserable enmity of mere party, political, literary or bookselling" (Hazlitt 1998: VII, xxv). In this respect, some contemporary reviewers identified the volume itself as a sign of the times, focusing on aspects that Hazlitt himself criticises, not just the vituperative party-spirit, but also the unreliability of current publicity. Thus, in February 1825 the (perhaps rather discerning) reviewer of the *Monthly Critical Gazette* complained of

> the same vicious tone which has characterized many public writings during the last seven years [...] we are pestered at every turn with animadversions written by Mr Campbell about Mr Lambe; by Mr Lambe about Mr Campbell; by Mr Jeffrey about Mr Gifford; and by Mr Gifford about Mr Jeffrey: [...] the same ball is bandied about by [...] these egotists. [...] Which of these egotists wrote the present volume, or whether each one contributed the article about himself, or one for the other, can only be known to the printer or editor. (Hazlitt 1998: VII, xxvii)

So according to *reviewers*, Hazlitt's book had features similar to those identified in reviews of Arndt's *Geist der Zeit* I: dealing with the "spirit of the times" and exhibiting its faults. Evidently the book was read, not unlike the individual essays when they were published separately, as a series of character descriptions that are loosely linked by the fact that the subjects were all – more or less – alive at the same time. And this determined much of the reaction to the text(s): agreement, or disagreement, with the assessment of the *individuals*, or approval or disapproval of Hazlitt.[70]

In his own review of *Spirit of the Age* Francis Jeffrey mixes praise and condemnation, and no doubt also reacts to his own portrait. After calling Hazlitt's writing "often powerful" and his ideas "generally original", he remarks that "a perpetual hunting after originality, and a determination to say every thing in a strange manner, lead him to paradox, error and extravagance, and give a tinge of self-sufficiency" (Jeffrey 1825). In this, Jeffrey too identifies Hazlitt's book as representative of the current age (and its faults) and refers, probably *not* inadvertently, back to Hazlitt's own pronouncements on the reasons for the popularity of German drama at present, their "paradoxical" nature.[71] But what Jeffrey sees as a failing can equally be interpreted as a refusal to consolidate complexity into easy coherence.

Much of this was no doubt lost on the book's readers, as we saw above. So was the "spirit of the age" simply "paradoxical", a disparate assembly of

---

[70] For a more complete overview of the initial reviews, see Hazlitt 1998: VII, xxiv-xxx.
[71] Hazlitt was not happy with this aspect of Jeffrey's verdict; in fact, he was so stung by this review that he composed a satirical poem about it (Grayling 2000: 315).

disagreements? James Chandler pointed out that "the irreducible multiplicity of representatives and representations of the spirit of the age in Hazlitt's great volume of 1825 aims precisely to refuse, or at least diffuse such an epitome and such a resolution" (1998: 185). He suggests that Hazlitt's book amounts to almost a debunking of the whole concept of the "spirit of the age".

> Reviewing the array of conflicting aspects and figures in Hazlitt's text, then, one might say that, if Hazlitt's own positing of the spirit of the age brings the operative contradictions to notice, then the contradictions in turn have implications for how "the spirit of the age" functions in the discourse of British Romantic [...] historicism. That is [...] that it bespeaks an "overdetermined" causality. [...] [*The Spirit of the Age*] might be taken to suggest that the contradictions of the new notion of culture under the aegis of the spirit of the age – culture as defined in the chronologically coded domestic manners of uneven social development – are not so easily contained. (1998: 183 and 185)

For Chandler, Hazlitt's achievement is pointing out that the spirit of the age, if it exists at all, cannot be reduced to one simple contradiction, because an age emerges from a multiplicity of historically contingent aspects. While it is patently true that Hazlitt presents a multiplicity of contradictions in terms of individual situation, motivation, and intention, which all interact directly and indirectly, I would argue that this multiplicity *does* turn on one basic contradiction, which is presented in action in multiple ways and from different angles. It is, unsurprisingly, the clash between "revolution" and the assertion of "liberty" on one side and the reactionary forces who wish to preserve the old order on the other. Hazlitt repeatedly identifies the (new) spirit as revolutionary, as demanding political and social reform, as "levelling". Going back to his pronouncements in *Lectures on the English Poets*, it is the spirit of the French Revolution, which is impeded by those who feel they have much to lose: the party of "Legitimacy" and its government. This clash produces a "warring" on different levels: political, personal, and intellectual. Every public individual – or those aspiring to be public figures – takes up position within this strife at their own risk, risking their personal integrity, their public reputation, their livelihoods, but equally standing to gain wealth, fame, or power. What is left undecided in the volume, left as slippage, is the question whether Hazlitt primarily focuses of the clash of ideas (revolution vs. Legitimacy) or on the war of public contestation, how power structures and new ideas interact in the public sphere by battling over control of public opinion. Again, he focuses on the "content" of the spirit and its dynamics at the same time.

> The spirit of the monarchy was at variance with the spirit of the age. The flame of liberty, the light of intellect, was to be extinguished with the sword – or with slander [...]. The war between power and reason was carried on by the first of these abroad, by the last at home. No quarter was given (then or now) by the Government-critics, the authorised censors of the press, to those who followed the dictates of independence. (1910: 203)

In the link between the content of spirit (battle between demands for popular enfranchisement and public accountability vs. ancien régime) and the way it expresses itself (contested public sphere) is the site of this slippage.

This slippage allows Hazlitt to describe how the public sphere works, it allows him to occupy a meta-position, while at the same time being able to take up a position within the public arguments and voice his acerbic criticisms of people and conditions. The slippage allows him to be critical of selfishness and party spirit – the root of the loss of public spirit – and be (fiercely) partisan himself. In this also rests Hazlitt's Romanticism, he may be cynical, but he is not without ideals: selfish self-interest destroys public spirit and the public good, which his criticism, ridicule, and savaging is designed to counteract.[72]

In his pursuit of rescuing the public good, Hazlitt critiques not just the corrupt elite of "Legitimacy", "Hierarchy" and "Monarchy" and their lackies, but equally the wrong-headed reformers, such as Godwin and Bentham. Both Godwin and Bentham on the one hand and the government on the other promote forms of mechanistic oppression, lacking both in public spirit and humanity. The way Godwin has been treated by the ruling elite is evidence of selfish oppression, but Godwin's and Bentham's theories, progressive as they are socially, themselves represent forms of rational despotism. In Godwin "Man was indeed screwed up, by mood and figure, into a logical machine, that was to forward the public good with utmost punctuality and effect" (1910: 186). Bentham "reduc[es] law to a system, and the mind of man to a machine" (1910: 172). Over-rationality neglects, even destroys, the individually concrete, the historically contingent. These are familiar Romantic concerns: over-powerful systems reduce life to abstractions and turn the human being, and the state, into

---

[72] While Hazlitt criticised the utter predictability of reactions to political statements from politically committed entities, his own approbation was granted largely on political lines, too. Those that oppose political reform are propping up an unaccountable and unjust elite; even worse are those that do so after a "conversion" from more liberal thinking (Southey, Mackintosh, and to some extent Wordsworth and Coleridge), but the worst of all are those that do so for personal gain within a system which only by accident allows them to benefit from favours of the unaccountable elite (Moore and Gifford). But reformers whom Hazlitt considers useless because they are ineffective are no good either (Cobbett).

"machines". They were common Romantic criticisms of the contemporary state, also voiced by Arndt (or Brandes). For Hazlitt, *both* forms of oppression neglect the concreteness of historical and human contingency. This deficiency makes both types inhuman and devoid of sympathy or public spirit, creating a public sphere that is shallow, venal, but inescapably controlling. Hazlitt illustrates this through the fate of (poetic) genius which had originally supported a new progressive liberalism, but was now cowed into acquiescence. "There is no other age or country of the world (but ours), in which such genius could have been so degraded." (1910: 234)[73]

Despite his awareness of historical and individual contingency, history has a clear tendency for Hazlitt: towards political and social change, towards Liberty, which is evinced by the revolution in France. But in his experience the success of this tendency depends on the outcome of the public contests over public opinion, which make, un-make, and re-make the spirit of the age. This is most evident in Hazlitt's discussion of the two best – but fragile – hopes for the tendency of history: Wordsworth and Francis Jeffrey, the two best representatives of the progressive spirit of the age. Due to individual contingency, they do not work together: Jeffrey did not recognise the importance of the *Lyrical Ballads*. Wordsworth, "whose writings could the least be spared: for they have no substitute elsewhere" (1910: 255), has become disgruntled and difficult by the slow pace of public recognition (1910: 260–261). Mr. Jeffrey, although "perfectly fitted [...] from knowledge and habits of mind to put a curb on [the] rash and headlong spirit [of the age]", is not forceful or partisan enough when it comes to exposing the dangers of corrupt elites. "Where there is so much power and prejudice to contend with in the opposite scale, it may be thought that the balance of truth can hardly be held with a slack or an even hand; and that the infusion of a little more visionary speculation, of a little more popular indignation into the great Whig Review would be

---

[73] "Genius stood in the way of Legitimacy, and therefore was to be abated, crushed, or set aside as a nuisance." (1910: 203) So "Mr. Coleridge sounded a retreat for them [...] who turned back disgusted and panic-struck from the dry desert of unpopularity" (1910: 204). Scott debases himself, "prop[ping] up the throne by nicknames, and the altar by lies", and "being [...] the finest, the most humane and accomplished writer of his age, associated himself with [...] the lowest panders of a venal press". "Having secured the admiration of the public, [...] [he] showed no respect for that genius that had raised him to distinction". Byron "has prostituted his talents" like no other (1910: 241). He "panders to the spirit of the age, goes to the very edge of extreme licentious speculation. [...] His Lordship's poetry consists mostly of a tissue of superb common-places; even his paradoxes are *common-place*." (1910: 242) This is because "the poets, the creatures of Sympathy could not stand the frowns both of king and people." (1910: 203).

an advantage both to itself and to the cause of freedom." (1910: 296) The shifting, hybrid, unresolved complexity of Hazlitt's writing is made possible by his pervasive use of (Romantic) irony. The ironic depth of his prose invites the reader to think and question, as the un-introduced collection and seemingly random positioning of the portraits invite the readers to make their own inferences and draw their own conclusions.

James Chandler makes a distinction between British Romantic historicism, which includes Hazlitt's approach, and the Hegelian sort, which relies on the existence of one underlying contradiction for its dialectical engine (Chandler 1998: 183–184). The manifold complexities Hazlitt presents are indeed different from simple antagonistic opposites, and there is little evidence in Hazlitt of Hegelian dialectics that aim, at least for a time, at the neutralisation of oppositional historical contradictions. But I would argue that Hegel in his *Lectures on the Philosophy of History*, which he was giving in Berlin at precisely the time that Hazlitt was writing his *Spirit of the Age*-essays in London, was grappling in his "systematic" ruminations on how ideas arise, clash, dominate, and are vanquished by new ones with the same question: how do ideas and human political and cultural activity interact with each other, and how do ideas and people (not necessarily peoples) relate to each other. Hegel's intellectual trajectory – German Idealism – was different from Hazlitt's "British Romanticism", but both describe the interaction between intellectual, political, and cultural activities as a process of "warring", of vying for dominance, of contestation. One wonders whether Hazlitt did not see this "warring" as the irreducible – essential – signature of progress, and its difficulty.

Two recurring themes run through Hazlitt's book, both intricately related to the idea of zeitgeist: the difficulty of a new idea to gain public and general acceptance in the face of resistant power structures and the malleability and power of public representation. Public images respond to the shifting instability of public opinion, which in turn is determined by powers that (manage to) control the public sphere. In the concrete historical terms of Hazlitt's context, the new idea was the critique of political and partisan selfishness. Such selfishness was considered exploitative, destroying public spirit and making social and moral responsibility unlikely. It was dominant because current social and political conditions favoured both its individual and collective variants. In this respect, selfishness is not presented as an inalterable human trait (although it may be innate), but as a viable practice suggested by the "situation", its predominance is contextual, the context is maintained by (approving) public opinion, which is controlled by those with power over the public sphere. In this circular way an idea and a related practice achieve and retain such dominance as to appear as the spirit of the age. If the public sphere is not (fully) despotically controlled, however, a new idea may challenge the established notion(s) and practices and replace them. Hazlitt's "gallery" is a representation of this contest, a contest that the German zeitgeist investigators described almost a generation earlier. Hazlitt's *Spirit of the Age* presents zeitgeist in action.

By discussing "popularity" (or the lack of it), i.e. reception and judgement by public opinion, and the individual's own handling of them, Hazlitt explores the dynamics of the "spirit of the age" as a public force impacting on its contemporaries. He was doubtful, just like Herder, Hendrich, Garve or Brandes, as to whether public opinion was an entirely positive force, especially when it is linked to forms of fashion and gullibility. In this, he joined the ranks of the many detractors of public opinion, who tended to come from the conservative end or the centre ground of political orientation. Unlike the radicals of the 1790s, Forster and Thelwall, Hazlitt professed to have little trust in the salutary powers of the public. In *Spirit of the Age* he presents publicity as a pretending and projecting, something that is shifting, yet powerful and effective. Public opinion is not always discerning, Hazlitt frequently identifies it as liking mediocrity, not out of self-interest, but out of shallowness. Elites in power, on the other hand, tend to have self-serving motives and will attempt to neutralise anyone who harms their interests.

Hazlitt does not cease to publicly expose un-public-spirited practices, using publicity very effectively for his own political ends, which *he* sees as supporting the much neglected public good, as a decided social and political intervention. Grayling has pointed out that Hazlitt was a "political polemicist and journalist" (Grayling 2000: ix) and for Duncan Wu Hazlitt "fed the new industry [of mass media]" in a "most gifted, [...] most percipient" way, which made him the "most articulate spokesman" of his age (Wu 2008: xxii). Hazlitt used current practices (periodical journalism) to *redirect* current affairs by combining a meta-perspective of the situation with direct intervention, which is only possible if there is a sense of the "spirit of history" as well as an understanding of the dynamics of collective social forces, both combining to shape a spirit of the age. Hazlitt did not primarily use the diachronic dimension of zeitgeist to contain a scary present or smooth a radical message, he used it to be able to keep the party-politics he indulged in in perspective.

Hare did not approve of Hazlitt; the *Liber Amoris* scandal blackened him as a lecherous libertine, which only confirmed his political libertinism as a Jacobin. Yet in terms of their assessment of what was "wrong" with Britain in the early 1820s they agreed: short-sighted self-interest was reducing social structures to functional forms for profitable exploitation, either in terms of materials or of power. Hare also agreed with Hazlitt about the significance of Wordsworth, and the reasons for the telling lack of popularity of Wordsworth's poetry. And they agreed that this state of affairs could only be changed through public intervention: both had a clear sense of the importance of the public sphere and how it worked. But, and perhaps like Jeffrey and Wordsworth, they could not quite see their agreement, obscured by the contingency of individual circumstance.

5.5 Thomas Carlyle – the "Age of Mechanism" and the French Revolution

In 1829 Thomas Carlyle (1795–1881) produced a definition of the spirit of the age with a clarity that Hazlitt had eschewed – for Carlyle his was the "Age of Mechanism". This definition applied to the content of the prevailing spirit and the way it worked. Carlyle's certainty was in fact based on a clear sense of the way in which this spirit permeated all contemporary human activity, which is one of the reasons why there is less of a sense of contestation in Carlyle's analysis. His focus is on how the *dominant* notions exert *control*, rather than on how a new idea challenges an established set of notions (although he does get on to that). With a decisive catchword – mechanism – he provided what many reviewers of Hazlitt's *Spirit of the Age* felt was missing. The idea of the "mechanical" as a dominant trait of the age was not original: Hazlitt, Coleridge, and Hare pointed it out before Carlyle,[74] but in Carlyle's analysis the idea of the mechanical, which in Hazlitt, Coleridge, and Hare was an aspect of the prevailing selfishness and lack of public spirit, turns from being a result of the prevailing spirit into the essence of the spirit itself.

However, this difference should not obscure the shared ground on this topic between these very different writers, which is perhaps particularly telling because Hazlitt and Carlyle subscribed to very different philosophical and political creeds, while Hare and Carlyle *shared* a belief in the need for religiosity. This fundamental difference illustrates the non-homogenous, and to some

---

[74] As we have seen, Hazlitt used the term "mechanical" in a derogatory way to describe very similar "negatives" already in 1806 (Hazlitt 1930: 117–118). In 1816 Coleridge castigated the "mechanical understanding" in the *Statesman's Manual*, it does not grasp the "translucence" of the ideal in the real, or the universal in the particular (Coleridge 1852: 32–33), and Hare employed this term in similar contexts, although less prominently, in *Guesses* in 1827.

extent un-co-operative nature of this "group", who nevertheless agreed on key concerns, which qualifies these concerns as characteristic of a "general spirit".

Carlyle and Hazlitt both delineate the overlap between what they see as the essence of the age (self-serving party spirit, egotism) and the social processes that determine the currency of this essence through the power of public opinion. For both, public opinion tends to conflate popularity and fame with being right and good. They agree that the absence of public spirit is the key difficulty of the age; for Hazlitt the absence of public spirit is linked to political conditions, while Carlyle focuses on the spiritual renewal of the individual to achieve its return. Both, however, promote the rebirth of ethical principles in public life. Hazlitt and Carlyle did not meet, Carlyle was beginning his career as a writer in the last few years of Hazlitt's life, but Hazlitt was a reference point for Carlyle, as we shall see.

Carlyle made his entry onto the literary and critical scene as a "Germanist", as a member of the busy "Germanic faction", as *Blackwood's* quipped in 1824.[75] His first publications on German topics were his essays on "Schiller's Life and Writings", which appeared between October 1823 and September 1824 in John Taylor's *London Magazine*,[76] in which Hare had also published his early essays on German literature. In 1825 Taylor and Hessey brought out an extended version of them as Carlyle' first book, *The Life of Friedrich Schiller – Comprehending an examination of his works*, which further underlines the Germanophile tendency of this publisher.[77]

Although Carlyle spent time in London, and visited Taylor's offices, he disliked the place, referring to it as "Babylon" in his letters of the mid-1820s. Writing to Taylor in February 1824, in advance of his first visit, he expressed the hope "to see you and your monstrous city", fearing however that "the smoke and tumult and unutterable horrors of the place might affright me" (1970: III, 28). He also did not seem to make much contact with the "set" of the

---

[75] "Well, the German faction is getting on, this gentleman [John Russell, author of *A Tour in Germany* 1828] and young Carlysle [sic] – he who translated Meister – are two pretty additions to Kempferhausen's battalion. To be serious, North, we shall run some risk of inundation." ("Ambrosian Nights" August 1824: 242) The figure of Philipp Kempferhausen was one of the spoof personages John Wilson impersonated, just like "Christopher North", to whom the above remarks are addressed.

[76] *London Magazine*: VIII (October 1823), 381–400; IX (January 1824), 37–59; X (July, August-September 1824), 3 instalments of part 3, 16–24, 149–163, 259–269. His Goethe translation also appeared in 1824, with G. and W. Whittaker in London and Oliver & Boyd in Edinburgh.

[77] Carlyle's correspondence with both Taylor and John Hessey about extending these essays into a book are extant in his letters (29 July and 6 August 1824), (1970: III, 117–120); he went with Taylor and Hessey, not before also offering the Schiller volume to the Whittaker brothers who published his *Wilhelm Meister* translation (20 July 1824), (1970: III, 110).

London Magazine, which regularly gathered at Taylor's house and included Hare, Lamb, de Quincey, Hazlitt, Thomas Campbell,[78] and occasionally Coleridge, although he got close enough to observe some of them in the flesh.[79] What he reported to Thomas Murray in August 1824 is so amusingly disrespectful that it would not be out of place in Hazlitt's writing.[80] That he has little time for de Quincey after the latter's negative review of his *Wilhelm Meister*-translation (which was also published in the *London Magazine*) is not surprising; his annoyance vents itself in moral(istic) censure.[81] There was, it seems, a decided intention on Carlyle's part to keep away.

One of the reasons for his reluctance to get involved with "the Literary World of London", "this rascal rout, this dirty rabble, destitute not only of high feeling or knowledge or intellect, but even of common honesty" (1970: III, 234), seems to be Carlyle's disapproval of their dissolute lifestyles and what he presumes to be their attitudes. After longer inspection, Carlyle expressed, in November 1831, a decided aversion to the prevalent ironic – paradoxical? – and often outrageous wit, which in his view was controversial, antithetical, and after a quick laugh.

---

78 Campbell was another Germanophile, who had travelled in Germany in the early years of the nineteenth century and was now editing the *New Monthly Magazine*.

79 Carlyle's correspondence around this time makes clear that he was friendly enough with Henry Crabb Robinson, who was also loosely attached to this circle around Lamb, Hazlitt, Hunt, and Coleridge, to ask his opinions on recent German literature and for his help in procuring German books (1970: III, 108 and 316).

80 "There is no significance in [Thomas Campbell's] aspect: his blue frock and switch and fashionable wig, and clear cold eyes and clipt accents and slender persifflage [sic], might befit a dandy better than a poet". "Hardship [...] has withered out the sensibilities of his nature, and turned him finally into a sort of whisking antithetical little Editor." (1970: III, 138–139) "Charles Lamb is a ricketty creature in body and mind, sprawls about and walks as if his body consisted of four ill-conditioned flails, and talks as if he were quarter drunk with ale and half with laudanum." (1970: III, 139) Coleridge is "a steam-engine of a hundred horses power – the boiler burst. His talk is resplendent with imagery and the shows of thought; you listen as to an oracle, and find yourself no jot the wiser. He is without beginning or middle or end. A round fat oily yet impatient little man, his mind seems totally beyond his own controul; he speaks incessantly, not thinking or imagining or remembering, but combining all these processes into one." (1970: III, 139) This assessment of Coleridge is rather similar to the one Hazlitt would publish a few months later.

81 On 20 December 1824 he wrote to Jane Welsh: "The dwarf Opium-eater (my critic in the London Magazine) lives here [London] in lodgings, with a wife and children living or starving on the scanty produce of his scribble, far off in Westmoreland. [...] Vanity and opium have brought him to the state of 'dog distract and monkey sick'". (1970: III, 233–234).

> I return from Enfield where I have seen Lamb &c., &c. Not one of that class will tell you a straightforward story, or even a credible one, about any matter under the sun. All must be perked up into epigrammatic contrasts, staggering exaggerations, claptraps that will get a plaudit from the galleries! (Carlyle 1898: 217)

This approach and practice are in many respects examples of what Hazlitt criticised as "extravagant singularity". That Carlyle detected this in Hazlitt's friend Lamb and in those around him illustrates, again, that particular contemporary "characteristics" were being picked up by observers of different political, moral, and aesthetic persuasions.

Carlyle's attitude towards Hazlitt was complex. He valued Hazlitt's work before he knew anything about him, in 1815,[82] and still once he had established himself, in the late 1820s. In 1828, he acknowledged him as "a man of talent" in a letter to Goethe (1970: IV, 364).[83] But in a letter to Murray in August 1824, after his first visit to London in the preceding spring, Carlyle quipped that Hazlitt "takes his punch and oysters and rackets and whore at regular intervals; escaping from the bailiffs as best he can, and writing when they grow unguidable by other means. He has married [lately] [sic] (for the second time, his first spouse and the tailor's daughter [Sarah Walker] being both alive)" (1970: III, 139). Carlyle was reporting second-hand information because he also indicates that he has not met Hazlitt, and no intention of doing so: "I never saw him, or wish to." (1970: III, 139) While Carlyle would reiterate criticism of Hazlitt in the above vein (1970: III, 234), Hazlitt was clearly an object of interest for him. A year after Hazlitt's death, in November 1831, he complained "I have heard a hundred anecdotes about W. Hazlitt (for example); yet cannot, by ever so much cross-questioning even, form to myself the smallest notion of how it really stood with him" (Carlyle 1898: 217). He read Hazlitt's work, as his notebooks show, and pitied him as a victim of the age. In October 1831 he noted: "The man has thought much; even intently and with vigour: but he has discovered nothing; been able to believe nothing. One other sacrifice to the Time!" (1898: 213) This particular bout of interest in Hazlitt may not *only* have been occasioned by Hazlitt's death, it occurred at the time when Carlyle had been closely engaging with the "spirit of the age" in his own work, his essays "Signs of the

---

[82] Letter to Robert Mitchell, 14 June 1815 (1970: I, 50), and again to Mitchell on 16 February 1818 (1970: I, 122).

[83] In the same letter Carlyle reports without qualification that Hazlitt's biography of Napoleon has been judged by an acquaintance to be superior to Walter Scott's (1970: IV, 364). He is, however, writing to Goethe, a correspondent with whom he might be less likely to indulge in displays of one-up-man-ship.

Times" and "Characteristics", which are discussed below, appeared in 1829 and 1831 respectively.

It is somewhat surprising that Hare does not feature in Carlyle's letters or his notebooks of the 1820s, given the fact that both were interested in spreading the salutary influence of German literature, that both translated romances, and that both were worried about the threat to specifically *religious* spirituality (not *just* the threat to primarily communal-social *political* spirit, which so concerned Hazlitt). Hare and Carlyle would eventually meet in 1835 (Distad 1979: 135), through their mutual friend John Sterling, and would entertain reasonably cordial relations until near the time of Hare's death. It appears Carlyle read *Guesses* only in 1836 (Distad 1979: 135). Nevertheless, their relationship appears to have been an uneasy one, and almost dissolved over their competing biographies of Sterling (Distad 1979: 174–183). Perhaps, in the early 1820s, Hare appeared to Carlyle, rightly or wrongly, as belonging to the London class of Hazlitts, Hunts, and Shelleys. His assessment of Hunt's journal *The Liberal*, although Carlyle read it with interest and passed it on to his bride Jane, is not dissimilar to Lady Jones' view of what was wrong with German books: atheism and political radicalism. But unlike Hare's aunt, Carlyle was interested in what the magazine says, albeit with a sense of superiority.[84]

Carlyle, the Germanist, began to learn German from 1819,[85] by the early 1820s he was proficient. So he could, like Hare, read any German work in the original and was not limited by reading translations, or their lack. For Carlyle this was a serious business. Even a cursory look at Carlyle's letters of this period reveals how passionately he engaged with his German reading.[86]

---

84 On 28 October 1822 he wrote to Jane: "Byron's Magazine, or rather Hunt's "The Liberal" is arrived in town; but they will not sell it – it is so full of Atheism and Radicalism and other noxious – isms. [...] I read it thro and found two papers, apparently by Byron, and full of talent as well as mischief." (1970: II, 190).

85 See the letters to Thomas Murray dated 19 February 1819 and to his brother Alexander dated 22 February 1819 (1970: I, 165 and 167).

86 See, for example, the letter to his brother John of 7 March 1828 (1970: IV, 332–339), which is liberally interspersed with German words and phrases. John was in Munich at the time, attending lectures by Schelling and others. He supplied Thomas with all kinds of information about things German, philosophy, literature, books, sketches (including one of Schelling). Carlyle was very keen on this mix of information: "Preserve your Journal! Preserve it however stupid; so it be only *full* enough. *Write down* whatever strikes you and as it strikes you." (1970: IV, 339, italics in original) John was to make the most of his acquaintance with Schelling: "Tell me more and more about Schelling, and get as well acquainted with him as you honourably can." (IV, 338–339) But Carlyle was equally eager to gather information about others, and books by them: "I have so many questions about German Books, that I know not where to begin. Gather stores of Knowledge which may avail us both. Is there such thing as a life of *Fichte*, or, if not, do you know

German also played a role in his courtship of Jane Welsh. Thomas and Jane used German words, or whole phrases, to create a playful intimacy in their letters. This appears to have been common among those intellectuals who could: Hare and Whewell did the same, at the same time.[87] Carlyle may also have intended German as a secret language which could not be deciphered by Jane's mother's vigilant eye.[88]

What drew Carlyle to German literature was similar to what had engaged Hare: it provided important pointers for understanding and improving the current "situation", both on a personal and a collective social level, which he felt he could not obtain from anywhere else. And like Hare, he felt he needed to introduce this writing to British readers for this reason. On the social level, Carlyle, who was fiercely opposed to the prevalent Benthamite utilitarianism and the rapidly developing capitalism of the 1820s and 1830s, i.e. to the externalization of life, here found inspiration for ways of safeguarding, or re-introducing, spiritual meaning and moral substance in(to) a secularised world. On the personal level, Carlyle, the Scottish Calvinist who had lost his faith and experienced the *Ever-lasting No*, here found evidence for the possibility of an Everlasting Yea. Similarly, Hare had felt around 1820 that German "books" were protecting his faith and sharpening his sense of the wrongs afflicting British public affairs, i.e. money-worshipping materialism and self-serving egotism.

Carlyle's propagation of things German was by no means indiscriminate, nor *entirely* evangelical. He was not uncritical (some romances were awfully gothic), nor undiscerning (Wilhelm Meister's *Wanderjahre*, a translation of which he had tentatively offered to Taylor, was after closer perusal "full of

---

anything about his history?" (IV, 338) And he entreated urgently: "Tell me also the title and character of Lessing's Biography [...] if there is such a work in print. [...] What is Fichte's Wissenschaftslehre to be had for? And when is Schelling to publish his bibliographi[es]." (IV, 338) Carlyle expressed the hope that he and his brother might become a Scottish version of the Schlegel brothers, casting himself as August Wilhelm and John as Friedrich (IV, 335).

87 See the exchange of letters between Whewell and Hare regarding Hare's accepting a position at Trinity in spring 1822 and their use of the German word "tüchtig" (Distad 1979: 41–42).

88 See the letter to Jane dated 1 September 1821 (Carlyle 1970: I, 383, also note 4). While Jane firmly rejected the idea that Thomas should write to her, as she felt this was deceitful (24 September 1821, 1970: I, 383–384) – throughout the autumn of 1821 she repeatedly rejected Thomas' ardent epistolary advances – their relationship was clearly sparked by their shared excitement over German literature and learning German (see their letters to each other between June 1821 and June 1822), and Jane continued to learn, read, and translate from German, and share this with Thomas throughout her period of wanting to be only Thomas' "friend".

genius, but [...] unfit for the British market"),[89] nor was he enamoured with the metaphysical speculation of German Idealism. His interest in Fichte did not extend to the latter's *a priori* philosophical system, instead it focused on spiritual salvation in an analytical-critical age, which could be achieved by analysing society and history. In other words, Carlyle was interested in the work of the post-Jena, the "Berlin" Fichte, who after the atheism controversy had turned his attention to a more practical type of philosophy. Carlyle's use, and dissemination, of German sources was eclectically selective (Harrold 1963: 7), and his reading of them thoroughly conditioned by his personal and national context. Divergences between what the source text author "meant" and what Carlyle "understood", or found worth propagating, seem less the result of intellectual errors, i.e. of a lack of understanding, than of Carlyle's specific perspective and needs (Oergel 2015: 70–71).

By the late 1820s Carlyle was fully engaged in assessing the "spirit of the age", which he presents in two essays, "Signs of the Times" (1829) and "Characteristics" (1831), both written following almost a decade of intense involvement with German texts.[90] The two essays deal, respectively, with the synchronic spirit of the age and with the diachronic spirit of history in which distinct epochs, animated by a specific epochal spirit, succeed one another; both appeared in the *Edinburgh Review*. "Signs of the Times" examines the condition of Britain; "Characteristics" deals with the alternating periods of doubt and faith in European intellectual history.

In "Signs of the Times" Carlyle continues the familiar critique of the machine-like nature of current society. His key criticism, which is the theme of the essay, focuses on the pernicious "genius of mechanism" (1899 [1829]: II, 62) which pervades the "age".

> To characterise this age of ours by a single epithet, we should be tempted to call it [...] the Mechanical age. [...] The mechanical genius of our time has diffused itself into quite other provinces. Not the external and physical alone is now managed by machinery, but the internal and spiritual also. (1899: II, 59–60)

Its externalisation and materialism are thorough-going. "Not for internal perfection, but for external combinations and arrangements, for institutions,

---

[89] As he remarked to James Hessey on 6 August 1824 (1970: III, 119).
[90] "Sign of the Times" (1899 [1829]: II, 56–82); "Characteristics" (1899: III, 1–43). Both essays are well known, variously described as "seminal" (Rosenberg 1985: 35) and "celebrated" (Ashton 1980: 72), but only Harrold observes a link to, or even dependence on, Novalis on the topic of mechanism (1963: 64–65).

constitutions, – for Mechanism of one sort or other, do they hope and struggle." (1899: II, 63) What characterises the spirit of the age and the process by which this "content" permeates the age have become indistinguishable. Hence any striving for internal perfection has been abandoned "because, cultivated on such principles, it is found to yield no result" (1899: II, 66): it is the "Age of the Machine", "of Machinery", of "Codification" (1899: II, 68). The mark of the age is the absence of spiritual content in favour of profit and material wealth on the one hand and "mechanical" political rights and equality on the other. The "wise men" of "former times" were "Moralists, Poets, and Priests" who were concerned about the "primary inward powers of men", now they are "Political Philosophers" and "Political economists" "occupying themselves in counting-up and estimating men's motives, [who] strive by curious checking and balancing [...] of Profit and Loss, to guide them to their true advantage" (1899: II, 69). They assume (reductive) motives, which are the "finite, modified developments" of "primary, unmodified forces and energies of man, the mysterious springs of Love, and Fear, and Wonder, of Enthusiasm, Poetry and Religion" (1899: II, 68). These energies Carlyle labels "dynamic", and the resulting vital dynamism is conceived as the opposite to "mechanism". In short, he thinks the "Machine of Society" is devoid of life, it lacks a genuine connective, a true *spirit*. However, this lack does not prevent this mechanical spirit from being effective.

It did not escape Carlyle that he was not alone in complaining about this, nor that others, too, tended to identify this connective as "public spirit": "In all manner of periodical or perennial publications" one can find laments that "Public principle is gone; private honesty is going; society, in short, is fast falling in pieces" (1899: II, 58). Identifying "mechanism" as socially pernicious and morally dangerous, because it instrumentalises selfishness to achieve mechanical "balance" and to control activity is, bearing in mind what Arndt, Brandes or Hazlitt have said, far from original. Carlyle sums up:

> Equally mechanical, and of equal simplicity, are the methods proposed by both parties for completing or securing this all-sufficient perfection of [political] arrangement. [...] Men are to be guided by their self-interests. Good government is a good balancing of these; and, except a keen appetite for self-interest, requires no virtue in any quarter. To both parties it is emphatically a machine: to the discontented a "taxing machine", to the contented a "machine for securing property". (1899: II, p. 67)

The time is devoid of moral virtue and spiritual values, on which public spirit relies. There is very little that is new here; it was well established that anti-communal, virtue-less egotism was the problem of the age, for many, and not just in German thinking. As we have seen, even the conceptual link between such anti-communal, virtue-less egotism and mechanical processes is not new. Carlyle may have taken over much from others, but, crucially, he managed to disseminate, not to say popularise, the idea of a socially pernicious mechanism among a wide audience. His explicit summation of all current ills *and* the manner of their operation under one clear-cut term, mechanism, was his own work. He created an effective catchword, which is probably the reason why Carlyle – rather than Hazlitt – is remembered as the chief *critical* investigator of the "spirit of the age". In the process of presenting this spirit he went some way towards formulating a theoretical understanding of its dynamics, which Hazlitt had practically, if obliquely, presented.

The point that had not been made with quite the same force and clarity was how complete the permeation of society with this (deadening) spirit was: "the age which, with its whole undivided might, forwards, teaches and practises the great art of adapting means to ends" (1899: II, 59). It permeates all areas of human activities, mental and physical, individual and collective.

> The same habit regulates not our modes of action alone, but our modes of thought and feeling. [...] Their [men's] whole efforts, attachments, opinions, turn on mechanism, are of mechanical character. We may trace this tendency in all great manifestations of our time; in its intellectual aspect, the studies it most favours and the method of conducting them, its politics, arts, religion, morals; in the whole sources, and throughout the whole currents of its spiritual, no less its material activity. (1899: II, 62–63)

For Carlyle the danger of "mechanism" lies in this: although its key characteristic is its lack of independent vital energy, it is capable of a kind of automatic perpetuation of frightening force and control, it "encircles and imprisons" (1899: II, 81): "'the deep meaning of the Laws of Mechanism lies heavy on us'; and in the closet, in the marketplace, in the temple, by the social hearth, encumbers the whole movement of our mind, and over out noblest faculties is spreading a nightmare sleep" (1899: II, 80).

It is questionable to what extent this force actually possesses the qualities of a "spirit", as it lacks the crucial power to animate. Although he does speak of the "*genius* of mechanism", Carlyle's describes it as a *system* that is fully established and focused on maintaining its state of permeation. The zeitgeist Carlyle is dealing with is not so much a *rising* force as a *ruling* one. The same is true of its grip on public (or indeed private) opinion. Carlyle makes the connection to public opinion in a more analytical way than Hazlitt did in his portraits.

Carlyle could have found views on the mechanical, machine-like nature of society and its link with selfishness and a dehumanising state in British sources (Hare, Hazlitt or Coleridge), but he chose to refer to German ones, especially

Novalis. "Signs of the Times" was written when Carlyle was working on his "German" essays for various periodicals,[91] and corresponding with his brother who was travelling in Germany (and Austria).[92] In the same year that "Signs of the Times" appeared Carlyle also published his essay on Novalis (Carlyle 1899: II, 1–55), which was based on his reading of the 1826 (fourth) edition of Friedrich Schlegel's and Ludwig Tieck's collection of their friend's *Schriften*, (which is, incidentally, the same edition that Hare owned, too). In "Glauben und Liebe" (1798), Novalis had put forward a similar critique of self-interested competition and materialism, paired with the conviction that machine-like mechanism is detrimental when applied to human affairs, that machines have dehumanising qualities, and that states run like machines are ultimately inhuman and self-destructive. Arndt and Brandes made similar points a few years after Novalis.

> So nöthig vielleicht eine [...] maschinistische Administration zur physischen Gesundheit, Stärkung und Gewandheit eines Staates seyn mag, so geht doch der Staat, wenn er bloß auf diese Art behandelt wird, darüber zu grunde. Das Prinzip des alten berühmten Systems ist, jeden durch Eigennutz an den Staat zu binden. [...] Aber der rohe Eigennutz scheint durchaus unermeßlich, anti-systematisch zu sein. [...] Durch die förmliche Aufnahme des gemeinen Egoismus, als Prinzip, [ist] ein ungeheurer Schade geschehen. (Novalis 1981 [1798]: 498, no. 35)

> [As necessary as perhaps a machine-like administration may be for a state's health, for strengthening it and for its agility, the state itself will perish if it is treated in this manner only. The principle of the good old system is to bind everybody into the state through self-interest. [...] But raw self-interest appears to be entirely immeasurable and anti-systemic. [...] By formally making common selfishness a [condoned] principle, incredible damage has been done.]

Novalis opened the above section by describing the administration of Frederick the Great's Prussia as a "Fabrik" [factory]. In his penultimate "Political Aphorism", he reiterates his abhorrence of the "great mechanism" in political processes, which inevitably ensues when self-interest rules.

> Ein großer Mechanismus wird sich bilden – ein Schlendrian – den nur die Intrigue zuweilen zerbricht. Die Zügel der Regierung werden zwischen den Buchstaben und den mannigfaltigen Partheimachern hin und her schwanken. Die Despotie des Einzelnen hat denn

---

91 Between 1827 and 1832 Carlyle published numerous essays on German literature and writers, starting with more contemporary topics (Jean Paul, Goethe, Novalis) between 1827 and 1829, mainly for the *Foreign Review*, before also including historically more distant topics for a number of other journals, such as the *Edinburgh Review*, *Westminster Review*, and *Frazer's Magazine*.

92 See above, note 86.

> doch vor dieser Despotie den Vorzug, daß man dort wenigstens an Zeit und Schuhen spart – wenn man mit der Regierung zu thun hat. (Novalis 1981: 506, no. 67)
>
> [A great mechanism will arise, which is only occasionally disrupted by intrigue. The reigns of government will sway back and forth between the letter [of the law] and the many different partisan interests. The despotism of a single despot is to be preferred to this kind because with the former at least one saves on time and shoes when dealing with the government.]

If government is not animated by "spirit", it will be based on the "letter" and partisan party-politics. Carlyle recorded the similarity in his Notebook: "Paper on Novalis just published in F.[oreign] R.[eview]. [...] Novalis is an anti-Mechanist; a deep man; the most perfect of modern spirit-seers. I thank him for somewhat." (1898: 140) The entry immediately following reads: "also just finished an Article on *The Signs of the Times* for Ed. Review" (1898: 140).[93] Novalis, too, uses the (Biblical) term signs of the times, "Zeichen der Zeit", in *Christenheit oder Europa* (1981: 534).

Carlyle would have found the same attack on dehumanising mechanism, which only serves those in power in their self-interested exploitation of those they rule, in Arndt, Hendrich, or Brandes, but there is no indication that he read them. Carlyle *could* have identified fellow fighters in the battle against community-corroding selfish mechanism in London, but, as we saw in his letters, he only grudgingly admitted Hazlitt's talent, remained dubious about Shelley,[94] and seemed to ignore, or be unaware of, Hare. Instead he preferred to seek out the same ideas across the channel in Germany. In the context of Carlyle's evident desire to keep a distance between himself and "this rascal rout, this dirty rabble, destitute [...] of high feeling or knowledge or intellect" (Carlyle 1970: III, 234), it seems likely that he deliberately avoided engaging with people he considered too tainted by a hedonistic secularism (Hazlitt, Lamb, de Quincey) or subject to an unhealthy mental overdrive (Coleridge) to be taken seriously in his spiritual quest.

---

[93] At the end of his Novalis-essay Carlyle quotes Jean Paul (Richter's) rueful prediction that, if the materialism of the mechanical age continues to hold sway, "of the World will be made a World-Machine, of Aether a Gas, and of God a force, and of the Second World – a Coffin" (1899: II, 54).

[94] In "Characteristics" Carlyle describes Shelley as "filling the earth with inarticulate wail" (1899: III, 31), an assessment he did not change; in a letter to Robert Browning he wrote in 1850: "Shelley. Poor soul, he has always seemed to me an extremely weak creature; a poor, thin, spasmodic, hectic, shrill and pallid being. [...] The very voice of him (his style &c.), shrill, shrieky, to my ear has too much of the ghost!" (1970: I, xxxviii).

In difference to the more established and more political 1820s intellectuals, for Carlyle the problem was not *primarily* political, but spiritual and intellectual. In "Signs of the Times" he inveighs with irony and scorn against the priority of constitutions and institutions, which has frequently led to him being cast as a political conservative.

> A good structure of legislation, a proper check on the executive, a wise arrangement of the judiciary, is *all* that is wanting for human happiness. [...] Contrive the fabric of the law aright, and without farther effort on your part, that divine spirit of Freedom [...] will of herself come to inhabit it; and under her healing wings every noxious influence will wither, every good and salutary one more and more expand.' (1899: II, 67–68)

This is, however, a difference of priority and perspective, not of essence or aim; Carlyle, too, puts forward the idea that the "noble People" should have political control. "Man is not the creature and product of Mechanism; but, in a far truer sense, its creator and producer: it is the noble People that makes the noble Government; rather than conversely". (1899: II, 72) Human spirit and human goodness must predate any good "system". There is a hint of the "revolutionary" notion of the incorruptible people who are being oppressed or misled by an inhumane and inappropriate system of government and who should really be their own legislators. In answer to the question of *who* the "noble people" are, Carlyle suggests that it should be a people that is morally inspired, and this includes revolutionary inspiration.

> Our English Revolution too originated in Religion. [...] The French Revolution itself had something higher in it than cheap bread and a Habeas-Corpus act. There too was an Idea; a Dynamic, not a Mechanic force. It was a struggle, a blind and at last an insane one, for the infinite, divine Right of Freedom and of Country. (1899: II, 71)

Carlyle proposes that spiritual foundations have to precede political changes, but the political ones must and will follow. The good state *is* the desired (political) outcome, but it must be a state built on spiritual, moral foundations. This is strongly reminiscent of the German mantra that moral reformation and cultivation must be linked to, and ideally precede, political reformation, put forward by Schiller and Fichte. By the end of the essay Carlyle arrives at the conclusion that a good liberal political system underpinned by dynamic moral spirit will produce salvation.

> Political freedom is hitherto the object of these efforts; but they will not and cannot stop there. It is towards a higher freedom than mere freedom from oppression by his fellow-mortal, that man dimly aims. Of this higher, heavenly freedom, which is "man's

> reasonable service", all his noble institutions, his faithful endeavours and loftiest attainments, are but the body, and more and more approximated emblem. (1899: II, 82)

While all – Thelwall, Burke, Hazlitt, Hare, Carlyle – identify the corrosion of public spirit as the key ill of the age, only Hare and Carlyle interpret the missing spirit in a more than quasi-religious way. In Hare and Carlyle, the lack of public *spirit* and public virtue comes to the fore as a lack of communal *spirituality*. Their professed anti-atheism lets them appear as political conservatives; yet they, too, wanted to reap the *political* benefits of the revolution and were keen to learn from any earlier short-sightedness. For Carlyle, revolution, even the French Revolution, was positive as long as it was based on a moral idea.

Like all zeitgeist investigators, Carlyle insists that ideas direct human activity and that "opinion" is the link between ideas and activity.

> We advert the more particularly to these intellectual propensities, as to the prominent symptoms of our age, because Opinion is at all times doubly related to Action, first as cause, than as effect; and the speculative tendency of any age will therefore give us […] the best indications of its practical tendencies. (1899: II, 66)

Ideas, the "speculative tendency", determine practice. In explaining the actual spread and grip of a "spirit", Carlyle identifies opinion as the cause of action, which in turn confirms (or changes) opinion, and thus follows the pattern that intellectual elites seek public acceptance for their ideas in the public sphere via the power of "public opinion", which is familiar from the debates starting a generation earlier.

"Signs of the Times" is obliquely focused on public opinion – one of its review items was the anonymously published *Rise, Progress and Present State of Public Opinion* by Alexander William Mackinnon (1828), a celebration of the growth of enlightened public opinion that has kept a check on social and economic despotism throughout history, using the familiar formula of surveying nations. Carlyle's views of course run counter to this positive assessment. His main concern about public opinion is its overwhelming force, for which he offers two explanations. On the one hand, public opinion has currently all the features of mechanical coercion. It is a soulless, self-perpetuating force, running through a public sphere mechanised by the machinery of public meetings, committees, prospectuses and other publications (1899: II, 61). Once established, its coercive grip on thought and feeling is enslaving, cancelling all free and independent activity: "we are shackled in heart and soul with far straiter [sic] than feudal chains", "we stand leashed together, uniform in dress and movement, like the rowers on some boundless galley" (1899: II, 79).

Carlyle links this uniform behaviour of automatons to the dominance of (mechanical) politics over (dynamic) morality, or of political benefits over moral ones: "Thus, while civil liberty is more and more secured to us, our moral liberty is lost." (1899: II, 79) Current public opinion is, in content and as a force, symptomatic of the Age of Mechanism, it is based on self-interest, materialism, and empty codifications. This public opinion is closely linked to "popularity" (1899: II, 79), alluding to Hazlitt's extensive treatment of his subjects' public standing: "What morality we have takes the shape of Ambition, [...]: beyond money and money's worth, our only rational blessedness is Popularity" (1899: II, 79). Gaining popularity is necessary to effect anything in public, but this public acclaim is empty and fickle, a temporary "huzzaing" (1899: II, 79).

On the other hand, there is a "dynamic" version of public opinion, a spreading of new ideas powered by strong communal emotions, such as "Fear" and "Hope", which Carlyle describes as the "springs of human energy" and which – in a fully functioning community – are closely linked to public spirit. This type is currently represented by the "Millennarians" on the one hand and the materialistic Utilitarians and "Millities", who quote Bentham rather than the Bible (1899: II, 58), on the other. The Millennarians are related to the other review items, the anonymously published *Anticipation; or A Hundred Years Hence* and *The Last Days. A Discourse on the Evil Character of these our Times* by the Rev. Edward Irving, the popular preacher who was the subject of one of Hazlitt's portraits. But in Carlyle's broken society this "dynamic" type of public opinion tends to produce only the wrong-headed enthusiasm of these two groups.

Evidently public opinion has dynamic and mechanical aspects. While the mechanical type spreads through the coercive force of the "Police of Public Opinion", the dynamic one disseminates through intense sympathetic emotion. Carlyle's ruminations reflect the familiar tension between coercion and free expression in (zeit)geist, which has remained unresolved since Montesquieu. The two types also reflect the tension between the beneficial impact of community spirit ("noble Sympathy") and the corrupting influence of selfish or purely materialistic motives. The intensity of dissemination – or put another way, the level of acceptance – depends on the emotional, rather than moral, condition of the public. In calm times any intensity eventually dissipates: "The grand encourager of the Delphic or other noises is – the Echo. Left to themselves, they will the sooner dissipate and die in space." (1899: II, 59) But in times of crisis public opinion spreads "dynamically" by "frenzied fury" as many people engage in "a rage of prophecy" (1899: II, 58) and turn an idea, preoccupation, or fear into an enormous power.

> Here [at such times] the prophets are not few, but many; and each incites and confirms the other; so that the fatidical fury spreads wider and wider [...]. For there is still a real magic in the action and reaction of minds on one another. The casual deliration of a few becomes, by this mysterious reverberation, the frenzy of many. [...] It is grievous to think that this noble omnipotence of Sympathy has been so rarely the Aaron's-rod of Truth and Virtue, and so often the Enchanter's-rod of Wickedness and Folly. (1899: II, 57)

Dissemination is based on the power of the word or argument to appear convincing and can be supported by either ubiquitous "mechanical" modelling or by emotional connection, "sympathy". Initially, there is a focus on reason and rationality, it is "minds" that engage with each other, but as the "dynamic" force increases, emotional fury and irrational "frenzy" set in. While it may run wild and destabilise governments or social cohesion, for Carlyle public opinion is always an effective force of social control.

> [Contemporary] superior morality is rather an "inferior criminality" produced not by a greater love of Virtue, but by greater perfection of Police; and of that far subtler and stronger Police, called Public Opinion. This last watches over us with its Argus eyes more keenly than ever. [...] This and that may be right and true; but we must not do it. Wonderful "force of Public Opinion"! (1899: II, 78–79)

Carlyle's "Force of Public Opinion" is a close match for the second half of Hendrich's title, *Über den Geist des Zeitalters und die Gewalt der öffentlichen Meinung*. While I have found no evidence that Carlyle knew Hendrich's book, there are some interesting parallels between Carlyle's and Hendrich's terminology and argumentation. Both draw parallels between the Reformation and the French Revolution as moments of historic change driven by abuses of power and public outrage,[95] but more specifically, both describe the manner in which ideas emerge and spread in similar ways. Hendrich had concluded:

> They [ideas] have such power because they create emotions, passions, enthusiasm. They form and develop quietly; through communication and intercourse between individuals they meet and catch fire from each other. As soon as these encounters have made them complete and given them structure [Haltung], they rush forth among the masses with irresistible force. (Hendrich 1797: 91–92)

When human minds think, and influence and affect each other, an idea ignites and develops its vehement force. The similarity to Carlyle's description is striking:

---

[95] Carlyle likens the "English Revolution" (the Reformation) to the French Revolution, in both "men did battle [...] not for Purse-sake, but for Conscience-sake" (1899: II, 71).

each incites and confirms the other; so that the fatidical fury spreads wider and wider [...]. For there is still a real magic in the action and reaction of minds on one another. The casual deliration of a few becomes, by this mysterious reverberation, the frenzy of many. (1899: II, 57)

Both refer to an elite which influences public opinion as an (invisible) church. The difference is that for Hendrich these elites are, in the beginning, wise and benevolent,[96] while Carlyle has only sarcastic censure for their bowdlerized affectation of priesthood. Carlyle, however, is speaking of the press, whose power over public opinion is church-*like*.

> The true Church of England, at the moment, lies in the Editors of its Newspapers. These preach to the people daily, weekly, admonishing kings themselves; advising on peace or war, with an authority which only the first reformers, and a long-past class of Popes were possessed of; inflicting moral censure; imparting moral encouragement, consolation, edification; in all ways diligently "administering the Discipline of the Church". (1899: II, 77)

In Carlyle's account, this "church" has turned entirely secular and is profaning its once sacred duties by pursuing self-serving agendas. In a British context, any reference to the Catholic Church – ("Popes") – would always conjure up notions of self-serving despotic organisations. While for Hendrich this "church" has at least partly beneficial intentions and impact, for Carlyle its workings create the thought police of Public Opinion. But public opinion is human-made, and hence its power can be broken: "Our spiritual maladies are but of Opinion; we are but fettered by chains of own forging, and which ourselves also can rend asunder" (1899: II, 80). Mechanism is only a "glass bell" that can be smashed (1899: II, 81). There are echoes of the opening of Rousseau's *Contrat Social* here, as well as of Arndt's reasoning in *Geist der Zeit*: man-made conditions may produce a zeitgeist, but conditions and opinion can be changed. Carlyle's essay, too, is a call for action; he believes that the historical process will assist in this, linking the diachronic and synchronic aspects of zeitgeist in a familiar way: mechanical and dynamic ages alternate in universal history and currently "many things have reached their height" (1899: II, 81). Carlyle invokes the diachronic spirit of history to contain the perils of a pernicious zeitgeist. Human contingencies can be influenced, power can be challenged, and it has all been done before.

---

96 "The principles of the Reformation did now exist, they could not be eliminated, on the contrary they were picked up by the brightest minds and developed further. As these constituted something of an invisible church." (Hendrich 1797: 125–126).

Carlyle's subsequent essay "Characteristics", also published in the *Edinburgh Review*, explores further the idea of historical progression and historical recurrence and where the present age fits in. It is another assessment of the condition of Britain, this time in relation to Germany and this country's more advanced intellectual progress. Ostensibly a double review of Thomas Hope's *Essay on the Origins and Prospects of Man* (1831) and Friedrich Schlegel's *Philosophische Vorlesungen* (1830), Carlyle uses the two books to present two very different opinions on the relation between the spiritual and material conditions of humanity in an age that has no established forms of spirituality. While both publications are presented as "Voices" from a transnational "stunning hubbub, a true Babel-like confusion of tongues" (1899: III, 33) and while they are the "latest utterances of European speculation", "representing the two Extremes of our whole modern system of Thought" (1899: III, 33), he has nevertheless chosen them as representatives of their national contexts: Thomas Hope "may painfully remind us [...] that England, the most calculative, is the least meditative, of all civilised countries" (1899: III, 34). Hope was a transnational Dutch émigré who made his home in Britain in the 1790s.[97] His book "could have originated nowhere save in England" (1899: III, 36). Schlegel, however, represents the more advanced "Metaphysics of the Germans" (1899: III, 40), even if he has reneged on his youthful radicalism, converted to Catholicism, and taken up a pensionable position in the reactionary Austrian government, he remained to the end "a high, far-seeing earnest spirit" (1899: III, 35). It is not surprising that Carlyle favours Schlegel's eloquent advocacy for spirituality. With Hope, there is "no Philosophical Speech; but a painful, confused stammering, and struggling after such" (1899: III, 34). In the end, Hope's book does, for all its serious endeavour, not accomplish anything, rather like Hazlitt. Both are tainted by the philosophising rejection of religious spirituality in favour of purely secular ends, while in German metaphysics at least credible efforts are being made to remedy the spiritual crisis (1899: III, 40–41).

In "Characteristics", the present age is defined not so much by the familiar evil of materialistic selfishness, but by incessant and unlimited inquiry and intellectual speculation. But the outcome is the same: "our era's" mechanical philosophy is the reason for the lack of spiritual values, communal spirit, and happiness. It is responsible for a predominance of "doubt", scepticism, and

---

[97] Thomas Hope (1769–1831), of Dutch-Scottish extraction, a member of a banking dynasty and socialite in Regency London, was a traveller, writer, and art collector with an interest in orientalism. His novel *Anastasius* was a huge success. His philosophical work took a secular approach to human culture, which was anathema to Carlyle.

paralysing self-conscious self-reflexivity.[98] For Carlyle, such inquiring speculation is unproductive, as perhaps he knows from personal experience, "it begins in No and Nothingness, so it must needs end in Nothingness" (1899: III, 27). Public spirit is lacking because there is nothing to believe in, to inspire; the lowest common denominator is the materialistic and political. This is a conclusion very similar to the social context Hazlitt describes in his portrait of Lord Eldon. Carlyle's criticism, however, is focused less on "un-public-spirited" personal behaviour than on collective political priorities in general.

> Which cunningly-devised "Constitution", constitutional, republican, democratic, sansculottic, could bind that raging chasm together? Were they not all burnt up like paper [...]? It is not by Mechanism, but by Religion; not by Self-Interest, but by Loyalty, that men are governed, or governable. (1899: III, 42)

While Carlyle sounds like a political conservative, his "Religion" is, at least in part, a metaphor for a general communal spirit:

> Every Society, every Polity, has a spiritual principle; [...] all its tendencies of endeavour, specialities of custom, its laws, politics and whole procedure (as the glance of some Montesquieu [...] can partly decipher) are prescribed by an Idea, and flow naturally from it, [...]. This Idea, be it of devotion to a man or class of men, to a creed, to an institution, or even [...] to a piece of land, is ever a true Loyalty; has in it something of a religious, paramount, quite infinite character; it is properly the Soul of the State, its Life, and like these working secretly, and in a depth beyond that of consciousness. (1899: III, 13–14)

This is redolent with Hazlitt's 1806 conclusions in *Free Thoughts*.

For Carlyle, "unconsciousness" is crucial. The essay outlines a historical progression of mind based on alternating states of intuition and analytical reasoning. The ages of inquiry and doubt are conscious ones, like the present (1899: III, 18), while ages of faith are unconscious ones. It is only possible to speak of, and meditate on, the "spirit of the age" because of the current highly developed level of consciousness. This may well be an allusion to Hazlitt and his book, not least because he makes an appearance a few pages on as "poor Hazlitt", the figure familiar from the Notebook comment, who "must wander on God's verdant earth, like the Unblessed on burning deserts; passionately dig wells, and draw up only quicksand; believe that he is seeking Truth, yet only

---

98 "Doubt storms-in on him [the youth of these times] through every avenue; inquiries of the deepest, painfullest sort must be engaged with; and the invincible energy of young years waste itself in sceptical, suicidal cavillings [sic]; in passionate 'questionings of Destiny', whereto no answer will be returned." (1899: III, 30).

wrestle among endless Sophisms, doing desperate battle as with spectre-hosts; and die and make no sign!" (1899: III, 32)

Carlyle links this unconsciousness with morality and virtue; these values only operate properly when they are not reflected upon, i.e. not the result of (self-interested) checks and balances. He detaches understanding from reason and replaces the latter with intuitive knowledge. "The healthy Understanding, we should say, is not the Logical, argumentative, but the Intuitive; for the end of Understanding is not to prove and find reasons but know and believe." (1899: III, 5) The mechanical understanding, as Coleridge termed it in 1816, cannot produce spiritual certainty.

> Man's misery is even this, that he feel himself crushed under the Juggernaut wheels, and know that Juggernaut is no divinity, but a dead mechanical idol. Now this is specially the misery which has fallen on man in our Era. Belief, Faith has vanished from the world. (1899: III, 29)

Carlyle identifies the rupture between scientific knowledge, produced by rational enquiry, and faith, which also concerned Hare.

It is often assumed that this essay's title is a nod to Shaftesbury's *Characteristics of Men, Manners, Opinions and Times* (1711), for which there is some evidence.[99] It is a popular term, Hazlitt, too, made it the title of a collection of shorter prose and aphorisms, which he, however, saw as a reference to François de La Rochefoucauld's *Réflexions*. Friedrich and August Wilhelm Schlegel also used the term for their *Charakteristiken und Kritiken* of 1801, a loose collection of essays and reviews. This term could equally be a reference to Johann Gottfried Fichte's *Grundzüge des gegenwärtigen Zeitalters*, lectures held in Berlin in 1804–1805 and published in 1806, a text Carlyle knew.[100] "Characteristics" is the translation of the German word "Grundzüge" and Carlyle's essay shares a number of key ideas and concerns with Fichte's lectures: the detrimental dominance of a merely instrumental understanding, a historical trajectory of

---

[99] In a letter to Robert Mitchell, which predates his reading of German sources, Carlyle asks the addressee whether he owns as copy of Shaftesbury's book, because he wants to read it. The editors of the *Letters* suggest that there is a link not just to the "Characteristics" essay, but also to "Signs of the Times". In the letter Carlyle suggests, indeed foreshadowing aspects of his later essays, that eras have their distinctive intellectual features and outlooks. In a satirical vein, though, he goes on to say that once a characteristic outlook has been adopted by the lowest social classes, it is superseded, as thinking minds, not least out of pride, turn towards something new (1970: I, 51, note 11).

[100] See Harrold 1963: 163–171. But Harrold, not without justification, remains cautious regarding Carlyle understanding history as the realisation of an *a priori* defined idea of reason (1963: 161).

revelation, the priority of the moral over the political (although politics *is* important), and the potentially damaging power of the press over public opinion.

Grundzüge is itself a contribution to the zeitgeist discussion around 1800. Fichte subscribes to the notion of permeation: "jedes mögliche Zeitalter strebt, die ganze Gattung zu umfassen und zu durchdringen; und nur inwiefern ihm dies gelingt, hat es sich als Zeitalter dargestellt" [every age strives to embrace and permeate the whole species, and only as far as it achieves this, has it presented itself as an age] (Fichte 1846 [1806]: 78). In *Grundzüge*, Fichte outlines the history of human intellectual and spiritual progress in five stages, but – in keeping with the title of his lectures – spends the majority of the seventeen lectures on the "present age", the third in his scheme. This broad approach is evidence not just of the Idealist philosophers' belief in a "Weltplan", but also in the common conviction that the present is a distinct epoch in a diachronic movement, which as a distinct epoch can only be properly understood as the "conflux" of past and future, an idea to which Carlyle also subscribes: "The poorest Day that passes over us is the conflux of two Eternities; it is made up of currents that issue from the remotest Past, and flow onwards to the remotest Future" (1899: II, 59). Fichte's progression moves from liberation from unquestioned authority, via self-confident rule of the human intellect, towards a new acceptance of the authority of reason, which will eventually allow the human race to realise its potential to live in reason and freedom. It is the historical teleology of German Idealism, which moves through liberation and strife to historical consummation. It underlies the philosophies of Schelling and Hegel, as well as Schiller's cultural histories.

For Fichte, the current era is marked by an over-reliance on the individual's own understanding and experience, its "basic maxim" is "durchaus nichts als seyend und bindend gelten zu lassen, als dasjenige, was man verstehe und klärlich begreife" [to accept nothing as existing or binding unless I can understand and clearly grasp it] (1846: 21). As for Carlyle, this focus on the understanding produces "scepticism" (1846: 225). This amoral dissolution of philosophical values erodes any interest in truth (1846: 11–12). While their takes on self-reflexivity illustrate the difference between Fichte and Carlyle – for Fichte there cannot be enough, for Carlyle it is destructive – their diagnosis of the erosion of moral value through the priority given to material and empirical understanding is very similar. If there is no generally agreed idea to inspire individuals, a focus on individual self-interest is inevitable, the only "virtue" is to "further one's own benefit" (1846: 30), which leads to prioritising the immediately and materially useful.

> Ein solches Zeitalter [wird] überall nur auf das unmittelbar und materiell nützliche, zur Wohnung, Kleidung und Speise dienliche sehen, auf die Wohlfeilheit, die Bequemlichkeit, und [...] auf die Mode; [...] und so wird sich ihm auch die [...] übriggebliebene Kunst zu einem neuen Gebiet für die Mode, und zum Werkzeug eines wandelbaren, und darum keinesweges der Ewigkeit der Idee angemessenen Luxus umschaffen.
>
> [Such an age will in everything only see to the immediately and materially useful, that which is serviceable for accommodation, clothing, food, or for comfort and what is cheap and common, or for fashion; [...] what is left of art will in such an age become a new terrain for fashion, and will thus become the tool of a transient luxury that is not appropriate for the idea of eternity.] (Fichte 1846: 29–30)

Carlyle observed, acerbically, in "Signs of the Times, "what wonderful accessions have thus been made [...] to the physical power of mankind; how much better fed, clothed, lodged and, in all outward respects, accommodated men are now" (1899: II, 60). Both texts exhibit the same focus on self-interested profiteering and materialistic concerns. Nevertheless, this age will be overcome, according to Fichte, by two periods of gradual redemption, the "science of reason" (Vernunftwissenschaft) followed by the "art of reason" (Vernunftskunst) (1846: 12). In "Characteristics", Carlyle, too, identifies doubt and scepticism as preparing the way, in the form of metaphysical speculation, for spiritual and moral purification. Contemporary German metaphysics, such as Fichte's, is for Carlyle leading the way:

> Metaphysical Speculation, if a necessary evil, is the forerunner of much good. The fever of Scepticism must needs burn itself out, and burn out thereby the impurities that caused it; then again will there be clearness, health. [...] Of Modern Metaphysics [...] may not this already be said, that if they have produced no Affirmation, they have destroyed much Negation? It is a disease expelling a disease: the fire of Doubt [...] consuming the Doubtful; so that the Certain come to light, and again lie visible on the surface. English and French metaphysics, in reference to this last stage of the speculative process, are not what we allude to here; but only the Metaphysics of the Germans. (1899: III, 40)

Carlyle's stages of development are less "philosophically" – one is tempted to say, "mechanically" – defined than Fichte's. Although Carlyle is concerned with historical progression, he remains attached to the principle of intuitive, vitalistic emergence. This foreshortens Fichte's process of gradual philosophical resolution into a historical revelation. It is likely that Fichte's religious language, which describes how (modern European) humanity moves from "Sündhaftikeit" [sinfulness] to "Heiligung" [sanctification] and in which his abstract philosophy of reason is couched, was deeply appealing to Carlyle, even if Fichte's intervening "Rechtfertigung" [justification], having the hallmarks of philosophical, not to say judicial, enquiry, may have been less so. Fichte and Carlyle share a sense of the qualitative difference between understanding and knowledge: understanding is merely instrumental (mechanical in Carlyle's terminology), while knowledge is linked to eternal entities, such as faith, or ideas, but also to intuition and imagination. Fichte expresses this in the term "Vernunft*kunst*", which is the final stage of reason. Carlyle transforms the German Idealist ideas into concepts of faith and intuitive moral virtue, which does not need self-reflexion because it is based on *knowing*, free from doubt.

There is also overlap between Fichte and Carlyle regarding the current priority of the political. Fichte diagnoses as characteristic of his *Zeitalter* a misunderstanding of political liberty and freedom of opinion, and especially of the function of the press, which is directly related to the reductive rationalism of the age. This misunderstanding amounts to a misuse of equality, which leads to the tyranny of public opinion. Fichte satirises "publicity", without denying its power:

> Falls aber gar jemand, der vor den Richterstuhl dieser Publicität einberufen ist, es verschmähte sich zu stellen, werden sie [die Journale] ganz irre in ihren Begriffen, und sie werden sich über den widernatürlichen Mann, der es über sich vermag, ihr Richteramt nicht zu respectieren, wundern [...]. Wie könnte doch ein vernünftiger Mensch diesem ihrem Denken die ehrfurchtsvolle Unterwerfung versagen? (1846: 83)
>
> [But if anyone who has been called before the tribunal of publicity, disdained to appear, they [the journals] find their notions confounded, and they are astonished by this unnatural man who can bring himself to disrespect their role as judges [...]. How could any reasonable person refuse to submit humbly to this their thinking?]

By 1806 Fichte registers his doubts regarding the usefulness of "Freiheit der Publicität" [freedom of publicity] (1846: 92), which results in everything being discussed and judged in the public sphere. Everything is "vor den Richterstuhl der Publicität gezerrt" [dragged before the tribunal of publicity] (1846: 93), which is largely run by the press, "die Journale" (1846: 82). This tribunal of the public-ness is similar to Carlyle's "police of public opinion", something Fichte's Scottish translator may have picked up. [101] In both Carlyle's and Fichte's view,

---

101 In his translation of *Grundzüge*, William Smith translated Fichte's term *Publicität* as "Public Opinion", capitalised like Carlyle's (Fichte 1848–1849). Smith translated Fichte in the late 1840s – *Characteristics of the Present Age* was published in 1848 – *after* Carlyle's essays had been widely received, and one cannot help suspecting that this is a reference to Carlyle's text, indicating an understanding that Carlyle's "Characteristics" is closely related to Fichte's *Grundzüge*, and that Carlyle's essay was possibly seen, at least by Smith, as a conduit of key German ideas, a link he wanted to emphasise. *The Popular Works of Johann Gottlieb Fichte* contains *Grundzüge* and *Reden an die deutsche Nation*.

such free-wheeling speculation, resulting in doubt, coupled with a tyranny of uninformed publicity, impairs the functioning of cohesive social structures. Fichte expresses reservations regarding the new French political experiments, which have made "constitutions" out of "luftige und gehaltleere Abstractionen" [airy and empty abstractions] and lack the power to rule, but he is equally unimpressed with the more established British practices, which rely on an irregular patchwork of past instances and have no genius (1846: 30). As we saw, Carlyle, too, focused on both France and England as places where political and philosophical experiments have not produced beneficial results. And he expressed concern about the prevalent belief, resulting from the Mechanical Age, in *political* salvation per se.

> What sound mind among the French, for example, now fancies that men can be governed by "Constitutions"; by the ever so cunning mechanising of Self-Interests, and all conceivable adjustments of checking and balancing; in a word, by the best possible solution for this quite insoluble and impossible problem, *Given a world of Knaves, to produce an Honesty from their united action?*" (1899: III, 43)

He had already asserted in "Signs of the Times" that "we might note the mighty interest taken in mere political arrangements, as itself a sign of the mechanical age. The whole discontent of Europe takes this direction. The deep, strong cry of all civilised nations [...] is: Give us a reform of Government!" (1899: II, 66–67)

For Carlyle, a specific spirit, in this case the "mechanical genius", permeates the age, making it a complex yet recognisable web of inter-connected views and activities. The spirit spreads as "opinions" and practices and achieves temporary coherence by conditioning minds, this impacts on public policy, e.g. government reform, which in turn may stimulate other activities, potentially for *and* against. These opinions and practices are replicated in all areas of human affairs according to the same maxims. As such "spirit" is an immaterial collective entity that produces material, tangible outcomes. In *Grundzüge*, Fichte repeatedly speaks of individuals as "Producte der Zeit" (1846: 18) and "Producte des Zeitalters" (1846: 72), the true "products of their age" are those "in denen diese Zeit sich am klarsten ausspricht" [in whom this age finds the clearest expressions] (1846: 13).

Understanding the content as well as the force of an immaterial consensus that enjoyed high levels of public acceptance acquired a new urgency in the post-revolution context. For Carlyle the French Revolution had lost none of its significance as a political event. And in 1830, the July Revolution, occurring between the publication of "Signs of the Times" and "Characteristics", reminded everybody that the outcomes of the first revolution remained up for debate, that this particular historical chapter was not yet closed. Carlyle would shortly begin work on the book that made him famous: *The French Revolution. A History*, which appeared in 1837. To him the Revolution was the "grand poem of our time" which needed to be "told right", as he wrote to J. S. Mill on 24 September 1833, if humanity was to benefit from this event (1970–1977: VI, 446). Into his narrative he wove not just his views on the revelatory nature of history. More importantly in our context, his conclusions on the workings of the spirit of the age, in the shape of a forceful public opinion driven by contextual conditions, play a key role in his interpretation of the events in France. His account of the revolution presents Carlyle's view of zeitgeist in action as a political and social force.

Like any student of the Revolution, Carlyle wanted to *explain* the Revolution: how did it come about, why did it turn out the way it did, and what did it mean? His explanation is based on his assessment of the spirit of the recent past. While he does not say that the Enlightenment caused the revolution – a hotly debated issue in the 1790s in German journals –, he does suggest that "French philosophism", itself a product of its time, is responsible for the Age of Mechanism with its emphasis on the material and political existence of the human being. This in turn paved the way, in the specific conditions in late eighteenth-century France, for the revolution to occur *there*. French "philosophism" led to scepticism and on to atheism, but worse still, it discredited as chimera anything not immediately "logical" or tangible, leaving the human being without a spiritual rock to anchor a moral compass.

> French Philosophism has arisen; in which little word how much do we include! Here indeed lies properly the cardinal symptom of the whole widespread malady. Faith is gone out; Scepticism is come in. Evil abounds and accumulates; no man has Faith to withstand it, to amend it, to begin amending himself. [...] What other thing is certain? That a Lie cannot be believed! Philosophism knows only this: her other Belief is mainly, that in spiritual supersensual matters no Belief is possible. Unhappy! [...] but the Lie with its Contradiction once swept away, what will remain? ([1934] [1837]: 13)

The current battle between scepticism (ultimately Unbelief) and Belief, which he diagnosed and delineated in "Characteristics", has its origin in eighteenth-century thought. The "mechanical genius", identified in "Signs of the Times", is inherent in this "Philosophism", an idea he outlines in his long essay on Diderot, published in 1833. Diderot is a "Mechanical philosophe" (1899 III, 236), a "fearless, all for logic, thoroughly consistent Mechanical Thinker" (1899: III, 237); he is a fine exponent of the "polemical philosophe" conditioned by the "Mechanical

Age". But Diderot had little choice, he had to "turn [...] to [...] Polemical Philosophism" because it "seemed the most promising and fitting" (1899: III, 229). He was a "product of his age" subject to the (mechanical) coercion of an established opinion, which was his misfortune, because Carlyle considers him a genuine thinker, who under his contemporary guise of mechanical philosophe had the attributes of a poet and prophet, but was doomed to "unhappy" atheism in a mechanically physical universe (1899: III, 230). This is a description not at all out of place in Hazlitt's *Spirit of the Age*, had he included historical personages. One wonders whether this was not also how Carlyle ultimately saw William Hazlitt, who "believe[d] that he is seeking Truth, yet only wrestle[d] among endless Sophisms, doing desperate battle as with spectre-hosts; and die[d] and [made] no sign!" (1899: III, 32).

With the idea of the gifted thinker trapped in an age inhospitable to their true genius Carlyle returns to the issue of whether contemporaries can break free of the conditioning grip of their times. In "Signs of the Times", he had insisted that individuals who "argue on the 'force of circumstances'" "argue[...] away all force from [them]selves" (1899: II, 79), which implies they are either lazy, corrupt, or making excuses. By 1833 Carlyle has shifted his position. Man

> makes the Circumstances, and spiritually as well as economically is the artificer of his own fortune. But [...] man's circumstances are the element he is appointed to live and work in; that he by necessity takes his complexion, vesture, embodiment, from these, and is in all practical manifestations modified by them almost without limit; so that in another no less genuine sense, it can be said Circumstances make the Man. (1899: III, 229)

Carlyle now focuses on the tension between the pressure of the collective and individual freedom, which had emerged in the eighteenth century and was in the 1830s no closer to being resolved. Carlyle's rendering of it is reminiscent of Arndt's description of the individual moulding their environment and their time while being moulded by them, a description that also appeared in Hare.

For Carlyle, the French Revolution is a product of its time, shaped in its content by the preoccupations of mechanism and animated by a dynamic spirit of liberation (which would, however, prove unproductive). While Carlyle championed "Belief", he did not believe that human actions were devoid of empirically verifiable causes. This is why the "real" historical details, the contingent elements of the historical situation, are so important in his account of the French Revolution and why they are presented meticulously: the bankruptcy of the state, the long-running disputes with parliament, the oppression of the poor, the exploitation of the middle classes etc. It is their combination with the intellectual conditions created by the Enlightenment, which had brought down the ancien régime. The new elites, the lawyers, the men of commerce, and, most powerful of all, the writers, had prepared and expedited its dissolution. It is a conclusion that Arndt had reached thirty years earlier. The anarchy that resulted, in spiritual, intellectual, and political terms, was in Carlyle's view still current. Even if Britain had had no revolution in the past forty years, it had not been short of political unrest, from the naval mutinies in 1797 via Luddite frame-breaking to Peterloo in 1819. And when Carlyle was writing the two essays discussed here, the Bristol Riots of October 1831, occasioned by the difficult passage of the first Reform Bill, were just around the corner.

In Carlyle's *French Revolution* the reader finds this ambiguous mechanical-dynamical zeitgeist, and its tangible effects, at work (Oergel 2015). It relies on public opinion, which has acquired a new, dynamic ferocity. Carlyle presents its violent power as driving the revolutionary developments. The public "consensus" expressed in it is the result of the preceding workings of the "mechanical philosophy", which, through the dissolution of the old regime, has freed the "Many" from their political suppression and given them a public voice. This is a commonplace in the 1820s, it had been invoked in a positive sense from Forster and Thelwall to Hazlitt and been presented as ominous from Burke to Brandes, and Blackwood's satirical "One of the Democracy" ("On the Spirit of the Age" 1830). For those who wanted or needed to control this force, their job had become much harder, because it had changed in nature and may require, and produce, different means of control. Carlyle asks:

> What is this Thing, called *La Révolution*, which, like an Angel of Death, hangs over France, noyading, fusillading, fighting, gun-boring, tanning human skins? La Révolution is but so many Alphabetic Letters; a thing nowhere to be laid hands on, to be clapped under lock and key: where is it? What is it? It is the Madness that dwells in the hearts of men. In this man it is, and in that man; as a rage or as a terror, it is in all men. Invisible, impalpable; and yet no black Azrael, with wings spread over half a continent, with sword sweeping from sea to sea, could be a truer Reality. ([1934]: 669)

He presents this ephemeral spirit as powerfully real. Its actions are linked to real individuals, but they are nameless, and each individual is at the same time part of a collective force, an image of the new "masses". The "thing" appears to be the revolution, it engenders an all-permeating "atmosphere". It is a force, pathological in this case, a "madness", but pervasive, because it makes sense of the situation for "many", in the moment and in a wider context.

> Nay, if we even had their thought, a fraction were that of the Thing which realized itself, which decreed itself, on signal given by them! [...] this Revolutionary Government is not a self-conscious, but a blind fatal one. Each man, enveloped in his ambient-atmosphere of revolutionary fanatic Madness, rushes on, impelled and impelling; and has become a blind brute Force. ([1934]: 669)

Here zeitgeist's ambiguity regarding its equally mechanical and dynamic nature is evident: the revolutionary government is a blind fatal force linked to pathological madness, and as such linked to the unconscious dynamic springs of human energy. This ambiguity relates back to the point he had made in "Signs of the Times" that even the French Revolution was a genuinely vitalistic occurrence, similar to the Reformation or the English Civil War. This vitality powers the immense force of public opinion at this time, which creates the wild sea on which the "ship" of the Convention, or indeed the ship of state, is being tossed about.

> The Convention, borne on the tide of Fortune towards foreign Victory, and driven by the strong wind of Public Opinion towards Clemency and Luxury, is rushing fast; all skill of pilotage is needed, and more than all, in such a velocity. Curious to see how we veer and whirl, yet must ever whirl around again, and scud before the wind. [...] To no purpose: so strong blows the wind of Public Opinion. ([1934]: 709)

This kind of public opinion is beyond control, by individuals or governments. It remains ambiguous whether its grip represents mechanical coercion or dynamic connection ("noble Sympathy"), whether the revolution develops its own mechanism or whether people, en masse, join willingly, whether individuals make a choice or follow blindly.

> The death of Robespierre was a signal at which great multitudes of men [...] rose out of their hiding places; and, as it were, saw one another, how multitudinous they were, and began speaking and complaining. They are countable by the thousand and the million, who have suffered cruel wrong. Ever louder rises the plaint of such multitude; into a universal sound, into a universal continuous peal, of what they call Public Opinion. [...] Force of Public Opinion! What king or convention can withstand it? You in vain struggle: the thing that is rejected as "calamitous" today must pass as "veracious" with triumph another day. ([1934]: 699)

Hume's "spirit of the times", which was the check of rulers, now appears as the caprice of the masses. Individuals discover a commonality, which allows them to bond, at least for the moment, into not just a unitary body but a will, whose force becomes difficult to re-direct. While Carlyle's interpretation of it is negative, its quality is dynamic, or at least fundamentally un-mechanical, because it is unpredictable, capricious. It is doubtful whether it is "free", although it breaks the chains of oppression, its collective force appears to create new forms of coercion. Despite its dynamic origin this force acquires, in Carlyle's assessment, full mechanical jurisdiction: on the penultimate page of the text, the "force of Public Opinion" becomes the "*law* of Public Opinion" ([1934]: 726). The terminology of law enforcement employed by Carlyle ("Police of Public Opinion") was not new: it had also been a feature in Fichte ("Richterstuhl der Publicität") and was the original basis for the eighteenth-century idea of the incorruptible public: it could *judge* because its collective reason could not fail.

For Carlyle, the mechanical and dynamic qualities of public opinion, and zeitgeist, depended largely on which stage of the historical process had been reached. Fully established public opinion works mechanically to coercively produce self-perpetuation, while emerging new opinion, if it is bound for success, works dynamically to achieve dominance. Revolutionary stages are dynamic, established systems are mechanical; both can occur within "revolutions" that take place over longer time-spans. These are the same conclusions that Hendrich had put forward in 1797, and with which Arndt, Brandes, Garve, and even Forster, had concurred. However, Carlyle's presentation of the forces that drive the French Revolution is fundamentally ambiguous.

Hazlitt and Carlyle have in the past not been considered very similar. And they no doubt would have considered themselves as very different from each other. Carlyle certainly saw Hazlitt as profoundly different from himself; to him Hazlitt was one of those representing the mechanical age, because he followed its philosophy and could not break out of its grip. A perceived lack of genuine "Faith" was one of the key reasons why Carlyle, instead of engaging fully with British sources in the 1820s, turned to German ones to map a way out of the present. He even avoided the term "spirit of the age", although it would have fitted much of what he says, perhaps because it was too associated with Hazlitt and *that* London set. Instead he favoured the slightly less idiomatic calque of the German *Zeitgeist*, "spirit of the time",[102] not "times", the term familiar from the eighteenth-century sources. He may also have preferred the hint of ambiguity inherent in "spirit of the time", also present in "Geist der Zeit" and "Zeitgeist", which makes it possible to establish a close link between the spirit of history and the spirit of the present age and suits his conflation of the nature of the present age with its place in the historical process. This ambiguous conflation amplifies the *tendencies* of an era by linking it, through its place in history, to historical continuities as well as discontinuities. We do not know – maybe have not yet discovered – what Hazlitt thought of Carlyle; Grayling's biography does not mention him.[103]

---

102 "Edward Irving's warfare has closed; if not in victory, yet in invincibility, and faithful endurance to the end. The Spirit of the Time, which could not enlist him as its soldier, must needs, fight against him as its enemy." "On the Death of Edward Irving", first published in 1834 in *Fraser's Magazine* 61 (1899: IV, 319).

103 I think it is unlikely that Hazlitt would have been unaware of the young writer who had published a book on one of his favourite German dramatists, Schiller.

From reading Hazlitt and Carlyle on zeitgeist in conjunction, and putting Carlyle's aversion to, and pity for, "poor Hazlitt" to one side, it appears that that there are considerable parallels not just of theme, but also of style and approach between the two. Both approach the spirit of the age through individual figures, portraits, or biography. Both favour a highly mixed style, in which assured pronouncements and pathos are tempered with irony; their writing preaches but equally sets out to amuse and teach. John Rosenberg described this – for Carlyle – as a tension between "scripture" and "journalism" (1985: 50). Both detect and delineate the lack of a vital moral spirit, which they see as a key feature of their age and which they blame on the absence of a unifying collective bond, public spirit. This lack, and all that flows from it, is for both the basis for the coherence of the age. Carlyle, too, is fond of pointing out the "paradoxical" nature of especially intellectual affairs, when he presents Thomas Hope and Friedrich Schlegel as "voices" in the "Babel-like confusion of tongues" (1899: III, 33). Both focus on the minutiae of everyday reality – looks, mannerisms, the weather – as well as the abstract import of developments or ideas, and both have a clear sense of the power and dynamics of public opinion.[104] Many of these similarities are of course due to the fact that both were writing at roughly the same time, for the same audiences, and publishing in the same or similar outlets. However, these similarities between these two in other respects very different writers also illustrate the intellectual coherence of their age. Both responded to the issues of their "age" with similar alarm and a determined will to rectify its faults; in doing so they generated, especially in hindsight, a fairly coherent social and cultural effect, which impacted on general opinion, or at least general parlance. It appears that their writing resonated with their audiences, who by 1830 increasingly referred to the "spirit of the age", if *Blackwood's Magazine* is anything to go by (see below, p. 219). The fact that the similarities between the two have not been focused on, on account of their different political and moral aspirations, shows how an understanding of zeitgeist can help tease out otherwise overlooked convergences and coherence, where they exist. Because, for all this focus on the similarities between the two, they *were* also very different, in terms of lifestyle, political persuasion, and attitude. *This* illustrates once more the non-homogenous, disparate nature of an intellectual elite who nevertheless were responding to the same issues and managed to create a cultural climate.

---

104 In his short essay on Edward Irving, occasioned by the preacher's death in 1834, Carlyle charts the waves of public esteem, "of popular Applause" in the preacher's career (1899: IV) in a way very similar to Hazlitt's in *Spirit of the Age* (1910: 204). Although Hazlitt is a great deal more sceptical about Irving, he, too, observed that he "has opposed the spirit of the age" (1910: 210).

5.6 John Stuart Mill – the "Spirit of the Age" and the "Age of Transition"

A few years after Hazlitt's efforts to capture the "spirit of the age", the young John Stuart Mill (1806–1873) presented his assessment of the times in a series of essays with the same title, which appeared in the *Examiner* between January and May 1831 (Mill 1942: xxvii); it was one of his first publications. Mill takes the existence of a spirit of the age for granted, it is based on "fixed opinions" commanding a general "assent" that approaches "unanimity" "while they continue in vogue" (1942: 6). Betokening its descent from Montesquieu's general spirit and British public spirit, the spirit expressed in these opinions is crucial for the functioning of society, for the interactions between its members, and Mill makes it the basis for his analysis of Britain's political and social issues.

Taking an approach different from Hazlitt's gallery of portraits and similar to Carlyle's in "Characteristics" (which would appear a few months later in December 1831), Mill describes the character of the present age and how it differs from preceding ones by making it part of a historical progression: it is an "age of transition", when ideas, ideals, and particularly forms of government, are in flux. "Mankind have outgrown old institutions and old doctrines, and have not yet acquired new ones." (1942: 6) There is no stability because there is no general consensus: "No fixed opinions have yet generally established themselves [...] no new doctrines, philosophical or social, as yet command, or appear likely soon to command, an assent at all comparable in unanimity to that which the ancient doctrines could boast of while they continued in vogue." The result is "intellectual anarchy". (1942: 12) In the context of this study, Mill is going over familiar ground. Nevertheless, Mill and his editor at the *Examiner*, a magazine with a reputation for intellectual and political radicalism (Mill 1942: xxiv), clearly felt this was a yet unexhausted topic. Carlyle would, in "Characteristics", soon confirm that historical speculation (such as his and Mill's) was under-developed in England (1899: III, 33).

Mill's essays are a response to the twenty-page "Letter to Mr Christopher North on the Spirit of the Age" in *Blackwood's Magazine*, which had appeared in December 1830, less than a month before Mill's first essay, and to which Mill refers as "the ravings of a party politician" (1942: 3).[105] One can safely assume that this "Letter" either galvanised him into action or spurred him on, if he had already started writing. The (relatively new) editor of the *Examiner* was Albany

---

[105] Mill clearly identifies the "Letter" when he is refers to "a late article in Blackwood's Magazine, under the same title which I have prefixed to this paper" (1942: 3).

Fonblanque, who had taken over from John and Leigh Hunt in 1828 and who may well have thought that the *Blackwood*-piece needed rebutting, perhaps not least because in it the Hunts come in for heavy criticism (1830: 902, 910). Fonblanque was well acquainted with the topic of Mill's essays, he had reviewed Hazlitt's effort – favourably – for the *Examiner* in 1825. The *Blackwood*'s "Letter", sarcastic and serious, identifies the "spirit of the age" as a political ploy used by diverse counter-cultural radical demagogues – who range from Brougham via the Hunts to Cobbett, incidentally all members of Hazlitt's gallery – to bring about a revolution in Britain. This revolution will destroy the fabric of the state and the ancient constitution and result in the despotic rule of the self-interested and the uneducated "people", who are unfit to govern. According to the "Letter", the term "spirit of the age" is part of "the slang of faction", i.e. political propaganda, used to persuade the gullible that its force is omnipotent and resistance pointless. The *Blackwood* writer describes a practice which Jost Hermand will nearly two centuries later call manipulative "Verschleierungstaktik" (Hermand 2007).

In terms of content, the "Letter" is itself a contribution to the (raging) contemporary zeitgeist debate. One long lament about the destruction of "paternalistic public spirit", which is a "bond of union and affection" between rulers and the ruled, it touches upon all significant issues of our context: who are the people, or the public, and what is their function; the power and the creation of public opinion, both good and bad; and the danger posed by self-interested, incompetent, or self-serving politicians. Diagnosing this state of unsettled affairs echoes the general findings of nearly all zeitgeist observers since the 1790s.

Mill's aim is to rescue the idea of a "spirit of the age" as a serious historical category, and history as a meaningful process. He presents this undecided and lawless state as part of a historical progression in which what he calls "natural" states of society and phases of transition alternate. This alternation is necessary for social and historical progress because once social systems and their underpinning ideas have ceased to be convincing, beneficial, and appropriate, they cannot, and should not, maintain themselves. This view is indebted to eighteenth-century historicism from Blackwell to Herder, and it had considerable currency at the time. It underpinned Claude Henri de Rouvroy, Comte de Saint-Simon's and Auguste Comte's historical schemes, which are usually given as Mill's inspiration. It was equally the basis for Hegel's philosophy of history of the 1820s, and for Fichte's (earlier) *Grundzüge* discussed above. It was in many respects the basis for nineteenth-century historicism and would shortly be the foundation for Marx's trajectory of communism. It also gives legitimacy to the call to change elites. The difference to both French and German (Idealist) frameworks of history is that, in his essays at least, Mill leaves open whether the historical progression is teleological, he merely suggests that it follows a discernible pattern, although historical specificity makes every development contingently unique. His strongly utilitarian background – his father James was, next to Jeremy Bentham, the most important thinker of utilitarianism – made him less susceptible to metaphysical theory and kept his focus on sociopolitical developments and needs, which makes him (appear as) more of a political or sociological thinker than an historical one.

Mill *was* influenced by French thinking on this, his involvement with St. Simonianism is well documented.[106] His exposure to German ideas tends to be stressed less, von Hayek, for example, only remarks that the Simonians' "philosophy of history [...] probably appealed to him for its obvious resemblance to certain German strands of thought with which he had recently become acquainted" (Mill 1942: xxviii).[107] In the late 1820s Mill was friendly with F. D. Maurice and John Sterling, both imbued with Hare's Germanising. At this time Mill was also in close social contact with John and Sarah Austin, who had just returned from a stay at Bonn, at whose university Arndt, A. W. Schlegel, Schleiermacher, the Welckers and Niebuhr were gathered, and where Hare would shortly be visiting. According to Sarah Austin's correspondence during their time in Bonn in the winter 1827–1828, the couple were in regular contact with both Schlegel and Niebuhr (Ross 1893: 67–73). Sarah Austin was the daughter of the Germanophile Unitarian radical John Taylor (of Norwich) and at the beginning of an influential career as a translator of German literature. Mill had been recovering from depression and personal crisis in the course of 1828 by engaging with the poetry of Wordsworth (Mill 1942: x-xi), championed by Hare as the new voice in English writing that could point the way out of British spiritual and social problems and by Hazlitt as the writer whose poetry "could least be spared" (Hazlitt 1910: 255). Edward Bulwer-Lytton would declare in 1833 that "Wordsworth's genius was particularly German" (1833: II, 97). All this put Mill in – albeit vague – contact with German thinking; it led him, eventually, to coin the term "Germano-Coleridgean" to describe such thought, which he defined as a reaction against aspects of Enlightenment thought (irreligious abstractions of progress) and as the basis for a philosophy of human culture, which was necessary to understand how human societies work because each is based on particular ideas.

---

106 See Friedrich von Hayek's introduction to Mill's *Spirit of the Age* (Mill 1942: xxvii-xxx), and Jerome B. Schneewind's introduction to Mill's text (Mill 1965).
107 More recently however, it has been pointed out that "[Mill] acquainted himself with both German Romanticism [...] and the French utopianism of Henri de Saint-Simon. Yet he fended off all attempts to recruit him as a disciple of these or other views." (Miller 2010: 8).

Mill proves himself as an astute observer of the zeitgeist phenomenon. He traces its emergence – based on the rise of the term "spirit of the age" – to about fifty years from his time of writing (1942: 1), i.e. to the years leading up to the French Revolution. He considers the uncertain and restless search for the spirit of the age the "dominant idea" of this period. Ernst Brandes reached similar conclusion in the introduction to his *Über den Zeitgeist* over twenty years earlier in 1808, when he spoke of the dominant "Geist der Unruhe". Mill links such thinking to the new notion of history and identifies it as typical of ages of transition (1942: 1). There is some ambiguity as to whether all ages of transition have this historical bent, or whether the present historical approach was owed to the extreme extent of the current upheaval and in fact an aspect of modernity. Mill's discussion suggests that the spirit of the age was reaching self-reflexivity. Unsurprisingly he identifies the current "intellectual anarchy" as a clash between potentially radical reform, embodied in the "march of intellect", and social conservatism, holding on the "wisdom of the ancestors" (1942: 1), a term the *Blackwood* Letter uses prominently (1830: 911).[108] In this constellation the contest comes across as a socio-political version of the *Querelle*, which was one of the starting points for the development of modern historicism.

Mill points out that, for all its political antagonism, the current intellectual anarchy is predicated on shared linguistic patterns. He astutely observes how the contemporary discussion has produced its own discourse und turns on the same phrases: the current "catch-words" are used by all sides in this partisan conflict, which ultimately deprives them of any clear meaning. "Each phrase, originally an expression of respect and homage, each ultimately usurped by the partisans of the opposite catchword, and in the bitterness of their spirit, turned into the sarcastic jibe of hatred and insult" (1942: 2). This study has produced copious evidence of this. While Mill sees this mainly as a devaluation of language and meaning, it is equally an expression of the shared concerns and the contested ground, where different solutions are being offered for the same concerns, each vying for acceptability among audiences in the public sphere. As we have seen throughout this investigation, every partisan claims to be the guardian of true public spirit and the public good.

Mill's interest focuses on the authority to govern with public consent, or at least with public acceptance, which is in his view the only way to govern authoritatively without having to resort to constant coercion. While this was of course an idea put forward nearly a century ago by Hume, picking it up represents Mill's

---

[108] In the same vein, Mill prominently uses "outgrown all its institutions" (1942: 6), which the "Letter" also employs (1830: 912).

most original contribution to the zeitgeist debate; he explicitly investigates the link between public authority and public opinion, or the mechanism that empowers, and potentially authorises, a governing or intellectual elite in a post-revolution context. Such elites, post- or pre-revolution, have been the crux of zeitgeist thinking, they are the instrument by which new ideas emerge, spread and are maintained, until they are themselves challenged. Their authority rests on public acceptance; Mill leaves open who – or how many – constitute the public, and he is not convinced that such acceptance is based on wisdom or rightness, as he is fully aware of the potential of demagogical abuses, "the influence of imposture and charlatanerie" (1942: 10–11).

All zeitgeist investigators since the French Revolution agreed on the key role of elites and public opinion, but they differed as to whether these two entities are, or can be, "virtuous". Their views tended to depend on their political convictions and how these convictions related to the current political landscape. Mill makes a conscious effort to rise above the general lamenting about the age (in which the *Blackwood* Letter indulges for political effect) and to take a more neutral look. It is this openness towards finding out what motivates people to support or oppose change that he (later) saw as the key achievement of the Germano-Coleridgean "school".[109]

The idea that the ruling "few" require the approbation of "many" of the governed had been a concern in English politician thinking since the late seventeenth century. Thinking about the way in which intellectual elites are effective went back to the eighteenth-century notion of an "invisible church". Mill makes these considerations his central issue, taking Arndt's descriptions of the types of people (writers) involved in maintaining a dominant spirit a step closer towards a conceptual understanding of zeitgeist by focusing on the links between social institutions, communal values, political and intellectual elites, and the governed. For him, this link is explicitly based on shared ideas maintained in the public sphere by shaping, expressing, and assenting to public opinion. In difference to Arndt, Mill's focus was slanted towards *ruling* elites rather than the role of intellectual ones. He did by no means ignore the latter, rather for him the two are merged, he discusses executive power and intellectual capital in conjunction. For Arndt the influence of the "writing" elite was the key lever of power in favour of change. While this difference is no doubt

---

109 "The peculiarity of the Germano-Coleridgean school is, that they saw beyond the immediate controversy, to the fundamental principles involved in all such controversies [...]. They thus produced, not a piece of party advocacy, but a philosophy of society [...], not a defence of particular ethical or religious doctrines, but a contribution, the largest contribution made by any class of thinkers, towards the philosophy of human culture." Quoted by Bantock (2011: 105).

evidence of the differences in political set-up between Britain and Germany, it is equally an expression of the increased readiness for political change among liberals who would not consider themselves radicals and in public opinion in general.

When society is not in a transitional phase, the ruling elite has, according to Mill, the willing support of the governed, who are happy to be ruled by them in terms of political setup (government), moral and spiritual values (established opinions) and intellectual approach (ways of arriving at "truth"). This support is based on the actual as well as the perceived "capacity" of the elite. Society is in its "natural" state

> [w]hen on the one hand, the temporal, or [...] the material interests of the community are managed by those of its members who possess the greatest capacity for such management; and on the other hand, those whose opinions the people follow, whose feelings they imbibe, and who practically and by common consent, perform [...] the office of thinking for the people, are persons better qualified than any others whom the civilization of the age and country affords, to think and judge rightly and usefully. (1942: 35–36)

Authority and legitimation are in a reciprocal relationship. The capability of the ruling elite needs to be obvious: they need to be – or believed to be – the "fittest" to rule, "worldly power, and moral influence, are habitually and undisputedly exercised" (1942: 35). This is the case in republican as well as monarchical systems. Mill revisits Montesquieu's taxonomy of good forms of government.[110] In times of transition, this relationship between ruling elite and the governed, or the people, is out of joint, which is currently the case in Britain. Mill considers the British "aristocracy", the "wealthy classes", "persons of rank and fortune", who after the Reformation inherited "worldly power from the Roman Catholic clergy" (1942: 86), too discredited to hold on to government. "The superior capacity of the higher ranks for the exercise of worldly power is now a broken spell." (1942: 90) "They have flung away their advantages" because they have not "preserved the confidence of the people in the integrity of their purposes, by abating each abuse, in proportion as the public conscience rose against it", not least because "they have not kept themselves on the level of the most advanced intellects of the age", so they "have been overtopped by the growth around them of a mass intelligence superior, on average, than their own" and lost "the moral ascendancy which an intelligent people never long

---

[110] The difference between the two systems is that in republics "holders of power are purposely selected for their fitness", while in monarchies "the possession of power of itself calls forth the qualifications of its exercise" (1942: 38).

continues to yield to mere power" (1942: 90). While Hendrich, Arndt, and Brandes argued that the government, i.e. the rulers, should learn, and behave differently, Mill, a generation later, suggests that the government needs to be replaced.

For all Mill's claims of neutrality in the first essay, there is in his thinking a strong legacy of the "salutary" correctness of public opinion, which had been propagated by 1790s radicals like Thelwall or Forster. By losing the confidence of the people, the ruling elite have forfeited their right to rule and to "do [the peoples'] thinking for them". In 1831 a managed reform from above – as envisaged by reforming moderates in the run-up to 1815 or 1819, – seems no longer possible to Mill. The difficult – readily obstructed – progress of the Reform Bill through the legislative chambers and the violent reactions in the streets to these difficulties in the course of the year seemed to confirm Mill's views. Crucially, the ruling class have lost their authority because they have been left behind, intellectually and socially, by the "age", or even history, by not noticing that the world was changing. Brandes expressed the same view in 1808 in relation to the German rulers' failure to read the signs of the times.

For Mill, "Old maxims" are now ineffective (1942: 7), i.e. no longer convincing. This is the reason why many people are ready to listen to ideas of radical reform. "It is not in human nature to yield a willing obedience to men whom you think no wiser than yourself, especially when you are told by those whom you do think wiser, that they would govern you in a different manner." (1942: 43) Mill himself comes down heavily on the side of political reform. Contrasting Britain's current leaders with "natural leaders of the people"[111] he concludes that

> The whole of their effect is the direct contrary – to degrade our morals, and narrow and blunt our understandings: nor shall we ever be what we might be, nor even what we once were, until our institutions are adapted to the present state of civilization, and made compatible with the future progress of the human mind. (1942: 58–59)

Values ("morals"), forms of enquiry ("understandings"), and political set-up ("institutions") are all linked and affected by the dominant principles. If the same principals are guiding all three, the peace of the natural state rules; if there are discrepancies, the disruption of transition will arise. (In contrast to Carlyle, such unanimity is not conceived as the rule of mechanical coercion.) Mill formulates a comprehensive picture not just of the link between prevalent

---

[111] Examples of such natural leaders were, according to Mill, the seventeenth-century parliamentarians (1942: 58–59).

ideas and their institutionalisation, but also of the effects of the prevalent ideas on the governed and the ruling elites. In the present context the latter "must be divested of the monopoly of worldly power" (1942: 93) not just because they have rendered themselves unfit to rule by failing to keep up with the "age", but because their continued rule is socially corrosive, they "degrade *our* morals" and "blunt *our* understandings". Their rule is no longer in the communal (national) interest, they prevent "us" from being what "we" could be. They are discredited by the (familiar) failings of self-interested materialism, which erodes public spirit and community, and devoid of "public virtue". Mill still promotes the term Blackwell used so approvingly a century ago, and that also dominated the legitimation of the Jacobins 1792–1794.

> Idolatry of certain abstractions, called church, constitution, agriculture, trade and others: by dint of which they have gradually contrived [...] to exclude from their minds the very idea of their living and breathing fellow-citizens, as the subjects of moral obligation in their capacity of rulers. [...] They do not love England as one loves human beings, but as a man loves his house or acres. (1942: 92)

One wonders whether Mill is deliberately echoing Hazlitt's 1806 pamphlet, which castigated a society dominated by irresponsible venality: "They will defend England as connected with her colonies, [...] but will they defend her [...] as their country? [...] They would defend their country not as her children, but as her masters, as a property, not as a state." (1806: 114)

This discredited ruling elite holds on to power through their effective control of public opinion. "They [the possessors of worldly power] retain [...] enough of that influence to prevent any opinions, which they do not acknowledge, from passing into received doctrines." (1942: 92–93) But this control is clearly being contested, otherwise Mill would not be able to publish his essays in a successful magazine, and people would not be listening to writers urging reform. Albany Fonblanque would not get the chance to publish Mill's essays because his magazine would be closed down, or go bankrupt from lack of sales, irrespective of whether Fonblanque thought Mill was right.

Despite his evident zeal for political reform, Mill is sceptical as to an immediate resolution of the age of transition, because no clear consensus of what should be done exists (yet). Although the number of individuals "in possession of knowledge to form sound opinions by their own lights" is increasing, the main "achievement of the present age is the diffusion of superficial knowledge" (1942: 10). This does not make the majority necessarily less liable to "sophisms and prejudice", as one set of such opinion has merely been replaced with another (1942: 11), which simply results in a greater reluctance to be "told".

This *has* achieved an "increase of discussion" (1942: 13), which is at the moment, however, mainly responsible for the "intellectual anarchy". A lack of clarity continues to prevail, because clarity cannot emerge while the clash of sectarian party-spirits is raging. Hendrich had reached very similar conclusions on 1797.

Mill remains uncertain about the potential new structures and new elites; he even begins to consider the power of (any) opinions to rely on a "charm" (1942: 7). Nevertheless, he holds that ideas *do* rule the world beyond direct individual action, although he does not clearly distinguish between ideas, opinions, maxims, or doctrines, all of which are subject to the same process of emergence, acceptance, maintenance, and eventual displacement. He stresses the power of the mental-spiritual, of the spirit of the age, over people and society in the opening essay, something to which he returns in the last: "The revolution which had already taken place in the human mind, is rapidly shaping external things to its own form and proportions." Like the other zeitgeist investigators, Mill believes that social institutions are shaped by intellectual changes. By the same token, the human being is shaped by their context, which they cannot escape.

> Whatever we think, or affect to think of the present age, we cannot get out of it; we must suffer with its sufferings, and enjoy with its enjoyments; we must share in its lot, and to be useful or at ease, we must even partake its character. (1942: 4)

Mill swayed between a detached meta-historical view and a (more activist) focus on the immediate present, between considering the spirit of history and the spirit of the age. He seems torn between active radicalism and detached scepticism. On the one hand he takes a historical view and traced the "Geist der Zeiten" from the Reformation to the Enlightenment, but on the other hand he presents the spirit of the age (instability and confusion in a period of transition) as overwhelming society and requiring immediate action. Change could be rapid, a proposition of "a few months ago" could soon be "the tritest truism" (1942: 93). Ultimately a moderate Hegelianism wins out: he proposes to trust in "futurity" (1942: 93, 34), the force of history, but it is perhaps less a Hegelian world spirit that will answer to the current problems than a contingent specificity. The aim, however, is clear: a new generally convincing consensus *must* be created, which will allow a new public opinion to develop. This will in turn allow a settling into a new "natural" state. A new elite needs to come up with a convincing and acceptable new idea (and ways of its implementation), behind which the public will unite. The new elite needs to be sanctioned by at least one of the following: eminent wisdom and virtue, religion, or deserved worldly power.[112] The new idea only has a chance to become an established opinion, if it makes sense, producing a "unity of moral influence" (1942: 64). It is not entirely clear whether Mill considers himself as belonging to this new elite, or whether it has not yet emerged.

Carlyle read these essays with great interest; he was so intrigued that he resolved to meet their author, which he duly did. It seems likely that their budding friendship left a trace on Carlyle's "Characteristics"-essay, which offers some hope to overcome the coercive mechanism presented in "Signs of the Times". The overlap of ideas between Mill's "Spirit of the Age"-essays and Carlyle's December contribution to the *Edinburgh Review* is considerable, especially regarding the current anarchy and the alternating phases of history.[113] It is quite possible that "Characteristics" was, among many other things, also a response to the *Blackwood* piece. Carlyle may well have read the "Letter's" sarcastic characterisation of the spirit of the age as an – allegedly – inescapable and all-permeating force as a hostile reference to his "mechanism" from "Signs of the Times".[114]

The more significant outcome from the close intellectual partnership between the staunchly anti-utilitarian Carlyle and the Bentham-educated reformer Mill over the next few years, however, was Carlyle's *French Revolution*. Mill's interest in the Revolution and its meaning may initially have been (even) greater than Carlyle's: behind all of Mill's ruminations in the above essays, inevitably, stood the French Revolution. It was the evidence that "mankind have outgrown old institutions and old doctrines", it was the reason why "almost every nation on the continent of Europe has achieved [...] a change in its form of government", and it had created the – so far negative – consensus that "our own country [...] proclaims almost with one voice that [...] they [old institutions] shall be renovated" (1942: 6–7). Jerome Schneewind reports that

> Mill turned Carlyle's thoughts toward France and especially toward the French Revolution, of which Mill had himself occasionally entertained ideas of writing the history. When Carlyle decided to write it himself, Mill helped him [...], lending him scarce books, making enquiries for him in France (Carlyle could not afford to go there himself). (Mill 1965: 183)

---

[112] "All bow down, with a submission more or less implicit, to the authority of superior minds, or the interpreters of the divine will, or of their superiors in rank and station." (1942: 62).
[113] The essays differ regarding Carlyle's insistence on faith, intuitive understanding, and the salutary nature of unconsciousness.
[114] The reference in the "Letter" to "Carlile", however, is not to Carlyle, but Richard Carlile (1790–1843), a prominent advocate of universal suffrage and publisher of political literature, who had joined Henry (Orator) Hunt on the hustings at St. Petersfield in August 1819.

This was the background to the oft-quoted letter by Carlyle to Mill of September 1833, when Carlyle formulates the need to "tell" the Revolution "right". The (somewhat curious) incident of Carlyle's first manuscript being accidentally burnt in the house of Mill's father James while Mill and Harriet Taylor were reading it – Carlyle had given it to Mill for comment – is well known. Similarly curious is the uncharacteristically mild response to this calamity by the famously irascible Carlyle.[115] When the book – rewritten – eventually appeared in 1837, Mill promptly reviewed it in the *London and Westminster Review* in July (Mill 1837). He feared the book's reception might not be favourable due to the volume's novel approach to history, the idiosyncratic way in which it was written, and perhaps most of all due to its tendency to "German mysticism" (still a problem, it appears), which Mill censures and thus no doubt hoped to neutralise. His review was a deliberate public intervention to manage the book's reception, as he explained in a letter to R. B. Fox in 1840. It was

> a book so strange and incomprehensible to the greater part of the public that whether it should succeed or fail seemed to depend on the turn of the die; but I got the first word, blew the trumpet before it at its first coming out, and, by claiming for it the honour of the highest genius, frightened the small fry of critics from pronouncing a hasty condemnation, got fair play for it, and then its success was sure. (Mill 1965: 184)

The review suggests to its readers that the book is original and astonishing, presenting the revolution as truly as possible in this novel way because it is a modern epic poem.[116] He points to techniques used by Schiller in *Wallenstein's Lager* to justify Carlyle's poetic treatment, which seeks capture the revolution and its age. Mill repeats what he had already said in the essays regarding the intellectual and political anarchy that followed the revolution and which informs Carlyle's treatment. In this respect, Carlyle's *History* is also a literary realisation of Mill's conception of the spirit of the age, not just Carlyle's own representation of how zeitgeist works in general. Mill's intervention in the book's reception illustrates his belief in the power of public opinion as well as his will to deliberately use this power. How aware he was of this (salutary) power is evident from a letter to Albany Fonblanque in 1831:

> The Press, which is our only instrument, has at this moment the most delicate and the most exalted functions to discharge that any power has yet had to perform in this

---

115 See Carlyle's letter to Mill of February 1835, quoted in Mill 1965: 183.
116 Mill promotes the emerging idea that history can only be fully represented by poetic means (Oergel 1998: 79–96).

country. It has at once to raise the waves and to calm them; [...]. With such words ringing in their ears, Ministers cannot waver even if they would. (Fonblanque 1874: 29)

In this, he quite consciously *behaves* like a member of the new elite.

5.7 Zeitgeist in Britain – politics and public opinion

At the end of this long chapter it is time to take stock and summarise what helped and what hindered Zeitgeist, term and concept, on its journey into Britain and why "spirit of the time" eventually became a "Modewort". The short answer is: politics and public outlook.

The term was initially introduced in a strictly political context, that of anti-Napoleonic propaganda with the aim to suggest that British and "German" military and political interests were similar. Grasping the "spirit of the times", as Peter Will translated it, was linked to making accurate political predictions: understanding the spirit of the present was useful to those planning (or supporting) political and military interventions and helped protecting and furthering one's polity's interests, (which are always presented as, and believed to be, the public good). Intervening in the political direction of the present was also the key aim for the German zeitgeist investigators discussed here. The complication regarding Schwabe's and Will's activities is that they appear to be covertly furthering Germany's "public good" in Britain, whose own public good they present as aligned with Germany's. The term, however, did not have an immediate impact in Britain, there appeared to be no need for it or its concept at this time (before 1815), because the crisis it pinpointed in German discussions was covered by "public opinion" and the "public" in British discourse. Other reasons were undoubtedly the contemporary suspicion of German intellectual and political thought as radical, tainted by Jacobinism, atheism and overblown metaphysics, which Schwabe's and Will's best efforts probably only imperfectly allayed.

"Spirit of the age" did become significant a decade and a half later. In the 1820s it became associated with the full range of zeitgeist "applications" familiar from the German context: critiquing society's political and cultural direction and using this critique to project political, cultural, and spiritual reform. Its association with political and cultural reform was bound up with the "Germanising" trend among a disparate group of intellectuals who were at this time active in British periodical journalism and who were reaching a wide British audience among the educated middle and upper classes. Among these intellectuals German thought had become associated with a new way of understanding what was wrong with society and how to remedy these ills. Politically, their critiques focused on contemporary reactionary conservatism, a prevailing materialism, and social selfishness. Investigating the spirit of the age was a way of justifying political reform and social and spiritual renewal. How radical such reforms should be and how to balance political changes and spiritual reawakening varied from writer to writer. Zeitgeist allowed each of them to make a compelling case for what was wrong with the "times" and how to change it, because the zeitgeist approach saw the present in relation to the past it had evolved from, in relation to history, and it triggered a close investigation of who had contributed to the current state of affairs and who might be best placed to bring about change. The zeitgeist approach allowed them to focus not just on the "what", but equally on the "how", because it linked cultural critique with a sociological approach that looked at whose interpretations of the present were believed and why.

For Hare, awareness of zeitgeist could link political reform to spiritual renewal, creating a social consensus that made these political reforms likely to succeed. For the young Mill, the "spirit of the age" was a way of justifying thorough political reforms by establishing a socio-historical perspective on the workings of political authority in society. For Hazlitt, it was a way of investigating and exposing the workings of the public sphere and public opinion, which were in his view obstructing radical political reform (although the same "organs" could under different circumstances support such developments, which is why he kept writing). And for Carlyle, it was a way of justifying the need for spiritual renewal before any political changes could be contemplated.

For all these writers, albeit to varying degrees, German thinking, in literature and philosophy, addressed the spiritual and cultural deficit which they had identified in Britain and which impeded the necessary political changes. While only Hare and Carlyle can with any justification be called proselytizers of German ideas, the other two had significant contact with German literature and thought. Recent German thought – and this is evident in both literature and philosophy – had a decided historical bent (Oergel 2006). Ideas of historicity and a historicist understanding of existence were useful to provide the crisis of the present with a historical safety net: the age of transition, foregrounded by Mill and Carlyle but treated by all of them, made it possible not just to mine the past for precedents and look for patterns, but also to project a better future, which could be achieved if conditions changed, or *were* changed by social, political, and cultural work (which they saw themselves as doing.) Linking zeitgeist to *Geist der Zeit*, or linking the spirit of the age to the spirit of history and playing on the zeitgeist concept's synchronic and diachronic aspects, made it possible to imagine that radical – revolutionary – political and cultural change could be safe, because it had happened before.

The concept of zeitgeist, as a spirit of the age that is generated in the public sphere and manifest in public opinion through which it affects political, social, and cultural developments, mapped without difficulty onto the existing British concepts of public opinion and the public. Attention to public opinion was especially welcome as its growing role in post-revolution politics in an increasingly literate society awash with print media was being recognised. What the English concepts of public opinion and the public lacked was a diachronic dimension. Zeitgeist and *spirit of the age* always evoked the eighteenth-century concept of *Geist der Zeit(en)* in German and *spirit of the times* in English, which maintained a link to the historical process, or even historical progression. This potential for projection was useful for both radical or moderate reform objectives. Although this potential could of course equally be utilised for conservative and reactionary ends, it served in this context the agenda of reform and renewal well.

The analysis for the spirit of the age bundled interlinking aspects of the workings of the public sphere in a way that was useful for publicly active intellectuals who considered themselves in one way or another as members of a new intellectual elite. Understanding how this spirit worked, helped making them conscious of their public roles and how to best pursue their aims. Analysing the spirit of the age and its workings in the public sphere clarified to them how societies worked as communities. While modern societies inherited from their early or pre-modern predecessors the need for communal bonds based on a shared identity and shared objectives, post-revolution (European) societies needed to take account of the changed political landscape in which demands for wider enfranchisement made a wider social engagement of all enfranchised members necessary if persistent party-spirit was not to turn all political activity into permanent social warfare. All the writers discussed here argued that public spirit needed to become (again) a key aspect of the new spirit of the age.

The content of Arndt's *Geist der Zeit I* was suitable to engage British public opinion in relation to shared political and military objectives towards the end of the first decade of the nineteenth century. (To what extent the book's introduction actually achieved this is another matter.) Its anti-Napoleonic content made sense in a belligerent climate fearful of French domination. The term, however, with its potential for radical social criticism and the concomitant political reform, which made so much sense before and during the Wars of Liberation in Germany, a disintegrating polity largely under foreign control, had little resonance, and hence little use, in a centralised nation-state defending its borders and its interests. Suggesting political and social reform at *this* stage would have been seen as treasonable and would be – indeed *was* – quashed as that. When during the five years between 1815 and 1820 it became clear that political and social reform would be obstructed by conservative forces intent on holding on to or restoring pre-revolution conditions, in Britain and on the Continent, a broadly acceptable "reform" movement began to develop in Britain, which needed a concept that could synthesise social and political critique with suggestions for a new way forward. Zeitgeist's ability to embed the spirit of the age in the spirit of history, making possible a "safe" vision of even extensive political and cultural change, began to make sense. This (long) chapter has traced how this concept took hold of public discourse in Britain, signalling broad public acceptance. Any such acceptance, however, always remains partial, and is readily contested, as *Blackwood's* satire on the "spirit of the age" of December 1830 shows.

6 How Ideas Travel (in Theory): The Zeitgeist Dynamic

Based on the case of Zeitgeist itself, this short chapter summarises the findings regarding the socio-cultural dynamics of the circulation and institutionalisation of new ideas. This investigation shows that "zeitgeist" was understood as an agent of transfer between conceptual, political, and cultural activity, which relies on the interaction between "elites" and their publics within a given historical context. In this interaction a new idea emerges, challenges established opinion, manages to establish itself and changes attitudes, outlook, and cultural practice. This study shows that this "zeitgeist" dynamic is not delimited by linguistic or national borders, transnational receptiveness depends to a large extent on the functionality of the idea for elites and their audiences in their specific contexts.

So how does zeitgeist arise and how is it maintained? In sum, the process by which ideas travel through disciplines, areas of social and political life, and across societies is this: contingent historical circumstances, such as social and political developments or events, cause individuals with access to publicity – members of one or different "elites" – to react to these events and developments by interpreting them and propagating their interpretation(s). Such a group may be more disparate than homogenous in terms of political persuasion or intentions and may become visible as a "group" only in hindsight. However, these individuals, who may or may not see themselves as associated, share similar concerns and produce similar ideas, which tend to be linked to specific key words. If their ideas, based on their interpretation of the present, meet with enough public acceptance, it is likely that new opinions will be formed and adopted, becoming "public opinion", which may become established opinion and solidify into values and maxims. If these ideas solidify into values, they will in turn influence public and private thinking and decision-making, and become "culture".

In a similar way ideas travel between languages and across political borders. If an idea meets with similar social, cultural, and political ambitions in a foreign context and if similar (not necessarily identical) political and social constellations produce similar debates, the idea, or key aspects of it, are likely to take root. Conversely, if there are few shared ambitions, it is unlikely to be taken up, and if political and social constellations are only broadly similar, the idea is likely to need adjustment and calibration, if it is to have an impact. The term "Zeitgeist" was for the first time consistently used to summarise and conceptualise these processes around 1800. The term captured the seemingly ephemeral "spirit-like" operations of these processes, which were, however, at this time identified as actually driven by human activity. The trigger for this recognition was the French Revolution.

The term and the concept of zeitgeist, however, predate the Revolution. They emerged out of discussions about the functioning of collectives, such as peoples and cultural communities, and increasingly, by the later eighteenth century, states and societies. "Zeitgeist" descends from the older term *genius saeculi* which was translated as "spirit of the times" into English and "Geist der Zeit(en)" into German. During the eighteenth century, these vernacular terms occurred in historical discussions of different peoples and their culture. Most generally, the term emerged out of the interest in historical developments and socio-political organisation from the seventeenth century onwards. It was from the start connected to two issues: firstly, to considerations about the identity and cohesion of collectives and, secondly, to the embodiment of historical time through the discernible cultural coherence of collectives. The former represents the synchronic, the latter the diachronic aspect of zeitgeist. These embodiments may form long-term units, such as "classical antiquity" or the "Middle Ages", or, increasingly, shorter generational "ages", such as the *Friedrizianische Zeitalter*, the *Goethezeit*, or the Elizabethan or Victorian Age.

In the eighteenth century a growing concern about despotism increased the interest in the functioning of collectives. In mid-century Montesquieu's highly influential taxonomy of types of government had identified despotism as a dysfunctional form of collective. Such despotically run social collectives were contrasted with those imbued with "public spirit", a term that accompanied the concern about despotism and also came to political and cultural prominence during the eighteenth century. In Montesquieu it appears as "l'esprit général", and it was a key element in eighteenth-century patriotism. German uses a calque to translate the French *esprit général* (which is also used to render the English "public spirit"): "(All)gemeingeist". The link between the concept of zeitgeist, as it was slowly emerging in the second half of the eighteenth century, and the concern about how best to organise and run collectives was the idea of "spirit", or "Geist". In the course of the eighteenth century *spirit* became a short-hand summary for the identity and animating energies of a given collective, which may be a temporal unit, such as an "age", or a more diachronic entity, such as a people, a nation, or a city. This spirit functions as a bond between the members of this collective and as a control mechanism mitigating abuses of power and the decline of the identity's positive core. "Public spirit" was the most general description of this entity.

"Spirit" derives its power from its efficacy to convince; members of the collective share its spirit and are bound by it. This results in the collective's permeation with the spirit, which in turn produces an observable contemporaneity and homogeneity of activities carried out in the same "spirit". Evidently, "public spirit" is based on shared beliefs and experiences. Such sharing can only take place in a communal, i.e. in a in some respect *public* space. Contemporary with the rise of interest in public spirit is an interest in the public sphere and in public opinion. Public spirit, public opinion, and the "general will", which also made its entry into European thinking at this time, were all names for the collective energies that attracted much attention from the middle of the eighteenth century.

The concept of "public" reaches back into medieval and early modern political thinking; it has always been linked with notions of legitimacy, especially the legitimacy of political power. This notion of legitimacy became attached to the eighteenth-century concepts of "the public" and "public opinion". Both were configured as checks on political, and cultural, power and invested with notions of incorruptibility. This incorruptibility derived from the belief in the rationality and reason of the members of the public, whose combined rational scrutiny would safeguard society against errors and abuses. Public opinion was also seen as indispensable for the permeation of society with public spirit.

Around 1800, the concern among progressive intellectuals about (political) despotism was joined by a cultural and spiritual concern about materialism in all its forms, about a general "externalisation" that focuses on the material needs of the body and the narcissistic and egocentric desires of the individual, such as social status expressed in wealth, influence and power. Such a focus on competitive external and material markers was increasingly criticised for promoting self-interest and eventually selfishness. Self-interest, in turn, was thought to undermine "good" public spirit, by setting individuals competitively against each other, and thus preventing public spirit from mitigating forms of political despotism. In fact, prevalent spirit and opinion were becoming seen as perversions of their public selves: a publicly supported and promoted dominance of self-interest was thought to serve despotism by encouraging the members of the social body to compete against each other for the wealth and power in the gift of the despot.

These concerns were voiced in Germany and Britain at similar times; in Britain they featured in the publications of John Thelwall and Edmund Burke in the 1790s, and in Julius Hare, William Hazlitt, Thomas Carlyle, and J. S. Mill in the 1820s and early 1830s. In Germany, similar discussions reached a peak between 1790 and the 1810s; the works of Johann Gottfried Herder, Franz Josias von Hendrich, Ernst Moritz Arndt, and Ernst Brandes are evidence of this.

While the "public" was conceived as a *relatively* inclusive entity which brings forth and supports the consensus of public opinion (although there was much discussion about the appropriate scope of such a public and the benefits and dangers of its extension), it was not normally seen as the instigator of new ideas. This function was ascribed to "elites" who, in the context of a reasonable public and a rational public opinion, were conceived as an "invisible church" of great minds. These "public" elites were largely self-appointed; socially they broadly emerged from the middle classes who were increasingly publicly active, institutionally they tended to "sit" within the expanding and increasingly powerful civil administrations of the emerging modern states, such as the German civil service (*Staatsbeamtentum*) and the Church of England, or the institutions of learning, such as the universities and the various proliferating academies. Outside the institutions of the state, they tended to come from the growing sector of public media, they were writers, public lecturers (who published their lectures), journalists, journal editors, and publishers. Many of them straddled both areas. Herder, Hendrich, Brandes, and Arndt held public office either as government administrators, in the Church (controlled by the sovereign), or the universities, Hare had a career in the Church of England, all five published voluminously throughout their lives. Hazlitt and Carlyle lived off their publications, while Mill could dedicate his time to his interests because he had private means. Self-appointed and watched with unease by the established (conservative) political elites, they needed access to political power beyond their influence on the reading public and public opinion, this they acquired through connections to and approval by open-minded members of the established ruling elites.

In their "public" work, such public elites are engaged in the interpretation of the current situation regarding its social, political, and cultural constitution and development. They identify current issues, formulate and present them, and may also formulate and propose solutions. Their "proposals" are then put to the "tribunal" of the public for acceptance. Because of their activities of interpreting issues and events, which can be slowly emerging changes or signal events, such as the French Revolution, German has, in the twentieth century, coined the terms "Deutungselite" for such groups, who have "Deutungshoheit" [prerogative of interpretation], defining their role and activities in this context. Twentieth-century Anglophone research into "institutions" tends to speak of "interpretive communities" (Stanley Fish) and authoritative "professional communities" (Frank Kermode) to identify the same functions.[1]

In later eighteenth-century thinking, the concept of zeitgeist was closely linked to the emerging notion of public opinion and the prominent notion of public spirit. But unlike the latter two, zeitgeist partakes, to some extent, of the grandeur of history. Its semantics was linked to longer-term historical processes, a link that was maintained into nineteenth-century "historicism",

---

[1] See Chapter 7, pp. 294–295 for more details.

where the spirit of history was evinced by the succession of "Zeitgeister", a notion not just found in Hegel, but also in the writings of the British Victorian historian Edward August Freeman (Freeman 1873). Public opinion, on the other hand, was conceived as focusing on short-term political, social, and cultural issues; without public opinion, however, the public elites could not circulate, let alone establish, their new ideas that challenged and countered established ones, so without it zeitgeist could not function. In zeitgeist, short-term current affairs are vaguely associated with the sweep of history, which allows containing the problems of the present in a historical progression and legitimising proposals for a different future through historical precedents. It made it possible to imagine that even radical political and cultural change could be safe, would not lead to total apocalyptic dissolution.

This suggestion of historical immanence, however, was merely suggested. In the main, public spirit, public opinion, and zeitgeist were conceived as contingent on their historical context and were not *primarily* seen as expressions of any form of historical providence. Their analysis was part of a vigorous investigation of the present to find out how the political, social, and cultural aspects of the current situation combined in their effects, i.e. how power relations, (pre-)existing preoccupations, and values interacted with the critical mass of opinion. The outcome of these investigations was an understanding of zeitgeist's immense power of permeation and a clear sense that, being contingent, it could be influenced by human action.

The perceived need for such analyses increased dramatically from the early 1790s onwards, as the revolution unfolded before enthralled observers in Britain and Germany. It was in this context that the term "Zeitgeist" became prominent on the discursive scene in Germany. It emerged as an ambiguous force because it was associated with public opinion, which was undergoing a change of status. In the wake of the *terreur*, the rapid succession of French constitutions, and the autocratic behaviour of the French committees, doubts were increasingly being voiced regarding the incorruptibility of the public and public opinion. A sense established itself that both these originally positive (because rational) entities were easily manipulated through demagogic means by self-serving (un-public spirited) groups. While zeitgeist became associated with this form of manipulation and indoctrination, it did not lose its emblematic ability to summarise contemporary coherence, which emerged as a new tool to investigate and understand modern society as it was emerging in the early nineteenth century. John Stuart Mill and Ernst Brandes very prominently used the zeitgeist concept in this way when they investigated the dangers and potentials of their "age", which illustrates the concept's usefulness for those interested in sociological developments.

Zeitgeist had for a long time been associated with a power to permeate, but around 1800 its effect was increasingly seen as illiberal and coercive. The tension between the free expression of identity and the collective coercion to conform to an identity had already been latent in the concept of a pervasive public spirit around the middle of the eighteenth century (for example in Montesquieu), but around 1800 this ambiguity emerged clearly. While the "spirit" can be the free expression of a collective's identity, it can equally be coercive, or at least a controlling entity that ensures desirable behaviour. Some of this coercion was of course necessary for the spirit to fulfil its function of checking political, or individual, power.

Zeitgeist's rise to discursive prominence was entirely contextual; it was triggered by the French Revolution. Discursive innovations of this sort tend to be triggered by a historical specificity, i.e. "events" and their consequences, some of which may emerge gradually. Such events may be a war, a (natural) disaster or a discovery of some sort; historical specificities may be created by a combination of events and their consequences: epochs are marked by game-changers. Debates ensue as to what these changes mean, which eventually, and only for a time, produce a publicly accepted interpretation of the present, of its features and it needs. This is the process by which public opinion changes, and zeitgeist arises. Acceptance and public consensus are often achieved more easily if an interpretation has the approval of (members of) the political elites. But if public opinion is strong enough, any opposition by ruling elites to this interpretation – to these new ideas – is likely to be overcome. If the political elite is not ready to compromise in line with public opinion, it will need to use force to crush the popular new idea. In extreme cases of this process, the ruling elite is overthrown. The French Revolution and its reception across Europe between 1790 and 1849 provided ample illustration of how these processes work. In this respect, zeitgeist's rise to prominence is an illustration of itself.

When new ideas become established opinions, they begin to influence, and possibly direct, public policy in their sphere of influence. Such a sphere of influence can be a particular social group, a whole society or a larger "federation of societies" that share similar social, political or economic ambitions and concerns. The zeitgeist concept itself travelled, in its newly constituted form, from Germany to Britain in the first three decades of the nineteenth century. "Spirit of the Age" did not become a widespread term in English until the 1820s, because in the 1790s there was little need for a term that associated "public business", its failings or new potentials, with a diachronic safety net, the terms "public" and "public opinion" sufficed to discuss the revolution and the rise of Napoleon. During the 1820s, however, social change and internal political challenges made such a concept useful. At slightly different points in time, German and British progressive elites, and increasingly their audiences, shared similar ambitions regarding political reform and spiritual renewal. Any German term entering British political discourse between 1790 and 1820 had to contend with associations of dangerous radicalism, such as atheism, Jacobinism, and mind-addling metaphysical speculation, which would hamper a quick and successful transfer. The extent of these barriers is evident from Peter Will's calibration of Arndt's text in 1808 and they were still noticeable in Hare's handling of German ideas in the 1820s. But the fact that the concept was not useful *until* the 1820s must be seen as the overriding reason why it did not catch on earlier.

It remains an open question whether circulating new ideas is a process that is as "free" and "rational" as the model of "good" incorruptible public opinion assumes or whether it is engineered by influential groups to serve particular purposes, self-serving or not. In any case, however, this process is intricately bound up with gaining and maintaining social, cultural, and political power. It is frequently a process of intense public contestation and it is ultimately about control of the public sphere. In this process two phases can be distinguished: the "rise" of the new idea, which is the expression of a transformative new "will" challenging established notions and searching for acceptance, and the period of "dominance", when social, cultural, and political permeation is taking or has taken place and a (potentially coercive) perpetuation of the idea, a holding on to power, is the aim. Carlyle called the former process dynamic, the latter mechanical.

After the mid-1790s the public sphere was no longer seen as just the communal space in which public spirit was generated and shared (although it never lost this aspect), it also became the space that needed to be controlled in terms of political power and cultural dominance, if any "spirit", and the power that went with it, was to be secure. Hendrich and Brandes made the point that this was a public "battle" over not just political and social issues, but also over controlling of their public interpretation. This was also the basis of Hazlitt's understanding of how the "spirit of the age" arises, impacts, and can be discerned. Such battles lay the public sphere open to demagogic manipulation, usurpation, and exploitation. Secret societies, which only a generation earlier were regarded as forms of a beneficent "invisible church", became suspect and the "invisible hand" could no longer be relied upon to be purely rational. By the same token, "the public" was no longer the incorruptible entity of final (rational) appeal; instead, there was increasing concern about which was the "right" public and whether any public was a just tribunal. At this point public spirit, which maintains the shared – often historically based – identity of a community, moves into the direction of political ideology. This development is most visible in Georg Forster. However, the public sphere remained the space in which public spirit, public opinion, and zeitgeist "existed". While the latter two were no longer seen as *necessarily* reliable guides to the public good, they were still considered indispensable for collective cohesion, and the belief in their effectiveness, in their power, was undiminished. Irrespective of whether they were perceived as "good" or "dangerous", their dynamics and mechanisms could be – and were – clearly observed. By the first quarter of the nineteenth century, these observations had reached a considerable level of sophistication.

This sophisticated view of the public sphere and public opinion was first and foremost the outcome of contemporaries studying the progress of the revolution in France, but any insights were quickly related to local situations, where and when this was appropriate. The different moments at which the term reaches prominence in Germany and Britain illustrates this. In Germany, this occurs more immediately in the wake of the revolution than in Britain, and it reaches a peak during Napoleon's ascendency. The debates about the necessity or undesirability of political and social reform coalesced around the term Zeitgeist, which subsumed different social critiques. These critiques could be the basis for calls for political and national reform or for conservative containment. The focus on zeitgeist signalled the awareness that change was being "proposed" at a time when change seemed eminently possible.

In Britain, this discussion focused, until the end of the second decade of the nineteenth century, on the term public, or popular, opinion. While the older versions *Geist der Zeiten* and "spirit of the times" occur fairly frequently in both languages in the middle of the eighteenth century, the English term "spirit of the age" only becomes prominent in the 1820s, between the revolutionary unrest in the "England of 1819" (Shelley) and the first Reform Act in 1832, when France was no longer a threat to national security and it was clear that political and social reform was being obstructed by conservative forces. At this point a fairly broad "reform" movement emerged, which had use for a concept that synthesised social and political critique with suggestions for a new way forward. Terms and concepts travel easily when social and political ambitions are similar and need a similar discourse.

The dynamics of zeitgeist, as a general principle, can only be evidenced through historically specific examples, i.e. through investigations into a *particular* zeitgeist, in the way the zeitgeist idea presented here has been distilled from the political conditions and public debates between 1790 and the 1830s. The socially and culturally transformative effect of this process, which the idea of zeitgeist summarises, can be tracked through its three ways of permeation: through new or newly inscribed ubiquitous *words*, the *concepts* behind them, which are picked up across different intellectual and social spaces, and the *activities* these words and ideas engender. This means the effects of zeitgeist can be explored through three different but interlinking aspects: the linguistic-discursive, the conceptual, and the institutional. The linguistic effect of zeitgeist, which perhaps yields the strongest visible evidence, is the appearance of catchwords or phrases and specific discourse patterns (such as Zeitgeist and "spirit of the age", to labour a point). The conceptual effect produces new interpretations; these can be re-interpretations or transformations of existing entities or new constructions of meaning: the eighteenth-century calques of *genius saeculi*, "Geist der Zeiten" and "spirit of the times", were re-made in the new terms of "Zeitgeist" and "spirit of the age", which now focused on doubts about the incorruptibility of public opinion and on concern about the rise and pernicious effect of "self-interest" on the one hand, and on social change and reform on the other. Finally, the institutional effect is evidenced by new cultural and social activity, it is frequently a putting into practice of the new conceptual interpretation, underpinned by the new discourse, which, together, produces new *Kulturmuster* (cultural patterns). This aspect is somewhat harder to see with "Zeitgeist" and the "spirit of the age", because these terms *eo ipso* focus on *process*. One may be inclined to suspect that the success of the Wars of Liberation or the first Reform Bill are tangible outcomes of the zeitgeist discourse, or that discourses about a changing society will be followed by institutional changes, but this is too close to conjecture to be persuasive. It will be more convincing to chart the three aspects in a more concrete case study, which forms the final section of this volume: the journey of the closely related ideas of the "Germanic" and "Gothic" into forms of cultural institutionalisation from the mid-eighteenth to the mid-nineteenth century in and between Britain and Germany. This case study highlights not only the successful circulation of an idea, but equally the reasons when and why ideas do not travel (just as Zeitgeist did not travel in the 1790s) and where significant "slippage" occurs on their journeys, i.e. when they come to mean (slightly) different things in their new contexts, either because their reception is very specific or because they have been adjusted to the target context to a significant degree.

7 How an Idea Travels (in Practice) – A Case Study

The Germanic and the Gothic – The Life and Times of the "Northern" Identity of Liberty and Duty in Germany and Britain 1770–1870

This chapter uses the zeitgeist approach to chart the rise, consolidation, and institutionalisation of the idea of a "Northern" identity, which was broadly identified as Germanic or Gothic. This identity underpinned the notion of a new social and cultural collective in Germany and Britain, which is largely, but not exclusively, that of the modern nation state, because at the heart of this late eighteenth-century construction was the idea of a new community of enfranchised citizens.

The process of constructing, legitimising, and institutionalising this identity will be presented by tracing the role of the newly prominent terms Gothic and Germanic in this construction, as they emerge under specific cultural, political, and social conditions in both countries. The emergence and circulation of this identity will be linked to the activities of elites, who formulated aspects of this new idea in response to specific historical contexts and managed to gain public acceptance for their proposals. This public acceptability and approval will be measured by the influence the idea exerts on intellectual and cultural practices, by its power to generate new cultural patterns and achieve forms of institutionalisation in both the German and the British national contexts. The analysis has two key areas of interest: the process of institutionalisation and the transfer of ideas and practices between Germany and Britain. Transfer occurred in both directions at different times, which will provide insights into the barriers to and accelerators of cultural transfer processes.

The "myth of the North" was created towards the end of the eighteenth century and became, in various forms, part of the self-definition of all modern nations across central, Northern, and Western Europe during the nineteenth century.[1] This aspect of modern European identity has been extensively discussed in relation to modern nationalism; it has not been sufficiently recognised as being part of a zeitgeist pattern in the above sense. The difference between discussing the "Germanic" as an aspect of the rise of nationalism and discussing it as a zeitgeist phenomenon is twofold: one, the zeitgeist approach

---

[1] Oergel 1996 and 2016; von See 1970, and Bohrer 1961.

https://doi.org/10.1515/9783110631531-008

takes a comparative *transnational* perspective by looking at how these terms and concepts fared across different national contexts (British and German in this case); and two, the zeitgeist approach focuses on the specific and concrete ways of dissemination and their contexts – propagating elites, their publics, and public approval leading to institutionalisation – rather than on more abstract historical causation, such as modernisation or secularisation (although these aspects remain of course crucial to explaining modern nationalism and historicism).

It is well recognised that communal identities rely on convincing reasons for their community's existence: who "we" are, what "we" do, and, often, where "we" come from.[2] The last question asks after origins, it involves history to establish – or "invent" – traditions.[3] The research into the invention of traditions and the imaginative nature of communal identities has been pursued for over a generation, and to some extent this case study confirms its findings. But, in this context, my point is not to show that the late eighteenth- and nineteenth-century Germanic identities discussed here are "not true", that they are either deceiving fictions or creative constructions serving ulterior motives. Instead, my point is to show *why* they are *convincing* at their point of emergence and during their subsequent period of "dominance", because it is their efficacy in this respect that makes them successful, i.e. gain public acceptance, and assume a logic, a form of truthfulness, which goes beyond mere manipulation and brain-washing demagogy. This *making sense*, for better or for worse, is the heart of zeitgeist.

This identity emerged in the later eighteenth century, it was fully formulated by the end of the 1820s. Its central tenet was the idea that modern European culture was based on the ethnic and cultural legacy of the peoples who were involved in, or affected by, the Great Migrations that followed the decline of the Roman Empire and their assimilation of the Christian religion. This identity construction focused predominantly on peoples of Germanic origin, or who were thought to be of Germanic origin, as it remained a matter for debate well into the nineteenth century who exactly was included in this group. Frequently no clear distinction was made between Northern and Southern Europeans, or between Celts and Germanics. The more important distinction was that between an established Greco-Roman culture and "new" (previously not dominant) "wandering" peoples. *Some* debate focused on the position of the Celts, who

---

2 Benedict Anderson's seminal book *Imagined Communities. Reflections on the Origin and Spread of Nationalism*, first published in 1983, serves as a representative here.

3 Similarly, Eric Hobsbawm and Terence Ranger's seminal collection *The Invention of Tradition*, published in 1984, is a key example of this body of work.

tended to be included,[4] but also on the Slavic peoples, who tended to be separated, but were acknowledged to share the key characteristics of being newly prominent, "wandering", and having assimilated Christianity.[5]

The amalgamation of Christianity with the indigenous culture(s) of the "new" peoples was thought to be complete between the beginning and the end of the "Middle Ages", a vaguely defined historical period that tended to include the Early Modern period. These Middle Ages came under particular scrutiny because they were considered the formative period of this identity, which, as *modern* European Christian culture, came to be seen as the successor and the "other" of classical antiquity. In this respect, the construction of this identity was the final stage of the Quarrel of the Ancients and the Moderns. The key characteristics of this post-classical European culture were defined as liberty in socio-political matters (a society of "free men") and personal integrity in spiritual matters as well as in matters of individual obligation, often summed up in terms such as loyalty and honesty, and expressed pithily by Walter Scott's character Cedric in *Ivanhoe* (1819) as: " I will die a Saxon – true in word and open in deed." (Scott 1986: 279)

This identity shadows the emergence and rise of the zeitgeist concept: it developed at roughly the same time and fulfilled the function of making sense of challenging new social and political situations at similar social and political crisis points. In this respect it is an aspect of zeitgeist "content" at this time and an ideal subject for a case study in this context. While the emergence and circulation of the zeitgeist idea is an illustration of itself, it is difficult to demonstrate this concept's cultural and social institutionalisation, because it describes a dynamic and a process. The Germanic, on the other hand, aims to describe a cultural "substance" whose cultural institutionalisation can be traced in different areas of social and cultural activity. The "content"-function of the Germanic for *the* late eighteenth- and early nineteenth-century zeitgeist is further illustrated by the fact that a number of key eighteenth-century texts that discuss communal spirit and communal identity deal with *both* the "spirit of the times" *and* with aspects of Northern identity, e.g. Percy, Hurd, and Herder. This indicates that public spirit and public opinion, both of which were, in eighteenth-century thinking, necessary to maintain collective identity, had not yet clearly divided into a long-term communal identity and a short-term political public opinion. It also illustrates the "identity-nature" of zeitgeist constructions. Whether longer-

---

[4] Wherever this appealed to the writer, as it did, for example, to Henri Mallet, a Francophone Swiss, and Walter Scott, a Scot.
[5] For example, in August Wilhelm Schlegel's *Vorlesungen zur Romantischen Literatur*, Hegel's *Philosophie der Geschichte*, or Thomas Arnold's *Lectures on Modern History*.

or shorter-term versions, both public spirit, the animating principle of a collective identity, and public opinion, the currently established consensus of a collective, purport and assume a social coherence. In terms of zeitgeist, which combines a synchronic with a diachronic perspective to project or consolidate a new idea, the Germanic gives the social critique around 1800, especially its call for social and political change, whether as reform or renewal, historical justification, because the two most salient aspects of the Germanic identity were defined as love of liberty and inalienable individual integrity.

7.1 The emergence of the terms Germanic and Gothic

The terms "Germanic" and "Gothic" are the most prominent ones used to describe this new cultural identity. Neither at its emergence nor during its period of dominance was this identity unchallenged, but as the following will show, it had a wide reach, impacting significantly on cultural areas as disparate as legal thought and architectural design. Although often vaguely defined, this identity will be shown to affect different levels of collective self-representation, the construction of historical narratives (national and European), the priorities of academic research, and general taste. Apart from "gothic" and "Germanic" in English and "germanisch" and, to a lesser extent, "gotisch" in German,[6] this identity coalesced also around terms like "Anglo-Saxon", "Teutonic", and "English" in English and "deutsch" in German, as well as Northern/Nordic/nordisch in both languages. All terms describe the same key characteristics, the value of "liberty" and personal integrity and reliability. The rather confusing terminological situation – ranging from more specific terms like Anglo-Saxon in English or gotisch in German to descriptors of modern nationality (deutsch, English) – is responsible for the identity's versatile applicability. It also obscures the links between these terms. Twenty-first-century Anglophone speakers may be surprised to find that English national identity was from the mid-eighteenth century to the 1840s frequently described as "German" in English texts. The lack of a clear distinction, at this point, between the terms "German" and "Germanic" is largely responsible for this notion. When Thomas Arnold declared in 1843 that the English are "German",[7]

---

6 The meaning of *gotisch* is much narrower than that of *gothic*.
7 "Our English race is the German race." (Arnold 1845: 26) It is evident from the context that Arnold uses German in the sense of Germanic. A generation earlier, in his *Essay on Chivalry*, Walter Scott spoke of "German chivalry" in the same sense: "The institution of chivalry has been often traced to the German tribes." (Scott 1887 [1815]: 2).

this should translate into twenty-first-century English as the English are (of) Germanic (origin). Similarly obscure for the contemporary German speaker is the term "angelsächsische Welt" [Anglo-Saxon world], which to the educated German denotes Britain and North America, when a literal-minded Germanophone might have expected this to refer to Northern Germany. The terminology of the "Anglo-Saxon world" emerged in the early twentieth century as a direct result of the nineteenth-century Anglophone Germanic identity.

The idea of the Germanic identity was successful, i.e. it found widespread public acceptance, in the eighteenth and nineteenth centuries, because it had the capacity to address contemporary issues and engage new elites and their publics. It was attractive, in the broadest sense, to the educated middle-classes and the literate lower classes, i.e. to those social sections who had at the time the strongest interest in greater social and political enfranchisement. It even had the capacity to engage some sections of the ruling elites at points of crisis (the French Revolution, the Napoleonic Wars, the first Reform Bill). In the course of the nineteenth century it made the transition from supporting a challenge to the existing order to consolidating (new) orders, eventually it supported conservative political interests.

In the 1760s, the preferred descriptor for these "Germanic" peoples in English texts was "gothic", so in Percy's *Reliques of Ancient English Poetry* (1765) and Hurd's *Letters of Chivalry and Romance* (1762). The use of the term "gothic" increased noticeably from the 1740s, peaking just after 1800 and again in the 1820s, but by the mid-nineteenth century it was conceptually replaced by the term Anglo-Saxon. The latter had been in use in the eighteenth century, but for obvious reasons in more specific applications. In the eighteenth century, "gothic" was generally used to describe cultural entities, such as architecture, language, and social customs, including forms of government, before it became a much vaguer term in English as the key depreciative descriptor for a new fashion in literature and taste, from which it recovered in the 1830s in the context of the Gothic Revival. Percy's and Hurd's usage is consistent with mid-eighteenth-century use. The semantic history of the term "gothic" in English has been traced by Samuel Kliger (1945), who pointed out its well-established connotation of political liberty in the seventeenth century, and for eighteenth-century Whigs. This link to liberty and liberation provided the basis for the appropriation of the term in the discourse of liberation from one-sided rationality in mid-eighteenth century aesthetics. Through its association with social customs and forms of government, it had not just a cultural, but a political connotation. In the later eighteenth century, the term was quite indiscriminately applied to "tribes" and "peoples" from the "Dark Ages" and the early "Middle Ages". The difficulty of subsuming a Celtic identity under it was circumvented by substituting it with "Northern", a practice evident in Percy's choice of title for his translation of Mallet, *Northern Antiquities. [...] Ancient Danes and other Northern Nations*, which takes account of Mallet's "inclusive" approach to the northern nations. A generation later, Walter Scott took a similar approach in his balladry, prominently in "The Harp of the North". In his widely read *Essays on Romance, Chivalry*, and *The Drama* for the *Encyclopaedia Britannica*, Scott still used the term gothic in much the same way as Hurd. He speaks of "our Gothic ancestors", "Gothic tribes" and "Gothic conquerors" who subdued the Roman Empire (Scott 1887: passim). At the same time, however, Scott also refers to "German warriors" in similar contexts and consistently speaks of the "German forests", a concept gleaned from Tacitus. He does not use the term Germanic in his *Essays*.

The efficiency of the term "Northern" in this context, beyond simply being a clever way of obfuscating distinction, derives from the influential sixteenth-century activities of national-minded Swedish researchers at the University of Uppsala, who, based on Jordanes' sixth-century history of the Goths, had projected the origin of mankind into Scandinavia. Jordanes speaks of a region "in the North", from where the Goths were said to have spread across the European continent (Kliger 1945: 108–109). This interest in Jordanes arose at the same time as central Europeans rediscovered Tacitus' *Germania*. For reasons rooted in his own historical context, Tacitus had propagated the idea of the exemplary nature of the "Germani", including their culture of "liberty". Both sources were used to construct identities based on origins and ancient traditions in the early modern period. In the case of Tacitus, researchers were utilising a Roman counter-construction originally intended as a cultural critique of Rome. The Roman term *Germanus*, and the idea of freedom and elective egalitarian *brotherhood* (germanus = brother) associated with it, were ethnically fairly unspecific Roman constructions, generated by the specific cultural and political situation of the Roman Empire at the time of their coining.[8] This lack of specificity of the Germanic, compared to the lesser ambiguity, in terms of tribal ethnicity, of terms like Saxon, Frank, or Swabian, increased the term's efficiency in our context: it could be freighted with various conceptual content.

In his *Letters*, Hurd favours "gothic", he uses neither "Germanic" nor "Teutonic", and "German" only once (albeit in a relevant context).[9] In Percy's

---

[8] The idea that Julius Caesar "invented" "die Germanen" goes back to the Danish historian Allan A. Lund; it has since been widely accepted. See "'Cäsar hat die Germanen erfunden'" 2013.
[9] He speaks of "German nations" in the context of chivalry ("gallantry") and their chastity at the time of Julius Caesar (Hurd 1762: 19).

translation of Mallet's *Histoire de Dannemarc* (1770), however, "Germanic" and especially "German" occur frequently.[10] Percy's use may have been influenced by Mallet's own frequent use of "germains", which quite generally refers to Germanic peoples at the time of Tacitus. Mallet also uses "gothique", less frequently, but significantly in relation to language ("la langue Gothique") and forms of government ("gouvernment gothique").[11] Checking through Google NGram, the term Germanic does occur in mid-eighteenth-century English texts, predominantly in connection with references to the German Empire, either explicitly as the "Germanic Empire" or as the "Germanic body", i.e. in quite technical usage. Occasionally, however, it refers to legal-constitutional aspects, foreshadowing later developments.[12]

In German, "got(h)isch" occurs in eighteenth-century texts predominantly in relation to language and architecture, i.e. in specific contexts, which indicates it was used as a mainly technical term. However, an anonymous essay in the *Neue Lausizische Monatsschrift* of 1800 sums up the traditional use of the word *and* its new potential, when it speaks of a "Gewölbe mit Rippen – *more teutonico* oder gothisch, weil die Römer alles, was über den Alpen war, gothisch nannten" [cross-ribbed vaults [i.e. gothic vaulting MO] – in the Teutonic or Gothic manner, because the Romans called everything north of the Alps Gothic] ("Über die sogenannte Gothische Baukunst" 1800: 361). Here a Tacitus-like general label for the "North" merges with a more specific term for architecture or a specific tribe. Since the phenomenal success of Horace Walpole's *Castle of Otranto. A Gothic Tale* (1764), however, gothic became associated with overwrought sentimentality, excess, and deviancy, attributes with which its detractors characterised the "gothic" novel. German did not make use of this term in this context.

"Gotisch" appeared in a seminal later eighteenth-century German text, which is salient in this context: Goethe's contribution to Herder's *Von deutscher Art und Kunst* (1773). In his essay "Von deutscher Baukunst" [Of German Architecture],

---

10 Percy also uses "Teutonic" to denote Germanic; see the subtitle of his "Translator's Preface" (Mallet 1770).
11 The denotation of gothic government as based on political liberty and even parliamentary democracy is borne out by Kliger's evidence from later seventeenth- and early eighteenth-century sources, which Mallet may have used (Kliger 1945).
12 In Charles Lucas, "To the Lord Mayor of Dublin" (1768), it occurs in the context of the loss of liberty through the presence of a large standing arm; in Samuel Squire's *Enquiry into the Foundation of England* (1753) "Germanic polity" refers to England and in a translation from the French of G.F.F. Raynel's *Philosophical and Political History of Settlements and Trade of Europeans in the East and West Indies* (1776) it is claimed that the Germans have lost their "Germanic constitution", while the English have kept it.

which appeared independently as an anonymous "Flugschrift" in 1772 (Herder 1988: 153), "Gothik", the Gothic style, is claimed to be German in nature. The "Germanness" Goethe describes here has the features that would become stock qualities in August Wilhelm Schlegel's, and indeed Fichte's, definitions thirty years later. This identity is defined by "das tiefste Gefühl von Wahrheit [...], würkend aus starker, rauher, deutscher Seele" [the deepest feeling of truth [...] emanating from their strong, rough German soul] (Herder 1988: 103); referencing the spiritual and individual integrity I described above. Herder himself, however, does not use this term in his own contributions to this programmatic publication, which was one of the key texts to launch the literary and cultural challenge to neo-classicism, the *Sturm und Drang*.

In German texts the use of the term "germanisch" increased in the 1790s, when it began to appear consistently in the context of cultural and linguistic descriptions, so in Daniel Jenisch's *Philosophisch-kritische Vergleichung und Würdigungen von 14 älteren und neueren Sprachen Europens* (1796), a Prize Essay of the *Preußische Akademie der Wissenschaften*, and in his *Geist und Charakter des 18. Jahrhunderts* (1800), which went into its second edition in 1803. Jenisch (1762–1804) was a Protestant theologian and pastor based in Berlin. Other examples include Johann Christoph Gatterer's *Allgemeine Weltgeschichte* (1792) and Johann Gottfried Eichhorn's *Geschichte der Cultur und Literatur des neueren Europa* (1799).[13] More examples followed in the first decade of the 1800s, which was also the time when the writer best known today for his widely received efforts to create this post-classical European Germanic identity, August Wilhelm Schlegel, changed his terminology from "deutsch" in 1803 ("deutsche Stämme" in *Romantische Literatur*) to "germanisch" in 1808 ("germanische Stammart" in *Dramatische Kunst und Literatur*).

By the 1760s, the English "Gothic" began to be used to denote the culture of the "Middle Ages" generally. Hurd laid the basis for this in his *Chivalry and Romance*, which was reinforced by Walpole's *Castle of Otranto*, which is set at the time of the Crusades. In both English and German (and most other European languages), a cognate of gothic became the established technical term for the predominant architectural style of the period between the late twelfth and the late fifteenth century, covering the high to late medieval period.

---

[13] Gatterer uses "germanisch" in connection with Germanic tribes settling in Northern Africa (1792: 520), Eichhorn uses "germanisch" and "Germanier" throughout, beginning on p. 1 (Germanier) and p. 5 (germanische Stämme) (1799: II).

7.2 The "Germanic-Gothic" identity project 1770–1830 – a social and cultural challenge

The two terms denote an idea of historic liberty which made it possible to mount social and cultural challenges that addressed contemporary issues and which at the same provided reassurance that these challenges were legitimate and appropriate. Its purpose was determined by its social, political, and cultural context.

Emerging from the eighteenth-century context of modern cultural and political self-determination and social emancipation, this identity could effectively accommodate the contemporary socio-cultural critique of despotism, selfishness, and social corrosion by providing a "Kollektivsymbol" (Jürgen Link) for a newly defined and historically appropriate identity that could not just symbolise, but also *legitimise* challenges to aspects of the existing order. These challenges targeted the prevalent neo-classicism, identified with oppressive prescription in the arts, which reflected the prevalent oppressive social structures. This contestation was two-pronged, with both approaches, the socio-political and the socio-cultural, interlinking. The socio-political approach related to the concern about political despotism, which was formulated in Montesquieu's highly influential *L'esprit des Loix* (1748). The socio-cultural approach developed out of the *Querelle* and crystallised in Blackwell's *Enquiry into the Life and Writings of Homer* (1736), in which early Enlightenment historicism paved the way for synthesising the two opposing positions of the ancients and the moderns by making the culture of classical antiquity historically contingent, i.e. the result of its specific historical conditions, which allowed thinkers to investigate the social and cultural conditions that produced different forms of culture in different contexts. This set the stage for constructing a "modern antiquity" out of the vague notion of the "Middle Ages" (as well as constructing, incidentally, a Biblical Hebrew antiquity out of the Old Testament). In this discourse, "antiquity" came to denote the earliest cultural stage of any civilisation, it created the idea of a "foundational antiquity" from which an authentic culture could develop. This notion of "earliness" allowed this concept to become representative of youthfulness, vigour, innocence, the uncorrupted, and notions of "natural" societies. This formulation took place in the context of mid-eighteenth-century discussions of "nature", the "sublime", the "noble savage" and "sentiment".

The "Germanic-Gothic", based on such foundational authenticity, challenged the existing social and cultural order by propagating social and cultural emancipation and social inclusion. This is borne out by its investigators' prominent interest in forms of "low culture", folk songs and tales, ballads, or oral traditions of lays and heroic epics in different vernaculars. Such specimens of folk culture were seen as remnants of an original and authentic culture of modern Europe, which was conceived to varying degrees as both mono-cultural (based on Christianity, chivalry, and ancient cultural legacies) and multi-lingual. A key feature of this early, original culture was its assumed social inclusiveness, all social classes enjoyed listening to such forms of poetry, before and after they were written down. Crucially its "texts" (poetic or legal) were expressed, frequently orally, in a communal language and enacted in a communal place, to which all listeners had access. This was conceived as a deliberate challenge to neo-classicism, which was regarded as an exclusive culture of intellectual and cultural refinement. The identity's thrust was both cultural and political, based on a cultural critique: refined civilisation with its excessive and calculating rationality bred cynicism and had a debilitating and corrupting effect on a natural humanity, which was believed to be innately moral and good. Such refined civilisation was identified with hierarchical court-culture, based on intrigue and competition, with a jaded appetite for the exquisite and a preference for the inauthentic, be this pretence, feigned politeness, or hypocrisy. "Low cultural" art and literature, on the other hand, did not only represent uncorrupted and authentic culture, but had egalitarian and national-communal undertones. It had the potential to enfranchise a new collective, initially perhaps only in a cultural sense.

The political and cultural concerns underlying the interest in the "Germanic-Gothic" intersected with the general interest in the structures and dynamics of social collectives. Interest focused on how collectives worked, how they were maintained, and how they could be made most inclusive and fair. Laws and the forms of government and society they produce (Montesquieu) were brought into close association with poetry and language, which reflect and perpetuate this society (Blackwell), producing the eighteenth-century interest in "culture". Blackwell's contextualisation of language, literature, and society and his notion that the perfect age for poetry lies at the intersection between primitive and civilised culture informed cultural thinking from Hurd to Herder, and beyond. A joint interest in legal, linguistic, and poetic traditions is – famously – obvious in the work of Jacob Grimm, but overlapping interests in political and legal customs on the one hand and in poetic and cultural achievements on the other was already clearly visible in the work of Richard Hurd.

In his *Letters of Chivalry and Romance*, Hurd had not only identified English liberty as a "Saxon" legacy, but drawn parallels between Homeric "heroic" culture and that of "Gothic" times, which rested not just on "ignorance and barbary", but on the similarity of a "*civil* condition" (Hurd 1911 [1762]: 103). His ideas were embedded in the contemporary context of the "long" *Querelle*, he initially postulates an analogy between the political and social conditions in Homeric epics and the "forgotten" Middle Ages (1911: 107),[14] parallels which he qualifies in the course of arguing for modern superiority. Hurd pronounces on the parallels between "the heroic and the Gothic manners" in the context of establishing what makes favourable conditions for the creation of poetry. Already in the *Dialogues*, he had asserted that the best conditions occur in the period of overlap between primitive original culture (marked by martial strife in an insecure society) and the first stirrings of civil society, and had proceeded to identify such an overlap in the Elizabethan Age. In *Chivalry and Romance*, he extends this fruitful post-classical period further back in modern history, to the "Middle Ages", and claims that the *Christian* Gothic times have the edge on their pagan predecessors, due to their "improved gallantry" and their more humane religion, the "superior solemnity of their superstitions": "The *gallantry*, which inspirited [inspired] the feudal times, was of a nature to furnish the poet with finer scenes and subjects of description in every view, than the simple and uncontrolled barbarity of the Grecian." (1911: 108) Hurd fuses different aspects of the *Querelle* in his argument: original, "ancient" culture is a powerful basis for poets (which was the case in early classical antiquity), but modernity is morally and aesthetically superior to classical antiquity at any time. While the barbarism may have been similar in both antiquities, the Christian Middle Ages awoke "gentler and more human affections" (1911: 109). In Chapter 2 we saw how, for Hurd, Germanic law was the basis of English liberty and England's exemplary legal and political institutions. Christianity and Germanic customs combined to create (a superior) modernity.

The interpretation and deployment of the Germanic-Gothic were continuously affected by political and social events, most prominently the French Revolution and the Napoleonic Wars, with which they stand in a reciprocal relationship. But there are also more subtle political deployments, which are less obvious to a non-contemporary reader and which predate the cataclysmic political events at the end of the century. When Percy composed his lengthy correction of Mallet's view that Goths and Celts were closely related – Percy puts forward

---

[14] "The two poems of Homer express in the liveliest manner [...] the capital mischiefs and inconveniences arising from the political state of Greece: The Iliad, the dissensions that naturally spring up amongst a number of independent chiefs; And the Odyssey, the insolence of their greater subjects, more especially when unrestrained by the presence of the Sovereign. [...] And can any thing more exactly resemble the conditions of the feudal times, when, on occasion of any great enterprize, as that of the Crusades, the designs of the confederate Christian states were perpetually frustrated [...] by the dissensions of their leaders; and their affairs at home as perpetually distressed and disordered by the rebellious usurpations of their greater vassals?" (Hurd 1911: 106).

sound linguistic reasons for his correction (Mallet 1770: ii-iv)[15] – at least part of his motivation for making a distinction between Germanics and Celts appears to be political: he distinguishes Gothic liberty (Mallet 1770: xii) from Celtic obscurantism and considers the latter evident in the practices of the Druids (Mallet 1770: xviii). His wording reads as a thinly veiled reference to Irish Catholicism.[16] He was evidently keen to create a close cultural link between German and English peoples (Goths) and a corresponding gulf between English and Welsh or Irish language and culture (Mallet 1770: xxii). While it may have suited Percy to talk up the differences between the Goths and the Celts in specific contexts, he nevertheless engaged in creating a fairly integrated early European culture by strongly suggesting that as far as poetry, or the social position and practice of culture, was concerned, the Gothic scalds and the ancient British (Celtic) bards had similar offices, and fulfilled very similar cultural functions. The following passage from Percy's "Essay on the Ancient Minstrels in England" touches, as far as terminology is concerned, on much I have discussed above, linking the "North" with "Europe" and both with the early indigenous culture of Gothic-Teutonic and Celtic tribes.

> The Minstrels seem to have been the genuine successors of the ancient Bards, who under different names where admired and revered, from the earliest ages, among the peoples of Gaul, Britain, Ireland, and the North; and indeed by almost all inhabitants of Europe, whether of Celtic or of Gothic race; but by none more than our own Teutonic ancestors, particularly by all the Danish tribes. Among these they were distinguished by the name of Scalds. (Percy 1794 [1765]: I, xxii)

From the end of the eighteenth century, the "European" Germanic-Gothic was in both Britain and Germany increasingly set against a Roman, Romance or Southern France, while at the same time the more inclusive Northern identity, based on a united post-classical Christian Europe, was never abandoned. But as intra-European divisions came to the fore, establishing "supremacy" soon became an area of contestation.

---

[15] Percy's "Translator's Preface" is subtitled (in the Table of Contents) as "Proofs that the Teutonic and Celtic Nations were ab origine two distinct Peoples", and Percy censors Mallet's error of not distinguishing between Goths and Celts when he points out that their languages have different roots (Mallet 1770: ivff). Percy foreshadows, however amateurishly, Jacob Grimm or Max Müller on linguistics and culture. For Percy, the Germans, Scandinavians, Saxons, and Belgians are Goths, while the British, Irish, and Gauls are Celts (Mallet 1770: ix).

[16] "What particularly distinguishes the Celtic institutions from those of the Gothic or Teutonic nations, is that remarkable air of Secrecy and Mystery with which the Druids concealed their doctrines from the laity; forbidding that they should ever be committed to writing." (Mallet 1770: xvii).

In the wake of the French Revolution and the Napoleonic Wars, this modern cultural identity, which was believed to have descended from "Germanic-Gothic" antiquity, acquired overt political meaning, although its eighteenth-century formulation had been by no means unpolitical. The overtly political aspects of the "Germanic-Gothic" were related to its close association with liberty and freedom in British and German thinking, both in terms of individual independence and equality and liberal processes of communal decision-making. This association with liberty and independence was already present in the mid-eighteenth-century uses of "Germanic" in constitutional contexts mentioned above. This aspect became politically potent in the late eighteenth century, when it featured in discussions of constitutionalism and political enfranchisement. It was integral to the German resistance movement against Napoleonic occupation and control and to the British understanding of the "Defence of the Realm" against a French invasion, both in military and political (Jacobin) terms, especially in Edmund Burke. There is, however, a key difference, which is clear from the preceding chapters. While in Germany conservative forces interested in preserving a pre-revolution situation and politically progressive forces interested in establishing constitutional states (briefly!) worked together to defeat Napoleon, in Britain these forces were opposing each other (Burke vs Thelwall), even though both British sides utilised the discourse of Germanic-English freedom.

In the course of the first half of the nineteenth-century, the Germanic identity with its European "medieval" origins and its contemporary efficiency to define a modern collective established itself to such an extent that it turned from challenge to being a consolidating force and began to underpin mainstream cultural patterns. In nineteenth-century England "gothic" became the defining term of the so-called "Gothic Revival", the widespread preference for medievalised architecture and furnishings. This medieval turn is associated with the new Anglican High Church religiosity and with consolidating social conservatism, and the mid-century High Church movement was indeed a clear sign of the identity working to consolidate rather than challenge, although the socially and culturally challenging aspects did not fully disappear. Around 1800, however, the "medieval" still represented a cultural and political challenge. Even aspects now frequently associated with backward-looking, anti-progressive tendencies, such as presenting pre-industrial and pre-capitalist medieval social structures as alternatives to current early capitalist ones, as for example Novalis or William Cobbett do, represented political radicalism that charged a "selfish" establishment with the destruction of paternalistic social structures which had obliged the powerful to accept a duty of care.

The perceived "deviancy" of the gothic novel is part of this challenge in its anti-utilitarian, un-practical emotional excessiveness. However, in its move towards emotional excess and conservative spirituality, the medieval became increasingly detached from its seventeenth and eighteenth-century "gothic" narrative of Germanic liberty. The politically more liberal aspects of the concept were, largely but not exclusively, transferred to the term (Anglo-)Saxon, which became crucial in the Victorian master-narratives of the English history of liberty and parliamentary government, continuing what has been identified long ago as the Whig interpretation of history (Butterfield). The term "Saxon" was already used in Percy's title of Mallet's *Histoire* as well as in Hurd's discussion of Saxon law, and the "Anglo-Saxons" became the subject of Sharon Turner's four-volume study of *The History of the Anglo-Saxons* (1799–1805), which covers the period from "their first appearance above the Elbe" to the Norman Conquest and dedicates volume 4 to their "manners, landed property, religion, government, laws, poetry, literature" and "language", i.e. their "culture".[17] In the early nineteenth-century, "gothic" and "Anglo-Saxon" identities were both based on the amalgamation of a "Northern" cultural legacy with Christianity. By the middle third of the nineteenth century, the medievalist Gothic Revival *tended* towards a Catholic or High Church Christianity, whereas the Anglo-Saxonist historiography *tended* to celebrate the liberating Protestant Reformation and Low Church approaches. *But* both these interpretations of the Germanic-Gothic evince the process of moving from challenging existing cultural and political hierarchies to being employed for purposes of cultural and political consolidation. Both approaches, the Catholic-medievalist and the Protestant-liberalist, claim the Germanic as their essential co-element.

During this identity-building process, the English "gothic" makes its journey from connoting Germanic liberty to its current meaning of connoting high medieval culture, without entirely losing the meaning of dark emotional excess. In German the term "gotisch" became linked, within a similar timeframe, to a gradually more clearly defined Gothic ethnicity, relating to the language and culture of the Goths, and to medieval architecture. The general Northern identity became increasingly denoted by the term "germanisch". Both Anglo-Saxon and "germanisch" push the root of this identity back to pre-Christian times, but none of this affected the idea that the Germanic-Christian culture of the Middle Ages was the place and time when European culture emerged as a distinct identity.

---

[17] It was a successful book, further editions appeared in 1807, 1820, 1823, and 1852. The term "Saxon" had been in use, with connotations of "liberation" and cultural origin since the Tudor Reformation and played a part in the seventeenth-century political struggles in England; at the end of the seventeenth century it was used in *this* context by William Temple (Kliger 1945).

7.3 National self-determination and social emancipation – the Germanic Europe, chivalry, and constitutionalism

The Germanic identity served to mount a challenge to existing social and cultural hierarchies in order to enfranchise a new modern collective. This challenge was, before the advent of the *Communist Manifesto*, largely framed in a *national* context. In this respect it was – of course – part of the story of nineteenth-century nationalism. But whether as a *social* challenge and consolidation or as a *national* construction, it was about new enfranchisement and new demarcations. Such demarcations always have the potential to disenfranchise others. The co-existence of inclusiveness and hierarchies, which are both inherent in the different applications of this conceptual identity, illustrates this clearly.

In the second half of the eighteenth century, the Germanic-Gothic identity had a fairly inclusive reach: Mallet did not clearly distinguish between Celts and Goths,[18] Percy – for all his corrections of Mallet on this matter – closely aligned (Celtic) Bards with (Scandinavian) Scalds. A generally Northern antiquity was a foundational part of post-classical European culture. That the general reading public at this time did not distinguish between ancient Celtic and ancient Gothic, that both could inhabit an ancient North, is borne out by the Ossian "phenomenon", which was gathering pace in the early 1760s. James Macpherson published his first edition of *Fragments of Ancient Poetry* in 1760, a second edition appeared within months, and was followed by *Fingal*[19] in late 1761 and *Temora* in 1763, with a collected edition of *The Works of Ossian* in 1765. There is a wealth of literature dealing with "Ossian", its reception history and controversies.[20] The Ossian phenomenon illustrates the cultural polyvalence of this Celto-Gaelic material as generally "Northern", something that had not been intended or expected by Macpherson or his backers in the Edinburgh Enlightenment elite, most prominent among them Hugh Blair and John Home. *Their* aim had been first and foremost to preserve the remnants of a disappearing Gaelic-Scottish identity and to present this quite specific material to their contemporary audience as a cultural and ethical, but also a national,

---

[18] Mallet considers the Celts to be the ancestors of the Gothic peoples as well as of their British descendants.
[19] The full title runs *Fingal, an Ancient Epic Poem in Six Books, together with Several Other Poems composed by Ossian, the Son of Fingal, translated from the Gaelic Language.*
[20] Excellent starting points are Wolf Gerhard Schmidt, *"Homer des Nordens" und "Mutter der Romantik". James Macphersons Ossian und seine Rezeption in der deutschsprachigen Literatur* and the work of Howard Gaskill on this topic.

experience (Schmidt 2003: I, 74–76, especially note 72).[21] Its endangered status was due to the dominance of Anglo-British cultural and political power. But Ossian's appeal went far beyond Scottish, Gaelic, or Celtic contexts; it aroused intense interest across Europe, as evidence of an exotic but *shared* pre-history. The difference between the intentions of the Edinburgh circle and Ossian's actual reception illustrates the persuasiveness of a "Northern" antiquity vis-á-vis a more ethnically based folk culture.

Macpherson's undertaking was also not the only one of its kind. The intentions of Percy's *Reliques of Ancient English Poetry* of 1765 were similar, as is its title, which seems to be more than a nod to Macpherson's first collection. Both Macpherson and Percy used early modern manuscripts as sources for their publications, and both "improved" their ancient materials for publication. But while Macpherson's motivation included a (perhaps forlorn) hope for national liberation – his effort was closely linked to the final defeat of the Jacobites, the clearance of the Highlands, and the decline of spoken Gaelic as it was being replaced by English – Percy's context was focused more on cultural and potentially moral, rather than national, recovery, for which there was less need.

The same cultural dynamic that moved Percy or Macpherson, despite their differing motives, also drove the Zurich group of cultural innovators around Johann Jakob Bodmer and Johnn Jakob Breitinger, who were active from the 1730s to the closing decades of the century. Both Macpherson and Bodmer were keen readers of Blackwell's *Enquiry*.[22] Bodmer was responsible for resurrecting the medieval *Nibelungenlied* in the 1750s, which he identified, along with other thirteenth-century Middle High German poetry, as original national epics that had been nearly lost. Bodmer was interested in cultural and spiritual reform, in which uncorrupted Swiss-German Protestant culture was to pave the way towards a morally responsible society based on national-local traditions. This reform was aimed against over-civilised (and foreign) neo-classicism, which was corrupting local traditions. This was the context of the *Literaturstreit* between Zurich and Leipzig in the 1730s, or between Bodmer/Breitinger and Johann Christoph Gottsched, in which the newly emerging "cultural centre" of Switzerland

---

21 According to Gerald P. Tyson (1969), "Fingal expressed the Scots' desire for the supremacy of Gaelic literature over British examples. Its nationalistic significance resided in the alternative it presented to the English (Scandinavian) usurpation of Scottish culture as well as the example it offered to English readers of literary value unique to Scotland." The line between these two aims seems rather porous: While Home for example was famous for his nationally minded Scottish tragedies, he also took early versions of material eventually published in the *Fragments* to London to show to interested and enthusiastic readers (Schmidt 2003: I, 74).
22 See Chapter 2 and Oergel 2017.

was challenging the established leadership role of Saxony's Leipzig. Gottsched's own approach to establishing a national German literature was based on adhering largely to neo-classical principles. But Gottsched, too, wanted to help facilitate a national literature and attempted to write a heroic epic on a medieval Christian topic at the same time as Bodmer produced his *Noah. In zwölf Gesängen* (1752), based on the Old Testament (Hentschel 2007: 187–199).

In 1770s Germany, the *Sturm und Drang*, inspired by Percy, Hurd, and Ossian, focused on working out the most appropriate cultural tradition from which a modern national literature and culture with a high cultural impact and socially wide reach could develop. Herder and Goethe, the young prime movers in this thinking, were also influenced by the Zurich group. In *Von deutscher Art und Kunst*, edited by Herder, all these concerns were assembled: the historical difference between the modern North und the classical (and pre-classical/ Homeric) South, which was based on different geographical and historical conditions that had produced a different mindset and culture, the idea that culture found expression in poetry, laws, language, and architecture, and the belief that early cultural sources represented foundational antiquities and encapsulated authentic culture, fresh and uncontaminated by elitist, degenerate, or imported influences.[23] Herder's concept of *Volkspoesie* was a direct product of this thinking. The cultural tradition of the North, which the book foregrounds through two exponents, Shakespeare and Ossian, is historically, but not structurally, different from classical and pre-classical southern antiquity. Neither Shakespeare nor Ossian were in any way Herder's or Goethe's "discovery", both are the subjects of current literary and aesthetic controversies, and this was a key reason for choosing them. The editor Herder joins the discussion on the side of the newly constituted "party" of the historicist moderns, descending from Blackwell and Montesquieu and seeks to provide pointers for an inclusive collective culture that can animate a newly configured community.

---

23 Herder's *Shakespear* essay outlines the differences between post-classical modern literature and early classical Greek drama and the historically different cultures they "grow" from. His *Ossianbriefe* makes the same point, cultural authenticity, by focusing on the different modes of creativity: imported, rule-bound neo-classicism versus free and original genius presenting its native environment and culture. Goethe's "Von deutscher Baukunst" introduces the Strasbourg Minster as an example of original Northern culture; Herder, in dialogic fashion, juxtaposes Goethe's essay with a translation of the neo-classically minded piece "Versuch über die gothische Baukunst" by ("nach") the Italian Paolo Friesi. Herder closes the volume with Justus Möser's Introduction to his *Osnabrückische Geschichte*, entitled "Deutsche Geschichte". Möser's book emerged in the context of the legalistic *Nationalgeistdebatte* of the 1760s and was part of the mid-century Montesquieu reception (see Chapter 2). Its introduction discusses the legal and constitutional history of the German Empire.

Herder's efforts to collect all kinds of European folk poetry followed in the footsteps of British antiquarians and modernisers such as Percy, but far outstripped their activities, not least because his ambition was transnational. His vaguely defined concept of *Volkspoesie*, which became so influential for both German and British Romantic poetry, was premised on the idea of an inclusive cultural collective in which all classes participated. Its demise was the mark of over-civilised, aristocratic, absolutist societies. Both Herder's and Goethe's output of the 1770s, which serves as a shorthand for *Sturm und Drang* here, is equally marked by social concerns. Werther's critique of over-civilised, courtly, and deadly competitive culture as destructive is well known, as are his author's ambivalent views about these issues.

English Romanticism is considered closer to German *Sturm und Drang* than to German Romanticism (Mason 1959). This view is based on the similarly iconoclastic approach to the merits of established culture and society, which eventually finds expression in Britain in, for example, the *Lyrical Ballads* (1799) and which was preceded by the enthusiastic reception of German *Sturm und Drang* literature by a generation of frequently young, sometimes radical, literary hopefuls. This enthusiasm is exemplified by Coleridge's, Southey's, or Hazlitt's excited response to Schiller's *Räuber* in the 1790s, or by the excitement caused by "gothic" German literature, which enthused the young Walter Scott and enthralled the readers of G. A. Bürger's *Lenore*. However, during the Napoleonic Wars the engagement with a Germanic or gothic identity decreased in Britain, not least because the effective conservative propaganda, of which *The Anti-Jacobin* was the most famous purveyor, made anything *termed* Germanic or gothic, or indeed culturally German, suspect, or even treasonable, as Chapters 3 and 5 discussed. Instead, the cultural and political focus shifted, temporarily, towards an exclusively *English* liberty. This is an example of a contextually motivated new demarcation: gothic becomes (modern, contemporary) German, and one's own share in the (inclusive) Northern identity is rebranded. But as we shall see in the following, this Englishness was again closely aligned with the Germanic in the nineteenth century, when English liberty was claimed to represent the truest and purest form of the Germanic freedom Tacitus had described.

By the end of the Napoleonic Wars the Germanic-Gothic returned to the cultural fray in Britain through the reception of August Wilhelm Schlegel's *Dramatische Kunst und Literatur* (1808), lectures given in Vienna, which were translated in 1815, in the wake of Mme de Staël's *De l'Allemangne* which had appeared in London in 1813. Schlegel's *Dramatische Kunst* was avidly received by readers as politically diverse as Walter Scott, now fully Tory, and William Hazlitt, who continued to believe in the ideals of the French Revolution. In these lectures,

7.3 National self-determination and social emancipation — 261

Schlegel repeats what he had already put forward in greater detail in his lectures on *Romantische Literatur* in 1803–1804 in Berlin. In *Romantic Literature*, he first formulated what I described as the central tenet of the new modern tradition above, the amalgamation of the Germanic legacy with Christianity, which, in his view, produced *Ritterkultur*, the culture of chivalry. *Ritterkultur* represented the original and defining identity of modern (post-classical) Europe, the history of which was only beginning to be understood.

> So [...] bewährt sich das Christentum demnach als Grundprinzip der Einheit Europas; das andere Element war die deutsche Stammesart. Aus diesem beidem zusammen mit den Trümmern des klassischen Altertums muß die neuere Geschichte konstruiert werden. [...] Aus der Kombination der kernigen und redlichen Tapferkeit des deutschen Nordens mit dem Christentum, diesem religiösen, orientalischen Idealismus, ging der ritterliche Geist hervor, eine glänzende, wahrhaft entzückende, in der Geschichte bisher beispiellose Erscheinung. (A.W. Schlegel 1965: IV, 82–83)

> [So accordingly, Christianity is the foundational principle of European unity; the other element was the German(ic) identity (Stammesart). Modern history has to be constructed from these two elements, and the ruins of classical antiquity. [...] Combining the German(ic) North's strong and honest braveness with Christianity, this religious, oriental idealism, produced the spirit of chivalry, a glorious, truly delightful phenomenon, which is without equal in history.]

In these lectures Schlegel formulates the most coherent and explicit exposition of the idea that the Germanic legacy and Christianity have produced post-classical Europe and that due to this foundational fusion Europe shares one culture. There is no point, Schlegel says, in trying to provide a history of "neueuropäische Poesie" [modern poerty], "wenn nicht anerkannt wird, daß [...] Europa im Mittelalter wirklich *ein* Land gewesen sei" [if it is not recognised that during the Middle Ages Europe was really *one* country]. (1965: IV, 22, italics in original). This unity was evinced through chivalry, a shared cultural heritage *and* a common patriotic interest: "durch das Rittertum [...]; durch große Übereinstimmung in der Denkart, den Sitten und Gesinnungen; endlich durch das Gefühl eines gemeinsamen Interesses, einen wahrhaft europäischen Patriotismus [through chivalry [...]; through extensive agreement in the mode of thought, in manners and attitudes; finally through the sense of a common interest, a truly European patriotism] (1965: IV, 22).
He continues:

> In der Poesie selbst werden wir einen Beweis dieser behaupteten Einheit sehen: denn nicht nur diente eine ritterliche und christliche Mythologie ihr überall zur Grundlage, nicht nur gefielen die in der zuerst ausgebildeten Sprache, der Provenzalischen, gedichteten Lieder in einem großen Teile Europas, sondern wir bemerken noch weit später die auffallenden Analogien in den Ko[m]positionen von Dichtern. (1965: IV, 22)

[We can see evidence of this proposed unity in poetry itself: not only did a chivalric and Christian mythology serve everywhere as poetry's foundation, not only were the songs written in Provençal, the first modern language, popular across large parts of Europe, but we also remark the noticeable analogies between compositions by different poets in much later times.]

The reference to a Christian mythology of chivalry, which once supported the young European identity, indicates the implicit context of the lingering *Querelle*. But Schlegel's words equally clearly indicate that chivalric culture underpinned an inclusive social project, "gemeinsames Interesse" and "wahrhaft europäischer Patriotismus". The use of the eighteenth-century key term patriotism, so crucial in the contemporary debates about new (national) collectives, suggests a direct link to these debates and their concerns. Schlegel suggests the possibility of a non-classical European culture, fully equal to that of classical antiquity, and a European patriotic, i.e. non-absolutist, non-despotic state, both deemed fairly radical cultural and political endeavours at the time. Schlegel reiterates his characterisation of post-classical European culture as resting on German(ic) essence and Christianity, which in combination have produced the culture of chivalry, in *Vorlesungen über dramatische Kunst und Literatur* (1923 [1809]: 13–25). In 1808, however, Schlegel did not repeat the overtly political terminology of a European patriotism.

Between the Berlin lectures in 1803–1804 and the Vienna lectures in 1808, there was another shift: that from German ("deutsch") to Germanic. In Berlin, Schlegel speaks of "deutsche Stämme" [German tribes] in this European context and reserves the term "Germanier" for pre-medieval times, for example, "heidnische Germanier" [pagan Gemanics] (1965: 41) or the "Germanier" of Tacitus and Julius Caesar (1965: 40), who were alive when Rome was still powerful and classical civilisation dominant. By the time Rome was declining, he calls these people "deutsch".

> Deutsche Stämme waren es, welche durch den Umsturz des abendländischen Römischen Reiches im Süden, dann durch Ausbreitung im Norden das neuere Europa gründeten und erfüllten. Auf dieser Seite des Erdbodens waren die Deutschen nach den Römern die zweiten großen Welteroberer. (1965: 21)
>
> [It was German(ic) tribes who, by toppling the Western Roman Empire in the South and then spreading across the North, founded modern Europe. On this side of the globe, the German(ic)s were after the Romans the other great conquerors of the world.]

In 1803–1804, chivalry is "of German origin and much older [i.e. pre-Christian MO] than is commonly thought" (1965:37).[24] The characteristics of the "deutsche

---

24 "deutschen Ursprungs und viel älter als man gewöhnlich glaubt".

Stammesart" are love of freedom and independence, honesty, loyalty, earnestness, valour, and courage.²⁵ These characteristics, which also feature in Fichte's *Reden* and Hegel's *Philosophy of History*, proved very durable.²⁶ In Fichte and Hegel, they coalesce around the term "Gemüt" [a form of "soul"], a word Schlegel also uses. By the time Schlegel gave his Vienna lectures, the term "deutsch" tended to be replaced by "germanisch" in identical contexts. In Vienna he says: "Nächst dem Christentum ist die Bildung Europas seit dem Anfang des Mittelalters durch die germanische Stammart der nordischen Eroberer [...] entschieden worden." [After Christianity, the culture of Europe was from the beginning of the Middle Ages decided by the Germanic identity of the northern conquerors.] (1923 [1809]: I, 11)

This early nineteenth-century polyvalence of "deutsch" and "germanisch" has had unfortunate consequences when it came to describing Europe's ethnic composition. As the meaning of *deutsch* narrowed and acquired exclusively national connotations, its shrinking reach and lessening polyvalence made it easy to instrumentalise terms such as "deutsches" or "germanisches Europa" in later nationalistic discourse. It seemed, on the one hand, to legitimise claims of a German-controlled Europe and, on the other, allowed reading such constructions as evidence of a single-minded, predatory nationalistic aggression reaching from Herder straight to Hitler and postulating a thorough-going contamination of modern German thinking. This is not to suggest that such a "line" does not exist, but it is one reading among others and does not do justice to the complexity of the semantic situation and its cultural and political context around 1800. While this polyvalence largely rests on the overlap between the words Germanic and deutsch – exacerbated in English by the closeness of Germanic and German – I discussed above that behind this terminology stands a history of political and cultural considerations reaching back to the Humanists and a history of aesthetic discussions reaching back to the early eighteenth century.

Based on the semantics of the Germanic North, the notion of a Germanic Europe resting on a culture of chivalry was to have a long career in both

---

25 Schlegel speaks of "alter Biedersinn, Einfalt der Sitten" und "kräftiger Freiheitssinn" (1965: 38). These features were also associated with the early martial cultures and societies run by warriors and warlords, which Blackwell described in *Enquiry* and Hurd in *Chivalry and Romance*.

26 The specificity of the combination of independence/freedom and loyalty and honesty has very recently been endorsed again as "Proto-Indo-European", which is an ethno-cultural construct that covers a range similar to that of the nineteenth-century Germanic. The archaeological anthropologist David W. Anthony (2007) puts forward that the notion of the verbal oath which is absolutely binding in a social context of personal liberty is a specifically PIE concept evidenced by comparative linguistics.

nineteenth-century Germany and Britain. Such ideas were disseminated to a large British readership through Scott's *Essays on Chivalry,* on *Romance,* and on *the Drama,* which appeared in the supplement of the fourth, fifth, and sixth editions of the relatively new *Encyclopaedia Britannica* between 1815 and 1824. In many respects, they are also formative for Scott's novel *Ivanhoe* (1819). While Scott no doubt found much of Schlegel prefigured in Hurd, Mallet, or Percy, he did read both August Wilhelm and Friedrich Schlegel. His Abbotsford Library holds the first English and French translations of August Wilhelm's *Dramatische Kunst und Literatur* as well as the first edition of Friedrich's *Geschichte der alten und neuen Literatur* (1815), and its first English translation (1818).[27] *Geschichte der alten und neuen Literatur* is based on Friedrich Schlegel's 1812 lectures. Lectures 7 and 8 summarise his brother's points from above and give chivalry a central position in the "Geist des Mittelalters" [spirit of the Middle Ages] (F. Schlegel 1842 [1815]: 225). At the opening of his *Essay on Chivalry,* Scott reiterates Schlegel's key points: early versions of chivalry originate in the "German forests", they become "blended" with Christianity, along with the Christian religion chivalry distinguishes the moderns from the ancients, its development goes hand in hand with the "establishment of the modern states of Europe on [Rome's] ruins", it is a key cultural marker of "modern Europe" and "its effects may still be traced in European manners" (Scott 1887: 1–5).[28]

William Hazlitt used the idea of the German(ic) and Gothic "muse" – i.e. what radical German literature has to offer for revolutionising society – in his lectures on the "Dramatic Literature of the Age of Elizabeth" in 1819–1820. Although he does not suggest that a Germanic identity is to enfranchise a new collective, he clearly proposes that German writers and German literature, the latter largely in its "gothic" incarnation, increase the chances of such a (in his view) much needed social enfranchisement. "The same [German] writers [...] have made the only incorrigible Jacobins, and their school of poetry is the only real school of Radical Reform." (1931 [1820]: 362)

At the same time as A. W. Schlegel was holding his lectures in Vienna, the philosopher Johann Gottfried Fichte was addressing the public in the *Rundsaal* of the Berlin Academy of Sciences with his *Reden an die deutsche Nation,* his

---

[27] The English translation of *Dramatische Kunst und Literatur* is by John Black (1815), *Geschichte der alten und neuen Literatur* was translated by Scott's son-in-law John Lockhart (1818) (Catalogue of the Library at Abbotsford 1838: 200); the French translation of *Dramatische Kunst und Literatur* is Mme Necker de Saussure's (1814) (1838: 40).

[28] I have traced the conceptual and semantic overlap between August Wilhelm Schlegel and Scott's *Essay on Chivalry* (Oergel 2016: 109–111). It *is* feasible that Schlegel himself drew on Hurd and that Scott had found much of this already in *Letters on Chivalry and Romance.*

lengthy outline of an education plan for the German nation, and the rest of humanity. In many respects the lectures reflect the desperate situation of Prussia and the other German territories after Napoleon's decisive victories in 1806. One of the key objectives of Fichte's lectures is to explain to his audience that the (Protestant) German cultural and philosophical heritage needed to survive if the liberty and earnestness of philosophical enquiry was to have a future. In this context Fichte also identified the European cultural heritage as based on the amalgamation of the "liberal", freedom-loving traditions of the Germanic peoples with Christianity, which initially created a unified and inclusive Europe that then became, intellectually and politically, stuck in Catholicism. For Fichte, the signature event in European history is not the emergence of chivalry, but the Reformation, when Germanic seriousness and its love of freedom broke the shackles of a corrupt and repressive – a despotic – Catholic church. For Fichte, the Europeans are divided into Catholics and Protestants, i.e. into those who (re-)instated and embraced the liberty of conscience (and the spiritual, moral, and intellectual independence and self-reliance this implies) and those who did not. This division runs along linguistic lines: those Germanic peoples who speak a predominantly Germanic language had (largely) become Protestant, those who had taken on forms of vernacular Latin and developed the Romance languages had tended to remain Catholic, because, according to Fichte, their intellectual self-reliance was restricted due to their thinking and speaking a language they did not fully understand (1846 [1808]: 311–327). Regarding this linguistic partition, Fichte agreed with August Wilhelm Schlegel, who had made a similar distinction between neo-Latin and Germanic languages in *Romantische Literatur* in 1803–1804. However, Schlegel had also pointed out the close kinship between Germanic and Romance European languages through their shared element of the Germanic, which in the Romance vernaculars had resulted in hybridity (1965: 36).[29] The idea of an internal linguistic division among the Germanics had been in circulation for over a decade; it had been formulated before Schlegel by the Berlin-based pastor Daniel Jenisch in 1796 (Jenisch 1796) and made an appearance in Goethe's *Wilhelm Meister* at the same time (1977 [1795–1796]: 367).[30] Hegel would take up this linguistic segregation in his lectures on the *Philosophy of World History* in the 1820s, where, again, the Romance languages, due to their hybrid nature, are made the reason why the majority of southern Europeans did not become

---

29 Taking the Indo-European approach to languages, Schlegel also stressed the common root shared by the Germanic languages, Latin, and Greek (1965: 21).
30 See Aurelie's criticism of Lothario's use of French; and Oergel 2006: 208–209.

Protestants, a key disadvantage in Hegel's historical theodicy, in which Protestantism represents progress (Hegel 1986: 413–508).[31] By the 1820s, Hegel's idea of the Germanic was coalescing into his historical teleology of the realisation of the world spirit, which was prefigured in his *Phenomenology* (1807) and in Fichte's *Reden*. Hegel's lectures were given over a number of years and published posthumously in 1837. In the context of the 1820s, the new idea of the Germanic Europe or of the European Middle Ages as a unified geographical, cultural, and spiritual entity retained its pervasiveness (as it did in Britain). It would remain the backdrop for any contestation of supremacy within this identity beyond the middle of the century.

How is this European Germanic identity used to further social emancipation and national self-determination? In Germany, the Germanic legacy was effectively politicised in the run-up to and during the Wars of Liberation, i.e. between the Austrian and Prussian defeats of 1805–1806 and the first victory over Napoleon at the Battle of Leipzig in 1813. During the *Befreiungskriege*, German cultural heritage was mobilised by Arndt, Friedrich Ludwig Jahn, the *Burschenschaften* and the *Turnerbewegung* in support of a general "national" resistance against French occupation, against Napoleon's version of the outcomes of the Revolution, and against despotic German princes. This mobilisation has been summarised as *Deutschtümelei*, or Teutomania.

However, the powerful appeal of the famous *Lützower Jäger*, a free corps of young volunteers, was, for all their military insignificance, based on their contribution to the struggle to create military and political conditions that might make a new Germany possible, which would be created after Napoleon was beaten. The "movement" managed to unite, however briefly and outwardly only, three groups: moderate and radical liberals hoping for different levels of constitutional reform, reformers within state governments, and a weakened aristocracy and monarchy. This broad "coalition" fractured almost immediately after Napoleon's final defeat, with fissures becoming visible already during the Congress of Vienna, but the concept of a German(ic) national heritage continued to be invoked to register protest against the conservative restoration inaugurated by the Congress. This heritage was employed to symbolise and legitimise the demand for constitutional reform and a new egalitarian (by the standards of the day) collective, the modern nation of free citizens. The *Wartburgfest* of 1817 was a signal event in the context of keeping these hopes alive, and was

---

[31] He opens the section "Die germanische Welt" with the programmatic statement: "Der germanische Geist ist der Geist der neuen Welt. [...] Es wurde diesen [Völkern] aufgegeben, im Dienste des Weltgeistes, den Begriff der wahrhaften Freiheit [...] in der Welt aus dem subjektiven Selbstbewußtsein frei zu produzieren." (1986: 413).

understood, and feared, as such by the conservative authorities. This fear was the reason why the Follen brothers' draft of an all-German constitution, the "Grundzüge für eine künftige Reichsverfassung" (1817), was considered by conservatives as a highly seditious document. The *Burschenschaftlers'* "altdeutsche Tracht" [old German dress] had a similarly seditious image. Its vaguely sixteenth-century appearance was a reference to the Reformation, to which the largely Protestant radical *Burschenschaft*, being familiar with Fichte's work, attached much significance. This self-representation is an example of the pattern of using cultural history to legitimise demands for social and political change.

The German(ic) cultural heritage was a vital ingredient in the radicalisation process that took place between 1815 and the assassination of the conservative writer and diplomat August von Kotzebue in 1819, the event that triggered the repressive Carlsbad Decrees and silenced the national liberal movement for at least a decade. An interpretation of this Germanic-Christian legacy resonates in the protests of the Protestant Arndt as well as the Catholic Joseph Görres, which voiced the thwarted constitutional hopes. Arndt's commitment to Christianity as part of German culture has been pointed out in Chapters 4 and 5. Here I will focus on Arndt's deployment of a German(ic) identity to support and legitimise political reform.

In *Geist der Zeit II*, published in small numbers in 1809, and re-issued with part 3 in 1813, Arndt invokes the original Germanic heritage of a united Europe, "unser Ältestes" [our most ancient] is shared by the Germans, Scandinavians, French, Spanish, Italians, and most British peoples (1813 [1809]: 220–221). The figure of Hermann (Arminius), who repelled the Roman army in the legendary battle in the Teutoburg Forest in 9 AD, represented a stand for (Germanic) freedom, independence, "unser eigenes Recht" [our own law] and "eigene Sprache" [our own language] (1813: 223), which suggests more than a cultural liberation, preparing the ground for the constitutional exhortation of the final chapter, "Letztes Wort an die Teutschen (gesprochen im Herbst 1808)" [Last Word to the Germans, spoken in autumn 1808]. Here, Arndt again holds the princely rulers responsible, castigating the "Sorglosigkeit und Schwächlichkeit derer, die eure Sprecher und Vertreter seyn sollten" [the carelessness and weakness of those who should be your voice and your representatives] and the "Hülflosigkeit eurer Verfassung" [helplessness of your constitution] (1813: 288, also 429), descriptions which have clear revolutionary undertones. Arndt concludes: "Laßt uns vergehen für unser Land und unsere Freiheit, auf das unsere Kinder ein freies Land bewohnen! [...] Ihr dürft nicht leben als Sklaven." [Let us die for our country and our freedom, so that our children may live in a free country! [...] You must not live as slaves.] (1813: 441). While this has been primarily read as call to fight

Napoleon – the speech gives plenty of encouragement to do this (1813: 439) – it is, bearing in mind the weak and careless princes, also as a call for constitutional change based on taking power from aristocratic rulers and their class. Before the concluding oratorical orgy of hatred against the French and their leader, Arndt proposes a new constitutional arrangement for a united Germany under a form of representative government in which the nobles are not abolished but accountable to the people. "Wir wollen uns und unser Land nur einrichten, wie wir müssen, wenn wir nicht Knechte werden wollen." [We want to arrange our country in a way that ensures that we will not be slaves.] (1813: 430) Arndt's proposal is vague and provides no mechanism for producing representation other than stipulating appropriate proportions between the people and the nobility. *But* it does stake a claim for enfranchisement – the people who have fought for their liberation from the French are to make decisions: "*Wir gesellen* [die größeren Fürsten] den beiden größten Häusern zu." [*We* arrange for the greater princes to join the two greatest aristocratic houses.] (432, italics mine) Arrangements of who leads them will be made by the majority, "wir". He continues: "Auch für den kleinen Adel, wenn er bleiben sollte, müßten strengere Ordnungen und Satzungen gemacht werden." [For the lesser nobility, should it remain, stricter order and rules would have to be made, too.] (1813: 433) The lesser nobles would hold their lands as administrators and the nobility will form an advisory upper chamber, a kind of House of Lords.[32] "Das Vaterland", a clear echo of "la patrie", is more important than any aristocratic rulers. These proposals are, Arndt assures his readers, not insurrection and revolution, but for the common good and patriotic, they are *not* "Ungehorsam gegen die Fürsten, sondern [...] Gehorsam gegen das Vaterland" [disobedience against the princes, but obedience to the fatherland] (1813: 430). No doubt he is also mindful that he, in 1808–1809, was co-operating with the princes. However, he issues a clear challenge to the existing order: division into different territories is to be abandoned (1813: 428) and unity will be based on "fraternity" "zu lange vergessene Bruderschaft" [brotherhood – or fraternity – forgotten for too long] (1813: 432).

> Ihr müsset ungerechte Vortheile, ungleiche Ansprüche aufgeben; ihr müsset gleich arbeiten, gleich opfern für die heilige Freiheit und das liebe Vaterland. Das sei das Vorrecht: der Ersten, vordest zu stehen in der Schlacht und im Rath, vorderst zu stehen in rastloser Arbeit, in schlafloser Wachsamkeit [...] in des Vaterlandes glorreichem Dienst. (1813: 428–429)

---

[32] "Die kleinen Fürsten, Grafen und Herren bekämen [...] ihre Abtheilungen und Schlösser als stehende Majorate [...]; [...] sie säßen als geborne Räthe nebst den Fürsten vom Blute den Königen zur Seite. Sie und die Fürsten vom Blute bildeten eine Art von rathendem Körper, oder Oberhaus in dem Volke. Ihre Zahl wäre nach dem Verhältnis der Volksmenge bestimmt; sobald eine Pärsfamilie ausginge, erhöbe der Regent eine neue Familie zur Pärie." (1813: 432–433).

[You should have to give up any unjust advantages and unequal claims; you should have to work in the same way and make the same sacrifices for sacred freedom and our dear fatherland. That should be your prerogative: to be the first, in the front line in battle, at the forefront of restless work, in sleepless watchfulness [...] in the glorious service of the fatherland.]

These descriptions of a collective of newly enfranchised citizens retains distinct aspects of French Revolution rhetoric.

Joseph Görres (1776–1848), whose *Rheinischer Merkur* has been described as "Sprachrohr der deutschen Verfassungsbewegung" [mouthpiece of the constitutional movement in Germany]), was a seasoned publicist by the time he put the above into circulation in January 1814, three months after the battle of Leipzig. The *Merkur* was intended to contribute to the "Ablösung der souveränen Willkür durch gesetzliche Herrschaft" [change from arbitrary sovereignty to the rule of law] (Roegele 1964: 533). Arndt, Clemens Brentano, Henrik Steffens, and Freiherr vom Stein were among its contributors. In the late 1790s Görres had been a dedicated supporter of the revolution and promoted the annexation of the Rhineland to the French Republic in order to guarantee the new French freedoms in his home region. Becoming disillusioned with Napoleon, he turned to the Germans themselves to bring about German liberation. While this publication's anti-Napoleonic stance was still welcome in 1814, by late 1815 his constitutional and national commitment had made Görres many enemies among the princes and conservatives who had no longer anything to fear from Napoleon, and on 3 Januray 1816 the *Merkur* was closed down by the Prussian authorities. When Görres presented a 5000 signature-strong petition demanding the realisation of the constitutional promises for the Rhineland to the Prussian government in 1818, this triggered the criminilisation of petitions (Roegele 1964: 533). Görres responded defiantly with his *Teutschland und die Revolution* (1819), attacking the selfishness of the reactionary governments and the "pale" union of the 1815 German Confederation (Deutscher Bund) that had been negotiated at the Congress of Vienna. He had to flee into exile to Strasburg to evade arrest. While in 1806 Arndt had to run from Napoleon, in 1819 Görres had to flee from German conservative governments. In *Teutschland und die Revolution*, Görres, not unlike Arndt, demands that the princely rulers respond to the "Geist der sich emanzipierenden Zeit" [spirit of the times which is emancipation] (1819: 197) and accept the new political ideas. In doing so, they would demonstrate common sense and show themselves worthy of their (constitutional) authority. Demanding enfranchising constitutions for German territories could, in theory, be a generally *liberal*, rather than *national*, endeavour. Görres' constitutional vision, however, was premised on a united all-German territory, including Austria.

Görres relied on German traditions in a way similar to Arndt. He is perhaps best remembered as a key figure of later German Romanticism, as the editor of *Teutsche Volksbücher* (1807), a collection of folk wisdom. Görres utilises what he considers ancient German(ic) traditions to legitimise a new constitutional start. His all-German constitution was to be based on a restitution of the *Reich*, but on the basis of modern ideas, animated by "bürgerliche Tugend" [civic virtue] (1819: 193). The imperial structure is appropriate for Germany because it is the original German political structure and the only one that can cope with German federalism and accommodate the different regional entities, while at the same time assuring that they do not turn into absolutist despotic states. Görres outlines a complex system for a federal constitutional monarchy in which top-down majestic "legitimacy" intertwines with bottom-up popular local democracy. Popular local democracy, he argues, is "altgermanisch", a surviving tradition of Germanic freedom (1819: 160). At the top, his constitutional model features a two-chambered "Reichsparlament" [Imperial Parliament] (1819: 10). There is now an anti-French note when it comes to political theory: French thinking is too materialistic and focused on human fallibility ("Schlechtigkeit") (1819: 198–199).

Görres was, in 1819, well aware of the different approaches to German history in the liberal constitutionalist camp: one "Partey" was focusing on the "Middle Ages", while the other looked to the Reformation (and the revolution), a difference generally linked to the division between Catholicism and Protestantism (1819: 85–90). Görres takes a fairly ecumenical view and reviews the constitutional demands of the Protestant *Burschenschaften* in Jena and Göttingen (1819: 104) and their political professors, his explicit example is Lorenz Oken (1819: 82), generally favourably. He castigates the criminalisation of "Teutschtümeley", which may be silly, but is an effort by the young to register their protest, and disappointment (1819: 98–99). While in exile in Strasburg, Görres increasingly turned to the Middle Ages and, rejecting secular liberalism, he eventually returned to a more traditional Catholicism. During the 1820s, he promoted the newly emerging Christian-democratic movement and connected with the Catholic renewal movement in Vienna. By 1827 he was rehabilitated enough to be appointed to the chair of general and literary history at the University of Munich (recently moved to the Bavarian capital from Landshut), where he remained until his death in 1848.

In Britain, the discourse about English liberty and the "ancient constitution" stretched from the 1790s to the 1820s. It featured in the radical circles of the *London Corresponding Society*, as we saw in Thelwall's work, it was part of Hare's private denunciations of Lord Castlereagh in 1816, and of Shelley's public denunciations of the ruling elite in his "Mask of Anarchy" in 1819. But as

Britain experienced, during the first decade of the new century, no Napoleonic conquest and subsequent struggle for liberation, the urgency of this discourse was (slightly) less intense, and its nationalism less virulent than in Germany during the *Befreiungskriege*. This is one of the reasons why the British discourse on the Germanic has been studied in much less detail than its counterpart in Germany, although its *Germanic* nature was a key aspect of *English* liberty, which was, and remains, a central concept in English and British identity constructions.

The narrative of Germanic-European history, as well as Germanic purity, would be of key importance for the mid-Victorian English historians of the Germanist group. They put forward the idea that, while *not* having preserved Germanic purity linguistically, England, compared to fellow European nations, *had best* preserved its Germanic inheritance in constitutional and legal terms. Its polity was the historically grown model of modern democracy and representative, non-despotic government (of which more below). The championing of the Germanic in Britain and Germany is the basis for the contestation of Germanic supremacy within European Christendom, or Germanic Europe, which relies on the purest tradition of Germanic liberty. Despite these dividing lines, which make the claims to supremacy possible, the Germanic remained a shared element in the post-classical European identity.

7.4 Paths to institutionalisation in Britain and Germany – *Germanistik*, the Christian gentleman, and the Gothic Revival

7.4.1 *Germanistik* – traditions of liberty in laws and poetry

In Germany, discussions about linguistic and cultural identity focused not just on religious, but equally on legal-social identity; Arndt had identified "unser eigenes Recht" [our own law] and "eigene Sprache" [our own language] (1813 [1809]: 223) as key aspects of the historical and future German identity. Both the linguistic-cultural and the legal-social identities were anchored in independence and liberty. This interest in a tradition of independent liberty, which could be traced in legal and constitutional history, produced the mid-eighteenth-century interest in legal traditions. The intellectual activities of the Brothers Grimm are a case in point. They were preoccupied with a submerged inclusive culture in which (folk) poetry and ancient legal traditions were linked. As these poetic and legal traditions were associated with a German(ic) legacy, they were implicitly connected to notions of individual and collective liberty. The Grimms' linguistic and historical research into ancient German and European legal and poetic documents continued eighteenth-century activities, but in the first decades of the nineteenth century this research into European vernacular traditions became institutionalised in university curricula and university posts, which in both Germany and Britain were in the gift of the state. In Germany, this inaugurated the academic discipline of *Germanistik*, originally very much concerned with both literary-linguistic and legal antiquities. The first German university chair of "Altdeutsche Literatur" was established at the new University of Berlin in 1810. This approach to cultural history spawned the sister disciplines of *Romanistik* (the study of Romance-language antiquities) and eventually *Anglistik*, which split off from *Germanistik* in the course of the century. In Britain, this kind of academic institutionalisation occurred slightly later, but still before 1830, with the setting up of university chairs of English Studies at the new London colleges. These institutionalising activities created many of the modern disciplines of the humanities and refocused the conception of knowledge from classics, law, history and theology towards "culture".

The wide-spread activities of collecting the remnants of ancient poetic and legal documents of a submerged, and nearly lost indigenous culture between 1750 and 1830 needs no reiteration here. The fashion of subtly, or not so subtly, modernising extant poetic materials, which had produced Macpherson's Ossian poetry and Percy's *Reliques*, was giving way to careful editions, while imitating old forms became a genre in itself, although "edited" versions of old material did not disappear. This is the time when Jacob and Wilhelm Grimm published *Deutsche Haus- und Kindermärchen* (1812–1815) and *Deutsche Sagen* (1816), Arnim and Brentano brought out *Des Knaben Wunderhorn* (1805–1808) and Walter Scott published his *Minstrelsy of the Scottish Border* (1802–1803). Scott's initial literary fame rested on his imitative ballad poetry of the 1790s and the first decade of the nineteenth century. Scott was a lawyer, a profession he, after a troubled start to academic study, chose not least due to his academic engagement with the history of law.

In 1816, Jacob Grimm proposed an explicit connection between ancient poetic and legal texts by identifying a reciprocal relationship between poetry and laws in his essay "Von der Poesie im Recht": both are based on language and language is the basis of cultural tradition (Grimm 1816). This identification of language, laws, and poetry as original culture had been prepared by the eighteenth-century work on foundational antiquities: Hebrew antiquity had been discussed in this manner by the Biblical scholars Robert Lowth, Johann David Michaelis, Johann Gottfried Eichhorn, and Herder, Greek antiquity by classical scholars from Blackwell to F. A. Wolf, and Northern post-classical antiquity by writers from Hurd to Herder. John Mitchell Kemble, who collaborated with Jacob Grimm in the 1830s, would, a generation later, make his academic reputation by producing the first modern edition of the Anglo-Saxon poem *Beowulf* and editing Saxon legal codices before suggesting that the Germanic heritage was the foundation of the modern British polity. I will return to Kemble below.

Jacob Grimm's essay appeared in the context of the codification controversy (Kodifikationsstreit) of 1814, in which legal *traditions* (originally Roman and canon law) were pitted against *new* positive legislation, such as new constitutions or new legal codices. New positivist legislating had initially occurred in the wake of the Enlightenment and its concern for natural laws based on reason and leant towards universal human rights. Frederick the Great's *Allgemeines Landrecht* for Prussia, drafts of which appeared 1784–1788, the final version in 1794 (Ziolkowski 1990: 79), is an example of this, as is the *Code Napoléon*. These were clear attempts at legal modernisation and enfranchisement, not least because both the *Landrecht* and the *Code* were written in the vernacular to make them accessible to all (literate) citizens, taking the law out of the sole custody of a particular class, the Latin reading lawyers.

On the side of tradition, Roman and canon law was, according to Theodore Ziolkowski, preferred by the aristocratic classes because it seemed to form a bulwark against any form of modernising legislation. One flashpoint was the landed aristocracy's need for dependent peasants, which the *Allgemeines Landrecht* did not interfere with, but against which Arndt had famously inveighed in his first publication. Ziolkowski identifies traditional – organically developed – law codes as favoured by anyone with conservative leanings (1990: 95). However, it is not borne out by this investigation that all laws that can be identified as historically traditional were *necessarily* used to legitimise socially conservative endeavours. The traditional German law that Grimm investigates in his essay, and which the Jena, Gießen, and Göttingen *Burschenschaftler* wanted to (re-)instate *in tyrannos*, stands precisely at the crossroads of this difference. The legal traditions Grimm investigated as "traditional", as part of an organic historical development, were valuable not just because of their cultural appropriateness (they were indigenous), but because they developed from a liberal tradition. The very same Germanic cultural traditions were at the time inscribed as revolutionary liberal forces that could liberate the oppressed "nation" from French domination and despotic German princes and lay the basis for the new constitutional collective of the new German nation, as discussed above. Celebrating Anglo-Germanic liberty was of course also the strategy of Edmund Burke's anti-revolution defence of English liberty, *but* this tradition of ancient English liberty was equally the basis for Thelwall's appeal against the current despotism of the powerful few, and it inspired Hare to inveigh against the conservative politics inaugurated at the Congress of Vienna.

In Germany, Germanic studies were being institutionalised as *Germanistik*, the text-based historical study of (German) language and culture. This interest manifests itself institutionally in the founding of the first (extra-ordinary) chair of "Altdeutsche Literatur" at the new University of Berlin in 1810, mentioned above, to which Friedrich von der Hagen was appointed, whose work, incidentally, differed from the scientific philology of Jacob Grimm by focusing on content and storylines in relation to revelatory mythology. Karl Lachmann was made extra-ordinary professor of Latin and German philology at Berlin in 1825, Ludwig Uhland was appointed at Tübingen University to a chair of "Deutsche Sprache und Literatur" in 1829, and Jacob Grimm was called to a chair at Göttingen in 1830 (where he officially taught *Rechtswissenschaft*), his brother Wilhelm followed him in 1831. In 1837 both Grimms moved to the University of Berlin, following their resignations from Göttingen (more on this below). The first *Deutsches Philologisches Seminar* was established at the University of Rostock in 1858.

At roughly the same time as in Germany, chairs of English Language and Literature and of English literature and history were created in Britain, too. The introduction of *English Studies* marked the same turn towards "one's own" culture and tradition as part of a post-classical European culture, which was now not just on a par with classical antiquity, but thought more relevant. While in Britain this development had the same identity-driven focus that ultimately exalted modern "Liberty" as in Germany, the chairs of English were created in a context that is specific to the pre-Reform Bill decade: a clash between liberal secular innovation and Anglican conservatism, the story of which is worth telling in more detail.

The first two chairs of English were set up in London, at the new rival institutions of University College and King's College. University College was founded in 1826 and admitted its first students in 1828; it was the result of utilitarian (and to some extent dissenting) interests to establish a higher academy of secular education, Jeremy Bentham and James Brougham were prime movers in this scheme. The curriculum was to include useful subjects, such as sciences, modern languages, and English language and composition. King's College, which had its first intake in 1831, was the conservative response. It was set up as an institution that served Tory and Anglican interests and was committed to the established Church, but it was based on a similar sense of educational reform.[33] The antagonism between the two colleges focused, ultimately, on civil liberties: the dissenting utilitarian interests promoted social enfranchisement on a practical and

---

33 In the following I rely on D. J. Palmer's study (1965: 15–28).

liberal basis, while the conservative establishmentarianism sought to protect established English liberty enshrined in the "glorious" compromise of constitutional monarchy and the established Church. "Liberty", however, was key for both, as it had been in a different context for both Burke and Thelwall.

Both institutions shared with the new Prussian universities of Berlin and Bonn a sense of the need for new subjects and a general broadening of the curriculum beyond "classical" learning. While models of teaching language and literature could certainly be taken from the Scottish universities – and Brougham was a product of the Scottish system – the German models were closely looked at. Thomas Campbell, who was involved in the founding of University College, contributed his knowledge of German developments to the discussions about the new foundation and even undertook a research trip to Berlin to gather information.

King's College and University College approached English Studies slightly differently: University College focused on skills of composition and the more scientific study of language and its history, while King's College focused on literature for the purpose of moral and spiritual improvement. The philological tradition did eventually establish itself at University College, although not for a decade. Despite the College's secular orientation, the first incumbent of the Chair of English language and literature was the Cambridge-educated Rev. Thomas Dale, who combined a successful career in the Church of England with academic posts. His curriculum focused on traditional aspects of composition, rhetoric and translations from classical authors. He was aware of the new Anglo-Saxon scholarship that Kemble was producing but remained convinced that there was little merit in studying *Beowulf* because the culture it represented was uncouth (Palmer 1965: 24). In 1835 Dale took up the chair of English literature and history at King's College, where he taught the history of English literature from Chaucer onwards. A philologist in the German vein was appointed to the University College chair with Robert Gordon Latham in 1839, who had studied with Rasmus Christian Rask at Copenhagen, like the Anglo-Saxon scholar Benjamin Thorpe.

The influx of continental philological ideas into England was accompanied by arguments over whether the new German methods were useful, or welcome, which continued throughout the century, and beyond, in the perennial discussions on whether German *Anglistik*, which was eventually divided off from *Germanistik*, was compatible with English interests. German scholarship was increasingly seen as pedantic, deadening the moral and enlivening spark of literature and language (Utz: 2009). This may be read as an aspect of the struggle for Germanic supremacy, which is equally evident in the wrangling over who had the purest Germanic traditions, which underlie, with varying intensity, the Victorian "Histories" of English legal and constitutional traditions from populist Kingsely to scholarly Stubbs.

The relations of the different Germanic peoples to each other were closely studied in Germany, too. The somewhat bifocal approach of the Germanic Europe and the German position within it worked its way into the study of literature and history. Ludwig Uhland's researches into medieval Western European literature were based on this idea, as was Leopold von Ranke's first work *Geschichten der romanischen and germanischen Völker 1494–1514* (1824). Ranke (1795–1886), the "founder" of modern historical research (based on sources and their contexts), emerged as a cultural thinker from the context of the Germanic Europe, as it had been defined by Schlegel and Fichte, and accepted by Hegel for his plan of world history. Ranke's book on the emergence of modern Europe on the eve of the Reformation – which brought him to the attention of the Prussian king Frederick William III and which preceded the publication of Hegel's lectures on history – outlines in its introduction the idea of the kinship of the nations of central and Western Europe. They descend from the Germanic peoples of the Great Migrations and assimilated Christianity, and with it a respect for Latin culture, especially Roman law. Slavic peoples are Christian, but explicitly different (Ranke 1885 [1824]: V). For Ranke too, this amalgamation produced chivalric culture and a shared outlook. This outlook finds expression in common enterprises: the crusades and colonial expansion (1885 [1824]: XVI-XXX).[34] A. W. Schlegel had also identified the crusades as a key feature of European history in 1803 (1965: 32), as had Hurd before him. The Germanic legacy was evidently assigned a key role in history. Ranke regarded Hegel's approach as ahistorical, because it did not pay enough attention to the unique value and self-sufficient meaning of individual epochs by arranging them in a "march of history". To him, this amounted to holding on to an Enlightenment belief in universal progress. This criticism is similar to Hare's and Carlyle's condemnation of the "march of mind" at very much the same time, in the 1820s and 30s.[35] Although Ranke meticulously prioritises contemporary context over a universal teleological approach in the chapters that follow his preface and introduction, it is far from clear that he does *not* narrate a historical development that – *a posteriori* – presents a teleology of the Germanic, despite spending much of his early career distancing himself from Hegelian teleology.

---

[34] "Vorrede zur ersten Ausgabe" and "Zur Einleitung" respectively.
[35] It is also worth noting that Carlyle's life spans the same decades as Ranke's; Carlyle, like Ranke, had little time for universal historical speculation, believed in the superiority of sources based on the testimony of eyewitnesses, and, most importantly, sought the hand of god in history to shore up a modern faith that could proceed to an everlasting yea. Both Carlyle and Ranke rose to similar positions of fame and cultural authority in their respective societies, based on their ability to draw, and spread, spiritual solace through writing history.

Within the Historical School, legal-constitutional research continued, too. From the mid-1840s, Ranke's pupil Georg Waitz began publishing his *Deutsche Verfassungsgeschichte* (1844–1878), which investigated medieval German institutions and constitutional history and would run into eight volumes. Waitz began publishing at the same time as Kemble was bringing out his Anglo-Saxon legal codex and preparing his *Saxons in England*; his first volume (1844) covers similar ground as Kemble, focusing on property rights, communal organisation, and early kingship. Weitz' last volume appeared just after William Stubbs' *Origins and Development of the Constitution of England*.

7.4.2 The Christian gentleman and English liberty – Kenelm Henry Digby's *Broad Stone of Honour*, J. M. Kemble's *Saxons in England* and the Germanist historians at Oxford and Cambridge

Despite the nominally Protestant hegemony presented by the established Church, *both* the "Germanic-medieval" and the "Germanic-Reformation" approach to cultural and social identity had high currency in Britain. As in Germany, both interpretations of the foundational traditions deeply influenced intellectual activity and produced effective cultural patterns. In Britain as in Germany, the focus was on cultural, including legal, traditions, which would form the basis for the identity and spirit of a new collective, a modern nation with an important role in the world. In British historical narrative, Germanic freedom and independence appeared as political (English) liberty and individual and national prosperity, the latter achieved through economic self-determination and (free) trade. Such liberties were envisaged to come with social responsibilities. These responsibilities were linked to the emerging concept of the Christian gentleman who lives by a chivalric code of honour. Such socially responsible individuals were presented as the upholders of "English" ways and values at home and as exporters of them abroad. The concepts of liberty and self-determination underpinned political reform at home and legitimised the expansion of the British Empire abroad, by conceiving the imperial drive as a civilising force. This is the reason why, frequently, political reformers in home affairs were committed imperialists abroad. A case in point is Charles Wentworth Dilke (1843–1911), who supported the early labour movement, municipal self-regulation, and (limited) female suffrage, but believed in the political and cultural mission of the British Empire (Oergel 2012). This vision of Germanic liberty and legal inheritance was not uncontested, it was opposed by the "Romanist" historians around Francis Palgrave, who maintained that a Roman legacy, especially Roman law, was formative in the make-up of English law. This contestation mirrors the differences between the Grimms and Savigny's understanding of the composition of German legal traditions.

Both the medieval strand and the Reformation strand of the Germanic identity received a decisive impetus from the 1820s members of Trinity College Cambridge. Perhaps it was no coincidence that in Julius Hare's library not just Arndt's books were numerous, but also Joseph Görres'.[36] The Reformation strand influenced key British historians and the historiography they produced, finding strongest expression in British Victorian historiography. This is the group of Germanist historians, or Anglo-Saxoninsts, around Thomas Arnold, Charles Kingsley, William Stubbs, and Edward Augustus Freeman. All, except Kingsley, were Oxford graduates, but all of their work was indebted to the Germanic efforts of John Mitchell Kemble (1807–1857), a prominent member of the Cambridge Apostles and Trinity graduate, who had gone up to Trinity College in 1825. The medieval strand was promoted through the work of Kenelm Digby (1795/6–1880), Trinity graduate and life-long friend of Hare's. Irish-born Digby, whose family descended from Leicestershire gentry, started spending his summers travelling on the Continent (Germany, France, Switzerland, and Italy) while he was still a student. He was particularly fascinated by medieval culture and architecture. His book *The Broad Stone of Honour, or, Rules for the Gentlemen of England*, the first edition of which appeared in 1822, makes the case for a behavioural code for the modern (English) gentleman, adhering to ideals of truthfulness, honour, valour and, crucially, public service. Much of the 1822 volume is a tirade against "refined selfishness", familiar from Chapters 2–5, evincing a "degeneracy of mind, united with ambition" (1823 [1822]: 32). His "rules" are designed to mitigate these contemporary social evils, he is providing a rule book to educate "the youth of gentle breeding", and "make them ever mindful of their duties" (1823: x). The book addresses the same audience as Hares' *Guesses*, but is intended as a practical rather than intellectual guide. The behavioural code it advocates takes its legitimacy from being indigenous, originating from the common traditions of European medieval culture.

> We date the origin of our order from the early institutions which took place in Europe after the Christian Religion had been generally received: and it is therefore in the principles of ancient chivalry, in the characters of the knights and barons of the middle ages that we must look for the virtues and sentiments that are to be our inheritance. (1823: 31)

As the concept of the English gentleman it had a profound influence on the ethos of a number of public schools, first and foremost Rugby under Thomas

---

[36] The Trinity College Library catalogue records fourteen individual titles by Görres in the Hare collection.

Arnold's headmastership (see below pp. 300–301), on the Young England movement, a religiously minded group with strong High Church leanings,[37] the Oxford Movement, and the Pre-Raphaelites (Oergel 1998: 112–113).

The title of Digby's book refers to the castle ruins of Ehrenbreitstein on the Rhine, which Digby is likely to have visited on his travels and which is emblazoned on the first page of every volume of the enlarged edition. Remaining in residence at Trinity throughout the 1820s, he re-wrote the book, which had gone into its second edition in 1823, turning it into a five-volume oeuvre between 1826 and 1829 and changing its subtitle to "The true Sense and Practice of Chivalry". From expounding an ethos, Digby moved on to bolstering his behavioural code with a "philosophic history" (Digby 1827–1829: I, 1).

The book's first edition proposes, or seeks to resurrect, a universal code of rules that transcends history. While it clearly references a medieval "chivalric" code, through the chivalric romances and epics mentioned in its early pages, there is room for chivalry in ancient times. It is a "religious doctrine" that has "flourished wherever a sense of religion prevailed" (Digby 1823: xxiii). Accordingly, Digby speaks of "Sir Hector" and "Sir Ajax" (1823: xxiv) and is particularly fond of pointing out Hector's chivalry (1823: xxv-xxvii). In the extended edition, these direct equivalences between ancient and modern times have disappeared; instead Digby points out that it was the medieval writers, rather than he himself, who seem to have thought there was an ancient chivalry comparable to their own.[38] As he is now writing a "philosophic history of chivalry", his approach becomes decidedly more historical. He concludes that the chivalric rules only achieve full realisation under Christian conditions. Clearly Digby had meanwhile read up on recent historical research on the Middle Ages, much of which would appear to be by Friedrich Schlegel, who is referenced numerous times in volume 1 alone.[39] While Digby does not mention August Wilhelm Schlegel in the four-volume work, he quotes liberally from Friedrich Schlegel's *History of Literature*, which contains the key points his brother made regarding the Middle Ages, including that Europe had been one country during the

---

[37] Charles Whibley called it the Movement's "breviary" (1925: I, 133).
[38] "So far it only appears that the chivalrous writers, during the middle ages, assumed that those gentle knights, Sir Hector, Ajax and Alexander, were gentle and chivalrous like themselves." (1876–1877 [1827–1829]: I, 98).
[39] Among them, *History of Literature*, *Philosophie des Lebens*, and *Wisdom of the "Ancients"*. As *Philosophie des Lebens* is repeatedly referred to by its German title, it is possible that Digby – in true Trinity fashion – could read German, had perhaps learnt it in those reading sessions while the Debating Union was suspended. The *History of Literature* he refers to is Friedrich Schlegel's *Lectures on the History of literature: ancient and modern* of 1818, translated by John Lockhart.

medieval period (I, 177–178). Between the early and the late 1820s Digby also changed his mind about the benefits of philosophic systems. While in 1822 he had denounced the "monstrous system of moral philosophy" (1823: xx), by 1827 he conceded that a "philosophic" history of chivalry was required to fully understand European – his own – history (1827–1829: I, 2).

The idea of the unified Christian Europe is evident in both editions of *Broad Stone of Honour*, but has, like chivalry, also become more historical in the second version. While Digby states in 1822 that for the "Christian gentlemen" "Europe *is* a common country" (1823: xi, italics mine), by the end of the decade he hopes

> that men might learn to emulate the virtues of their famous ancestors, and as Christian gentlemen, to whom Christendom *was* a common country, to follow the examples of those ancient worthies who were the defenders of the Church, the patrons of the poor and the glory of their times. (1827–1829: I, 4, italics mine)

Rather like the Hare brothers' *Guesses at Truth*, Digby's book is largely forgotten today, but, and again like *Guesses*, it had a huge contemporary reception. The four-volume version was reprinted in the 1840s. The wide availability of this edition on digital platforms today is testimony to the book's wide circulation. Hare warmly recommends the book (in this case the first edition) in *Guesses* I(1827: I, 151–152), Digby returns the compliment (1827: I, 8). Digby converted to Catholicism in 1825 (at the same time as Görres returns to it), a conversion that in no way dimmed Digby's friendship with the Anglican vicar Hare.

John Mitchell Kemble, son of a British father and an Austrian-French mother, combined religious fervour with revolutionary zeal, with what D. J. Palmer referred to as the "complex interaction between the spirits of Utilitarianism and Evangelicanism" which characterise the "spirit of reform in nineteenth-century England" (1965: 29 and 15). After a spell in Germany in 1829–1830 and participating in the Spanish insurgence against Ferdinand VII in 1830–1831, in which he was joined by other young Cambridge radicals, Kemble returned to Cambridge to study the Germanic heritage of England. He was particularly interested in Germanic legal and linguistic identities, and researched Anglo-Saxon texts. He published the first modern scholarly edition of *Beowulf* in 1833, and six volumes of Anglo-Saxon legal charters between 1839 and 1848, known as the *Codex diplomaticus aevi Saxonici*. In 1834 he spent time at Göttingen University to work with Jacob Grimm, whose research corresponded closely with Kemble's own interest in Germanic laws, language, and literature, and the two became friends. Kemble's most influential book is based on his extensive knowledge of Anglo-Saxon language, culture, and history. *The Saxons in England. A History of the English Commonwealth till the period of the Norman Conquest* (1849) presents the evolution of the

English "commonwealth", utilising his own research and Benjamin Thorpe's editions of Anglo-Saxon sources (Thorpe had collaborated with R. C. Rask at Copenhagen).

As a Germanic people the Anglo-Saxons partook of the original Germanic culture of communal property, which enfranchised the members of small agricultural communities. This idea is summed up in Kemble's "mark theory" and his view of Anglo-Saxon local democracy. The latter was institutionalised in the "witena gemot", which he sees as an early and rudimentary form of parliamentary structures. While these social and political structures were, according to Kemble, developed and amended to adjust to the progress of history and civilisation – key stages in this process were the arrival of Christianity in England, the advent of larger populations, and, in modern times, greater commerce –, they remained essentially English, i.e. Germanic. Although such ideas were potentially a political challenge, Kemble takes the political sting out of his points by suggesting these political traditions are the reason why there is less revolutionary fervour in mid-nineteenth-century Britain than elsewhere in Europe: there was less need. As he explains in the preface to the first edition, his book was ostensibly intended as a contribution to keeping the peace in Britain during the unstable years of 1848–1849, when even the famously obedient and loyal Germans were taking to the streets in revolt, "thrones totter" and "shot and shells sweep the streets of capitals" (1849: v). It is his duty as a "patriotic [British] citizen" (1849: viii) to point out "that which is great and glorious in her [England's] history" (1849: viii) firstly to his "countrymen" and secondly "for the admiration and instruction of her neighbours". The English are lucky because "their institutions have given to them all the blessings of an equal law" (1849: v). Pointing this out to others presumably allows them to learn how to achieve the liberal grail of "solv[ing] the problem of uniting the completest obedience to the law with the greatest amount of individual freedom" (1849: vi). However, some controversy was clearly still associated with Kemble's way of studying Old English and its political legacy, as Kemble did not manage to secure a permanent position at Cambridge.[40]

---

[40] Some of Kemble's inability to become established may be due to personal reasons. Fellow Anglo-Saxon scholar Benjamin Thorpe was given a civil list pension in 1835 – very near the *beginning* of his career. This suggests a keen royal interest in the Germanic years *before* Victoria came to the throne and Albert of Saxe-Coburg-Gotha arrived. Thorpe held no academic posts, but produced an enormous quantity of publications, many of them scholarly editions of Anglo-Saxon texts, some translations from German, and a number of books intended for a general readership, such as *Northern Mythologies* and *Yuletide Stories*.

In the first decades of the nineteenth century, interest in the Germanic legacy was extended across a wide range of contexts, from collections of folksy materials, such as Görres' *Teutsche Volksbücher* (1807), and Digby's chivalric code (1822) at the more populist end to academic research, such as the Grimms' or Kemble's, or political agitation like Arndt's. While the critical methods of researching historical sources developed, driven by increasing philological knowledge and a wider availability of source texts, the *aims* of what the Germanic legacy should prove and stand for changed little from Schlegel's lectures in the first decade of the century: it remained a vital part of the modern European identity and provided cultural continuity from the time Germanic peoples appeared on the frontiers of the Roman Empire to the present. By the same token, its focus on liberty and independence continued the eighteenth-century constitutional discussions in Germany and the eighteenth-century celebrations of the English constitution and English liberty enshrined in the Whig interpretation of English history in Britain. The constitutional discussion remained alive in Germany throughout the 1830s and 1840s up to the elected national assembly in Frankfurt's *Paulskirche* in 1848, to which Jacob Grimm, Uhland, Arndt, Jahn, and Waitz were all elected. In Britain, the Germanic legacy of freedom and independence was believed to have safeguarded constitutional liberty since the Glorious Revolution, if not the Reformation (Burrow 1981), but at the same time it had been invoked to legitimise political change, in a radical vein by English Jacobins like Thelwall, and in a more moderate way by reformers like Hare.

Thomas Arnold, John Mitchell Kemble, Charles Kingsley, William Stubbs and Edward Augustus Freeman all subscribed to the idea that the combination of the Germanic legacy with Christianity formed a new, generally European identity, which was the basis of modern European history, much in the manner that Schlegel had outlined. Arnold, the oldest of them, focused perhaps most explicitly on the idea of the Germanic Europe in his Inaugural Lecture in 1842. While Christianity is important, the new, dynamic, and defining spark that ignites modern history, is the Germanic.

> The importance of this [Germanic] stock is plain from this, that its admixture with the Keltic [sic] and the roman races at the fall of the western empire has changed the whole face of Europe. [...] the other elements of modern history are derived from the ancient world. If we consider the roman empire in the fourth century of the Christian era, we shall find in it Christianity, [...] all the intellectual treasures of Greece, all the social and political wisdom of Rome. What is not there was simply the German race, and the peculiar qualities that characterize it. This one addition was of such power, that it changed the character of the whole mass: the peculiar stamp of the Middle Ages is wholly German [...]. That element still preserves its force and it is felt for good or for evil in almost every country of the civilized world. (1845: 26–27)

Communal identity rests on culture, the place where traditions, language, institutions and religion interlink. While the modern European identity has inherited many things from antiquity, the Germanic legacy is its defining feature.

What in Arnold's view may be an influence "for good or evil" is in Charles Kingsley's assessment twenty years later decidedly positive, as it was in Kemble's, which is roughly contemporary with Arnold's. Kinglsey rejoices, not unlike Kemble:

> Happy for us Englishmen, that we were forced to seek our adventures here, in this lonely isle; to turn aside from the great stream of Teutonic immigration [towards Rome], and settle here [...] to till the ground in comparative peace, keeping unbroken the old Teutonic laws, the old Teutonic faith and virtue. (Kingsley 1864: 17)

Kingsley's interpretation is clearly more separatist, contesting the amount of Roman legacy in English culture. While Kemble was prepared to accept quite a measure of "Roman" influence in the course of history, Kingsley aims to minimise this. His lectures on *The Roman and the Teuton*, which were given during the 1860s, while he was Regius Professor of Modern History at Cambridge, and published in 1864, aim to delineate between these two cultures. Rome stands for a decadent, over-civilised empire as well as a largely corrupt and universalist Catholic Church, which during the Middle Ages tried to abolish Germanic law (1864: 271–295) and displaced English Christianity, until it resurfaced victoriously at the Reformation. Images of two "yokes" are prominently invoked: Norman feudal despotism began to be checked as early as the Magna Charta, while the "ultramontane yoke", representing the meddling despotism of a centralist Church (Kingsley, 1864: 294), lasted until the Reformation.

Kingsley's lectures on this topic were legendary; contemporary sources suggest that they were given to enthralled audiences in packed halls (Kendall 1947: 160–161). Max Müller reports in his Preface to the 1875 edition that

> these lectures, it should be remembered, were more largely attended than almost any other lectures at Cambridge. They produced a permanent impression on many a young mind. [...] According to the unanimous testimony of those who heard them delivered at Cambridge, they stirred up the interest of young men, and made them ask for books which Undergraduates had never asked for before at the University libraries. (Kingsley 1913: x-xii)

Kingsley commemorated this reciprocal engagement between speaker and audience in his dedication of the published version of the lectures to "The Gentlemen of the University who did me the Honour of attending these Lectures", to his audience of students, who did not share the widespread harsh criticism heaped on the lectures by the other historians. The lectures were reprinted eight times between 1875 and 1913 and appeared in German translation in 1895.[41]

At the same time Edward Augustus Freeman published the first volume of his *History of the Norman Conquest. Its Causes and its Results* (1867), which he announces in his preface to the first edition as a balanced assessment of the Conquest, intended to rectify the earlier and, in his view, one-sided accounts of Augustin Thierry's *Histoire de la conquête de l'Angleterre par les Normands* (1825)[42] and Francis Palgrave's *History of Normandy and of England* (1851–1864) (1870 [1867]: x-xi). Palgrave had argued for a strong legacy of Roman law and culture in England following the Middle Ages, while Thierry had advanced the view that the Norman Conquest had done little to undermine the Germanic identity of English culture. However, while Freeman allows for a strong Romance imprint on the vocabulary of English as far as institutions are concerned, modern English, nevertheless, (re-)emerges between the reigns of Edward I and Edward III as a Germanic language and the English as a Germanic nation. He takes the view that the Conquest is an episode of cultural influx which did not produce a lasting cultural change. "Englishmen before 1066 were the same people as Englishmen after 1066." By the fourteenth century the Normans had been absorbed, "The Norman Conquest, instead of wiping out the race, the laws and the language, which existed before it, did communicate to us a certain foreign infusion in all three branches, which was speedily absorbed and assimilated in the pre-existing mass." (1870: xii) Their rule, however, did bring England into closer contact with the continent, England joined Europe, with closer ties to continental social structures and continental Christianity. The Norman Conquest brought England into line with important historical developments in Germanic Europe (Freeman 1876).[43]

In the early 1870s, soon after his appointment as Regius Professor of Modern History at Oxford, William Stubbs published *Origins and Development of the Constitution of England,* a three-volume comparison of the political institutions of the "four great nations of Western Christendom": Germany, France, Spain,

---

[41] Including the first edition in 1864 all editions are by Macmillan, they appeared in 1875, 1877, 1879, 1884, 1887, 1889, 1891, and 1913. From 1875 they have a preface by Max Müller. The translation appeared in Göttingen: *Römer und Germanen. Vorträge gehalten an der Universität zu Cambridge.* Autorisierte Übersetzung nach der 9. Auflage des Originals von Maria Baumann. Göttingen: Vandenhoeck and Ruprecht, 1895.

[42] Thierry's account was immediately translated into English as *History of the Conquest of England by the Normans* (1825).

[43] See especially chapter 14 "Political Results of the Norman Conquest" and chapter 15 "The Effects of the Norman Conquest on Language and Literature".

and England. (Western in this context denotes sharing the legacy of the *Western* Roman Empire.) Stubbs concludes that the institutional and constitutional structures of all four nations have descended from Germanic origins (Stubbs 1891: 2–6, 11), but that the English constitution has preserved its Germanic nature in the purest form.

> The result of this comparison is to suggest that the polity developed by the German races on British soil is the purest product of their primitive instinct. [...] The chain of proof is to be found in the progressive and persistent development of English constitutional history from the primeval polity of the common fatherland. (1891: 11)

By the last quarter of the century, Palgrave's Romanist interpretation was being marginalised. Stubb's preparatory work for his study coincided with Kingsley's lectures at Cambridge.

The Germanic legacy was also instrumentalised to legitimise the British Empire. Charles Wentworth Dilke opens his *Greater Britain* (1868–1869), the travelogue of his grand tour which took him around the globe via North America, Australia, and India, with the following lines:

> My fellow and my guide [on my travels] [...] is a conception, however imperfect, of the grandeur of our race, already girdling the earth, which it is destined, perhaps, eventually to overspread. In America, the peoples of the world are fused together, but they are run into an English mould: Alfred's laws and Chaucer's tongue are theirs whether they would or no. [...] Through America, Britain is speaking to the world. (1868–1869: I, viif)

Again, laws and language make up culture, they are the guarantors of cultural, social, and political coherence, they enable the public spirit of a polity. The English spirit is, in Dilke's view, of global humanitarian importance; he concludes volume 2: "The ultimate future of any one section of our race, however, is of little moment by the side of the triumph as a whole, but the power of English laws and English principles of government is not merely an English question – its continuance is essential to the freedom of mankind." (1868–1869: II, 404) His travelogue was enormously successful, its *eighth* edition appeared in 1885, sixteen years after the first. It fused British liberalism and imperialism and linked emancipatory progress to imperial ambition. Dilke was a political intellectual, but first and foremost a Liberal politician, winning, aged twenty-six, the seat for Chelsea, in the year volume 2 came out. At one stage tipped to be the next prime minister, his politics were soundly imperialist as well as socially liberal: he supported the widening of the franchise and helped pass the laws that gave the vote to (some) women in municipal elections and that legalised the labour unions (Oergel 2012: 99–101). Dilke was an undergraduate at Cambridge between 1862 and 1866, the time when Kingsley was giving his lectures on "the Roman and the

Teuton". It is more than likely that Dilke's was one of the young minds on whom they made, in Max Müller's words, an impression. Even if he did not attend the lectures, it is unlikely that he would not have been aware of them.

In Britain, the Germanist historians were stimulated by German ideas (Oergel 2012: 96–97). This influx of German historicist thinking also had a philological basis, going back to Trinity College Cambridge and the influence of Julius Hare and Connop Thirlwall. German historicist thinking flowed through the conduit of classical studies: the Germanophile centre at Trinity brought into Britain the work of Barthold Georg Niebuhr, whose *Römische Geschichte* was crucial in this context. Niebuhr himself could only conduct his controversial literature-based research into Roman constitutional history in the context of the Romantic research into the connection between poetry and laws within a linguistically fixed collective cultural space. Precisely this cultural space was being developed in the research trajectory that produced the work of the Grimms, but its origin lies in the eighteenth-century historicism of works like Blackwell's. A key point of cross-over of "modern-Germanic" and "classicist" philological studies, which both fed the creation of cultural identities, was the Anglo-German intersection at Trinity College: Thirlwall and Hare brought Niebuhr's work and Kemble the Grimms' philological studies into British academia.

7.4.3 The Gothic Revival – the Palace of Westminster and Cologne Cathedral

The Germanic-Gothic identity also found expression in general taste. Under the name of medievalism it has been discussed in the history of art and literature. The medieval is one key aspect of the Germanic identity that is discussed in this chapter, and irrespective of whether the Reformation is the focus of Germanic liberty or whether the culture and ethics of chivalry are its products, the "Middle Ages" were believed to be the foundational culture of post-classical Europe. A taste for the medieval is evident across virtually all nineteenth-century arts, in terms of subjects in literature (e.g. Scott's *Ivanhoe*), opera (e.g. Richard Wagner),[44] painting (e.g. Pre-Raphaelites), or in decorative crafts (e.g. William Morris). The championing of medieval forms is perhaps nowhere more evident than in nineteenth-century neo-gothic architecture, where it found long-lasting and visible expression. In our context it is significant that it became particularly

---

[44] In Wagner's oeuvre the overlap between Germanic and medieval themes is particularly palpable: his operas create a cultural collage of Germanic legend (*The Ring*) and Christian mythology (*Parsifal*) (Oergel 1998: 208–293).

popular, not to say *de rigeur*, for *public* buildings, which suggests it functioned as an affirmation of a collective identity. The Gothic Revival in Britain and *Neugotik* in Germany are, from the middle third of the nineteenth century, responsible for the medieval look of numerous new builds, from parish churches to state buildings. Civic buildings (Hamburg telephone exchange 1902–1907), railway stations (London's St. Pancras, 1860s) or the new Houses of Parliament in London, rebuilt in the 1830s after a fire, are prominent examples of this. The completion of the unfinished medieval cathedral in Cologne between 1842 and 1863, with 60% of the cost paid for by public subscription,[45] is another. The *Kölner Dom* is a *Catholic* cathedral, but it was completed in a strongly ecumenical spirit that regarded the building as a monument of *national* history and identity. Many of the advocates for its completion, who began promoting the idea in earnest the 1820s, were Protestant, such as Goethe and Eichendorff; unsurprisingly the Catholic Joseph Görres was among them, too. The Boisserée brothers Sulpiz and Melchior had been collecting money for the upkeep of the building since the Napoleonic wars, and became key figures in the "rediscovery" of the importance of medieval art and architecture. The first stone of the completion was laid by the Prussian king Frederick William IV, himself a Protestant with a keen interest in the medieval past.

The story of the design for the rebuilding of the London Houses of Parliament after 1834 illustrates the powerful pull of the neo-gothic, when it came to choosing the most appropriate historical reference. The competition for the design of the new build was won by the architect Charles Barry who specialised in neo-Renaissance structures. Italian Renaissance styles were often favoured for ministerial buildings (Gombrich 1978: 396). However, as the art historian Ernst Gombrich told the story in the mid-twentieth-century with evident incredulity, an Italianate building was not to be:

> It was found that England's civil liberties rested on the Middle Ages, and that it was right and proper to erect the shrine of British Freedom in the Gothic style [...]. Accordingly, Barry had to seek the advice of an expert on Gothic details, A. W. N. Pugin (1812–1852), one of the most uncompromising champions of the Gothic revival. (Gombrich 1978 [1950]: 396)

It goes beyond the boundaries of this study to explore the relationship between the neo-gothic and the neo-Romanesque in architectural design, save to say that the neo-Romanesque is part of the same medievalising impetus.

The trajectory of neo-gothic architecture accompanied the progress of the Germanic from being the preoccupation of an intellectual elite to public

---

45 See <https://www.koelner-dom.de/home> (accessed 10 February 2018).

representativeness. The origins of the Gothic Revival, as later nineteenth and early twentieth-century cultural criticism named this phenomenon, lie in mid-eighteenth-century England; they appear around the same time as Macpherson's Ossian and Percy's *Reliques*. One of this new taste's first expressions was the medievalised architecture of the country houses of the landed aristocracy and gentry, such as Horace Walpole's Strawberry Hill House (1749–1776). A less expensive way of acknowledging an connection with the emerging antiquity of modernity were the newly popular fake medieval ruins, the "follies", in country house parks and gardens. An early transfer of this trend to Germany was the Nauener Tor in Potsdam, commissioned by Frederick the Great in 1755. This origin in aristocratic taste set it apart, to some extent, from the more (although by no means exclusive) middle-class preoccupation with ancient ballads and epics, which aimed to create a new, broader, collective identity. The impetus, however, was the same: to establish historically an indigenous, and hence legitimate descent that proclaimed a "true" identity. As required, this identity could then legitimise different forms of liberation from different kinds of constraining dominance or hierarchy: over-bearing reason, classical antiquity, or absolutist rule. By the middle of the nineteenth century, this style was seen as the true expression of (Germanic) national identity, rather as Goethe had suggested it should be in "Von deutscher Baukunst" in 1772.

7.5 The "Germanic-Gothic" identity project and its cultural patterns – summary

An emerging new idea has initially only a tentative claim on public support. As a project, it will only succeed if it can enlist more and more supporters and colonise more and more areas of public activity. The beginning of the chapter focused on the context and the reasons for the emergence of this identity, on the socio-political and cultural challenge it articulated. The project employed the new (eighteenth-century) idea of "culture", which had been identified as the life-blood of a functioning collective, necessary to formulate a broadly relevant "public spirit" (a Germanic identity of liberty and integrity) that could engage *ideally* the whole community and *practically* those sections that were most relevant to the elites that were undertaking its propagation. These "relevant" social sections were different entities for Hurd and Percy on the one hand, or Arndt and Görres on the other, or for the Schlegel brothers, or indeed for Stubbs and Freeman. As disparate as the aims of the above writers were the levels of minimum inclusiveness

7.5 The "Germanic-Gothic" identity project and its cultural patterns — 289

each formulation of this identity aimed at. The idea's efficacy, and its success, rested on its ability to cover this wide spectrum.

Before taking a closer look at the elites involved in propagating the Germanic-Gothic identity, it is time to summarise the different aspects of this identity project. Its starting point was the perceived need for a new (or revived) public spirit, which came to the fore in the eighteenth-century discussions of "selfishness" and "despotism". Public spirit creates *and* relies on a functioning communal identity. Much has been written about the rise of European identity politics in the late eighteenth and nineteenth centuries. This study bears out that around 1800 the impetus for creating such a public spirit of collective identity and social purpose was both political and religious. It was driven by the need to address a newly enlarged social collective. Politically, it was to address declining social coherence in a society increasingly viewed as insincere and selfish. This social critique became overtly political, i.e. linked to increasing political enfranchisement, in the wake of the French Revolution, which seemed to set a precedent for the possible range of such enfranchisement. At the same time this identity addressed a key religious issue: the increasingly evident rupture between faith based on revealed religion on the one hand and reason based on critically and/or empirically verified knowledge on the other, a rift that had been deepening as the Enlightenment advanced throughout the eighteenth century.

There was yet one other impetus, which is connected to both the political and the religious drivers: the aesthetic-psychological. Critiquing the current environment as over-rationalistic, the project seeks to (re-)enfranchise the emotions and the imagination. It is the driver foregrounded in traditional discussions of the rise of Romanticism in all its guises, from *Sturm und Drang*, sentimentalism, the ballad revival, and the sublime to Romanticism proper in the early nineteenth century. This impetus occupies the middle ground between the political and the religious: its anti-rationalist stance mitigates the reason-based natural law approaches to political enfranchisement, facilitates religious revivals based on intuitive knowledge, and supports essentialist notions of collectives, without itself promoting religious or essentialist approaches. It makes possible an emotional engagement with rationally based political enfranchisement. This is useful for collectives based on egalitarian, anti-aristocratic ideas, because such collectives do not only need a rational basis for their revolutionary demands, but also an (emotive) public spirit that engages members to *believe* in the collective's purpose. This is why in "Romantic nationalism" both hard-nosed political enfranchisement, folksy communality, and historically legitimised manifest destiny can, perhaps need to, co-exist.

The Germanic project was constructed to address, and provide solutions to, all these different needs and requirements, which, although almost opposing (revolutionary enfranchisement and national traditions), were inter-connected. This interconnectedness is indicated by the materials used to distil it. The idea of the Germanic was based on historical investigations into laws and language; the materials used were not just legal documents, but largely literary ones, i.e. ancient "national" poetry. The historical study of (Germanic) law allowed constructions of legal traditions that could underpin claims of individual civil rights (the free-born *English*man) and of constitutional legitimacy (Görres' or Follen's *Reichstag*, Thelwall's or Burke's ancient English constitution). The collective communal identities based on these traditions could be democratic republics, "prince-and-people" popular monarchies or constitutional monarchies in which the enfranchised groups (who they were was debatable) control the monarchical executive. Montesquieu's legacy is evident: all of these diverse forms are designed to oppose "selfish" despotism.

All legal traditions discussed here are traditions of liberty. They aim at enfranchisement. Collective identities were defined as underpinned by linguistic, legal, and literary heritage, and history was used to support and legitimise such cultural identities. Initially the enfranchisement was cultural: culture must be (made) relevant and address the entire community; this was the view from Herder to Arndt or Görres, from Hugh Blair to Scott, or from Percy to Thomas Arnold. Cultural and linguistic enfranchisement was essential for moral improvement and intellectual development, the critical role of an accessible language in such forms of improvement runs from Herder to Fichte, the importance of an appropriate moral code exercised Digby as much as Arnold. The power of indigenous language and literature for moral and intellectual improvement inspired the foundations of the new colleges in 1820s London and the new universities in Berlin and Bonn. Such improvement was supposed to keep the collective strong and safe. Cultural enfranchisement, and the moral improvement it brings, became the basis for greater political enfranchisement, a theme that runs from Herder via Schiller and Fichte to the Victorian social reformers of the nineteenth century.

Much of the success of the Germanic concept rests on its plasticity, not just politically, regarding forms of government, but also in terms of cultural identity. It could be moulded to suit notions of a common European culture (whether this is a Germanic Europe or European Christendom) or it could be narrowed to distil a superior national identity within this large identity, such as English laws or German linguistic transparency. It can suggest fully inclusive collectives, a *Volk* where everybody is equal *or* belongs together (which is not the same); Karl Follen's "Künftige Reichsverfassung" [future constitution of the

Empire] of 1817 was distinct in its political intentions from more paternalistic approaches, such as Novalis' in "Glauben und Liebe" (1800) or Young England's medievalism, or Frederick William IV's understanding of political legitimacy, which comes to the fore in his rejection of the "crown from the gutter" in 1849.

By the same token, exclusion was never far away. Exclusion in this context was frequently based on reduced "purity", something is not as "good" because it has absorbed, but not fully assimilated, something designated as foreign, such as the Latin language, Roman laws, classical culture, or the wrong kind of Christianity. Change was considered necessary, especially adapting to changing circumstances, and hybridity was not a problem *per se*, as the celebrated joining of the Germanic peoples and Christianity illustrates. But creative constructions could, for example, exclude the French due to their supposedly reduced share in the Germanic heritage, which was held responsible for their aristocratic, materialistic, abstract culture and seen as evident in their only semi-Germanic language. At the same time, the French could be included (and readily included themselves, Augustin Thierry's work is an example) *through* their share in the Germanic-Gothic identity and its foundational culture of chivalry. Exclusions tended to be motivated by contemporary circumstances. The exclusion of the French in German thinking after 1800 was the result of the military and political constellation of the German *Befreiungskriege*, before it became enshrined in Hegel's philosophy of history of the 1820s.

The division between Protestantism and Catholicism within a greater (Western) Christendom was a similarly adjustable demarcation. While Christianity was shared by the entire "Germanic Europe" (or even the entire European continent), for the Protestant vision of manifest destiny only Protestant Christianity retained the original in revitalised form (Fichte, Kingsley, Hegel). Such views, however, did not dim the enthusiasm for medieval culture as the foundational expression of a Germanic-Gothic identity. Similarly, Germanic laws were being traced all over Europe, but in the Victorian version of the Whig interpretation of history they had retained their purest form only in England (Kingsley, Stubbs, Freeman).

This adjustable inclusiveness was also the reason why this idea was so easily transferable between Britain and Germany, and at the same time so contested between the two. While the mid-eighteenth-century impetus to investigate the "Goths" certainly came from Britain to Germany, in the early nineteenth-century interest in "Germanic", rather than just English or Anglo-Saxon, culture was stimulated in Britain by German influences. The sources presented here evidence both the inclusive Anglo-German(ic) identity and the separatist claims to English or German superiority. This plasticity is equally responsible for the concept's successful transition from being a radical – a "left-wing" – challenge to established political order towards becoming a convincing argument for a conservative social and imperial consolidation. This was a gradual and by no means uniform or consistent process. The Germanic retained its challenging edge into the 1840s, but its mainstream status, reached by the 1840s, allowed its mobilisation for national and imperial consolidation. Once an established identity, the Germanic-Gothic served from the 1840s onwards to consolidate and legitimise "empire"; in Britain in the context of colonial expansion (Dilke), in Germany in the renewed efforts to create a unified German state. The endeavours of 1848–1849, following the 1848 revolution, still had much of the radical political edge of the constitutional ideas of the *Befreiungskriege*. This political radicalism was proclaimed by the black-red-gold tricolour that was flying on the barricades in Berlin in March 1848, but also bedecked the interior of the *Paulskirche* for the sessions of the Frankfurt Parliament, where conservatives sat alongside the rehabilitated "revolutionaries" of the Wars of Liberation and younger radicals. These colours commemorated the *Lützower Jäger* and had in 1817/1818 signalled to contemporaries the same politics as the French tricolour. There is no room here to trace the fully "imperial" instrumentalisation of the Germanic for the eventual *Reichsgründung* in 1871, but it is significant that the imperial flag did not feature the revolutionary colours of black-red-gold, but black-white-red, a combination created in 1866 for the Biskmarckian *Norddeutscher Bund*.

The Germanic-Gothic project's focus on Christianity as one of its two key cultural ingredients offered the opportunity to bring religion back into contemporary culture, under historically legitimised, cultural auspices. As the most appropriate religion for European culture it had *historical* legitimation, which went some way towards fending off the doubts occasioned by reason. It followed that (Neo-)Gothic churches were fitting places of worship for European Christians. The power invested in history to legitimise culture also provided an alternative answer to the issue of religious revelation: revelation could be considered immanent in the historical process, and satisfy the need to believe, rather than to doubt, so obvious in Carlyle's battle with the Everlasting No and in Ranke's approach to history. The historicisation of religion, begun by Michaelis, Eichhorn, and Herder, which read revelatory religious texts as cultural history, sanctified culture as human revelation, and allowed the rise of literature as quasi-sacred texts, which required academic study (*Germanistik*), especially if it was appropriate, i.e. nationally or culturally relevant, literature in the first place. The rise of the academic study of *one's own* cultural and literary history originates in this context, with the first chairs in German and English literary and linguistic history appearing between 1810 and the 1830s. Again, these new disciplines were not exclusively separatist: *comparative* legal, linguistic, and literary studies remained a corollary and flourished at the same time, producing integrationist tendencies.

While the religious revival of the mid-nineteenth century was in tune with medievalism, it equally had a social edge. Deteriorating social conditions in the first half of the nineteenth century, driven by advancing market-based economics, provoked social concern, which found expression in the thinking of Christian Socialism and the Young England-movement. The search for functioning and nurturing collectives in the historical past, which was one of the starting points for the interest in the Germanic-Gothic, provided options to historically legitimise different forms of responsible states.

The "Germanic-Gothic project" was attractive to multiple distinct, sometimes overlapping groups with different political and cultural objectives. All objectives, however, relied on the key idea contained in the terms Germanic and Gothic, i.e. the idea that the Germanic heritage bequeathed an identity of liberty and personal integrity, which from the late eighteenth to the later nineteenth century animated political and cultural discourses alike and which from the later eighteenth century began to address two of the most pressing issue(s) of the time: the extent of political enfranchisement and the question of a new Faith. Through this, the Germanic-Gothic acquired its central status.

The cultural identity of the Germanic-Gothic, in connection with the specific social, cultural, and political conditions that facilitated its rise, was responsible for a number of cultural patterns. Its new centrality in political and cultural thought led to different forms of institutionalisation. In the academies, it produced the "identity studies" of *Germanistik* and *Romanistik* in Germany and its counterparts of English Studies and culturally oriented historical studies of nationhood in Britain. In German and British thinking, it bolstered a sense of manifest destiny based on the realisation of liberty in a responsible and caring polity, which enfranchised its members (it was always debatable who counted as a full member) and which expected a sense of duty and commitment to its "public spirit" in return. These political and social aspirations reflected the key characteristics of the Germanic: an innate sense of liberty and personal integrity. This sense of personal integrity informed favoured forms of social behaviour and was responsible for the concept and ethos of the Christian gentleman, who is conceived as a modern "knight", honest, brave, and loyal, dedicated to selfless service and social justice (protecting the "weak"). In general taste, the Germanic-Gothic project produced medievalism, which was thought to express this identity appropriately. The neo-gothic style favoured in nineteenth-century public architecture is a particularly salient example of this.

How did the "propagators" and supporters of this project relate to existing power structures? How were they able, beyond capturing a large readership, to engage those with political power, which was necessary to consolidate these ideas into cultural patterns? In other words, in what way can these supporters be described as "elites", whose role has been identified as crucial in the zeitgeist process? The following – and final – two sections trace and describe these elite groups in both countries, as they emerge and become established, along with their "concept", while all the while remaining liable to being "challenged".

7.6 The propagators of the Germanic-Gothic identity – the profile of an "elite"

Such elites are in the main what is in German described as "Deutungseliten", who possess, for various and manifold reasons, "Deutungshoheit", the legitimate right of interpretation. Such interpretation, broadly, engages in producing world views and perspectives on values that make sense in a given situation to a given audience. The difficulty of delineating manipulation from less "operative" forms of presenting meaningful constructions of sense is evident. The term "Deutungselite" emerged in German in the 1970s and became widely used from the 1990s, it is a term linked to postmodern theory, but the phenomenon itself is a social function of human collectives, and as old as these. Such elites, and the processes they initiate, come under scrutiny at times of social, cultural, and political transition. Whenever existing interpretations are challenged, competing groups scrutinise each other, and in this scrutiny insights into the processes behind transitions are gained, by them and by later investigators.

A (postmodern) evaluation of intellectual influence capable of translating into social power also developed in American and British thinking from the 1940s to the 1970s. It emerged from the institutional approach in the social sciences, which surfaced at the end of the 1940s in the United States in the work of Harry Levin (Ziolkowski 1990: 6–7). It was developed by Frank Kermode for literary criticism as the "institutional control of interpretation" in 1979, which is, Kermode continues, exerted by a "professional community which has the authority (not undisputed) to define (or indicate the limits of) a subject; to impose valuations and validate interpretations."[46] Kermode observes that there are analogies to ecclesiastical or other institutions (Ziolkowski 1990: 7). At the same time (1980) Stanley Fish speaks of "interpretive communities" and asserts that "our mental operations" are "limited by the institutions in which they are

---

[46] "Institutional Control of Interpretation", *Salmagundi* 43 (1979), quoted in Ziolkowski 1990: 7.

embedded". These institutions shape their interpretive community, whose members only have access to the "public" and "conventional sense they [the institutions] make" by "inhabiting them".[47]

The elites involved in the rise, circulation, and consolidation of the Germanic were predominantly, and perhaps unsurprisingly, of middle-class origin. In both Britain and Germany, they came from the educated classes who either did not have sufficient independent means to not "work" or who saw education as preparation for the "professions" (law, medicine, the Church, public administration), as a path towards "work" in higher social positions. Practically this meant that these social groups depended or relied on forms of civil service for social advancement. Many originated from families of civil servants or professionals.

In Britain, this "civil service" was, until the second third of the nineteenth century, broadly equivalent with the established Church, which also had sole control of the two universities in England, Oxford and Cambridge, until the two new London Colleges, University College and King's College, provided secular alternatives. Outside the Church, the professional options tended to be the Law, medicine, and the armed forces, or teaching posts in the Dissenting Academies. "Professional" careers in politics did not develop until the middle of the nineteenth century. While clerics were debarred from a political role in the House of Commons, bishops and arch-bishops had direct political power through their seats in the House of Lords.

In Germany, the civil service was located in the administrations and institutions of the different principalities and included the clergy, the universities, and the armed forces. The most emblematic organisations of this type of public service were perhaps the Prussian civil service and the Prussian army, the latter had, by the late eighteenth century, acquired a legendary status similar to that of the British Royal Navy. Because the armed forces do not primarily engage in intellectual activity, these military organisations are less interesting in this context, although their ethos did utilise the discourse of "service" to the public good. It is likely that educated middle-class individuals were attracted to civil, and indeed "public", service by the meritocratic element in these organisational structures, even though meritoriousness was only an aspiration; there was no guarantee of meritocracy. Connections and patronage continued to play a key role, but the meritocratic element provided entry points into the "system" for those that were not yet part of it.

---

47 Fish 1980: 331–332.

For all individuals discussed here, the starting point for their involvement with the idea of the Germanic was personal interest in this subject. All produced publications that had high circulations and engaged a wide readership and all were linked to the cultural patterns discussed above. This suggests their ideas were connected to emerging or newly dominant tastes, preoccupations, and outlooks, which is obviously a precondition for being relevant in a zeitgeist context. All evinced an interest in the Germanic "projects", social and cultural, and propagated a new cultural and social direction.

7.6.1 The British "elites"

The career trajectories of the British elites involved here started in most cases from a grammar or public school education, moved on to an Oxbridge degree followed by a college fellowship and in many cases a church living, often one in the gift of the college. This applies to Richard Hurd, Thomas Percy, Julius Hare, Thomas Arnold, William Stubbs, Charles Kingsley, and John Mitchell Kemble, establishing a pattern that spanned at least three generations. Hurd, Percy, Hare, Kingsley, and Stubbs became bishops or high-ranking divines. E. A. Freeman did not take the "ordained" path, he was the first among those treated here who after an Oxford education made his way to cultural power by being an academic historian only; he was also the first in this list to attempt a career in politics, standing (unsuccessfully) for parliament. Kenelm Digby opted out of this route altogether; after attending school at Petersham (Surrey) and Trinity College Cambridge, he converted to Roman Catholicism. While still in his twenties he inherited, after a series of deaths, the entire family wealth and in 1833 married well, which allowed him to live comfortably on a private income. The route through the established Church was not open to Hazlitt who had a dissenting background and positioned himself directly in opposition to existing power structures.

Richard Hurd (1720–1808) descended from well-to-do Staffordshire yeoman farmers and rose via Cambridge through the ranks of the Church, holding various college positions and livings before reaching the upper levels of the hierarchy. His writing activities in the 1750s and 1760s were partly driven by the need to develop an intellectual reputation which would help a career aimed at the higher echelons of the ecclesiastical structure. His interests lay in establishing a modern cultural identity, based on Christianity and independent of classical antiquity, without denigrating ancient, perhaps especially classical, achievements. To him, such an identity was in rudiments visible in "gothic times" and experienced its first flowering in the "age of Elizabeth".

Within this modern context, his *Dialogues* advocate the Whig interpretation of English liberty that was based on Anglo-Saxon heritage: English liberty could not lastingly be subjugated by despotic monarchs, such as Charles I. In the middle of the eighteenth century, the seventeenth-century English civil war, the Restoration, and the Glorious Revolution were still the most recent formative political events, and the eventual compromise of constitutional monarchy represented a progressive liberal solution, especially in a century when most European states tended towards autocratic absolutism. Hurd's emphasis was firmly on the legacy and rightfulness of (English) liberty. Together, Christianity, a superior religion compared to its pagan predecessors, and the superior legal traditions of the Anglo-Saxons formed a modern (English) identity that was inclusive for aspiring middle-class Englishmen, like himself, without threatening the established structures of state and church, nor orthodox religious views. Hurd himself remained committed to revealed religion and the link between church and state.

Hurd enjoyed the friendship and vigorous patronage of William Warburton (another Protestant conservative), gained through his edition of Horace's *Ars Poetica* (1749), Hurd's first major publication. Warburton opened doors, first to a preacher's position at Whitehall in 1750, then made Hurd his own chaplain, and in 1760 to the position as preacher at Lincoln's Inn. In Hurd's career the Church, the Law and politics combine: the position at Lincoln's Inn turned out to be a launch-pad to the very top. With royal approval (George III) Hurd was appointed Bishop of Lichfield in 1775, made preceptor to the Prince of Wales in 1776, and moved on to the See of Worcester in 1781 (Ditchfield and Brewer 2008). As his career developed, Hurd expressed increasingly conservative views, condemning first the American revolution, then the French, and affirming the priority of monarchy over republican liberty. While he believed in religious freedom, he was opposed to enfranchising dissenters. Dissenters could not hold public office, because he equated, like many conservatives in the final decades of the eighteenth century, religious dissent with secular libertarianism. Although his championing of "barbaric" gothic culture as an ingredient of European, and English, identity set him at odds with large parts of the refined and civilised contemporary culture of the educated and the upper classes, it did not stop him from holding conservative views when the British political and religious compromise was threatened. The "revolutionary" aspects of his ideas (providing a potential basis for enfranchising all social classes of a nation) would only be realised one to two generations later.

Thomas Percy's career trajectory was similar to Hurd's. The son of a Shropshire (small) businessman, a grocer, Percy (1729–1811) attended a local grammar school and secured an "exhibition" (scholarship) to go to Christ

Church, Oxford. After graduation he proceeded to various church posts in the gift of his college and was mindful to acquire aristocratic patrons. One wonders whether his decision to spell his name as we know it – earlier records show Pearcy and Piercy (Palmer 2006) – was influenced by establishing a link to his most influential patrons, the Percys, Duke and Duchess of Northumberland. In the 1750s Percy became interested in balladry, having found and eventually borrowed a "battered" seventeenth-century volume of ballads (Palmer 2006), which would be the main source for the publication that would, in 1765, make his name and his career, the *Reliques of Ancient English Poetry*. Through his connections to the Duke of Northumberland – he was appointed chaplain and secretary to the Duke and tutor to his son in 1765 – Percy gained access to the royal household and became chaplain-inordinary (a small post) to George III in 1769 (Palmer 2006). In 1770 his widely read translation of Mallet's *Histoire de Dannemarc* appeared as *Northern Antiquities*, consolidating his fame as a man of letters in touch with current trends. During the 1760s and 1770s his connections at court and in London's literary and intellectual circles allowed him wide-ranging exchanges, and influence. While initially his interest in "northern antiquities" and rustic or ancient ballads was met with condescension by critics who found them uncouth and with outrage by more antiquarian minded collectors such as Josef Ritson (Palmer 2006, Oergel 1998: 37–38), the wide circulation of the *Reliques* and *Northern Antiquities* tells a different story. Percy was mindful of the potentially subversive aspect of a civilised gentleman spending his intellectual efforts on such low-culture entities, calling himself depreciatingly a "scavenger for the public", and he took his moral and aesthetic obligations very seriously: "As Virgil found Gold among the Dung of Ennius, from all this learned Lumber I hope to extract something that shall please the most delicate and correct Taste."[48] Although Percy did not reach the top level of the "church and state" establishment compared to Hurd – Percy eventually became Bishop of Dromore in Ireland in 1782 – the circulation and cultural impact of the *Reliques* was enormous, reaching beyond Britain. Herder and Goethe both treasured the book. What is most interesting in *this* context is the extent to which Percy adjusted his novel, and somewhat risqué, material to pass the muster of public acceptance, making his amendments in a deliberate and premeditated way, which involved considerable research. His collection not only engaged the reading public, but also satisfied the reviewer of the *Gentleman's Magazine* in 1765: Percy "has with great judgement selected such specimens [of ballads] as either shew the gradation of our language, exhibit the progress of

---

[48] Letters from Dr Percy to T. Astle, esq., quoted in Palmer 2006.

popular opinion, display the peculiar manners and customs of former ages, or throw light on our early classical poets" (Palmer 2006).

Walter Scott (1771–1832) was the son of an established Edinburgh solicitor, who himself was the son of a "prosperous" border sheep farmer, i.e. his father's trajectory is not dissimilar to Hurd's or Percy's; Scott's mother was the daughter of a well-travelled Edinburgh professor of medicine. He attended the High School in Edinburgh (1779–1783), which provided him with a wealth of connections, and a useful network for later life (Hewitt 2008). The young Scott was interested in (Scottish) early modern history, and Percy's *Reliques* made as deep an impression on him as they had on Goethe and Herder. After one false start in Classics at university and another as a legal apprentice to his father, Scott embarked on university study again in 1789, this time with great profit. He studied moral philosophy, history, and law. Among his teachers was Alexander Fraser Tytler (history), the first translator of Schiller's *Räuber*. Scott qualified as a lawyer ("advocate") in July 1792. Scott was very much keyed into the current intellectual interest in "culture", the mix of literature, history, and law. He co-founded the Literary Society in 1789 and became a member of the Edinburgh Speculative Society in 1790, he found the study of law interesting due to "the way in which law was simultaneously antiquarian and political, historical and contemporary" (Hewitt 2008). This is in line with Savigny's and later Grimm's approach to legal antiquities. Scott's formative phase around 1790 fell into the period of the influx of German "Gothic" literature, which in Scotland is dated to Henry Mackenzie's lecture on German theatre given to the Royal Society in Edinburgh in 1788 and which brought Schiller's *Räuber* to the attention of his audience (Koch 1927: 36–37). Scott bought a copy of Tytler's translation of Schiller in July 1792 (Clark 1969: 269, note 7), within weeks of it appearing. He was enthralled by Bürger's *Lenore* in 1795, on the theme of which some of his own early balladry focuses. Although keen to disavow his interest in things German in 1827, he was still prepared to admit that he *had* been "German-mad" at this time.[49] David Hewitt (2008) points out the conspicuous silence about the French Revolution in Scott's autobiography and memoirs, and suggests that Scott may have been sympathetic to the ideals of Revolution in the early 1790s. By early 1793, however, Scott was politically firmly on the anti-Revolution side; he volunteered as a gentleman constable (to help prevent popular uprisings in Edinburgh) and served in the Royal Edinburgh light dragoons from its

---

49 Letter to Mary Ann Hughes, 13 Dec 1827 (Hughes 1904: 224).

formation in 1797. In 1808 he was instrumental in founding the *Quarterly Review*, the conservative counterweight to the liberal *Edinburgh Review*.

I will now turn to those born in the 1790s, Hare, Carlyle, Thomas Arnold, all three born in 1795, Digby, possibly born the same year, and the youngest of this group, Kemble. These individuals came to intellectual consciousness towards the end of the Napoleonic Wars, and it was from this generation, with the exception of the slightly older Hazlitt, that the key propagators came, not just of the idea of a spirit of the age (Carlyle, Hazlitt and Hare), but of the early versions of the Germanic-Gothic as the basis of liberty and public duty (Arnold, Kemble and Digby).

Thomas Arnold (1795–1842) was the son of the postmaster of the Isle of Wight, he attended Winchester College before winning a scholarship to Oxford, where he proceeded to a fellowship (Reeve 2014). Religious doubts made him hesitate to be ordained and accept the Thirty-nine Articles at the same time as Hare debated these issues with himself. Like Hare, Arnold eventually submitted to the religious test. Like Hare in the early 1820s, Arnold was also attracted to Niebuhr's work, his *Römische Geschichte*, which forms the basis of his own work on Roman history (*History of Rome*, 1838–1843). Arnold learnt German to study Niebuhr in depth. Instead of a career at Oxford or at the new London colleges (he withdrew his application for a post there), Arnold chose a career in school teaching, becoming headmaster at Rugby in 1827. Arnold was an Anglican liberal of Broad Church persuasions, a staunch supporter of the Reform Bill and Catholic emancipation, with strong leanings towards social justice, for which he was vilified by the conservative press as "teaching revolution" in the 1830s (Reeve 2014). At the same time, he was enamoured with the idea of the Christian gentleman, "his aim was to make Rugby a Christian school producing Christian gentlemen" (Reeve 2014). His priorities were "1st, religious and moral principles; 2ndly, gentlemanly conduct; 3rdly, intellectual ability" (Stanley 1846 [1844]: 95). His closeness to Digby's ideas in *The Broad Stone of Honour* are inescapable. Arnold expected his staff at Rugby to embody this ideal. Not unlike Digby in 1822, Arnold had a universalist concept of the gentlemanly code: his *History of Rome* was intended as a school textbook to further *Christian* ideals (Stanley 1846: 162). Like Digby, and to some extent Scott before them, he considered Christian chivalry, as a mindset and behavioural code of unparalleled virtue and integrity, a universal phenomenon that was independent of religion, *but* that flourished best under Christian conditions. His own (re-established) faith was of the Hegelian kind: history was a divine revelation, an idea shared with Carlyle and Ranke. Arnold was anti-secular and anti-revolution, but for an evolution towards a liberal Christian democracy that was perhaps not very different from what Arndt and some of the *Burschenschaftler* imagined. There are some intriguing parallels between Arnold's reforms at Rugby and Karl Follen's idea of schools and universities as miniature *Freistaaten* which provide training grounds for responsible modern citizens (Oergel 2018a), especially the partial self-governance Arnold introduced through the prefect system. Similarly, Arnold's focus on physical education, especially organised games, has a parallel in Follen's and Ludwig Jahn's thinking. Arnold's influence on a generation of Victorians endeavouring to realise the ideals he preached is well known (Reeve 2014).

John Mitchell Kemble (1807–1857) did not succeed in securing a permanent academic position, but contributed significantly to establishing emerging ideas. His biography is a useful corollary to the success stories above, because it sheds light on why some individuals, although they propagate similar ideas and work in many respects on the same "project", achieve no socially consolidated status. Although arguably the greatest influence on careers are the contingencies of chance and luck, and sheer power of circumstance, such discrepancies in terms of social success often also highlight perspectives from which ideas were judged by contemporaries and which may in hindsight have become obscured. No doubt his reckless and self-indulgent nature played a role in the erratic stops and starts of his biography. Equally, his passionate and deeply political nature, which tended towards radical spiritual and social reform, did not easily enter into pragmatic arrangements with given situations of power, a pragmatism that had led Hare and Arnold to accommodate themselves with the "system", submitting to the Thirty-nine Articles. Kemble's belief in the need for comprehensive reform, starting with the education system, never lost its edge, retaining the radicalism of a Thelwall or an Arndt. Kemble's irreverent and cynical attitude and his uncompromising commitment to reform leap off the page in a letter to W. B. Donne of 25 October 1836:

> All reform is misplaced, which does not begin by reforming our system of *education*, from the lowest to the highest and from the dame school to the University. I do thank God that I for one escaped the soulkilling and ruinous effects of a University education: I hated and despised them, and I owe them nothing. Yet if accident should ever set me up on a pedestal and raise me to a name, they will claim me. Education must be taken out of the hands of the parsons, till the parsons are educated for their task of educating others. The *clerisy* of the land must no longer be the parsonage of the land. (Allen 1978: 164)

His friend Alfred Tennyson, a fellow member of the Cambridge Conversazione Society, expected Kemble to become a "latter Luther" "spurr'd at heart with fieriest energy / To embattail and to wall about thy cause with iron-worded proof". "Our dusted velvets have much need of thee".[50]

---

[50] Tennyson, "Sonnet to J.M.K." (1830).

Born into the famous Kemble family of actors and theatre owners, the son of a German-speaking Viennese mother (Maria Theresa de Camp), Kemble embarked on the standard path: Bury St. Edmunds Grammar School and then Trinity College Cambridge, which he entered in 1824/1825 and where he cultivated a large circle of friends, among them Frederick Denison Maurice and John Sterling, familiar from Chapter 5. Kemble was elected to the "Apostles" and became president of the Cambridge Union in 1828 (Haigh 2015). In 1827 he was at the Inner Temple, together with Maurice, who was well-connected in the London periodicals circles of the mid- and later 1820s (see Chapter 5), and Kemble contributed to the *Athenaeum*.

Kemble was a radical liberal, a staunch Benthamite, who turned "mystic" but kept his revolutionary tendencies. He put the latter into practice in 1830, in the context of the general revolutionary activity of those months, on the ill-fated expedition to support the Spanish insurgency against King Ferdinand VII. The expedition was organised out of Cambridge by John Boyd, Sterling's cousin, and Richard Trench, another Trinity student who, notwithstanding a radical youth, went on to become Archbishop of Dublin and Anglican primate of Ireland. After his revolutionary excursion, Kemble abandoned his plan of being ordained, decided against a career in law, and settled on an academic career. Inspired, not least by Jacob Grimm's *Deutsche Grammatik* (Haigh 2015), Kemble became interested in German ideas of Germanic legal and linguistic identities and began to research Anglo-Saxon texts. He published the first modern scholarly edition of *Beowulf* in 1833 and, between 1839 and 1848, the six-volume *Codex diplomaticus aevi saxonici*. He began to lecture at Cambridge, initially to packed rooms, but audiences dwindled and established scholars considered him too influenced by Danish and German methods (Haigh 2015). In 1834 he spent a few weeks in Göttingen, working with Jacob Grimm, whose research corresponded closely with Kemble's own interest in Germanic laws, language, and literature. Failing to establish an academic career, Kemble turned to journalism. In 1848, just before publishing *The Saxons in England*, his most influential work, he moved to Hanover, at a moment of momentous expectations regarding liberal change in Germany. In the 1850s, in Germany, Kemble was again working at the forefront of scientific developments, turning to the new area of scientific archaeology; he died in Dublin in March 1857 where he had addressed the Royal Irish Academy "On the utility of antiquarian collections".

Both **William Stubbs** and **Edward Augustus Freeman** were born in the 1820s. Stubbs William (1825–1901) was the son of a Yorkshire solicitor; he attended Ripon Grammar School, went to Trinity College Oxford and via the usual beginnings in the Church – a fellowship at Trinity, a church living and a spell as librarian at Lambeth Palace – advanced to a bishopric (first Chester, then Oxford). He made his intellectual impact before his arrival at the top of the Church establishment, as a scholar of Anglo-Saxon and medieval English legal antiquities. Stubbs was Regius Professor of Modern History at Oxford, a post he held from 1866–1884 (Campbell 2005). West Midland-born Freeman (1823–1892) descended from mixed middle-class parents. His father belonged to the new business-class, he owned a coal mine, which provided the orphaned Edward Augustus, who had lost both parents before his second birthday, with a private income of £600 a year, while his mother had a vaguely noble ancestry and traced her lineage to seventeenth-century English nobility. Freeman arrived at Trinity College Oxford in 1841, three years before Stubbs; like Stubbs, on graduation Freeman proceeded to a fellowship (Barlow 2011). Freeman's leanings were towards politics, he unsuccessfully stood for parliament, and was an outspoken liberal, supporting various independence movements, especially in the Balkans against the Ottoman Empire. He was a successful academic, even if he was only eventually appointed as Regius Professor of Modern History at Oxford in 1884 on Stubbs' departure to the see of Chester. Both Stubbs and Freeman were decidedly High Church and supported a conservative religious revival. Stubbs' appointment as Regius Professor took place amid assurances that he was politically and religiously "trustworthy" (Barlow 2011), i.e. moderate and conservative, at a time when Freeman, who had also applied in 1866, was believed less so. While both were, according to contemporary accounts, uninspiring lecturers, their historical publications were widely read. Both, as we have seen, presented a Greater Germanic Europe in which England, and by extension Britain, had a privileged place due to its legal and constitutional Germanic legacy. Their religious conservatism did not preclude liberal political views, especially in Freeman, but by the 1860s and 1870s the Germanic heritage of the English was firmly in the service of Empire and becoming a consolidating force. However, that it had not fully lost its liberating edge is evidenced by Freeman's support, at least in principle, for the national self-determination of others, including the Irish, and by Dilke's efforts to enfranchise (property-owning) women at municipal level (Oergel 2012).

Charles Wentworth Dilke's biography has already been sketched above. A flamboyant and eccentric character, his path was more unconventional than those of the others. A sickly child, he did not attend any school, but grew up among the varied cultural influences of a well-to-do, intellectual, middle-class metropolitan household in early Victorian London. He entered Trinity Hall Cambridge in 1862, studying maths and law. Dilke was an active debater in the Cambridge Union. He professed a liberal political creed that combined tentative republicanism with keen support for the Empire and imperial ambition, because the Empire's Germanic nature was crucial for salutary political and cultural development worldwide. His *Greater Britain* impressed both Gladstone, who annotated his copy, and J. S. Mill (Jenkins 2008).

Charles Kingsley (1819–1875) was low-church and Broad Church and a dedicated supporter of what his patron F. D. Maurice would in 1852 name "Christian Socialism".[51] In the "Hungry" 1840s, Kingsley argued for more social justice and participation; he attended the Chartist demonstration on Kennington Common in 1848 and was involved in setting up working men's colleges (Vance 2009). While a youngster at Clifton College, Kingsley had been an eye-witness to the Bristol Riots in 1831. His career path was standard: the son of a Hampshire country gentleman turned vicar, he was grammar-school educated and went to King's College London before moving on to Cambridge, from where he proceeded to a ministry in the Church. In a spectacular rise, paralleled in this collection of biographies perhaps only by Thomas Percy, Kingsley became one of Queen Victoria's chaplains in 1857 and private tutor to the Prince of Wales in 1861, while holding the Regius Professorship of Modern History at Cambridge (1860–1869). Here Kingsley gave his lecture series on "The Roman and the Teuton" to full houses of enthralled students, unlike Stubbs and Freeman in Oxford. As all three propagated a similar vision of a Germanic Christendom in which Britain, due to its traditions of liberal constitutional government, took pride of place, it is unlikely that the subject itself had much to do with the empty Oxford lecture rooms, but that instead it was a case of Kingsley's – the novelist's – superior story-telling. His literary output had initiated his preferment. Both Prince Albert and Freiherr von Bunsen had been impressed with his (early) *Saint's Tragedy* (1848), which propagated Christian Protestantism. After his time as Regius Professor at Cambridge, he was first a canon at Chester, then at Westminster Abbey. Like Arnold before him, Kingsley also suffered a crisis of religious faith (around 1840), which was eased – like Arnold's – by reading Coleridge and Carlyle (Vance 2009). Arnold was a keen admirer of the Lake Poets in general; Hare's and Hazlitt's insistence on Wordsworth's spiritual importance is borne out in these biographies. Kingsley wanted to overcome the rift between faith and science and took great interest in Darwin's theory of evolution, which *he* found compatible with a Christian faith. Like Arnold, he demanded the unity of politics and religion. It remains somewhat astounding that his employment by the royal family was not adversely affected by his social and intellectual reformism. Royal favour did, however, not protect him from the inevitable savaging as a radical in the conservative press.

---

51 Kingsley secured his first lecturing post at the newly founded Queen's College through Maurice.

7.6 The propagators of the Germanic-Gothic identity — 305

The survey of these somewhat repetitive career trajectories illustrates the central position of the established Church in the British structures of social power. The Church also had a central role in fostering and disseminating new ideas, once they had been identified as useful and consolidating. The survey also shows that diversity of opinion was common among the propagators of the Germanic, even within the same generation there are numerous different political and religious opinions, which do not prevent the individuals from holding positions of public influence or stop them from broadly supporting the same new idea. This biographical survey bears out to what extent the idea of the Germanic, and its eventually powerful discourse, was linked to the pre-existing idea of English liberty. This constellation allowed challenging as well as consolidating tendencies: because Germanic liberty was understood as based on ancient customs it could be used for conservative consolidation; as a "birth right" that had been lost, it could equally it be used to legitimise agendas of enfranchisement. Its "revolutionary" element of spiritual and political reform (something lost that needed to be reinstated) is the reason for the predominantly *liberal* political attitudes of especially the nineteenth-century propagators.

By the 1860s, the Germanic had been harnessed to support British imperial ambitions, still in the guise of liberation, and helped consolidate colonial power rather than challenge it. Ironically, the very idea of the inalienable rights of an enfranchised, culturally homogenous national collective, on which the challenging potential of the Germanic around 1800 was based, would in the twentieth century drive the independence movements in the crumbling colonial empires. Nevertheless, even in the mid-Victorian period the Germanic did not fully lose its challenging edge, Kingsley, for example, combined his views on English superiority with Christian Socialism.

These biographies also show that the established Church should not be viewed as monolithic. Although its hierarchy was generally socially and religiously conservative, intent on retaining the existing social power structures, on which its "established" status and wealth rested, and keen to protect orthodox theology, which made it averse to intellectual challenge, it had nevertheless developed the breadth to accommodate a wide political and intellectual diversity. After the effective emancipation of Catholics and dissenters in 1828, the liberal reform movement – the Broad Church – consolidated. It was itself both joined and challenged by the Oxford (reform) Movement, which criticised the conservative side of the "courtly" Anglican Church, but, being radically conservative, sought to restore the received doctrines and rituals. Both movements are testimony to the renewed religious fervour in the middle third of the nineteenth century; both were attempting to overcome, firstly, the rift between knowledge and faith that so preoccupied Victorian thinkers and, secondly, the (prevalent) social and individual selfishness by public-spirited faith.

In Britain, intellectual life took place to such an extent under the aegis of the established Church that the contestations that are the subject of this investigation would necessarily start here, until secular academic and political paths became established routes to social and cultural power for emerging elites. The process in which professional career options which lead to positions of social influence moved from the Church to secularised academies and politics occurred during the Victorian period. It is exemplified by the role of the Cambridge Apostles during the nineteenth century, whose networks and influence have been traced by Peter Allen (1978) and W. C. Lubenow (1998).

Founded at St. John's College Cambridge as the Conversazione Society in 1820, their centre of gravity soon moved to Trinity College. Intended as an intimate private club for frank and honest debate – removing the barriers that public acceptability and ulterior motives set up – their early members addressed themselves to political, intellectual, and religious issues. Both Hare and Thirwell had considerable influence on the first generation of "Apostles", many of whom were devotees of Wordsworth. Kemble, D. F. Maurice, and John Sterling were Apostles. Their ethos of public service, based on moral responsibility and intellectual integrity, developed out of their concern about the corrosion of public spirit and public service that were so formative for the zeitgeist discourse. Moral responsibility within a modern, newly enfranchised collective was also a key concern in the constructions of the Germanic identity. As we have seen, Trinity was one of the centres where this thinking developed. Allen has pointed out that especially in the first half of the century the Society functioned as a place where its members could connect the "non-topical curriculum of university studies and current social and political issues" (1978: 20). Similarly, Lubenow (1998) has focused on the link between ideas and action, which its members so actively sought to cultivate, in connection with the social status of authority. The Apostles were a self-conscious and self-consciously meritocratic elite who, because of their scepticism of established authority, preferred, in a direct challenge to this authority, to link liberalism and enfranchisement to a form of public service that was based on a sense of public duty, or public spirit.

7.6.2 The German "elites"

In Germany, the relevant biographies and career trajectories show similar congruence with each other, but are marked by more extreme "career events", such as suspensions, dismissals or exile, which reflects the more intense political power struggles *within* social and professional hierarchies. This to some extent confirms the received opinion of the more "troubled" political history in Germany, but whether this made for a more varied development of ideas is another matter. Despite these differences, there are considerable parallels between Britain and Germany regarding the aims of the public propagators of the Germanic: in both contexts they promoted this identity as representing and serving responsible but unalienable "liberty" within a shared European heritage.

Among the German propagators there, too, are considerable parallels regarding social background and career trajectories. The German elites propagating the Germanic recruited themselves from the same social strata as in Britain: the educated middle classes. All of the fourteen individuals surveyed in this section[52] descended from members of the professions (predominantly civil servants and clergy) or from parents involved in commerce or crafts. Slightly different are Arndt and Fichte: Arndt's father was a liberated serf who now worked in rural manorial administration and Fichte's forebears were smallholders and ribbon makers. All attended schools, and all (except Görres) attended universities as students, Görres joined higher education as a teacher. The majority studied either theology or law, suggesting intended careers in the church or the legal professions. Unlike in Britain, all except one (Goethe) held teaching positions at one time or another, eleven out of the fourteen held university chairs for long periods of their careers; *all* of them held "public" office, i.e. occupied positions in the administrations of territorial states. When in Britain a career in the Church was the preferred professional trajectory, in Germany it was the academic route of a university career. One is almost tempted to say that the bishopric's equivalent is the university chair.

Another feature that is markedly different between the two contexts is the greater number of different *centres* of activities. While in Britain there was a strong gravitation towards the capital(s), London (and Edinburgh), and to the two English universities (Oxford and Cambridge), in Germany there were not only more centres, gravity shifted between them, from the eighteenth-century centres Göttingen, Halle/Leipzig and Zürich towards Jena/Weimar, Berlin, Bonn, the southwestern university towns and Munich from 1800 onwards. Vienna, on the other hand, maintained its commanding position in the southeast in both centuries (and beyond). Another centre that blossomed relatively briefly in the second half of the eighteenth century, but does not continue to

---

[52] Herder, Goethe, Fichte, Hegel, the brothers Schlegel and Grimm, Arndt, Görres, Uhland, Ranke, Follen, and Bodmer.

hold a commanding position throughout the nineteenth, was Königsberg (now Kaliningrad) in East Prussia. The rise of the north-eastern regions towards the end of the eighteenth century reflects to a considerable extent Prussia's rise to political and cultural prominence.

These shifts should, however, be regarded as very gradual processes, which were accompanied by decades of interactions, not necessarily in terms of rivalries, but in terms of networking and fruitful exchanges. Göttingen, for example, remained a force well into the 1830s with close links to Jena and Berlin, Herder in Weimar was close to Heyne at Göttingen, August Wilhelm Schlegel studied at Göttingen before he embarked on his long trek around almost all centres mentioned. His brother Friedrich studied at Göttingen and Leipzig before making an impact at Jena and Berlin, and eventually settling in Vienna. The Grimms only moved from Göttingen to Berlin after their dismissal in 1838. Leipzig remained an eminent and popular place of study among the individuals in question, from Goethe in the 1760s (although Goethe went at his father's behest) through to Ranke fifty years later in the 1810s. Fichte provided a link between Zürich and Jena and Berlin, the Schlegels between Jena, Berlin and Vienna, and Görres between the Southwest, Munich, and Vienna. More research is needed to work out more clearly the "directions of travel" and the impact of this polycentric German set-up on intellectual, cultural, and political developments. Did it, for example, produce more (job) opportunities and a wider breadth of opinion? It evidently reflected the federal nature of Germany. One other detail emerges clearly in the German biographies, too: while upper-class patronage was common in the eighteenth century, it was increasingly replaced (although not obliterated) by more institutionally driven appointments from the Napoleonic period onwards.

Politically, the German propagators share with their British counterparts a generally liberal outlook and an interest in constitutional government. Depending on their dates, they tended to support the French Revolution, either in its initial stages, or in terms of what *they* took to be its "ideals". Their view of Napoleon was conditioned by this: while some initially still wondered whether he might be the carrier of liberation (Görres, and Hegel perhaps as late as 1806), virtually all who lived beyond 1806 concluded that he was an oppressive conqueror who had betrayed the ideals of liberty and equality and needed to be opposed. Many of them felt the force of repression after 1819: Arndt, Görres, Follen, the Grimms, and Uhland lost their jobs for political reasons at some point in their careers; Fichte might well have done, had he not died of typhoid in 1814. (Fichte did of course experience this in a different context, being removed from his chair at Jena in 1799 for "atheism".) However, those that survived into mid-century were all rehabilitated (Arndt, the Grimms, Görres, Uhland) and were, to a man, elected as members of the Frankfurt Parliament in 1848–1849, where their (too) broadly liberal constitutional efforts on a national level came to virtually nothing.

While liberal tendencies continued to be associated with the Germanic in the middle of the century, the consolidation moment that was observed around mid-century in the British context can also be made out in Germany. The rehabilitation of the old radicals is one aspect of this. This consolidation was facilitated by the changing interpretation of the Middle Ages, or perhaps more accurately, the changing face of medievalism. Mid-century medievalism had lost most of the radical challenge it had posed to the absolutist and early capitalist "mechanism" of modern society and to the "degenerate" refinement of aristocratic society, which it had embodied for Novalis, Arndt, and the *Burschenschaftler*. Instead it began to postulate chivalric and paternalistic ideals in a way that mixed social reform with nostalgic social conservatism. In Germany, the anti-Romantic rhetoric of the writers associated with *Junges Deutschland* expedited this shift, as the *Jungdeutschen* delineated their own social radicalism from this earlier form by suggesting the latter was conservative or unpolitical. The medieval, then, appeared not just less threatening, but also suitable for conservative consolidation. However, this is not a clear-cut division, Büchner's *Hessischer Landbote* shares many features – religious language and justification, recourse to medieval political structures – with the rhetoric and aims of Arndt's or Novalis' texts. This mirrors, to some extent, the development of medievalism in Britain. Here the Young England movement, unlike its German namesake, presented the concept of a paternalistic, chivalric, and Christian society in a socially conservative way, although they too were critiquing an unjust and broken society. What both "young" movements shared with each other and their radical political forebears, such as Arndt and Novalis, was their social conscience, which in all cases was its driving force. Finally, I will take a more detailed look at individual biographies, focusing particularly on social background, education, careers, political outlook, and generational coherence.

The oldest writer discussed in this chapter is **Johann Jacob Bodmer** (1698–1783). He belongs to the generation of Thomas Blackwell and Hugh Blair, who were crucial in paving the way for understanding the function and historicity of "culture" and who prepared the ground for Macpherson, Hurd, and Percy, and Herder and Goethe respectively. Bodmer was Swiss and as such a citizen of a territory that had been independent from the *Reich* since 1648 and forged a distinctive identity of its own, which rested on political independence and original democratic structures (so admired by Julius Hare's parents). Switzerland was also a European crossroads. While German-speaking Zurich looked to Germany, Necker's and Mme de Staël's Coppet looked to France, as did Mallet's Francophone Geneva. Bodmer was based in Zurich. During his lifetime, Switzerland was very much reinventing itself as an authentic and natural place, whose unrefined and uncorrupted culture and "sublime" landscape could rival the Scottish Highlands, or other such places. In this respect it slotted into the mid-eighteenth-century discourse on aesthetics and was part of the "pre-Romantic" intellectual landscape. Bodmer's family were long-standing members of the Calvinist Zurich bourgeoisie, his father was a pastor and his mother descended from merchants. He engaged in the typical mix of teaching, writing, publishing, and civic activities. He held a teaching post (professorship) at the Zurich "Gymnasium", the *Carolinum*, for over half a century and was a member of the *Großer Rat* [Great Council], the Canton-based legislative. His historicist outlook shaped his interest in the power of authentic culture. To this end he translated Milton and Homer, was instrumental in getting Wieland's Shakespeare translations published (Seybold 2005: 226–227), and brought medieval German poetry to the attention of a wider audience. Before Herder, he favoured Shakespeare and Milton over French neo-classicism and engaged in a well-known "Literaturstreit" with Gottsched on that matter in the early 1740s. At the Carolinum he taught Swiss history. His Calvinist faith and Enlightenment thinking created his fervour for moral and political rectitude and a keen support for Swiss republicanism. To these ends he was a vigorous writer and publicist, together with his school friend and compatriot Johann Jakob Breitinger he published the cultural-educational weekly *Discourse der Mahlern* in 1721–1723. Bodmer received key inspiration from early to mid-eighteenth-century Britain, his close reading of Blackwell was part of this (see Chapter 2). During the 1750s-1770s, Zurich became a magnet for those young writers in the ambit of the pre-romantic *Sturm und Drang*: Klopstock, Goethe, Haller, and Wieland (Seybold 2005 and Hentschel 2007). When Fichte reached Zurich in 1788, five years after Bodmer's death, it was through the educated burgher circles that had been Bodmer's environment that he met not just his future wife, but also Lavater and encountered Kant's *Critiques*, the crucial catalyst for his own philosophical work.

Johann Gottfried Herder (1744–1803) originated intellectually in the Königsberg of Kant and Hamann, who both influenced him. He descended from an East Prussian family of master craftsmen and church officials, attended the local Lateinschule, and found patrons to finance his studies at Königsberg. After a false start in medicine (he fainted at the first dissection he attended), he turned to theology and philosophy. Until he settled in Weimar in a comfortable church post – as *Generalsuperintendant* he was the principality's highest-ranking clergyman – Herder's CV was typical of the itinerant eighteenth-century intellectual who had to follow the opportunities that his education afforded him. Turning down a teaching post in St. Petersburg, he accepted a post at the cathedral school in the large Hanseatic port-city of Riga, which a generation ago had been acquired by Russia from Sweden. Ambitious, he knew he needed to publish to be noticed; similar calculations had motivated Hurd's writing and publishing efforts at roughly the same time. Herder's *Fragmente* were self-confidently styled as "Beilagen zu Briefen die neuere deutsche Literatur betreffend", aligning himself with one of the most progressive and talked-about publications on German literature and culture at the time. Herder's connections with the Riga merchants Berens, members of Riga's self-confident and educated Hanseatic German bourgeoisie, who had enabled Hamann to visit Britain (in their service), made it possible for Herder to embark, together with the young Berens, in June 1769 on his famously documented voyage to France, which took him via Nantes to Paris. In 1770 he was engaged as a companion-tutor for the Prince of Eutin, heir to the small Duchy of Eutin in North German Holstein, for the latter's trip to Italy. On this trip the party stopped at Strasbourg, where Herder remained from September until the following spring, making close friends with the young Goethe, who was completing his law studies there. Together they hatched the plan for what became *Von deutscher Art und Kunst*. It was Herder's positive write-up of the recently deceased Thomas Abbt, who had been a *Konsistorialrat* (top clergy) in the small Duchy of Bückeburg, that opened the Bückeburg *Konsistorialrat*-position to him: Duke Wilhelm of Schaumburg-Lippe felt moved to offer Abbt's post to the up-and-coming young writer and thinker. On a research trip to Göttingen, financed by the Duke for his trophy civil servant, Herder became friendly with Christian Gottlob Heyne, established classical philologist and university librarian of similarly lower middle class origin as Herder, and both worked to secure a professorship in theology for Herder at Göttingen. Their plan was foiled by worries over Herder's "atheist" racialism, and the offence he had given to two resident professors Michaelis (theology) and especially Schlözer (history) in earlier determinedly strident publications (Maurer 2014: 81–82). In 1776, his friend Goethe, who had meanwhile secured a very comfortable position at the Weimar court, managed to get Herder the post of *Generalsuperintendant* and court preacher at Weimar, which made Herder financially secure and able to pursue his intellectual career in more enlightened environs.

Goethe's biography is perhaps too well known to be rehearsed here, but it is instructive to point out the features that are key in my context. Goethe (1749–1832) descended from wealthy Frankfurt merchants on his father's side and well-established lawyers and civil administrators on his mother's. His parents belonged to the upper echelons of the city's ruling elite, who represented an older, imperial, enfranchised bourgeoisie. In the mid-eighteenth-century, Frankfurt's status as a free imperial city, and with it its history as the administrative centre of the old Empire, was still very much alive in the minds of its burghers who saw themselves as representatives of traditional imperial "liberties" that protected them from aristocratic or absolutist take-overs. Against this background, Frankfurt was the scene of the coronation of emperor Josef II in 1764, an event that the fifteen-year-old Goethe witnessed. Goethe was to pursue a career in law; although he would have preferred to go to the modern new university in Göttingen, he was sent to the traditional, and high-status, University of Leipzig (1765–1768) and, after his mental and physical collapse, completed his studies in Strasbourg in 1770–1771. He trained further at the Imperial Court of Law (Reichskammergericht) in Wetzlar, one of the two remaining imperial-level institutions of the old Empire, before practising in Frankfurt from 1771–1775, and his departure to Weimar. His "call" to Weimar was occasioned, not unlike Herder's to Bückeburg, by a prince, or his mentors, liking what he wrote. Goethe had attracted some attention with *Götz von Berlichingen* and his contributions to *Von deutscher Art und Kunst*, but he was made famous almost overnight through *Werther* in 1774. His writing provided the opportunities to make intellectual contacts (Lavater and Klopstock visited him in Frankfurt in 1774, as did the literary Count von Stolberg, who took him on a trip to the newly interesting Switzerland). The tutor of the two Weimar princes, Karl Ludwig von Knebel, also paid the young writer a visit, creating an acquaintance between his pupil and Goethe, which in September 1775 resulted in the eighteen-year-old, freshly created Duke Karl August of Saxe-Weimar offering the twenty-six-year-old Goethe a post at Weimar, where he remained, not just writing the majority of his works, but holding a string of offices and some considerable cultural and political power.

Johann Gottlieb Fichte (1762–1814) descended from craftsmen and smallholding farmers in the Saxon region of Oberlausitz; his background is traditionally described as humble. But the picture of the parental farmhouse at Rammenau shows a substantial building with two complete storeys and a tall loft, and his family were engaged in the local administration. His forebears on both sides practised the craft of ribbon weaving, *Bandweberei*. His paternal grandfather held a local magistrate's position (Geschöffe) (Zeltner 1961). However, no formal education has been recorded for his parents and there was no money for his, so he depended on patrons. His first was Ernst von Miltitz (Kühn 2012: 29–32). First placed with a local vicar, Fichte then attended the *Stadtschule* in Meißen, before going to Schulpforta in 1774, the famous Saxon *Fürstenschule* that had been preparing boys for university entrance to study Protestant theology (and become pastors) since the Reformation. In 1780–1781 he studied theology at Jena, then at Leipzig before lack of funds forced him to take a series of private tutor posts. Many university-educated young men took, while they were waiting to secure posts as academics, clergymen or administrators, positions as private tutors, "Hauslehrer", whose lot varied from being little more than domestic servants to offering intellectual companionship to their employers. It was such a well-placed position in the home of Zurich *Ratsherr* Ott – a member of the educated upper-middle-class urban bourgeoisie – that allowed Fichte in 1788 to connect with wealthier and more intellectual social circles. Here he met the Bodmer-Breitinger-educated Lavater as well as his future wife Sophie Rahn, the daughter of another wealthy *Ratsherr* who himself had married Klopstock's sister. Here Fichte engaged with Kant's *Critiques*, which led to the publication that made him famous, the 1791 *Versuch einer Critik aller Offenbarung*, and took him to Königsberg, Berlin, and eventually his chair at Jena in 1793. Fichte remained a keen supporter of the French Revolution and its ideals of liberty and equality into the mid-1790s. His radical thinking about thinking, the *Wissenschaftslehre*, already formulated in rudimentary form by 1793, first published in 1794–1795, and re-written throughout his life, provided enough ammunition for his enemies to suspect him of atheism, which led, in part, to his dismissal in 1799. In his defence Fichte appealed to the tribunal of the public with his "Appellation an mein Publicum" and "Verantwortungsschrift". At this point he had not lost his faith in an incorruptible public, but this faith was waning by 1804, at least as far as "journals" are concerned (see Chapter 5, pp. 211–212). Fichte moved from Jena to Berlin in 1799, but was not admitted to the *Akademie der Wissenschaften*. In 1806 he fled to East Prussia with the Prussian court; by then, his attitude to Napoleon, and France, was intensely negative, the French had, in his view, betrayed the Revolution. It was up to the Germans to save themselves (and the ideals of the revolution), a conviction that found expression in his *Reden an die deutsche Nation*. When the new university at Berlin was opened in 1810, Fichte received a chair, headed the *Philosophische Fakultät*, and was elected as the institution's first *Rektor* [chief executive], although by 1811 he resigned the *Rektor*-position. Fichte was fiercely committed to German resistance against Napoleon and had already in 1806 offered to serve as a "Feldprediger" [army chaplain] to the Prussian forces; he did so again in 1813 and he joined the training of the *Landsturm* (milita). To some extent, his death from typhoid in January 1814 was the result of his involvement in the armed struggle: his wife Sophie was volunteering as a nurse in field hospitals where she contracted the disease, which she passed on to her husband. She recovered, he did not (Kühn 2012: 566–567).

August Wilhelm's and **Friedrich Schlegel**'s father, a native of Meißen in Saxony, had also been a pupil at Schulpforta, as had his more famous brother, the poet Elias Schlegel. Schlegel senior, a writer in his own right, moved on to study theology at Leipzig and had a successful career in the Protestant Church. After a series of preaching appointments (one at his old school in 1751), he secured a key post at the Marktkirche in Hanover, where both sons were born, and concluded his career as *Generalsuperintendant* of the principality of Calenberg (von Kloeden 2007: 37–38). The older son August Wilhelm (1767–1845) studied theology at Göttingen from 1786 and, after a spell as *Hauslehrer* in a merchant's household in Amsterdam, moved to Jena, headhunted by Schiller to contribute to his journals. After completing advanced research (his assessed *Habilitation*), August Wilhelm was called to a chair in philosophy at Jena in 1798, but after falling out with Schiller and resenting Fichte's dismissal, he followed his younger brother Friedrich, and Fichte, to Berlin, where he gave public lectures, his so-called Berlin lectures, in which he constructed the "Germanic Europe" and the mythology of chivalry. Instead of further pursuing an institutional academic career, Schlegel joined Mme de Staël as her companion on her travels around Europe from 1804 and stayed in her employ until her death in 1817. In 1818 he was offered the professorship of literature and art history at the new Prussian university at Bonn, where he remained until his death in 1845 (John 2007: 38–40).[53] His younger brother Friedrich (1772–1829), after giving up training as a merchant and banker in Leipzig, joined him at Göttingen in 1790 to study law, but moved on to Leipzig in 1791 to study history and philosophy instead. Friedrich completed advanced research (his *Habilitation*) at Jena University in 1800, but soon left for Berlin. He then spent two years each in Paris (1802–1804), where conducted his Sanskrit researches, and Cologne (1804–1806), where he joined the Boisserée brothers in their medievalist activities. Friedrich converted to Catholicism in 1808 and in 1809 joined the Austrian civil service as a secretary at the *Hof-* and *Staatskanzlei* under Prince Metternich. Schlegel remained in the employ of the Austrian state until his death; he produced conservative constitutional proposals for the Congress of Vienna in 1814 and attended the *Bundestag* of the German Confederation in Frankfurt in 1819 (which unanimously ratified the repressive Carlsbad Decrees) as Austrian *Legationsrat*.

Ernst Moritz Arndt's career trajectory has already been touched upon. His upwardly mobile father, an emancipated serf, was able to send Arndt to the *Gelehrtenschule* in Stralsund and on to the university at Greifswald (with a spell a Jena) to study theology (as well as geography, sciences, and language) between 1789 and 1794. Both Stralsund and Greifswald were in Swedish

---

[53] See also Paulin 2016.

Pomerania, which had been under Swedish administration as "Reichslehen" (imperial fief) since the end of the Thirty Years War. The complex story of the return to, effectively, serfdom from the early modern situation of a free peasantry in North Eastern Germany cannot be told here. Arndt (1769–1860) took from this a strong sense of the need for social and political change. After a period as private tutor on his native Rügen, Arndt embarked on a tour of Europe 1798–1799, which took him, via Jena, to Austria, Hungary, Italy, and France, before securing a lectureship in history and (classical) philology at Greifswald University in 1800 (Müsebeck 1914: 71); he was called to a chair of history in 1806. He had to leave his academic career behind when he fled into Swedish exile from Napoleon's advancing armies in late 1806, on account of the views expressed in *Geist der Zeit I*, published in the spring. Arndt was eventually called to another university chair in 1819 at Bonn, from which he was suspended in 1820 (on account of *Geist der Zeit VI*) for the next twenty years, retaining his salary, but unable to supplement his income from lecturing fees. In 1840 he was rehabilitated by the new Prussian king Frederick William IV and remained in Bonn until his death in 1860. Between 1807 and 1813, Arndt was active in the German resistance movement, travelling around Europe, eventually in the service of Freiherr vom Stein, and frequently along similar routes as August Wilhelm Schlegel and Mme de Staël.

Similarly, **Joseph Görres's** biography has also been touched upon. Görres (1776–1848) was born in Koblenz, in the imperial Archbishopric of Trier, into a family of merchants and master craftsmen, his mother hailed from the Italian-speaking Swiss canton of Ticino. Some ancestors had (lower-ranking) civil service positions (Schultheiss, Schöffen). The archbishop of Trier was one of the seven electors of the medieval empire and *Kur-Trier's* set-up and privileges were a remnant of the imperial past. The court seems to have instilled a strong aversion against all forms of aristocratic privilege in the young Görres, who supported the Cis-Rhenish Republic in the mid-1790s and was an active publicist on behalf of the ideals of the revolution; he travelled as representative for Koblenz to Paris in 1799–1800. Görres had attended the Gymnasium in Koblenz but did not go to university. After his first disillusionment with politics in 1800, he took a teaching position at his old school. Through his school friend Clemens Brentano Görres was brought to Heidelberg, where he taught at the university from 1806 across a wide range of subjects. During this period, his Romantic works appeared, and his interest in medieval and old German developed. From 1810 he re-entered the political arena as a publicist, from 1814 with renewed vigour on the side of the national constitutionalists, before having to escape across the border to Strasbourg in 1819, as the conservative Restauration took hold. Here he turned, through his interest in the medieval, to Catholicism. In

1827, he accepted a call to the Bavarian university of Munich, recently moved to the Bavarian capital from Landshut, where he remained as professor of general and literary history until his death. Görres' call was part of a wave of new appointments at Munich, which included Schelling in the same year and Lorenz Oken, the natural scientist, *Burschenschaft*-supporting liberal, and philosopher, all of whom arrived in Munich in 1827. Görres' appointment was controversial, he was too revolutionary, too German-national, too Catholic (Roegele 1964: 534), which illustrates the complex mix of political agendas in the first two decades of the nineteenth century yet again. His appointment was part of a strategic move to bring exciting new teachers to the Bavarian institution, and it would appear his early lectures had very large audiences (Roegele 1964: 534). This was, incidentally, the Munich university that Carlyle's brother visited in the late 1820s. Although Görres turned more conservative, he remained an adherent of European Christendom and retained his commitment to a constitutional approach to national unity, which for him needed to include (Catholic) Austria.

Georg Friedrich Hegel (1770–1831) was born into a Stuttgart family of civil servants, his father was an "Expeditionalrat", his paternal grandfather an "Oberamtmann" (Fetscher 1969: 207). Hegel attended the Karlsgymnasium in Stuttgart and from 1788 the *Tübinger Stift*, an institution similar to Schulpforta: a secularised monastery, it had been turned into a seminary for Protestant clergy after the Reformation and primarily served to train new pastors for the local rulers. The *Stift* of the 1780s and 90s was well known for its liberal atmosphere and openness to French thought, pre- and immediately post-revolution. Inevitably, Hegel studied theology, he graduated in 1793 and moved on, perhaps also inevitably, to positions as "Hauslehrer" in Berlin (1793) and Frankfurt (1797–1800). He used this time to study Kant and Fichte and stayed in touch with two of his Tübingen friends, Schelling and Hölderlin. When Hegel inherited some money in 1799, he was able to move to Jena for his *Habilitation*, which he finally completed in 1807. In the same year he left Jena, the last of the canonical Romantic thinkers to move on from this place. Hegel first went into journalism, from 1807–1808 he was editor of the *Bamberger Zeitung*, a newspaper; he then secured a reasonably well-paid post as the headmaster of the Ägidien-Gymnasium in Nuremberg where he remained until 1816, when he was finally offered a university chair at Heidelberg in his native Württemberg, before being called to (Fichte's vacant) chair at Berlin in 1818. Hegel remained at Berlin until his death from cholera in 1831, like Fichte, leading the university as *Rektor* in 1829–1830. Throughout his life, Hegel remained keenly interested in constitutional politics.

Politically, Hegel moved from a radically liberal, pro-French Revolution position in the 1790s to a more conservative stance in his later years, most noticeably perhaps in his Berlin period. Much has been written about Hegel's view of the need for a powerful state and his ultimately conservative and determinist theodicy of history. But what kind of conservatism might this be? His concept of the state and of citizenship was strongly rationalist and he was in favour of positive constitutions, rather than traditional ones. He considered the English constitution irrational ("irrationales Zufallsprodukt", 1831), echoing Fichte's assessment of 1804 in *Grundzüge des gegenwärtigen Zeitalters* (See Chapter 5, p. 212). In 1817, while at Heidelberg, Hegel intervened in the constitutional discussions in Württemberg, where the traditional estates were blocking a (liberal) constitution proposed by the monarch, because it curtailed *their* privileges, or "old liberties". In his essay on the constitutional negotiations of the Württemberg estates, Hegel attacked the selfish insistence of the "bourgeois aristocracy" for obstructing a more rational constitution focused on prince and people in the hope of holding on to dated, and unfair, rights (Hegel 1817). In terms of constitutional law, this was an eighteenth-century rationalistic approach, not based on organically developed traditions. Evidently in Württemberg, too, the discourse of political and constitutional liberty was divided into an organically traditional wing and a rationalist positive one. These views were no doubt the reason why Hegel's appointment in Berlin in the following year was frowned upon by such organicist legal historians as Savigny, and perhaps why the young Ranke felt the need to distance himself from Hegel's approach to history.

In this constitutional quarrel in Württemberg, Hegel's younger compatriot **Ludwig Uhland** (1787–1862), who was elected to the Württemberg parliament in 1819, took the side of the *Landstände*, the estates. He supported the "Altes Recht", the traditional rights and powers of the corporate estates (established bourgeoisie and clergy), but at the same time insisted on greater independence of the estate-based representative body from monarchic rule. Such support for organically and collectively developed constitutions, in which the governmental (princely) executive was checked by selected social groups (who were assumed to represent the people), was in principle Burkean, and the basis for constitutional monarchy. Uhland's views were based on his interest in German(ic) traditions in poetry and, to a lesser extent, law, which he researched in both medieval German and French sources. His interest in ancient legal traditions was the basis for Uhland's later more "left-wing" political approach, when he consistently supported democratic opposition to unchecked central powers, both in the *Landtag*, and later in the *Nationalversammlung* in the Paulskirche. Uhland was the author of the appeal to the people, issued by the "rump parliament" in 1849, the hardcore democratic constitutionalists, after the rulers of the larger German states had declared the parliament dissolved and recalled their representatives following the failure of the *Kaiserdeputation* to the Prussian king Frederick William IV and the impasse on the Reichsverfassung [German constitution]. The "rump" moved to Stuttgart in an attempt to continue its constitutional work and even formed a "Reichsregentschaft", an imperial regency, which Uhland as a less radical member of the rump opposed (Fischer 1895). The rump delegates were soon locked out of their meeting room by the Württemberg government (who had initially been the first to accept the imperial constitution). Uhland was, however, part of the protest procession of the last remaining parliamentarians through the streets of Stuttgart until they were dispersed by military forces.

The complex nature of the political "colouring" of early nineteenth-century constitutional reform becomes obvious when comparing Hegel and Uhland, or indeed Burke and Thelwall in 1790s Britain. All share an aversion to princely absolutism, but they strongly disagree on the mechanism of checking such absolutism and on the make-up of political representation.

Uhland's biography is typical in this context. Born into a family of middle-class clergymen and academics, he attended the Tübingen Lateinschule (1793–1801) and won a scholarship to the *Tübinger Stift* in 1801, where he pursued philological studies, but eventually studied law. He completed his studies as Dr. juris in 1810, while also building up a reputation as a poet sympathetic to the endeavours of the *Befreiungskriege*. He practised law in Tübingen and Stuttgart, with a brief spell in an honorary position at the Stuttgart ministry of justice, and was elected to the Württemberg *Landtag* in 1819, remaining a parliamentarian until the 1830s. In 1829 he secured his university chair (for German language and literature) at Tübingen, which he had to resign in 1833 in order to fulfil his parliamentary role. He was forced to choose between his academic and political roles when, in the wake of the post-1830 fear of revolution, his sovereign revoked the right to leave from duty for civil servants when attending the "chamber". Uhland chose politics, on the opposition-side (Fischer 1895).

Uhland's interests in poetic, linguistic, and legal antiquities were shared by **Jacob** and **Wilhelm Grimm**, (1785–1863) and (1787–1859) respectively. Uhland and the Grimms were of the same age, born in the mid-1780s. All three were elected to the 1848 Frankfurt Parliament. The Grimms' forebears were Hessian clergymen and civil servants. Both Jacob and Wilhelm attended the Lyceum Fridericianum in Kassel (1798–1802/1803), from where both went to the University of Marburg to study law. Here they met the young Friedrich Karl von Savigny (1779–1861), the rising star of the historical study of (Roman) law. The latter's influence on them and their collaborations is well known. Jacob was able to conduct his own research at the Paris *Bibliotheque Nationale* in 1805, five years before Uhland made it there, while working as Savigny's assistant. Both brothers returned to Kassel, now in the Kingdom of Westphalia, newly created by Napoleon, to take up civil service positions, first under the French ruler, Napoleon's brother Jérôme Bonaparte, from 1813 under the reinstated German Hessian prince. Both attended the Congress of Vienna in official roles. In 1816 Jacob secured a high-ranking position in the Hessian national library as "second Landesbibliothekar", with Wilhelm soon joining him as library secretary. In 1830 Jacob was called to a chair at the Hanoverian University of Göttingen, Wilhelm in 1831, but both lost their posts in early 1838, after they had protested against the autocratic annulment of the Hanoverian constitution of 1833 by the new British king of Hanover, Ernst August, as members of a group of "liberal" professors who are remembered as the "Göttingen Seven". Jacob and Wilhelm (who were not Hanoverian subjects) were served with deportation orders and returned to Kassel, from where both followed calls to Berlin University in 1840. As we already noted with Arndt, the new Prussian king was creating a climate of rehabilitation for former nationalist "radicals" who had an interest in German history and national (especially medieval) traditions. While Frederick William IV turned out to be vehemently opposed to liberal politics and constitutional liberation, he was keen on organic traditions, especially medievalised feudal ones.

That a conservative paternalist happily rehabilitated former radical liberals, who twenty years ago had been associated with revolution, succinctly illustrates the tensions within the Germanic-Gothic in the second quarter of the century, between the original social and political challenge this identity represented and its growing use for conservative consolidation. When Frederick William (1795–1861) acceded in 1840, liberals invested considerable hope in him, justified by his immediate amnesty for those restrained in some form by the Carlsbad legislation and his interdicting the activities of the *Bundeszentralbehörde*, the federal security and surveillance authority, in Prussia, which had investigated suspect, i.e. national and liberal, political activities since 1820 and overseen the implementation of the Carlsbad Decrees. He also enthusiastically supported the completion of Cologne Cathedral, which he saw as a symbol of (a medieval and Christian) German unity, and commissioned numerous neo-gothic buildings himself. His interest in the Middle Ages, a conservative medievalism that focused on how a modern society might emulate (imagined) pre-industrial paternalistic social structures, earned him the soubriquet "Romantiker auf dem Thron".

There was, it seems, room for overlap between liberal and conservative visions of the Germanic-Gothic. Frederick William believed in the sacred unity of prince and people, which would be disturbed by positive legislation and modern constitutions. This belief was a factor in the vehemence with which he rejected the imperial crown, when it was offered to him by the Frankfurt Parliament. In this conception, selfish aristocratic privilege was, along with any other selfish competitiveness and advantage, opposed to the true "legitimacy" of the caring, impartial sovereign. Here it is easy to see how the challenging "traditionalism" of a Follen or an Arndt was turning into backward-looking nostalgia, which was easily instrumentalised for social conservatism. And yet, the idea of the union of prince and people was not so far removed from Napoleon's notion of being a *Volkskaiser*, Emperor *of the French*, rather than *France*, a concept rejected by Frederick William's younger brother William in 1871, when it was his turn to refuse to be proclaimed "Kaiser der Deutschen", preferring "Kaiser von Deutschland". The compromise solution was to proclaim him "deutscher Kaiser".

Finally, both **Leopold Ranke** (1795–1886) and **Karl Follen** (1796–1840), born in the mid-1790s, were a decade younger than Uhland and the Grimms, and separated by almost a generation from Fichte and the older "Romantics", whose births fall into the 1760s and early 1770s. Ranke and Follen were the same generation as Julius Hare, Kenelm Henry Digby, Thomas Arnold, and Thomas Carlyle, (and indeed Frederick William IV). Ranke and Follen closely fit the profile that has emerged for the propagators of the Germanic-Gothic, but their biographies are strikingly divergent regarding their political persuasions and (eventual) status in society.

Both Ranke and Follen descended from well-established families of civil servants who could trace their professional lineages back to the seventeenth century. The Rankes had been lawyers and clergymen in Saxony and Thuringia, the Follens had been (almost exclusively) lawyers in Hesse. Ranke attended Schulpforta from 1807 to 1814 and studied theology and classical philology at Leipzig from 1814–1817. In 1818 he passed the newly established Prussian teaching examination (Examen für das höhere Lehramt) in Berlin, before taking up a (school) teaching post for history and classical languages in Frankfurt an der Oder. His first book on *Germanische and Romanische Völker* (1824) attracted the attention of Frederick William III and brought him – almost immediately – a post as extra-ordinary professor of history at the University of Berlin. Ranke remained at Berlin, in the Prussian civil service, until his retirement in 1871.

In 1814, the teenage Follen volunteered to fight in the *Befreiungskriege*, although he saw no action (Mehring 2004: 28–32); to join up, he interrupted his law studies at Gießen. At school in Gießen he had been taught by Friedrich Gottlieb Welcker, who was actively supporting the resistance against Napoleon and avidly politicised his students. (Welcker joined up himself in 1814). Welcker was teaching at both the *Gymnasium* and the University in Gießen, and that Follen and his brother August joined the military campaign was not least due to

Welcker's influence (Mehring 2004). This is the same Welcker whom Hare would visit in Bonn in 1828.

Follen graduated as Dr. juris in 1818, the same year that Ranke took his teaching exam in Berlin. Follen held teaching posts (Privatdozenturen) in law, first at Gießen, then at Jena, and was an important influence on the *Burschenschaft* movement between 1814–1818 (Oergel 2018a and Mehring 2004). Following the assassination of August von Kotzebue by *Burschenschaftler* Karl Sand in 1819, who had been part of Follen's circle, Follen fled into exile to escape arrest, first to Strasbourg, then to Paris, and on to Switzerland, where he was eventually offered a university post in law at Basel in 1821 (Mehring 2004: 96–97). Continuing his political agitation, he was persecuted beyond the borders of the German Confederation and forced to emigrate to the United States in late 1824, the year Ranke secured his extra-ordinary professorship at Berlin. Follen settled in Boston and married into the upper echelons of Boston society. He set up German Studies at Harvard College, from which Harvard University developed, and taught at Harvard between 1826 and 1835, first as an instructor and from 1830 as the first chair of German language and literature in the United States. Fervently Christian, he turned towards Unitarianism and eventually became ordained as a preacher. On his arrival in the United States, Follen had still entertained hopes of creating a liberal German Christian *Freistaat* [free state] in the new world along the same lines he had imagined for a united Germany in his draft constitution in 1817. Increasingly, though, he focused his political activities on abolition. In the United States Follen is mainly remembered as an abolitionist. In 1835 his political activities cost him his chair at Harvard. Follen's life was cut short in a shipwreck off Long Island in 1840.

Ranke pursued his academic career as a ground-breaking innovator of historical studies at Berlin University, as a civil servant. He developed a close relationship with the Prussian establishment and the court; as a young historian he enjoyed the friendship of the conservative Friedrich von Gentz and the patronage of Prince Metternich. As the founding editor of the (Prussian) *Historisch-Politische Zeitschrift* he followed a conservative line, in 1841 he became Historiographer Royal, and in 1882, at the end of his life, he was made a "Preußischer Geheimrat". Ranke clearly acceded to the established Prussian elite, which in the second half of the nineteenth century supported conservative politics. Follen's biography, on the other hand, is that of a political radical committed to making his vision of social and political change reality; as a result, Follen was unable to establish any form of regular career in Europe and eventually floundered in the New World, too. And yet *both* used the same idea of specifically Germanic and Christian traditions of liberty and duty for their political visions of history and society.

7.6.3 Elites, ideas, and getting established

Why can the British and German individuals discussed here be considered as belonging to (intellectual) "elites"? All of them rose to positions of cultural or political prominence, often to positions of both, most of them by holding, sometimes in combination, high-ranking academic, administrative or clerical posts. This gave them influence, not just over rulers, but over their audiences, if they were writers, over the next generation, if they were teachers, or over policy, if they were administrators. The identity they propagated, and the (different) ideas that became associated with it, were not uncontroversial. Cultural and political prominence attracted back-lash. Quite a few experienced intimidation, persecution, public vilification or marginalisation, which is evidence of the contested nature of their ideas at different junctures in political developments. At the same time, many eventually found recognition and esteem, without necessarily having drastically changed their "ideas". This development demonstrates the establishment of the idea, its institutionalisation, and acceptance. However, it should be noted that those individuals in whose biographies the change from feared radical to esteemed elder intellectual is most marked *did* often change key aspects of their propagation. An obvious example of such a change is the increased focus on acceptable forms of "religion": Friedrich Schlegel and Joseph Görres turned to Catholicism, Hare foregrounded religiosity, not politics, Kinglsey took to a *Christian* Socialism. (A religious focus *per se* did not necessarily grant establishment status, Karl Follen is a case in point.)

Institutionalising the Germanic was in the course of the nineteenth century also driven by its usefulness for state- and empire-building. While the Germanic had, from its radical and challenging origins, always been used to establish, animate, and legitimise collectives, it became possible, as its political and social challenge decreased, to utilise it for non- or less liberal collectives, such as the Bismarckian German nation state, or the British Empire (although in Dilke's conception the latter *was* of course a liberal empire). This development follows the trajectory of the idea of "the nation", which also lost much of the radical, enfranchising nature it had possessed between 1789 and 1830 and became a consolidating notion set against the new enfranchising challenges from socialism and communism.

The review of biographies shows that individuals became institutionalised as members of an elite when they reached influential positions within their social set-up. They arrived in those positions through individual and institutional patronage just as much as by individual ability, (with historical contingency, i.e. being in the right place at the right time, of course also playing its part). The aristocratic, or princely, patronage common in the eighteenth century was in the early nineteenth century giving way to more institutional forms of preferment. In the end, *all* patronage, personal, and institutional, depended on (personal) connections and networks. While Herder and Goethe were given the posts that secured their careers – Herder in Bückeburg, Goethe Weimar – by rulers of (very) small German principalities, and while Herder's and Fichte's education had depended on the largesse of local aristocrats, a generation later, the Grimms, Uhland, and Ranke were appointed by institutions. This is of course a matter of degree, not of fundamental change, because frequently academic institutions implemented the representational agendas of rulers or governments, in both centuries. The Dukes of Bückeburg and of Saxe-Weimar were motivated to appoint Herder and Goethe, because they wanted to enhance the cultural clout of their courts through trophy intellectuals and poets. A similar wish for cultural or scholarly kudos to reflect positively on the intentions and nature of their (royal) government motivated Frederick William III of Prussia from the beginning of century, his son in 1840, as well as Maximilian II of Bavaria in 1827, to support the appointments of a string of upcoming or famous scholars to their universities.

A similar trend can be observed in England: while Percy and Hurd needed individual, well-connected patrons to get to the posts that made their careers, by the time Stubbs or Freeman were appointed to their chairs, this was done by institutional committees. To be sure, these committees were influenced by many forms political and governmental pressures, but it was less likely that one absolutist, princely view could over-rule all others, as might have been the case in Bückeburg, Saxe-Weimar, or George III's Britain.

Another key marker of social and political "arrival", and evidence of institutionalisation as part of an elite that was recognised and esteemed, is the ennoblement of individuals. All individuals reviewed here were born into untitled, middle-class families, Arndt and Fichte were struggling to be even middle-class. Many of them ended their lives as members of the "Beamtenadel" [civil service nobility] in Germany, or as peers of the realm in Britain. In Britain, this was mainly achieved through the Church, bishops sit in the House of Lords. Hurd, Percy, and Stubbs are examples. Kingsley, through royal favour, became a canon of Westminster, Hare became archdeacon of Lewes. In Germany, Goethe, Herder, both Schlegels, Görres, and Ranke were ennobled, i.e. entitled to add "von" to their surnames. Herder, however, does not appear to have used the "von". Fichte was not ennobled, but his son Immanuel was in 1863, which is a considerable social climb from ribbon-making in two generations. Ennoblement is an indicator of the acceptability of the ideas and the political and cultural position the ennobled individual is seen to represent. It indicates that their "ideas" have entered the mainstream, are publicly approved and may even have consolidating tendencies. Their ideas and views succeed because they are convincing to a large audience and because the political rulers agree, or have to be seen to agree, with them.

7.7 How an idea travels (in practice) – conclusion

This case study demonstrates how an idea, based on key terms and a concept, emerged, travelled, was consolidated and institutionalised. A combination of social, political, intellectual, and spiritual needs, resulting broadly from secularisation and revolution, generated a productive idea (Germanic liberty and moral integrity) that was capable of expressing and eventually implementing an agenda (enfranchising and identifying a new collective) that addressed these needs.

The idea of Germanic liberty and moral integrity was convincingly presented as appropriate for the (re)organisation of society at the point when modern social structures were developing in the run-up and the wake of the French Revolution. The belief that a social re-organisation was necessary drove the processes that led up to the French Revolution and informed the various receptions of the revolution and its fallout over the next generations. These different receptions created the varied political, intellectual, and spiritual issues that became identified as needing attention, the most prominent was the restoration of public spirit to counter-act despotism and "selfishness". One overriding consideration was that any (re-)organisation should be based on historical appropriateness. This set the scene for the idea of a Northern-Germanic-European identity to be formulated and to take centre-stage in these considerations. In this process, the idea of the Germanic, in the broadest sense, supported a social reorganisation based on historical legitimation and appropriateness. Gradually, the idea of the Germanic as indigenous, essential, and progressive became prescriptive, it attained value, or the status of "truth". It could then operate as a means of justification, legitimation, and explanation. The idea of the Germanic could justify, legitimise, and explain the need for a variety of social and cultural projects, which in turn supported the social and cultural institutionalisation of the Germanic. It was capable of legitimising the need for a German nation state, liberal-democratic or authoritarian; it could equally legitimate a growing British Empire, civilising or exploitative. Similarly, it could justify the need for national education programmes from village school to universities, teaching appropriate subjects (national and European history, Germanic and European legal and literary antiquities) to increase awareness of traditions, to explain identity and how tradition and idenity (should) shape the future. It could explain why building a physical environment of medievalised architecture appropriately reflected these projects and the identity they generated. And it explained the need for an inspiring culture of personal integrity that would support communal prosperity and individual independence, summed up in the Christian gentleman and the meritocratic elite. Its institutionalisation saw the Germanic-Gothic implemented across a wide range of social, political, and cultural activities.

In the case of the Germanic, the implementation of liberty and duty based on moral integrity in a civic society was also accompanied by a nostalgic retrospection; a pre-industrial paternalistic "medieval" society was by many believed to be harmonious. But this did not stop the idea from supporting the establishment of modern social structures. By the turn of the twentieth century, the *modern nation* states of Britain and Germany each understood themselves as uniting and representing a *national* collective, i.e. a people who shared a language, history, and culture based on Germanic German and English traditions. Both societies were by this time moving towards universal suffrage and equality before the law of all recognised citizens, both are demands with which the "Germanic" around 1800 was associated. Similarly, the understanding of the role of the state as collectively protecting its citizens and their rights and setting a framework for education and social provision is based on the concept of public spirit. This state is to be made possible by all citizens contributing to the common good and being entitled to share it. The case study demonstrates how the expanding public sphere(s) prepared the mass involvement in politics that developed in the course of the nineteenth and early twentieth century.

The processes of propagation, by which ideas emerge, travel, and are institutionalised have become clearer; they are largely the processes that this investigation has identified as the zeitgeist dynamic. A disparate group, or even disparate groups, of articulate individuals with access to publicity formulate issues and interpretations of them, which resonate with a larger public. If this resonance, public credence and acceptance are wide-spread enough, or attract the support of political or cultural power, the interpretation, and the solutions that may be drawn from these interpretations for the way forward, will influence collective and individual thinking and activity. In the first instance, the resonance relies on broadly shared notions of what the issues are, in this case poor (despotic and unaccountable) government and social corrosion due ambitious and venal selfishness caused by a lack of public spirit at all social levels. In the second instance, public acceptance relies on the extent to which the interpretations of the issues make sense to their audiences, to what extent they share the ambitions articulated and assent to the remedies proposed.

To be specific: the case study bears out that the idea of the Germanic was "proposed" and propagated by broadly middle-class groups and individuals who supported some form of participatory politics, some form of communal checks on the political executive, and a public-spirited polity. Many were – or had been at some stage – supporters of the French Revolution, or any subsequent revolution up to 1850, or they were moderate reformers. Among those to whom the "idea" made sense, there was not necessarily agreement regarding political orientation or specific social objectives. The case study shows that terms and concepts *that make sense generaqlly* are likely to be employed by potentially opposing contenders in the battle for public approval. Liberty, public spirit, and traditions were key, but it was debatable *whose* liberty, *what kind* of public spirit and *which* traditions they were.

Some of these individuals and groups would (eventually) link their politics overtly with Christianity (Friedrich Schlegel, Digby, Görres) or others would seek a more secular creed focused on historical revelation (Hegel, Ranke, Freeman, Arnold). Virtually all agreed on the need for and value of education, all had attended educational institutions, and their education had made possible their social rise to public prominence. All realised the importance of the expanding public sphere, and its many sub-spheres, and all engaged with print media as authors, many as editors and as public speakers. The majority of them were involved in some form of teaching, either at university or as private tutors. All were successful authors in their life-times, most of them highly esteemed. With the exception of Follen, and perhaps Digby and Dilke, all acquired some form of canonical status that outlasted their lives. Gaining social status though public posts, ennoblement, and lasting renown is evidence of the acceptability and institutionalisation of the ideas they put forward.

The Germanic-Gothic identity discussed here is complex, it has a difficult history and has produced a divided legacy. While the aspects of social *and* European inclusiveness that the Christian post-classical Germanic offered were a corollary of the contemporaneous efforts to lay the basis for a civic and more egalitarian society, these efforts were hampered by the inherently divisive potential of the Germanic, which only theoretically and partially projected a non-national, European ideal and was easily instrumentalised for ideas of national superiority, in both Germany and Britain, and for cultural supremacy globally.

Works Cited

[anon] (1800) "Über die sogenannte Gothische Baukunst", *Neue Lausitzische Monatsschrift 5*, 350–367.
[anon] (1806) "Ohne Angabe des Druckorts und Verleg.: Geist der Zeit, von Ernst Moritz Arndt u.s.w. (13. October 1806)", *Allgemeine Literatur-Zeitung (Halle)* 245, 81–88.
[anon] (1806) "Ohne Angabe des Druckorts und Verleg.: Geist der Zeit, von Ernst Moritz Arndt u.s.w. (14. October 1806)", *Allgemeine Literatur-Zeitung (Halle)* 246, 89–93.
[anon] (1806) "Ohne Druckort. Geist der Zeit, von Ernst Moritz Arndt (25. August 1806)", *Göttingische Anzeigen von gelehrten Sachen* 136. Stück, 2. Band 1806, 1352–1359.
[anon] (1806) "Ohne Druckort: Geist der Zeit, von Ernst Moritz Arndt (28. July 1806)", *Jenaische Allgemeine Literatur-Zeitung* 177, 185–192.
[anon] (1824) *The John Bull Magazine and Literary Recorder* vol. 1 (London: James Smith).
[anon] (1824) "Noctes Ambrosianae No. XVI (August)", *Blackwood's Edinburgh Magazine* 16, 231–250.
[anon], (1829) "St. Petersburgh. A Journal of Travels to and from that Capital etc.", *Quarterly Review* 77, 1–40.
[anon] (1830) "Letter to Christopher North on the Spirit of the Age. By one of the Democracy", *Blackwood's Edinburgh Magazine* 28, 900–920.
Allen, Peter (1978) *The Cambridge Apostles. The Early Years* (Cambridge: Cambridge University Press).
Allen, Peter and Clive Want (1973) "The Cambridge Apostles as Student Journalists. A Key to Authorship in the *Metropolitan Quarterly Magazine*", *Victorian Periodicals Newsletter* 6, 26–33.
Anthony, David W. (2007) *The Horse, the Wheel and Language. How Bronze Age Riders shaped the Modern World* (Princeton: Princeton University Press).
Arndt, Ernst Moritz (1806) *Geist der Zeit I* (no place of publication: no publisher).
Arndt, Ernst Moritz (1807) *Geist der Zeit I*, 2nd edition (no place of publication: no publisher).
Arndt, Ernst Moritz (1808) *Ardnt's [sic] Spirit of the Times, translated from the German by the Rev. P.W. Being the Work for the Publication of which the Unfortunate Palm, of Erlangen, was sacrificed by Napoleon, the Destroyer; containing Historical and Political Sketches etc.* (London: Thiselton).
Arndt, Ernst Moritz (1813 [1809]) *Geist der Zeit II*, 2nd edition (London: Boosey).
Arndt, Ernst Moritz (1813) *Geist der Zeit III* (London: Boosey).
Arndt, Ernst Moritz (1815) *Der Wächter. Eine Zeitschrift in zwanglosen Heften* (Cologne: Rommerskirchen).
Arndt, Ernst Moritz (1818) *Geist der Zeit IV* (Berlin: Reimer).
Arnold, Thomas (1845) *Introductory Lectures on Modern History, with the Inaugural Lecture* (London: Fellows).
Ashton, Rosemary (1980) *The German Idea. Four English Writers and the Reception of German Thought* (Cambridge: Cambridge University Press).
Bal, Mieke (2002) *Travelling Concepts in the Humanities. A Rough Guide* (Toronto: University of Toronto Press).
Bantock, Geoffrey (2012 [1984]) *Studies in the History of Educational Theory Volume 2: The Minds and the Masses 1760–1980* (Abington/New York: Routledge).

https://doi.org/10.1515/9783110631531-009

Barclay, John (1631 [1614]). *The Mirrour of Mindes or Barclay's Icon Animorum, Englished by T. M.* (London: Thomas Walkley).
Barlow, Frank (2011) "Edward Augustus Freeman", in *Oxford Dictionary of National Biography* (Oxford: Oxford University Press) <https://doi.org/10.1093/ref:odnb/10146> (accessed 22 June 2018).
Becker, Ph. August (1904) "John Barclay", *Zeitschrift für vergleichende Literaturgeschichte* 15, 32–118.
Bergk, Adam (1795) "Bewirkt Aufklärung Revolutionen?", *Deutsche Monatsschrift* 3, 268–279.
Blackwell, Thomas [anon] (1735) *An Enquiry into the Life and Writings of Homer* (London: no publisher).
Blackwell, Thomas [anon] (1736). *An Enquiry into the Life and Writings of Homer*, 2nd edition (London: no publisher).
Blumenberg, Hans (1998) *Begriffe in Geschichten* (Frankfurt am Main: Suhrkamp).
Bodmer, Johann Jakob (1943 [1743]) "Von den vortrefflichen Umständen für die Poesie unter den Kaisern aus dem schwäbischen Hause", reprinted in *Das geistige Zürich im 18. Jahrhundert. Texte und Dokumente von Gotthart Heidegger bis Heinrich Pestalozzi*, ed. Max Wehrli (Zurich: Atlantis), 67–76.
Böhler, Erich (1973) *Psychologie des Zeitgeistes* (Bern: Herbert Lang).
Brandes, Ernst (1808) *Betrachtungen über den Zeitgeist in Deutschland in den letzten Dezennien des vorigen Jahrhunderts* (Hanover: Hahn).
Brandes, Ernst (1810) *Über den Einfluß und die Wirkungen des Zeitgeistes auf die höheren Stände Deutschlands, als Fortsetzung der Betrachtungen über den Zeitgeist in Deutschland* (Hanover: Hahn).
Brendon, Piers (1975) *Hawker of Morewenstow. Portrait of a Victorian Eccentric* (London: Jonathan Cape).
Bulwer-Lytton, Edward (1833) *England and the English. In Two Volumes* (London: Richard Bentley).
Bunsen, Karl Freiherr von (ed) (1854) *The Life and Letters of Barthold Georg Niebuhr. With Essays on his Character and Influence* (New York: Harper).
Burke, Edmund (1892) *Selected Works. Four Letters on the Proposal for a Peace with the Regicide Directory of France*, new edition, ed. E. J. Payne (Oxford: Clarendon Press).
Burkhardt, Johann Gottlieb (1798) *Kirchen-Geschichte der deutschen Gemeinden in London* (Tübingen: Fues).
Burn, John Southerden (1846) *The History of the French, Wallon, Dutch and other Foreign Protestant Refugees settled in England* (London: Longman, Brown and Green).
Burrow, John (1981) *A Liberal Descent. Victorian Historians and the English Past* (Cambridge: Cambridge University Press).
Burrows, Simon (2000) *French Exile Journalism and European Politics 1792–1814* (Woodbridge: Boydell).
"Cäsar hat die Germanen erfunden". *Spiegel*-Interview mit Mischa Meier (2013) *Der Spiegel Geschichte* 2, 22–27.
Campbell, James (2005) "William Stubbs", in *Oxford Dictionary of National Biography* (Oxford: Oxford University Press) <http://www.oxforddnb.com/view/article/36362> (accessed 22 June 2018).
Carhart, Michael (2007) *The Science of Culture in Enlightenment Germany* (Cambridge MA: Harvard University Press).

Carlyle, Thomas (1898) *Two Note Books of Thomas Carlyle. From 23rd March 1822 to 16th May 1832*, ed. Charles Eliot Norton (New York: The Grolier Club).
Carlyle, Thomas (1899) *Critical and Miscellaneous Essays*, 5 vols (London: Chapman and Hall).
Carlyle, Thomas (1899 [1829]) "Signs of the Times", in *Critical and Miscellaneous Essays*, (London: Chapman and Hall), vol. 2, 56–82.
Carlyle, Thomas (1899 [1830]) "Characteristics", in *Critical and Miscellaneous Essays*, (London: Chapman and Hall), vol. 3, 1–43.
Carlyle, Thomas (1899 [1833]) "Diderot", in *Critical and Miscellaneous Essays* (London: Chapman and Hall), vol. 3, 177–248.
Carlyle, Thomas and Jane (1970–1977) *The Collected Letters of Thomas and Jane Welsh Carlyle* 6 vols (Durham NC: Duke University Press).
Carlyle, Thomas. (n.d.) [1934] *The French Revolution. A History* (New York: Cerf and Knopfler).
Cassin, Barbara (ed) (2004) *Vocabulaire européen des philosophies: Dictionnaire des Intraduisibles* (Paris: Éditions du Seuil and Le Robert).
Chandler, James (1998) *England in 1819. The Politics of Literary Culture and the Case for Romantic Historicism* (Chicago: University of Chicago Press).
Clark, Arthur Melville (1969) *Sir Walter Scott. The Formative Years* (Edinburgh/London: William Blackwood).
Coleridge, Samuel Taylor (1852) *Lay Sermons. The Statesman's Manual*, ed. Derwent Coleridge (London: Moxon).
Coleridge, Samuel Taylor (1956–1971) *The Collected Letters of Samuel Taylor Coleridge*, ed. Earl Leslie Griggs (Oxford : Clarendon).
Digby, Kenelm Henry (1823 [1822]). *The Broad Stone of Honour, or, Rules for the Gentlemen of England*, 2nd edition (London: Rivington).
Digby, Kenelm Henry (1826–1829) *The Broad Stone of Honour: or the True Sense and Practice of Chivalry*, 5 vols (London: Quaritch).
Digby, Kenelem Henry (1876–1877) *The Broad Stone of Honour: or the True Sense and Practice of Chivalry*, 5 vols (London: Quaritch).
Dilke, Charles Wentworth (1868–1869) *Greater Britain. A Record of my Travels in English-speaking Countries*, 2 vols (London: Macmillan).
Dilthey, Wilhelm (1923 [1883]) *Einleitung in die Geisteswissenschaften. Versuch einer Grundlegung für das Studium der Gesellschaft und der Geschichte*, 2nd edition (Leipzig: Teubner).
Distad, Norman Merrill (1979) *Guessing at Truth. The Life of Julius Hare (1795–1855)* (Shepherdstown: Patmos Press).
Ditchfield, Grayson M. and Sarah Brewer (2008) "Richard Hurd", in *Oxford Dictionary of National Biography* (Oxford: Oxford University Press) <http://www.oxforddnb.com/view/article/14249> (accessed 7 July 2016).
Eichhorn, Johann Gottfried (1796–1799) *Allgemeine Geschichte der Cultur und Literatur des neueren Europas*, 2 vols (Göttingen: Rosenbusch).
Erhard, Walter and Arne Koch (eds) (2007) *Ernst Moritz Arndt (1769–1860). Deutscher Nationalismus – Europa – Transatlantische Perspektiven* (Tübingen: Niemeyer).
Fetscher, Iring (1969) "Georg Wilhelm Friedrich Hegel", in *Neue deutsche Biografie* (Berlin: Duncker and Humblot), vol. 8, 207–222.
Fetscher, Justus (2000–2005) "Zeitalter/Epoche", in *Ästhetische Grundbegriffe. Historisches Wörterbuch in sieben Bänden* (Stuttgart: Metzler), vol. 6, 776–810.

Fichte, Johann Gottfried (1846 [1806]) *Grundzüge des gegenwärtigen Zeitalters*, in *Fichtes Sämmtliche Werke*, ed. Immanuel Fichte (Berlin: de Gruyter), vol. 7, 1–256.
Fichte, Johann Gottfried (1846 [1808]) *Reden an die deutsche Nation*, in *Fichtes Sämmtliche Werke*, ed. Immanuel Fichte (Berlin: de Gruyter), vol. 7, 259–499.
Fichte, Johann Gottfried (1848–1849) *The Popular Works of Johann Gottlieb Fichte, with a Memoir of the Author*, trans. and introd. William Smith (London: Chapman).
Fischer, Hermann (1895) "Ludwig Uhland", in *Allgemeine Deutsche Biographie* (Berlin: Duncker and Humblot), vol. 39, 148–163.
Fish, Stanley (1980) *Is there a Text in this Class? The Authority of Interpretive Communities* (Cambridge MA.: Harvard University Press).
Flad, Ruth (1921) *Der Begriff der öffentlichen Meinung bei Stein, Arndt und Humboldt. Studien zur Begriffsbildung in Deutschland während der preußischen Reform* (Berlin: de Gruyter).
Fonblanque, Edward Harrington (1874) *The Life and Labours of Albany Fonblanque* (London: Bentley).
Forbes, Duncan (1952) *The Liberal Anglican Idea of History* (Cambridge: Cambridge University Press).
Forster, Georg (1967–1971 [1794]) *Parisische Umrisse*, in *Georg Forster. Werke in vier Bänden*, ed. Gerhard Steiner (Leipzig: Insel), vol. 3, 729–769.
Forster, Georg (1991) "Über die öffentliche Meinung (Fragment eines Briefes)", in *Georg Forsters Werke. Sämtliche Schriften, Tagebücher, Briefe*, ed. Gerhard Steiner, 2nd edition (Berlin: Verlag Akademie der Wissenschaften), vol. 8, 365.
Freeman, Edward Augustus (1867–1879) *The History of the Norman Conquest of England. Its Causes and its Results*, 6 vols (Oxford: Clarendon Press).
Freeman, Edward Augustus (1870) *The History of the Norman Conquest of England*, 2nd revised edition, vol. 1 (Oxford: Clarendon Press).
Freeman, Edward Augustus (1873) *Comparative Politics. Six Lectures Read Before the Royal Institution in January and February 1872, with the Unity of History, the Rede Lecture Read Before the University of Cambridge, May 1872* (London: Macmillan).
Freeman, Edward Augustus (1876) *The History of the Norman Conquest, its Causes and its Results*, 2nd revised edition, vol. 5 (Oxford: Clarendon Press).
Fulda, Daniel (2010) *Kulturmuster der Aufklärung* (Halle: Mitteldeutscher Verlag).
Gamper, Michael and Peter Schnyder (eds) (2006) *Kollektive Gespenster. Die Masse, der Zeitgeist und andere unfassbare Körper* (Freiburg im Breisgau: Rombach).
Garve, Christian (1974 [1802]) "Über die öffentliche Meinung", repr. in *Christian Garve. Popularhistorische Schriften über literarische, ästhetische und gesellschaftliche Gegenstände*, 2 vols, ed. K. Wölfel (Stuttgart: Metzler), vol. 2, 293–334 [1263–1306].
Gatterer, Johann Christoph (1792) *Versuch einer allgemeinen Weltgeschichte bis zur Entdeckung Amerikas* (Göttingen: no publisher).
Goethe, Johann Wolfgang (1977 [1795–1796]). *Wilhelm Meisters Lehrjahre*, in *Sämtliche Werke in 18 Bänden* (München: Deutscher Taschenbuchverlag), vol. 7.
Goethe, Johann Wolfgang (1988 [1773]) *Von deutscher Baukunst*, in Herder, Goethe, Frisi, Möser. *Von deutscher Art und Kunst. Einige fliegende Blätter*, ed. Hans Dietrich Irmscher (Stuttgart: Reclam), 93–104.
Gombrich, Ernst Hans (1978) *The Story of Art*, 13th edition (Oxford: Phaidon).
Görres, Johann Joseph (1819) *Teutschland und die Revolution* (Koblenz: Hölscher).
Grayling, Anthony Clifford (2000) *The Quarrel of the Age. The Life and Times of William Hazlitt* (London: Weidenfeld and Nicolson).

Green, Georgina (2014) *The Majesty of the People. Popular Sovereignty and the Role of the Writer* (Oxford: Oxford University Press).
Grimm, Jacob (1816) "Von der Poesie im Recht", *Zeitschrift für geschichtliche Rechtswissenschaft* 2.1, 25–99.
Habermas, Jürgen (1990) *Strukturwandel der Öffentlichkeit. Untersuchungen zu einer Kategorie der bürgerlichen Gesellschaft*, new edition (Frankfurt am Main: Suhrkamp).
Haigh, John D. (2015) "John Mitchell Kemble", in *Oxford Dictionary of National Biography* (Oxford: Oxford University Press) <http://www.oxforddnb.com/view/article/15321> (accessed 30 May 2018)
Halem, Gerhard Anton von (1790) "Schreiben aus Paris an den Herausgeber des Teutschen Merkur", *Neuer Teutscher Merkur* 3, 381–410.
Hare, Augustus John C. (1872) *Memorials of a Quiet Life*, 2 vols, 5th edition (New York: Randolf).
Hare, Augustus John C. (1876) *Memorials of a Quiet Life. Supplementary volume* (London: Daldy, Isbister and Co).
Hare, Julius Charles (1816–1818) Commonplace Book, photocopy of manuscript held in Wren Library, Trinity College Cambridge, classmark Add.ms.c.205.
Hare, Julius Charles (1820) *Sintram and his Companions. A Romance. From the German of Frederick Baron de la Motte Fouqué, Author of Undine* (London: C. and J. Olliers).
Hare, Julius Charles (1829) *A Vindication of Niebuhr's History of Rome from the charges of the Quarterly Review* (Cambridge: John Taylor).
Hare, Julius Charles (1847) *Guesses at Truth by Two Brothers*, 3rd edition (London: Taylor and Walton).
Hare, Julius Charles (1867) *Guesses at Truth by Two Brothers. With a Memoir by Edward Hayes Plumptre* (London: Macmillan).
Hare, Julius and Augustus [anon] (1827) *Guesses at Truth by Two Brothers* (London: Taylor).
Hare, Julius Charles (1838) *Guesses at Truth by Two Brothers*, 2nd edition (London: Taylor and Walton).
Harrold, Charles Frederick (1963 [1934]) *Carlyle and German Thought 1819–1834* (reprint edition) (Hamden: Archon Books).
Hassinger, Erich (1978) *Empirisch-rationaler Historismus. Seine Ausbildung in der Literatur Westeuropas von Guiccardini bis Saint-Evremond* (Bern/Munich: Franke).
Hazlitt, William (1910) *Lectures on the English Poets and The Spirit of the Age*, introd. A. R. Waller (London/New York: Dent and Dutton).
Hazlitt, William (1930–1934 [1806]) *Free Thoughts on Public Affairs. Advice to a Patriot; in a Letter Addressed to a Member of the Old Opposition*, in *The Complete Works of William Hazlitt in Twenty-One Volumes*, ed. P. P. Howe (London/Toronto: Dent), vol. 1, 93–118.
Hazlitt, William (1930–1934 [1825]) *The Spirit of the Age*, in *The Complete Works of William Hazlitt in Twenty-One Volumes*, ed. P. P. Howe (London/Toronto: Dent), vol. 10.
Hazlitt, William (1930–1934 [1820]) *Lectures chiefly on the Dramatic Literature of the Age of Elizabeth. Delivered at the Surrey Institution*, in *The Collected Works of William Hazlitt in Twenty-One Volumes*, ed. P. P. Howe (London/Toronto: Dent), vol.6, 169–364.
Hazlitt, William (1930–1934 [1826]) *The Plain Speaker*, in *The Collected Works of William Hazlitt in Twenty-One Volumes*, ed. P. P. Howe (London/Toronto: Dent), vol. 12.
Hazlitt, William (1969 [1825]) *The Spirit of the Age or Contemporary Portraits*, ed. E. D. Mackerness (London: Collins).

Hazlitt, William (1998) *Selected Writings of William* Hazlitt, 9 vols, ed. Duncan Wu (London: Pickering and Chatto).
Hegel, Georg Wilheim Friedrich (1817) "Beurteilung der im Druck erschienenen Verhandlung der Versammlung der Landstände des Königreichs Württemberg im Jahre 1815 und 1816", *Heidelberger Jahrbücher der Literatur*, 66–68 and 73–77.
Hegel, Georg Wilheim Friedrich (1986) *Vorlesungen über die Philosophie der Geschichte*, ed. Eva Moldenhauer and Karl Markus Michel (Frankfurt am Main: Suhrkamp).
Helmcken, John Sebastian (1975) *The Reminiscences of Doctor John Sebastian Helmcken*, ed. Dorothy Blakey Lamb (Victoria: University of British Columbia Press).
Hendrich, Franz Josias von (1794) *Freymüthige Gedanken über die allerwichtigste Angelegenheit Deutschlands. Seinem und andern guten Fürsten desselben ehrerbietig zur Prüfung und Beherzigung vorgelegt von einem Freunde seines Vaterlandes* (Germanien [Zurich]: Orell, Geßner and Füßli).
Hendrich, Franz Josias von (1795) *Freymüthige Gedanken über die allerwichtigste Angelegenheit Deutschlands. Erster Theil*, 3rd edition (Germanien: no publisher).
Hendrich, Franz Josias von (1797 [facsimile reprint 1979]) *Über den Geist des Zeitalters und die Gewalt der öffentlichen Meynung* (Leipzig/Meisenheim: Hain Druck) (Scriptor Reprints).
Hentschel, Uwe (2007) "Zur malenden Poesie in der Aufklärung oder Wie die Schweizer die Sachsen besiegt haben", *Germanisch-Romanische Monatsschrift* 57.2, 187–199.
Herder, Johann Gottfried (1877 [1765–1767]) *Fragmente* [Über die neuere deutsche Litteratur], in *Herders Sämmtliche Werke*, ed. Bernhard Suphan (Berlin: Weidmannsche Buchhandlung), vol. 1, 131–548.
Herder, Johann Gottfried (1877 [1765]) *Haben wir jetzt noch ein Publikum und Vaterland der Alten?*, in *Herders Sämmtliche Werke*, ed. Bernhard Suphan (Berlin: Weidmannsche Buchhandlung), vol. 1, 13–28.
Herder, Johann Gottfried (1878 [1769]) *Kritische Wälder 1–3*, in *Herders Sämmtliche Werke*, ed. Bernhard Suphan (Berlin: Weidmannsche Buchhandlung), vol. 3.
Herder, Johann Gottfried (1880 [1798]) "Vorrede zu Majers Buch 'Kulturgeschichte der Völker'", in *Herders Sämmtliche Werke*, ed. Bernhard Suphan (Berlin: Weidmannsche Buchhandlung), vol. 20, 340–344.
Herder, Johann Gottfried (1891 [1774]) *Auch eine Philosophie zur Geschichte der Menschheit*, in *Herders Sämmtliche Werke*, ed. Bernhard Suphan (Berlin: Weidmannsche Buchhandlung), vol. 5, 475–594.
Herder, Johann Gottfried (1891) "Ursachen des gesunkenen Geschmacks bei den verschiedenen Völkern, da er geblühet", in *Herders Sämmtliche Werke*, ed. Bernhard Suphan (Berlin: Weidmannsche Buchhandlung), vol. 5, 595–655.
Herder, Johann Gottfried (1988 [1773]) *Herder, Goethe, Frisi, Moser. Von deutscher Art und Kunst. Einige fliegende Blätter*, ed. Hans Dietrich Irmscher (Stuttgart: Reclam).
Herder, Johann Gottfried (1991 [1793–1797]) *Briefe zur Beförderung der Humanität*, in *Johann Gottfried Herder. Werke in 10 Bänden* (Frankfurt am Main: Deutscher Klassiker Verlag), vol 7, ed. Hans Dietrich Irmscher.
Hermand, Jost (2007) "Moderne, Zeitgeist, Generation. Verschleierungstaktiken pseudo-demokratischer Ideologiebildungen", in Jost Hermand, *Utopie des Fortschritts. Zwölf Versuche* (Cologne: Böhlau), 66–78.
Hewitt, David (2008) "Sir Walter Scott", in *Oxford Dictionary of National Biography* (Oxford: Oxford University Press) <http://www.oxforddnb.com/view/article/24928> (accessed 15 July 2018).

Heyne, Christian Johann (1795) "Sind die Wissenschaften den Regierungen gefährlich?" *Deutsche Monatsschrift* 3, 3–28.
Hiery, Hermann (ed) (2001) *Der Zeitgeist und die Historie* (Dettelbach: Röll).
Hölscher, Lucien (1978) "Öffentlichkeit", in *Geschichtliche Grundbegriffe. Historisches Lexikon zur politisch-sozialen Sprache in Deutschland*, ed. O. Brunner, W. Conze and R. Koselleck (Stuttgart: Klett), vol 4, 413–467.
Hughes, Mary Ann (1904) *Letters and Recollections of Sir Walter Scott*, ed. H. G. Hutchinson (London: Smith, Elder and Co).
Hurd, Richard (1762) *Letters on Chivalry and Romance* (London: A. Millar).
Hurd, Richard (1788) *Moral and Political Dialogues with Letters on Chivalry and Romance*, 6th edition (London: Cadell).
Hurd, Richard (1911 [1762]) *Hurd's Letters on Chivalry and Romance with the 3rd Elizabethan Dialogue*, ed. Edith J. Morley (London: Frowde).
Jefcoate, Geoffrey (2015) *Deutsche Drucker and Buchhändler in London 1680–1811* (Berlin: de Gruyter).
Jeffrey, Francis (1813) "Mme de Staël's De la litérature considerée dans ses rapports avec les institutions sociales", *Edinburgh Review* 21, 1–50.
Jeffrey, Francis (1825) "The Spirit of the Age: or Contemporary Portraits", *Edinburgh Review* 42, 245–260.
Jenisch, Daniel (1796) *Philosophisch-kritische Vergleichung und Würdigung von vierzehn ältern und neuern Sprachen Europens* (Berlin: Maurer).
Jenkins, Roy (2008) "Sir Charles Wentworth Dilke", in *Oxford Dictionary of National Biography* (Oxford: Oxford University Press) <http://www.oxforddnb.com/view/article/32824> (accessed 22 June 2018).
John, Johannes (2007) "August Wilhelm Schlegel", in *Neue deutsche Biografie* (Berlin: Duncker and Humblot), vol. 23, 38–40.
Jung, Theo (2012) "Zeitgeist im langen 18. Jahrhundert. Dimensionen eines umstrittenen Begriffs", in *Frühe Neue Zeiten. Zeitwissen zwischen Reformation und Revolution*, ed. Achim Landwehr (Bielefeld: Transcript Verlag), 319–335.
Kemble, John Mitchell (1849) *The Saxons in England. A History of the English Commonwealth till the Period of the Norman Conquest* (London: Longman, Brown and Green).
Kemble, John Mitcell (1876) *The Saxons in England. A History of the English Commonwealth till the Period of the Norman Conquest*, new edition, revised by Walter de Gray Birch (London: Quaritch).
Kempter, Lothar (1990–1991) "Herder, Hölderlin und der Zeitgeist. Zur Frühgeschichte eines Begriffs", *Hölderlin Jahrburch/Iduna. Jahrbuch der Hölderlingesellschaft* 27, 51–76.
Kendall, Guy (1947) *Charles Kingsley and his Ideas* (London: Hutchinson).
Kingsley, Charles (1864) *The Roman and the Teuton. A Series of Lectures delivered before the University of Cambridge* (Cambridge/London: Macmillan).
Kingsley, Charles (1895) *Römer und Germanen. Vorträge gehalten an der Universität zu Cambridge. Autorisierte Übersetzung nach der 9. Auflage des Originals von Maria Baumann* (Göttingen: Vandenhoeck and Ruprecht).
Kingsley, Charles (1913 [1864]) *The Roman and the Teuton. A Series of Lectures delivered before the University of Cambridge*, new edition (London: Macmillan).
Kliger, Samuel (1945) "The Goths in England: An Introduction to the Gothic Vogue in Eighteenth-Century Aesthetic Discussion", *Modern Philology* 43.2, 107–117.

Kloeden, Wolfdietrich. von (2007) "Johann Adolph Schlegel", in *Neue deutsche Biografie* (Berlin: Duncker and Humblot), vol. 23, 37–38.

Koch, John (1927) "Sir Walter Scotts Beziehungen zu Deutschland", *Germanisch-Romanische Monatsschrift* 15, 36–141.

Konersmann, Ralf (1971–2007) "Zeitgeist", in *Historisches Wörterbuch der Philosophie*, 13 vols (Basel: Schwabe), vol. 12, 1266–1270.

Konersmann, Ralf (2006) "Der Hüter des Konsenses. Zeitgeist-Begriff und Zeitgeist-Paradox", in *Kollektive Gespenster. Die Masse, der Zeitgeist und andere unfassbare Körper*, ed. Michael Gamper and Peter Schnyder (Freiburg im Breisgau: Rombach), 247–263.

Kühn, Manfred (2012) *Johann Gottlieb Fichte. Ein deutscher Philosoph* (Munich: Beck).

Landwehr, Achim (ed) (2012) *Frühe Neue Zeiten. Zeitwissen zwischen Reformation und Revolution* (Bielefeld: Transcript Verlag).

Liesegang, Torsten (2004) *Öffentlichkeit und öffentliche Meinung. Theorien von Kant bis Marx* (Würzburg: Königshausen and Neumann).

Lubenow, William Cornelius (1998) *The Cambridge Apostles 1820–1914. Liberalism, Imagination and Friendship in British Intellectual and Professional Life* (Cambridge: Cambridge University Press).

Mackinnon, William Alexander (1828) *On the Rise, Progress and Present State of Public Opinion in Great Britain and Other Parts of the World* (London: Saunders and Otley).

Mallet, Paul Henri (1755) *L'introduction à l'histoire de Dannemarc où l'on traite de religion, des loix, des moeurs et des usages des anciens Danois* (Copenhagen: no publisher).

Mallet, Paul Henri (1756) *Monuments de la mythologie et poesie de Celtes, et particulièrement des anciens Scandinaves* (Copenhagen: no publisher).

Mallet, Paul Henri (1770) *Northern Antiquities, or a Description of the Manners, Customs, Religion and Laws of the Ancient Danes and other Northern Nations*, trans. and introd. Thomas Percy (London: Carnan).

Mason, Eudo (1959) *Deutsche und Englische Romantik. Eine Gegenüberstellung* (Göttingen: Vandenhoeck and Ruprecht).

Maurer, Michael (2014) *Johann Gottfried Herder. Leben und Werk* (Cologne: Böhlau).

McFarland, G. F. (1963/1964) "The Early Literary Career of Julius Charles Hare", *Bulletin of the John Rylands Library* 46, 42–83.

McFarland, G. F. (1964/1965) "Julius Charles Hare, Coleridge, de Quincey and German Literature", *Bulletin of the John Rylands Library* 47, 165–197.

McFarland, Thomas (1987) *Romantic Cruxes. The English Essayists and the Spirit of the Age.* (Oxford: Clarendon Press).

Mehring, Frank (2004) *Karl Follen. Deutsch-Amerikanischer Freiheitskämpfer* (Gießen: Ferbersche Universitätsbuchhandlung).

Meumann, Markus (2012) "Der Zeitgeist vor dem Zeitgeist", in *Frühe Neue Zeiten. Zeitwissen zwischen Reformation und Revolution*, ed. Achim Landwehr (Bielefeld: Transcript Verlag), 283–317.

Mill, John Stuart (1837) "Carlyle's French Revolution", *London and Westminster Review* 29, 17–53.

Mill, John Stuart (1942 [1831]) *The Spirit of the Age*, introd. Frederick A. von Hayek (Chicago: University of Chicago Press).

Mill, John Stuart (1965) *Mill's Essays on Literature and Society*, ed. Jerome B. Schneewind (New York and London: Collier/Collins).

Miller, Dale E. (2010) *John Stuart Mill. Moral, Social, and Political Thought* (Cambridge: Polity Press).
Montesquieu (Charles-Louis de Secondat, Baron de La Brède et de Montesquieu) (2011 [1748]) *Montesquieu's Spirit of the Laws*, ed. T. Adamo (Lakehurst NJ: Woodbine Cottage Publications).
Müsebeck, Ernst (1914) *Ernst Moritz Arndt. Ein Lebensbild. Erstes Buch* (Gotha: Perthes).
Nangle, Benjamin Christie (1955) *The Monthly Review. Second Series 1790–1815. Indexes of Contributors and Articles* (Oxford: Clarendon Press).
Niebuhr, Barthold Georg (1854) *The Life and Letters of Barthold Georg Niebuhr with essays on his Character and Influence* (New York: Harper).
Novalis (1981 [1798]) *Politische Aphorismen*, in *Werke in einem Band*, ed. Hans-Joachim Mähl and Richard Samuel (Munich: Beck).
Oergel, Maike (1996) "The Redeeming Teuton", in *Imagining Nations*, ed. Geoffrey Cubitt (Manchester: Manchester University Press), 75–94.
Oergel, Maike (1998) *The Return of King Arthur and the Nibelungen. National Myth in 19th-century English and German Literature* (Berlin/New York: de Gruyter).
Oergel, Maike (1999) "Ende der Querelle? Deutsche und britische Definitionen der modernen Identität im Kulturschatten der Antike 1750–1870", in *Unerledigte Geschichten. Der literarische Umgang mit Nationalität und Internationalität*, ed. Horst Turk and Gesa von Essen (Göttingen: Wallstein), 72–99.
Oergel, Maike (2006) *Culture and Identity. Historicity in German Literature and Thought 1770–1815* (Berlin/New York: de Gruyter).
Oergel, Maike (2012) "Germania and Greater Britain. German Scholarship and the Legitimization of the British Empire", *Angermion. Yearbook for Anglo-German Literary Criticism, Intellectual History and Cultural Transfers* 5, 91–118.
Oergel, Maike (2015) "'The Grand Poem of our Time': Carlyle, Zeitgeist and his *History of the French Revolution*", in *Critical Time in Modern German Literature and Culture*, ed. Dirk Göttsche (Bern: Peter Lang), 69–99.
Oergel, Maike (2016) "'Germanisierung' als romantisches Kulturmuster in der englischen Geschichtsschreibung des 19. Jahrhunderts", in *Praxis und Diskurs der Romantik 1800–1900*, ed. Norman Kasper and Jochen Strobel (Paderborn: Schönigh), 99–116.
Oergel, Maike (2017) "Die Verurtümlichung Homers – ein Beispiel transnationaler Antiketransformation. Die Rezeption des homerischen Barden in Großbritannien und Deutschland im 18. Jahrhundert", in *Topographien der Antike in der deutschen Aufklärung*, ed. Annika Hildebrandt, Charlotte Kurbjuhn, Steffen Martus (Bern: Peter Lang), 181–200.
Oergel, Maike (2018a) "Constitutionalism and Cultural Identity as Revolutionary Concepts in German Political Radicalism 1806–1819: The case of Karl Follen", *Comparative Critical Studies* 15.2, 183–205.
Oergel, Maike (2018b) "Politics, Radicalism and Anglo-German Relations. The Reception of Ernst Moritz Arndt in early 19th-century Britain", *Angermion. Yearbook for Anglo-German Literary Criticism, Intellectual History and Cultural Transfers* 11, 31–59.
Palmer, David John (1965) *The Rise of English Studies. An Account of the Study of English Language and Literature from the Origins to the Making of the Oxford School* (Oxford: Oxford University Press).
Palmer, Roy (2006) "Thomas Percy", in *Oxford Dictionary of National Biography* (Oxford: Oxford University Press) <http://www.oxforddnb.com/view/article/21959> (accessed 15 February 2018).

Paulin, Roger (1987) "Julius Hare's German Books in Trinity College Library", *Transactions of the Cambridge Bibliographical Society* 9.2, 174–193.
Paulin, Roger (2016) *The Life of August Wilhelm Schlegel. Cosmopolitan of Art and Poetry* (Cambridge: Open Book Publishing).
Percy, Thomas (1794) *Reliques of Ancient English Poetry*, 4th edition (London: Rivington).
Ranke, Leopold (1885) *Geschichten der romanischen und germanischen Völker 1494–1514*, 3rd edition (Leipzig: Duncker and Humblot).
Reeve, A. J. H. (2014) "Thomas Arnold", in *Oxford Dictionary of National Biography* (Oxford: Oxford University Press) < https://doi.org/10.1093/ref:odnb/686> (accessed 22 June 2018).
Reill, Peter Hanns (1975) *The German Enlightenment and the Rise of Historicism* (Berkeley/Los Angeles: University of California Press).
Roegele, Otto (1964) "Johann Joseph Görres", in *Neue deutsche Biografie* (Berlin: Duncker and Humblot), vol. 6, 532–536.
Rosenberg, John D. (1985) *Carlyle and the Burden of History* (Oxford: Clarendon Press).
Ross, Janet (1893) *Three Generations of English Women. Memoirs and Correspondence of Susannah Taylor, Sarah Austin, and Lady Duff-Gordon*, new, revised and enlarged edition (London: Fisher and Unwin).
Schlegel, August Wilhelm (1923 [1808]) *Vorlesungen über dramatische Kunst und Literatur*, ed. G. V. Amoretti (Leipzig: Schröder).
Schlegel, August Wilhelm (1965 [1884]) *Geschichte der romantischen Literatur*, in *Kritische Schriften und Briefe*, ed. Edgar Lohner (Stuttgart: Kohlhammer) vol. 4.
Schlegel, Friedrich (1818) *Lectures on the History of Literature, ancient and modern*, trans. John G. Lockhart (Edinburgh: Blackwood).
Schlegel, Friedrich (1822) *Geschichte der alten und neuen Literatur. Vorlesungen gehalten in Wien im Jahre 1812*, in *Friedrich Schlegels Sämmtliche Werke* (Vienna: Mayer).
Schlegel, Friedrich (1842) *Geschichte der alten und neuen Literatur. Vorlesungen gehalten zu Wien im Jahre 1812* (Berlin: Athenaeum).
Schlegel, Friedrich (1967) *Kritische Friedrich-Schlegel-Ausgabe*, vol. 2, ed. Hans Eichner (Munich/Zurich: Schönigh/Thomas Verlag).
Schmidt, Wolfgang Gerhard (2003) *"Homer des Nordens" und "Mutter der Romantik". James Macphersons Ossian und seine Rezeption in der deutschsprachigen Literatur*, 4 vols (Berlin/New York: de Gruyter).
Schoeps, Hans-Joachim (1956) *Was ist und was will die Geistesgeschichte. Theorie und Praxis der Zeitgeistforschung* (Göttingen: Musterschmidt).
Schöffl, Rainer (January 2018) *Franz Joseph von Wocher und das Nibelungenlied*. <http://www.nibelungenlied-gesellschaft.de/03_beitrag/gast/schoeffl/g-12_schoeffl.html> (accessed 22 January 2018).
Schwabe, Christian Anton [anon] (1806) "Geist der Zeit, &c. The Spirit of the Times by Ernest Moritz Arndt, 1806", *The Monthly Review or Literary Journal, Enlarged. From September to December inclusive 1806, with an Appendix* 51, 524–527.
Schwabe, Christian Anton (1809) "Arndt's Spirit of the Times", *Monthly Review* 60, 108–109.
Scott, Walter (1887 [1815–1824]) *Essays on Chivalry, Romance and the Drama* (London: Warne).
Scott, Walter (1986 [1819]). *Ivanhoe*, ed. A. N. Wilson (London: Penguin Classics).
[Scott, W] (1838) *Catalogue of the Library at Abbotsford*, compiled by John George Cochrane (Edinburgh: Constable).
See, Klaus von (1970) *Deutsche Germanenideologie. Vom Humanismus bis zur Gegenwart* (Frankfurt am Main: Athenaeum).

Seybold, D. (2005) "Johann Jakob Bodmer", in *Theaterlexikon der Schweiz*, ed. Andreas Kotte (Zurich: Chronos Verlag), 226–227.
Skalweit, Stephan (1956) "Edmund Burke, Ernst Brandes und Hannover", *Niedersächsisches Jahrbuch für Landesgeschichte* 28, 15–72.
Stadler, Ulrich (2006) "Zeitgeisterbeschwörung um 1800. Geschichtskritik und Gegenwartsklage bei Herder, Hendrich, Hölderlin und Brandes", in *Kollektive Gespenster. Die Masse, der Zeitgeist und andere unfassbare Körper*, ed. Michael Gamper and Peter Schnyder (Freiburg im Breisgau: Rombach), 265–284.
Stanley, Arthur Penrhyn (1846) *The Life and Correspondence of Thomas Arnold*, 6th edition (London: Fellows).
Steffens, Henrik (1817) *Die gegewärtige Zeit und wie sie geworden mit besonderer Rücksicht auf Deutschland* (Berlin: Reimer).
Stubbs, William (1891) *Constitutional History of England in its Origins and Development*, 3 vols, 5th edition (Oxford: Clarendon Press).
Thelwall, John (1795) *The Tribune. A Periodical Publication, consisting chiefly of the Political Lectures of J. Thelwall* (London: Printed for the Author. Sold at the Lecture Rooms Beauford Buildings, and the booksellers Eaton, Newgate St, Smith, Portsmouth St, Burke, Crispin St).
Thelwall, John (1796) *The Rights of Nature against the Usurpations of Establishments. A Series of Letters to the People of Britain on the State of Public Affairs and the recent Effusions of the Right Honourable Edmund Burke* (London/Norwich: Symons/March).
Turner, Sharon (1799–1805) *The History of the Anglo-Saxons from their first Appearance above the Elbe, to the Death of Egbert*, 4 vols (London: Longman and Rees).
Utz, Richard (2009) "Englische Philologie vs. English Studies: A Foundational Conflict", in *Das Potential europäischer Philologien. Geschichte, Leistung, Funktion*, ed. Christoph König (Göttingen: Wallstein), 34–44.
Vance, Norman (2009) "Charles Kingsley", in *Oxford Dictionary of National Biography* (Oxford: Oxford University Press) <http://www.oxforddnb.com/view/article/15617> (accessed on 22 June 2018).
Vazsonyi, Nicholas (1999) "Montesquieu, Friedrich Carl von Moser and the National Spirit Debate in Germany 1765–67", *German Studies Review* 22, 225–246.
Voltaire (François Marie Arouet) (2015) *Essai sur les moeurs et l'esprit des nations*, in *Les œuvres complètes de Voltaire*, vols 22–26 <www.voltaire.ox.ac.uk> (accessed 2 September 2016).
Wehrli, Max (ed) (1943) *Das geistige Zürich im 18. Jahrhundert. Texte und Dokumente von Gotthart Heidegger bis Heinrich Pestalozzi* (Zurich: Atlantis).
Whibley, Charles (1925) *Lord John Manners and his Friends*, 2 vols (London: William Blackwood).
Wieland, Christoph Martin (1857 [1799]) "Über die öffentliche Meinung", in *Vermischte Schriften. Sämmtliche Werke.* (Leipzig: Göschen), vol. 31, 309–351.
Wu, Duncan (2008) *William Hazlitt. The First Modern Man* (Oxford: Oxford University Press).
Zeltner, Hermann (1961) "Johann Gottlieb Fichte", in *Neue Deutsche Biografie* (Berlin: Duncker and Humblot), vol. 5, 122–125.
Ziolkowski, Theodore (1990) *German Romanticism and its Institutions.* (Princeton: Princeton University Press).
Zovko, Jure (2007) "Friedrich Schlegel", in *Neue Deutsche Biografie* (Berlin: Duncker and Humblot) vol. 23, 40–42.

Index

Age of Mechanism 190, 203, 213
Allgemeine Literatur-Zeitung (Halle) 58, 113, 113n48, 125, 125n60, 125n61
Allgemeine Literatur-Zeitung (Jena) 112, 125, 126
Anglo-Saxon 42, 246, 247, 256, 273, 275, 277, 280, 281, 281n40, 291, 297, 302, 303
Anti-Jacobin 138, 140, 163n49, 260
Arndt, Ernst Moritz 73, 84, 85, 86, 87, 88, 101, 104, 105, 106, 106n31, 107, 107n32, 107n33, 107n34, 108, 109, 109n38, 110, 111, 111n43, 112, 113, 114, 115, 116, 117, 117n52, 118, 119, 120, 121, 121n53, 122, 122n54, 123, 123n56, 124, 124n57, 125, 125n59, 126, 127, 128, 130, 131, 131n3, 132, 132n3, 133, 134, 134n5, 134n6, 135, 136, 137, 138, 139, 140, 141, 141n14, 142, 144, 145, 146, 148, 149, 150, 150n27, 151, 151n28, 152, 155, 158, 159, 159n41, 160, 161, 162, 162n48, 164, 165, 169, 178, 179, 184, 187, 197, 199, 200, 202, 205, 214, 215, 217, 221, 223, 225, 232, 236, 237, 240, 266, 267, 268, 269, 270, 271, 273, 278, 282, 288, 290, 300, 301, 307, 307n52, 308, 309, 314, 315, 319, 320, 323
Arnim, Achim von 272
Arnold, Matthew 154
Arnold, Thomas 166, 245n5, 246, 246n7, 278, 279, 282, 283, 290, 296, 300, 301, 304, 320, 326
Athenaeum (British magazine) 157, 302

Bacon, Francis 9, 10, 21, 23, 24, 24n36, 25, 26, 34, 44, 46, 173, 174, 175
Barclay, John 9, 10, 11, 12, 21, 21n24, 21n28, 22, 22n30, 22n31, 23, 25, 26, 32, 34, 113, 116, 123, 141n14, 174
Blackwell, Thomas 29, 35, 35n5, 36, 36n7, 37, 38, 39, 39n8, 41, 42, 43, 44, 47, 51, 52, 59, 71, 76, 85, 170, 173, 220, 226, 251, 252, 258, 259, 263n25, 272, 286, 309, 310
Blackwood's Magazine 141, 183, 191, 215, 218, 219, 219n105, 220, 222, 223, 228, 233
Bodmer, Johann Jakob 38, 39, 40, 41, 42, 44, 46, 47, 58, 258, 259, 307n52, 309, 310, 313
Boosey (publishers) 125n59, 139, 139n10, 140, 140n11, 151
Brandes, Ernst 85, 87, 88, 90, 91, 99, 100, 101, 102, 102n25, 103, 104, 105, 105n28, 106, 108, 109, 109n38, 111, 112, 113, 113n47, 119, 121, 122n54, 124, 127, 128, 130, 141, 142, 155, 187, 189, 197, 199, 200, 215, 217, 222, 225, 236, 237, 238, 240
Brentano, Clemens 269, 272, 315
Broad Church 144n17, 300, 304, 305
Burke, Edmund 63, 73, 74, 75, 76, 77, 78, 78n34, 79, 80, 82, 83, 86, 90, 95, 107, 123, 124, 124n57, 130, 141, 149, 150, 162, 164, 202, 215, 236, 255, 273, 275, 317, 318
Burschenschaft 107, 108n35, 152, 153, 154, 266, 267, 270, 273, 300, 309, 321
Byron, George Gordon, Lord Byron 179, 180, 187n73, 194n84

Carlyle, Thomas 1n2, 111, 129, 142, 143, 144, 146, 154, 155, 156, 157, 157n39, 166, 178, 190, 191, 191n77, 192, 192n79, 193, 193n83, 194, 194n86, 195, 195n86, 195n88, 196, 197, 198, 199, 199n91, 200, 200n93, 200n94, 201, 202, 203, 204, 204n95, 205, 206, 206n97, 207, 208, 208n99, 208n100, 209, 210, 211, 211n101, 212, 213, 214, 215, 216, 217, 218, 218n104, 219, 225, 228, 228n113, 228n114, 229, 229n115, 231, 236, 237, 240, 276, 276n35, 292, 300, 304, 316, 320

Castlereagh, Robert Steward, Lord Castlereagh 147, 270
Chivalry 11, 13, 46, 46n21, 174, 246n7, 248n9, 252, 257, 261, 262, 263, 264, 265, 278, 279, 280, 286, 291, 300, 314
Christian Socialism 293, 304, 305, 322
Church of England 145, 163, 168, 205, 237, 255, 274, 275, 277, 295, 296, 297, 302, 303, 304, 305, 306, 307, 323
Colburn, Henry 178
Coleridge, Samuel Taylor 130n1, 140, 142, 146n18, 156, 156n38, 166, 171n55, 178n65, 179, 182, 186n72, 187n73, 190, 190n74, 192, 192n79, 192n80, 198, 200, 208, 221, 260, 304
Comte, Auguste 220
Conversazione Society 157, 158, 301, 306

de Quincey, Thomas 143, 156, 157n39, 178, 192, 200
Deutungselite 237, 294
Digby, Kenelm Henry 277, 278, 279, 279n39, 280, 281, 290, 296, 300, 320, 326
Dilke, Charles Wentworth 277, 285, 286, 292, 303, 322, 326

Edinburgh Review 80, 140, 156n38, 167, 170, 181, 181n66, 182, 196, 199n91, 206, 228, 300
Eichhorn, Johann Gottfried 85n1, 131n2, 250, 250n13, 272, 292

Fichte, Johann Gottlieb 81, 84, 87n2, 99, 116, 122n54, 123, 130n1, 131, 146n18, 150, 177n61, 194n86, 195n86, 196, 201, 202, 208, 209, 210, 211, 211n101, 212, 217, 220, 250, 263, 264, 265, 266, 267, 276, 290, 291, 307, 307n52, 308, 310, 312, 313, 314, 316, 317, 320, 323
Follen, Karl 108n35, 114, 153, 267, 290, 300, 307n52, 308, 320, 321, 322, 326
Forster, Georg 53, 53n7, 57, 58, 58n16, 64, 64n23, 65, 65n23, 66, 67, 68, 69, 70, 71, 73, 74, 75, 77, 82, 84, 86, 103, 189, 215, 217, 225, 241

Frederick the Great 105n28, 124, 199, 273, 288
Frederick William I 105n28
Frederick William III 276, 320, 323
Frederick William IV 287, 315, 318, 319, 320
Freeman, Edward Augustus 77, 238, 278, 282, 284, 288, 291, 296, 302, 303, 304, 323, 326
Fries, Jakob Friedrich 153

Garve, Christian 57, 58, 58n16, 64, 64n22, 70, 71, 72, 73, 82, 89, 94, 127, 189, 217
Gatterer, Johann Christoph 250, 250n13
Gemeingeist 14, 19, 52, 52n4, 53, 235
Genius saeculi 3, 9, 11, 12, 13, 21, 21n25, 22, 22n31, 23, 25, 26, 27, 29, 31, 83, 123, 235, 242
Germanic Europe 257, 263, 266, 271, 276, 282, 284, 290, 291, 303, 314
Germanistik 271, 272, 274, 275, 292, 293
Goethe, Johann Wolfgang 89, 156, 157, 158, 162, 170, 172, 174n57, 177n61, 191n76, 193, 193n83, 199n91, 249, 250, 259, 259n23, 260, 265, 287, 288, 298, 299, 307, 307n52, 308, 309, 310, 311, 312, 323
Grimm, 252, 254n15, 271, 272, 273, 274, 278, 280, 281, 282, 286, 299, 302, 307n52, 318
Görres, Joseph 267, 269, 270, 278, 278n36, 280, 281, 287, 288, 290, 307, 307n52, 308, 315, 316, 323, 326
Göttingische Gelehrte Anzeigen 112

Habermas, Jürgen 56, 57, 57n12
Halem, Gerhard Anton von 57, 57n13, 58, 58n16, 59, 65
Hare, Julius 77n33, 85, 129, 142, 143, 144, 144n17, 145, 146, 146n19, 147, 147n20, 147n21, 148, 149, 149n23, 150, 150n27, 151, 151n28, 152, 153, 154, 154n31, 154n32, 155, 155n33, 155n35, 156, 156n37, 157, 157n39, 158, 159, 159n42, 160, 161, 161n46, 161n47, 162, 162n48, 163, 163n49, 164, 165, 166, 167, 168, 169, 179, 189, 190, 190n74, 191, 192, 194, 195, 195n87, 198, 199, 200, 202,

208, 214, 221, 231, 236, 237, 240, 270, 273, 276, 278, 278n36, 280, 282, 286, 296, 300, 301, 304, 306, 309, 320, 321, 322, 323

Hazlitt, William 21, 113, 124, 129, 142, 156, 156n38, 161, 166, 166n51, 167, 167n52, 168, 169, 169n53, 170, 171, 171n55, 172, 172n56, 173, 173n57, 174, 175, 176, 176n60, 177, 177n62, 178, 179, 179n65, 180, 181, 182, 183, 183n68, 183n69, 184, 184n70, 184n71, 185, 186, 186n72, 187, 188, 189, 190, 190n74, 191, 192, 192n79, 192n80, 193, 193n83, 194, 197, 198, 200, 202, 203, 206, 207, 208, 214, 215, 217, 217n103, 218, 218n104, 219, 220, 221, 226, 231, 236, 237, 240, 260, 264, 296, 300

Hegel, Georg Wilhelm Friedrich 1n2, 2, 4, 11, 27, 123, 130n1, 144, 146n18, 150, 188, 209, 220, 238, 245n5, 263, 265, 266, 276, 291, 307n52, 308, 316, 317, 318, 326

Hendrich, Franz Josias von 14, 63, 64, 75, 85, 87, 88, 89, 90, 91, 92, 93, 94, 95, 96, 96n11, 97, 98, 99, 99n17, 100, 102, 104, 105n28, 106, 111, 112, 113, 119, 121, 122n54, 123, 124, 127, 128, 130, 141, 142, 148, 155, 168, 178, 189, 200, 204, 205, 205n96, 217, 225, 227, 236, 237, 240

Herder, Johann Gottfried 1n2, 1n3, 8, 8n1, 9, 9n2, 11, 11n7, 13, 13n10, 13n11, 14, 14n13, 15, 15n14, 16, 16n15, 17, 17n16, 18, 18n17, 18n18, 18n19, 18n20, 19, 19n21, 20, 20n23, 21, 21n28, 23, 23n35, 24, 26, 28, 31, 32, 35, 35n6, 45, 48, 49, 52, 52n4, 53, 53n5, 53n6, 54, 60, 60n18, 61, 62, 70, 70n27, 81, 91, 100, 101n23, 111, 112, 113, 116, 122n54, 123, 127, 130n1, 150, 170, 171, 173, 174, 178, 189, 220, 236, 237, 245, 249, 250, 252, 259, 259n23, 260, 263, 272, 290, 292, 298, 299, 307n52, 308, 309, 310, 311, 312, 323

Heyne, Christian Gottlob 63, 308, 311

Homer 29, 35, 36, 39, 41, 42, 46, 47, 251, 253n14, 310

Hume, David 9, 58, 59, 59n17, 72, 76, 95, 96, 99, 99n18, 174, 216, 222

Hunt, Leigh 179, 192n79, 194, 220

Hurd, Richard 9, 38, 41, 42, 43, 45, 46, 47, 72, 76, 85, 173, 174, 245, 247, 248, 248n9, 250, 252, 253, 253n14, 256, 259, 263n25, 264, 264n28, 272, 276, 288, 296, 297, 298, 299, 309, 311, 323

Jacobin 64, 73, 75, 78, 90, 97, 98, 103, 120, 141, 142, 148, 162, 163, 164, 172, 180, 189, 226, 230, 240, 255, 264, 282

Jahn, Friedrich Ludwig 121, 121n53, 266, 282, 301

Jeffrey, Francis 80, 140, 179, 181, 182, 183, 184, 184n71, 187, 190

Jenisch, Daniel 250, 265

Kant, Immanuel 91, 99, 102, 104, 116, 310, 313, 316

Kemble, John Mitchell 157, 166, 272, 273, 275, 277, 278, 280, 281, 281n40, 282, 283, 286, 296, 300, 301, 302, 306

King's College London 274, 275, 295, 304

Kingsley, Charles 278, 282, 283, 285, 291, 296, 304, 304n51, 305, 323

Knight's Quarterly Magazine 143, 157, 158

Kodifikationsstreit 273

Kotzebue, August von 108n35, 122, 137n9, 154, 154n31, 172, 267, 321

Lamb, Charles 156, 179, 184, 192, 192n79, 192n80, 193, 200

Lessing, Gotthold Ephraim 172, 195n86

London Magazine 143, 156, 167, 177, 177n62, 178, 191, 191n76, 192, 192n81

Lowth, Robert 43n19, 272

Lützower Jäger 266, 292

Luden, Heinrich 153

Macpherson, James 257, 258, 272, 288, 309

Malden, Henry 157, 158, 162

Mallet, Henri 38, 43, 43n19, 44, 45, 46, 46n21, 47, 170, 245n4, 248, 249, 249n10, 249n11, 253, 254, 254n15,

254n16, 256, 257, 257n18, 264,
  298, 310
Maurice, Frederick Denison 154n30, 157,
  166, 221, 302, 304, 304n51, 306
Metropolitan Quarterly Magazine 157,
  157n39, 158
Metternich, Klemens von, Fürst von
  Metternich 314, 321
Michaelis, Johann David 43n19, 272, 292, 311
Mill, John Stuart 14, 23, 93, 129, 213, 219,
  219n105, 220, 221, 221n106, 221n107,
  222, 222n108, 223, 224, 225, 225n111,
  226, 227, 228, 229, 229n115, 229n116,
  231, 236, 237, 238, 304
Müller, Max 254n15, 283, 284n41
Montesquieu, Charles-Louis de Secondat,
  Baron de 10, 29, 30, 31, 32, 33, 34, 35,
  37, 38, 42, 43, 44, 51, 52, 54, 55, 59, 71,
  91, 96, 98, 102, 107, 107n32, 110, 136,
  159, 170, 203, 207, 219, 224, 235, 239,
  251, 252, 259, 259n23, 290
Monthly Review 58, 131, 139, 139n10, 183
Motte Fouqué, Friedrich de la 154

Napoleon (Bonaparte) 6, 56, 73, 88, 99, 107,
  107n34, 108, 109n38, 113, 119, 124, 125,
  130, 132, 133, 134, 134n5, 136, 139, 140,
  146, 147, 149, 150, 152, 153, 167, 168,
  169, 169n54, 193n83, 239, 241, 255, 265,
  266, 268, 269, 308, 313, 315, 319, 320
Nationalgeist 13, 31
Nationalgeist debate 53, 54, 60, 62, 102
Nationalgeistdebatte 259n23
Niebuhr, Barthold Georg 150, 162, 163,
  163n49, 163n50, 165, 166, 221, 286, 300
Niebuhr, Carsten 43n19
Novalis 101, 111, 111n42, 123, 155, 196n90,
  199, 199n91, 200, 200n93, 255, 291, 309

Oken, Lorenz 153, 270, 316
Ollier Brothers (publishers) 143,
  155, 170
Ollier's Literary Miscellany 156
Ossian 257, 257n19, 257n20, 258, 259, 272,
  288
Oxford Movement 279

Palgrave, Francis 277, 284, 285
Palm, Johann Philipp 124, 125, 134, 134n6,
  136, 139
Percy, Thomas 9, 38, 45, 46, 46n21, 46n23,
  47, 170, 174, 245, 247, 248, 249,
  249n10, 253, 254, 254n15, 256, 257,
  258, 259, 260, 264, 272, 288, 290, 296,
  297, 298, 298n48, 299, 304, 309, 323
Peterloo Massacre 6, 154, 215
Pitt, William 77, 80

Quarterly Review 162, 181, 181n66, 300
Querelle (des Anciens et des Modernes) 12,
  25, 26, 35, 38, 42, 46, 139, 222, 251,
  252, 253, 262

Ranke, Leopold 276, 276n35, 277, 292, 300,
  307n52, 308, 317, 320, 321, 323, 326
Rheinischer Merkur 269
Rousseau, Jean-Jacques 12, 48, 98, 205

Saeculum 10, 13
Saint-Simon, Claude Henri de Rouvroy, comte
  de 220, 221n107
Sand, Karl Ludwig 108n35, 154, 321
Savigny, Friedrich Karl von 278, 299,
  317, 318
Schiller, Friedrich 63, 79, 81, 123, 130n1,
  146n18, 156, 170, 171, 171n55, 172, 178,
  191, 191n77, 201, 202, 209, 217n103,
  229, 260, 290, 299, 314
Schlegel, August Wilhelm 150, 156, 156n38,
  170, 171, 174, 177n61, 195n86, 208, 221,
  245n5, 250, 260, 261, 262, 263, 263n25,
  264, 264n28, 265, 276, 279, 279n39,
  282, 288, 307n52, 308, 313, 314, 315,
  323
Schlegel, Friedrich 177, 195n86, 199, 206,
  218, 264, 279, 308, 314, 322, 323, 326
Schleiermacher, Friedrich 150, 151, 151n28,
  221
Schwabe, Christian Anton 131, 131n2, 132,
  132n3, 133, 137, 138, 139, 139n10, 140,
  141, 141n14, 158, 230
Scott, Walter 167, 177, 179, 180, 182n67,
  187n73, 193n83, 245, 245n4, 246n7,

248, 260, 264, 264n27, 264n28, 272, 286, 290, 299, 300
Shelley, Percy Bysshe 142, 142n15, 143, 156, 167, 176n60, 194, 200, 200n94, 241, 270
Southey, Robert 130n1, 142, 146n18, 171n55, 179, 186n72, 260
Staatsmaschine 100, 101, 105n28, 109, 110
Steffens, Henrik 55, 123, 155, 155n33, 269
Stein, Friedrich Freiherr vom 51, 51n1, 83, 106, 121, 269, 315
Sterling, John 143, 157, 194, 221, 302, 306
Stubbs, William 77, 275, 277, 278, 282, 284, 285, 288, 291, 296, 302, 303, 304, 323

Taylor, John (publisher) 143, 156, 170, 178, 191
Temple, William 58, 59n17, 95
Teutscher Merkur 57, 58
Thelwall, John 63, 73, 74, 74n30, 75, 75n31, 76, 76n32, 77, 77n33, 78, 79, 80, 82, 83, 84, 85, 86, 87, 88, 99, 107, 121, 124, 130, 141, 141n14, 142, 148, 149, 165, 168, 169, 189, 202, 215, 225, 236, 255, 270, 273, 275, 282, 290, 301, 318
Thirlwall, Connop 143, 150, 152, 152n29, 153, 156, 157, 163, 166, 286
Thorpe, Benjamin 275, 281, 281n40

Tieck, Ludwig 150, 155, 199
Trinity College Cambridge 145, 146, 147, 147n20, 156, 278, 278n36, 286, 296, 302, 303, 306
Turner, Sharon 256

University College London 274, 275, 295

Volksgeist 3, 18n17, 23, 31, 51, 51n1, 73, 74, 74n29, 83, 84, 121, 141n14, 145
Voltaire, François-Marie Arouet 1n2, 9, 10, 11, 12, 26, 26n38, 98

Wartburgfest 152, 154n31, 266
Welcker, Friedrich Gottlieb 150, 151, 151n28, 221, 320, 321
Whewell, William 152, 153, 156, 156n36, 195, 195n87
Wieland, Christoph Martin 57, 58, 58n15, 310
Will, Peter 136, 137, 138, 139, 140, 141, 146, 149, 158, 230, 240
Wordsworth, William 130n1, 142, 146n18, 156, 166, 179, 182, 183, 186n72, 187, 190, 221, 304, 306

Young England 279, 291, 293, 309

www.ingramcontent.com/pod-product-compliance
Lightning Source LLC
Chambersburg PA
CBHW031754220426
43662CB00007B/405